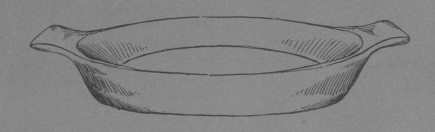
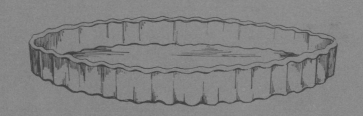
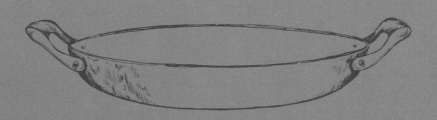

HELEN CORBITT
COOKS FOR COMPANY

ALSO BY
HELEN CORBITT:

HELEN CORBITT'S
COOKBOOK

HELEN CORBITT'S
POTLUCK

HELEN CORBITT
COOKS FOR LOOKS

HELEN CORBITT

COOKS FOR COMPANY

by Helen Corbitt

Illustrations by
Suzanne Cubberly Street

HOUGHTON MIFFLIN COMPANY BOSTON

1974

FIRST PRINTING C

Library of Congress Cataloging in Publication Data

Corbitt, Helen.
  Helen Corbitt cooks for company.

  1. Entertaining. I. Title.
TX731.C66   641.5′68   74–599
ISBN 0–395–18491–6

PRINTED IN THE UNITED STATES OF AMERICA

Dedicated to

Ann and Ann with an e, Barbara, Bertha, Binkie, Betty
and Billie M., Carla, Carolyn, Dollie, Eva Marie and
Evelyn, Fayetta, Geri, Hildegarde, Isabelle, Jean, Karen,
Liz, Lorraine, Louise and Lessie, Margaret, Marilyn,
Mimi, Marjorie, Muriel and Marcia, Nancy, Ollie Mae,
Patricia or Pat, Polly, Quinella, Rosemary, Sissie, Suzy,
Sharon, Tricia, Ursula, Virginia, Wendy, Xenia, Yari
and Zofia
and
Alfred, Anthony, Bert, Bob, Clarence, David, Dean,
Dan and Donald, Edward, Fred, George, Henry Earl,
Ike, Jabez, Jan and John, Kent, Larry, Michael, Mac,
Nathaniel, Oliver, Peter and Paul, Quincy, Raymond,
Stanley, Thomas, Ulysses, Vince, Wil, Xavier, Yves
and do you know a guy named Zeke?

Irish poets, learn your trade,
Sing whatever is well made,
Scorn the sort now growing up,
All out of shape from toe to top.

"Under Ben Bulben"
William Butler Yeats

Author's Note

EACH CHAPTER OF THIS COOKBOOK begins with a group of menus suitable
for various kinds and seasons of entertaining. Recipes for many of the
dishes suggested in these menus are contained in this book; some may
be found in other cookbooks, including my own *Helen Corbitt's Cookbook*, *Helen Corbitt's Potluck* and *Helen Corbitt Cooks for Looks*. The
names of dishes for which there are recipes in this book are capitalized.
The recipes are printed in the order in which they appear in the menus,
usually in the same chapter, otherwise elsewhere in the book. (If you
have trouble locating a recipe, just look it up in the index!)

I have planned the menus in three categories: expensive, less expensive
and inexpensive, for all types of occasions. For the reader's ease in
identifying the menus, I have chosen the cornucopia as a symbol.

Expensive — 3 cornucopias

Less Expensive — 2 cornucopias

Inexpensive — 1 cornucopia

The recipes, unless otherwise specified, are for eight people. In almost
every case the ingredients can be doubled or halved.

One ingredient in particular may need some definition: I refer to *half-and-half* in place of coffee or light cream and to *whipping cream* in place of heavy cream because some parts of the country designate them as such. For more bits of explanation, please refer to the Introduction and to Chapter 14.

H.C.

Contents

HELEN CORBITT

COOKS FOR COMPANY

Introduction
More Explanations Are
in Order

MY FRIENDS AND CO-WORKERS over the years have urged me to put down on paper the menus and recipes for the great many parties, large and small, which I have planned and executed.

The various people for whom I have handled parties have let me create my own climate, so to speak. As manager of the Houston Country Club, where every day was a party of some sort; at Joske's of Houston with its popular catering service for home entertaining so in favor in that city; at the Driskill Hotel in Austin, where politics and entertaining worked hand in hand, I was allowed to be as imaginative as time and money allowed. At Neiman-Marcus in Dallas, pleasing the discriminating tastes of urbane Dallasites and their guests in the Zodiac Room constantly presented opportunities to me and my employees to use our creative abilities.

This, then, is a book of the menus, recipes and ideas that have proved successful for me. It is a book for anyone who likes to entertain and who delights in sharing noteworthy food with his guests and his family.

I am an American. I like American food with a continental flavor. After all, that is what American food really is, is it not? We all came from somewhere else. Our mothers and grandmothers who taught us to cook had the culinary heritage of their foreign origins and adapted it to their own needs and tastes.

I have traveled extensively. I have looked over the shoulder of many a famous chef. I am tired of the overzealous gourmet cook who thinks only the French can cook. Everyone who really wants to and who is able to read can cook and cook well, regardless of nationality or sex. I think food should be uncomplicated and undisguised. A ham is beautiful to behold, but it has no business being decorated to look like a violin.

One of my most satisfying pastimes has been talking to people all over the country through illustrated lectures entitled "Fashions in Food." Wherever I have gone in the last twelve years I have found a new enthusiasm for food preparation and food presentation expressed by men and women of all ages. This hearty interest makes me very optimistic about the future of good food in America. I continue to enjoy a lively correspondence with people in all parts of the world comparing notes about cooking and serving food to our guests.

Many of the bread recipes came from the Wheat Institute in Chicago. The Institute provides the American housewife with excellent tested recipes. I have never found them to fail, and I used these recipes all during my professional life.

I hope I am right in thinking that people who like people derive much pleasure from inviting friends to break bread with them in their homes, regardless of how humble or how grand the homes may be. The hospitality Americans are noted for can be expressed either simply in the serving of a cup of coffee and a piece of cake or elaborately in a seated dinner.

Do not become bogged down with the worry of decorating your table. Do what comes naturally. If you are a gifted flower arranger, you can do your own. If you have the idea and the budget, order from your favorite florist, but the keynote of any table is simplicity. Margaret (Mrs. Eugene) McDermott of Dallas, whose taste I have always admired, uses a beautiful soup tureen or an artifact and no flowers. Her home has a restrained elegance and so has her table. Her guests look elegant because there is not the distraction of an overdecorated table.

Carolyn (Mrs. Dan) Williams for a Sunday brunch used a three-tiered compote filled with pots of blooming African violets. They were beautiful, fresh-looking and a nice thought to give each departing guest.

Do not be intimidated by the flamboyant illustrations in your current home magazines. The props that are used are inspiring and mouthwatering, but who owns them? After all, the magazines borrow from department stores. You do not need an elaborate collection of china, crystal and silver to set an interesting table, only a modicum of creativity and a touch of adventure in your soul. I feel that the food should be a part of the table decoration. Too little decoration is always better than too much.

I enjoy cooking all kinds of food. I love to entertain, but to entertain thoughtfully and well takes time. But don't you agree that everything we enjoy and which gives pleasure to others takes time? What, where and when you eat is your own business. It can be a peanut butter sandwich on the run if it is just your lunch and involves no one else. When you bring someone else in, even a member of your own family, you have a challenge and a responsibility whether you recognize it or not. The outlook of a weary husband or son can be much improved by a good simple meal carefully served. What someone else thinks of you is often tempered by the food you give him.

This is a very personal book, full of personal opinions, and I say many times that no one has to agree with me. My friends demanded the "I" approach, and I am glad they did because it is as casual and conversational as if we were sitting down to have a cup of tea together and to talk recipes and cooking.

The recipes and menus in this book for the most part were tested by me and my cooking classes. One class consists of fourteen good-looking (I wouldn't have them otherwise) men who for four years have been coming into my kitchen once a month to learn about all kinds of cooking. They are distinguished men in the community and have become what I call "gastronomical snobs." We cook, dine, wine and converse until midnight. I adore them! My women's class also numbers fourteen — fourteen interesting, versatile, talented women who happen to want to learn to cook superbly. Through our meetings we have become very good friends, and the women have realized their ambitions to cook well.

I farmed out some recipes to Margaret Hull of Huntsville, Texas, and to Annabelle Hill of Dallas, to prepare and criticize. Suzanne Street from Houston has contributed drawings which I think illustrate my conception of the finished product better than would photographs. Photographs are expensive, and she knew I did not want this book priced out of reach of the thousands who use my other books and have requested many of the special recipes and menus in this one. I want people to use this book as a cookbook and a menu guide, not as a coffee table showpiece, too costly to allow into the kitchen.

The cornucopia symbols printed above a menu indicate whether its preparation will be expensive, less expensive or inexpensive. Regardless of the cost of living index all ingredient costs are relative. One person's least expensive may seem costly on the thirtieth of the month. After payday or on the first Sunday of a new month, you might decide to splurge and have truffles no less.

I have no record of the number of recipes friends and readers of my three earlier cookbooks have sent me through the years — I have always thanked the sender at the time. If I have used one of your pet recipes, or one of your Aunt Clara's, I hope you are flattered that now countless readers will be able to enjoy it.

The Spanish have a dicho: *Haz todo con amor.* Do everything with love. Why not cook with love?

I

Mid-Morning Entertaining

To HAVE a successful morning coffee requires getting up at a devastatingly early hour and doing some of the preparation the day before. But early or not, a morning coffee is a great time to entertain a large or a small group of women. A man wouldn't be caught dead at one. It is the ideal time to introduce a visitor or a newcomer to your community, or for committee entertaining. You don't have to reveal that as a rule you are not good company before ten o'clock in the morning. Make an effort and be pleasant by nine — the earliest even a hard-working steering committee should gather. With chatter, gossip and good fellowship all animated by the aroma of rich coffee, you will be starting the day right for everyone.

The atmosphere should be gay and cheery. If the weather is not bright outside, the color in your home can compensate for what the weather lacks. The joy of color as a greeting is as important as a warm spoken welcome. If you have an informal sun room or an enclosed garden room it is refreshing to use brightly colored pottery. If it is too cool to stroll outside, the view of the patio and the garden beyond will be pleasant and interesting.

The food should be flavorful, simple or elaborate, but dainty in size. Buffet is the rule and the food should be part of the decoration. I often use daisies, poppies or ranunculus in basket arrangements for this time of day. If anemones are available I look no farther because they are favorites with their facelike blossoms saying a good-day to me. And lemon and lime trees are always a refreshing decorative theme.

Mid-Morning Menus

I like serving my guests something to sip before they go to the buffet table.

Hot chicken broth with floating slivered orange peel served
from a tureen into demitasse cups with Cheese Straws to pick up
is a good ice breaker.

On the Buffet Table

An arrangement of season-ripened fruits: small bunches of
sugared grapes, slices of papaya, mango or persimmon, fresh pineapple
fingers dusted with chopped fresh mint, whole berries and
sections of pink grapefruit and thin slices of melon
Lemon cups filled with blueberries (when available) and
twists of lime for a cool look
Parmesan and Cinnamon Bread Sticks
Mushrooms (large, canned) filled with sour cream and coarsely
chopped dry-roasted peanuts, or cottage cheese and walnuts

Open-Face Chicken Liver Sandwiches ("morsels for monarchs")
Dreamland Cake
Tea, hot or iced, with slivered candied ginger nearby
Coffee

Chablis in wine coolers (a good early-in-the-day eye opener)
or a bowl of Mimosa punch
Punch bowl of large fresh strawberries with puréed frozen raspberries
to spoon over, spiked with Grand Marnier if you like
Fresh pineapple fingers with hot rum for dunking
and sour cream mixed with brown sugar
Roquefort Mousse with Lahvash and Melba toast
Chafing dish of Crabmeat Lorenzo for small patty shells (Buy them
and scoop out the centers.)
or artichoke bottoms
Tiny Orange Muffins
Pecan Dainties (*Helen Corbitt's Cookbook*, page 315)

Cold Fruit Soup (*Helen Corbitt's Cookbook*, page 32) served from
a scooped-out melon shell — such as a watermelon, large casaba or

Spanish melon — or from a crystal bowl into crystal punch cups. I like to surround the melon with greenery, the edges dipped in slightly beaten egg whites and granulated sugar to give a frosty look (do the grapes the same way), or you may dip in simple syrup in place of egg whites. If I can find a water lily or a bunch of violets to tuck among the leaves I am ecstatic. I usually have a bowl of sour cream sprinkled with cinnamon to spoon in, too.

Lobster Quiche
Ham sandwiches made on thin slices of Sally Lunn,
spread with curry-seasoned butter
Chicken salad (combined with diced preserved kumquats
in place of celery) open-face sandwiches, piled high, cut in rounds
Glazed cashew nuts and Chocolate Chip Meringues
Coffee and Tea (Many prefer tea in the morning.)

A bowl of canned whole peeled apricots
with sour cream to spoon over
Casserole Sweetbreads and Dried Beef with artichoke bottoms
Toasted rolled mushroom sandwiches
English muffins, buttered and spread with lime marmalade,
oven toasted and quartered
Amaretti
Thin lemon butter cookies
Café au Lait

Hot Velvet Corn Soup, ladled into demitasse cups from a tureen,
with small watercress drop biscuits to munch on
Ham cornucopias filled with chicken salad
A tray of cherry tomatoes, celery brushes filled with mashed avocado
and chipped bacon, large black olives and fresh or preserved lichee nuts
Coeur à la Crème, flavored with preserved ginger,
surrounded by whole stemmed strawberries, and with it a tray of
toasted very thin unsalted crackers
Coffee and hot or iced Tea

White Sangria (in pitchers so guests can help themselves)
Fresh peach quarters or pineapple chunks
with bowls of sherried whipped cream to dunk them in
Mushrooms filled with sausage balls
Cheese tarts filled with Chicken Soufflé and baked
Cornmeal Biscuits with Green Chiles
spread with guacamole and pepper jelly
Poppy Seed Cake
Coffee and Tea

Punch bowl of milk punch or Cold Vegetable Consommé
Broiled Cheese Spread Sandwiches
Baked Banana Chunks Wrapped in Bacon
Corn Crisps
Chocolate Coconut Cookies
Coffee

Summer Soup served in demitasse cups
Melba Grapefruit Sections
Cream cheese loaf rolled in cinnamon and sugar,
served with toasted Triscuits
Hot biscuits filled with very thin sausage patties and chutney
Coconut Pound Cake
Orange Pecans

Sherry Frappé
Thin slices of avocado and fresh pineapple, drizzled with honey,
lemon juice and a dash of cinnamon
Croque Monsieur
Cream Puffs filled with chicken salad
Chocolate Fruit Bars
Coffee and Tea

CHEESE STRAWS
(*5 dozen*)

1 cup butter or margarine	1 teaspoon salt
1 cup grated sharp cheese	⅛ teaspoon cayenne pepper
2 cups flour	Parmesan cheese

Have butter and cheese at room temperature. Mix all ingredients and either put through a cookie press or roll out very thin and cut into narrow strips. Sprinkle lightly with Parmesan cheese. Bake at 350° for 15 minutes.

Sometimes I use grated Swiss Gruyère in place of the sharp cheese and add 1 teaspoon fines herbes. Especially nice with salads. Whatever kind of cheese you use, be sure you grate it finely.

CINNAMON BREAD STICKS

Sometimes I believe in letting packaged foods work for me. This recipe I use often.

¼ cup butter or margarine	½ cup sugar
1 package commercial bread sticks. I prefer the Grissini Motta brand	1 teaspoon cinnamon

Melt the butter and pour over the bread sticks that are one deep in a flat pan or on a piece of foil. Roll the buttered bread sticks in the mixture of cinnamon and sugar. Place on a cookie sheet or a piece of foil, shiny side up, and bake for 10 minutes in a 350° oven. Remove, cool and wrap in foil or wax paper until ready to use. I freeze them, then put back in the oven to heat.

There are all kinds of bread stick variations. Always pour melted butter over first and then roll in Parmesan cheese, or paprika and oregano, or finely chopped almonds, or just about any idea you have. But you *must* roll the sticks in the melted butter first, or your idea will roll off. I frequently use them buttered with no addition and serve hot in place of rolls. They are so crisp everyone likes them and forgets to count the added calories. You can follow the same procedure with day-old or brown-and-serve rolls.

OPEN-FACE CHICKEN LIVER SANDWICHES

½ pound chicken livers   Dash of Tabasco
½ cup milk   1 teaspoon onion juice
¼ pound butter   ½ pound bacon
½ pound mushrooms, chopped fine   Rye bread rounds

Soak chicken livers in milk for a few minutes. Drain. Melt the butter, add the chicken livers and sauté at medium heat for about 20 minutes. Remove, cool and mince. Add the mushrooms to butter and cook 5 minutes. Mix with the livers. Season with salt, pepper, Tabasco and the onion juice. Cut the bacon in small dice and cook until crisp. Drain and dry. Pile the chicken livers high on buttered rye bread rounds, sprinkle with the bacon.

DREAMLAND CAKE

Believe it or not, this recipe came from the Indiana University Medical Center in Indianapolis. I gave a talk there some time ago and came home with it. I use it for many occasions: a sweet for a cocktail party, a neighborhood gift at Christmas and with tea or coffee. Everyone likes it — calories and all — and you cannot fail. You may use it with or without an icing. If frosting, I use a lemon-flavored butter cream icing. Forget to count the added calories.

First Mixture: 1 cup flour   ½ cup butter
                          ⅛ teaspoon salt

Mix like shortbread and spread in 9-inch square cake tins about ⅛ inch to ¼ inch thick.

Second Mixture:

2 eggs   ½ cup coconut
1 cup brown sugar   ½ cup dates, chopped
1 teaspoon baking powder   ½ cup candied cherries
1 cup walnuts, chopped   1 teaspoon vanilla

Mix and pour second mixture over the first. Bake slowly about 40 minutes at 325°. Ice with butter icing if you wish. Cut in squares.

MIMOSA
(for 10 to 12)

I use this drink frequently for all-women gatherings, especially in the early part of the day. It doesn't tickle your nose as much as plain champagne, but it is better for you to start the day with a little Vitamin C.

    1 quart cold, freshly squeezed orange juice
    1 bottle chilled Brut Champagne

Mix and pour into stemmed glasses; and please, no maraschino cherry. If you have any mixture left, add softened unflavored gelatin (1 tablespoon for each pint liquid) to it and pour over a bowl of fresh fruit for a good dessert.

Cheese is not a must by any means for a mid-morning menu idea, but it helps, and Roquefort Mousse is yummy. Make the day before, freeze if there are any leftovers. I use it for many occasions — with a salad course at dinner, as a dessert with fruit, as an edible centerpiece for a cocktail table — oh, many ways.

ROQUEFORT MOUSSE

6 egg yolks	1½ cups cream, whipped
½ cup cream	3 egg whites, stiffly beaten
1½ tablespoons unflavored gelatin	
½ cup cold water	¾ pound Roquefort cheese

Beat egg yolks with cream, heat over hot water until creamy and thick. Add gelatin dissolved in the cold water. Remove from heat, add the cheese (put through a sieve) and cool. Fold into the whipped cream. Fold in the egg whites. Pour into a lightly buttered 1½-quart mold. Refrigerate overnight. Danish or American Blue cheese may be substituted, but the Roquefort is more delicate. Turn out onto a plate and decorate as you wish. I use only watercress — in a bunch — not spread out here and there.

Lahvash is an Armenian cracker bread, crisp and lower in calories than white bread. It is far more interesting than any cracker and can be used in place of either bread or crackers. This California-made bread is a very large thin cracker. Break it into pieces before serving. You can grind Lahvash into crumbs and freeze to use when needed.

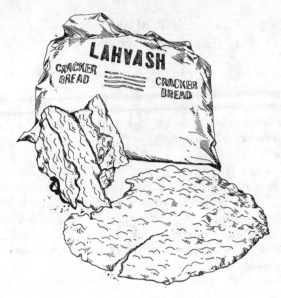

The delicate subtle flavor of crabmeat is always an addition to any table — and I like this for many occasions.

CRABMEAT LORENZO
(for 8 to 10)

½ cup finely chopped green onions
1 cup finely chopped mushrooms
½ cup butter
½ tablespoon Dijon mustard
½ cup dry white wine
1 cup Cream Sauce (1 tablespoon flour, 1 tablespoon butter, 1 cup milk)

½ cup half-and-half
½ tablespoon Worcestershire sauce
1 pound lump crabmeat
¼ cup finely chopped parsley
Salt and white pepper

Sauté onions and mushrooms in butter until soft. Add mustard, wine, Cream Sauce, cream and Worcestershire. Heat, add crabmeat and parsley, correct seasonings, and keep warm over hot water until served. King crab, shrimp or mixed seafood may be substituted.

ORANGE MUFFINS
(3 *dozen small muffins*)

1 cup butter or margarine	2 cups sifted flour
1 cup sugar	Grated rind and juice of 2 oranges
2 eggs	½ cup golden raisins
1 teaspoon soda	1 cup brown sugar
1 cup buttermilk	

Cream butter and sugar, add eggs and beat. Dissolve the soda in the buttermilk, add with the flour to the butter mixture. Add rind and raisins. Fill well-buttered muffin pans two-thirds full and bake in a 400° oven for 20 to 25 minutes. Mix orange juice with brown sugar. Pour over muffins and remove from pans immediately.

These could be used for a picnic dessert too. Sometimes ·I substitute pecans for the raisins.

LOBSTER QUICHE
(24 *small tarts*)

2 eggs	¼ teaspoon salt
1 cup half-and-half	¼ teaspoon dry mustard
2 cups grated Swiss cheese	Barque or tart tins lined with un-
1 cup cooked chopped lobster meat	baked pie crust

Beat the eggs, add the cream, cheese, lobster, salt and mustard. Mix and pour into the pastry-lined tins. Bake at 400° for 15 minutes. Remove tarts immediately from tins by running the tip of knife under one side and slipping out. Do not let them cool in the tins. For variation, add a bit of chutney before baking.

SALLY LUNN

1 cake or package yeast	2 eggs
1 cup milk	3½ cups flour
3 tablespoons butter	1¼ teaspoons salt
3 tablespoons sugar	

Soften yeast cake in lukewarm milk. Set aside. Cream together butter and sugar. Add eggs and mix well. Sift flour, to which the salt has been added. Add to shortening mixture alternately with milk-yeast mixture. Beat well. Let rise in a warm place until double in bulk. Knead lightly. Put into a well-buttered Sally Lunn mold or bundt pan. Cover. Let stand and rise again until doubled. Bake 1 hour at 300°.

CHOCOLATE CHIP MERINGUES
(2 dozen medium or 3 dozen small)

4 egg whites	1 teaspoon vanilla
¼ teaspoon salt	1 cup broken pecans
¼ teaspoon cream of tartar	1 6-ounce package semi-sweet
1½ cups sugar	chocolate bits

Beat egg whites until stiff, add salt and cream of tartar. Continue beating, adding the sugar a little at a time. Continue beating. Add vanilla, fold in pecans and chocolate bits. Drop by tablespoonfuls onto a pan lined with foil, shiny side up. Bake at 325° until dry. Cool slightly and pull off the foil.

Omit the nuts and chocolate for Kiss Meringues.

Your good butcher shops carry sweetbreads — use them!

CASSEROLE SWEETBREADS AND DRIED BEEF

2 pairs sweetbreads	2½ cups canned artichoke bottoms
Juice of ½ lemon	(usually 8 in a can)
½ cup butter	2 tablespoons Parmesan cheese
1 4-ounce jar dried beef	2 tablespoons grated Swiss
3 tablespoons flour	cheese
3 cups half-and-half or milk	

Soak sweetbreads in cold water for 30 minutes. Drain, cover with fresh cold water and lemon juice. Simmer just under boiling for 20 minutes. Remove, cool, discard membranes and slice as thin as possible without breaking. Melt the butter, add the sweetbreads and sauté until a light brown. Add dried beef cut into ½-inch strips. Heat only. Remove, add flour to the same pan, cook 1 minute. Add cream and cook until thickened, stirring with a French whip until you have no lumps. Return sweetbreads and beef to the pan and heat thoroughly. Correct seasonings. Place the drained artichoke bottoms in a buttered shallow casserole, spoon the mixture into them. Sprinkle with the cheeses mixed together and bake at 350° until bubbly. Run under broiler to brown if necessary. Substitute sliced hard-cooked eggs for the sweetbreads if you are budget-minded or substitute leftover ham for the beef. I'm extravagant at times — I use prosciutto ham!

The Italians invented Amaretti, or macaroons, and they are found all over Italy in various forms. The ones I liked were little almond-shaped ones put together with a chocolate fudge icing. I returned to Texas, and Amaretti à la Italianna Helen are still best sellers in the Neiman-Marcus bake shops. But you must plan on many when you serve them; they are like peanuts, you cannot take only one.

AMARETTI

1 8-ounce can of almond   1 cup sugar
  paste (you buy)   2 egg whites

Cut up paste into small pieces. Add sugar and the egg whites and mix until smooth. Drop from a teaspoon onto paper-lined cookie pans. Bake at 325° for about 30 minutes. Allow to cool, then wet back of paper to remove. Place the two flat sides together with chocolate fudge icing and let dry. Or buy the plain macaroons and do the same.
  or
Make macaroons from scratch:

1 cup unblanched almonds   ¼ teaspoon almond extract
1 cup sugar   ¼ teaspoon vanilla extract
2 large egg whites

Grind the almonds to a paste. Blend two thirds of the sugar and both the egg whites, adding a little at a time, until you have a soft mixture. Beat hard for about 3 minutes. Add almonds and flavorings. Drop from teaspoons or a pastry tube onto the paper-lined pan. Sprinkle with rest of sugar. Bake 15 to 20 minutes at 375° until the tops are cracked and light brown.

VELVET CORN SOUP
(*for 8 to 12*)

¼ cup butter   1 egg, beaten
¼ cup finely chopped onion   1¼ teaspoons salt
3 cups fresh or frozen corn   ½ teaspoon white pepper
4 cups half-and-half

Melt the butter, add the onion and sauté until soft but not brown. Add the corn and cook for 5 minutes, but do not brown. Add cream and beaten egg. Cook until mixture begins to boil, stirring constantly, about 3 minutes. Add seasonings. Let cool slightly, put in a blender and whip until creamy. Strain and reheat. This also makes a delicious cold soup. Try it — very cold!

COEUR A LA CREME

8 ounces cream cheese
⅓ cup confectioners' sugar
⅛ teaspoon salt

¼ cup slivered preserved ginger
2 cups whipping cream
1 quart large strawberries

Whip cheese with electric mixer until fluffy. Add sugar, salt and ginger. Whip the cream and mix with the cheese mixture. Pour into a 1½-quart heart-shaped mold, or 2 smaller ones, lined with wet cheesecloth. Refrigerate overnight. Unmold on a serving tray, peel off the cheesecloth and surround with berries. Put a few berries in a blender, slightly sweeten and pass the sauce with the coeur. For a less caloric coeur, substitute 2 cups of cottage cheese for the whipping cream and beat until the consistency of whipped cream.

There are several ways to make Sangria and only a few ways are good. The classic recipe is the best.

SANGRIA BASE

2 large oranges, sliced
3 lemons, sliced
3 limes, sliced

3 quarts water
2 pounds sugar

Slowly boil mixture for 3½ hours or more until it is reduced by one-half. Cook until syrupy and a bitter taste begins to appear. Cool at room temperature.

To make Sangria for 8: Spoon ⅓ cup of the Base into a pitcher, add 1 bottle of an inexpensive red wine. Add 1 dozen ice cubes and about half of a 10-ounce bottle of soda water. Stir well and add diced peaches, strawberries, cherries or whatever fresh fruit you wish, and thin slices of lemon, oranges and limes. There is a great difference between the taste of this Sangria and the simple kind. For a white Sangria use a dry white Burgundy wine in place of the red. You may also add brandy or vodka, 1 cup for each bottle of wine.

The simple Sangria, either red or white:

2 oranges, thinly sliced	1 bottle wine
2 lemons, thinly sliced	5 ounces soda water
1 lime, thinly sliced	12 ice cubes
½ cup sugar	Fresh fruit, if you wish

Crush the oranges, lemons and lime with the sugar and refrigerate for a couple of hours. Remove, add wine, soda water and ice cubes. Stir well and pour. Of course, add brandy or vodka, 1 cup for each bottle of wine. I sometimes serve this drink in tall glasses over ice with fresh fruit added and a sprig of mint — a type of Planter's Punch.

This keeps indefinitely in a jar refrigerated.

CORNMEAL BISCUITS WITH GREEN CHILES
(4 dozen small biscuits)

1 cup flour	½ cup milk
1 cup yellow cornmeal	¼ cup chopped green chiles (Ortego brand is the most common — buy whole and chop.)
1 teaspoon salt	
⅓ cup shortening (half may be butter)	

Mix flour, cornmeal and salt together, cut in shortening. Add milk and chiles, stir and turn out on floured board. Pat to ½ inch thick. Cut into biscuits. Place on an ungreased cookie sheet. Bake at 450° for 12 to 15 minutes.

Cakes without icing are becoming the usual, and this was a recipe sent to me many years ago. I have used it for entertaining, a neighborly gift, and for travelers to munch on. It freezes well and wrapped in clear plastic will keep for days in the refrigerator.

POPPY SEED CAKE

¾ cup poppy seeds
¾ cup milk
¾ cup butter, margarine or vegetable shortening
1¼ cups sugar

3 eggs
1 teaspoon vanilla
2 cups flour
2 teaspoons baking powder
½ teaspoon salt

Soak poppy seeds in milk overnight. Set aside. Cream butter and sugar. Add eggs one at a time, beating well after each addition. Add vanilla, milk and poppy seeds, then flour sifted with the baking powder and salt. Mix well. Pour into a well-buttered 9-inch tube or bundt pan and bake at 375° for 30 to 40 minutes. For a lighter cake, separate the eggs and fold in the stiffly beaten egg whites at the end. This cake may be served plain, with confectioners' sugar sifted over or with a lemon juice and granulated sugar glaze.

VEGETABLE CONSOMME

4 cups chicken consommé, beef consommé, or half of each
½ cup thinly sliced cucumber, chopped
½ cup peeled and seeded tomatoes

½ cup diced avocado
2 tablespoons minced green onion
1 tablespoon wine vinegar
1 teaspoon olive oil
Salt and pepper

Mix, season and chill. Serve very cold. Sometimes I add diced fresh mushrooms, any kind of seafood or cooked chicken.

CHEESE SPREAD SANDWICHES
(3 dozen)

1 pound Tillamook or similar cheese, grated
1 cup finely chopped onion
1 clove garlic, minced
1 4-ounce can Ortego green chiles, seeded and chopped
1 4-ounce jar stuffed olives, chopped
2 tablespoons vinegar
1 8-ounce can tomato sauce
1 teaspoon Worcestershire sauce
2 tablespoons salad oil (I prefer peanut oil)
French bread or baguettes

Mix together, spread on thin slices of French bread. I buy the baguettes that are about the size of a silver dollar in circumference. Broil, as far away from the heat element as possible, until bubbly and edges of bread are brown. A good cocktail snack also. The spread keeps well and is nice to have on hand.

BANANA CHUNKS WRAPPED IN BACON

Bananas are passed by too frequently. Cut them into 2-inch chunks and wrap in bacon that has been blanched in boiling water for 10 minutes and thoroughly dried. Sprinkle with brown sugar and bake on a rack at 350° until bacon is crisp and sugar slightly caramelized. Good with beef entrées too!

CORN CRISPS

1 cup boiling water
⅞ cup cornmeal
½ teaspoon salt
2½ tablespoons melted butter
⅛ teaspoon cayenne pepper
Poppy seeds

Pour boiling water over cornmeal and stir. Add salt, melted butter, and cayenne. Drop from teaspoon onto a buttered cookie sheet; then flatten with a spatula dipped in cold water. Brush with melted butter. Sprinkle with poppy seeds and bake at 350° until brown around the edges.

CHOCOLATE COCONUT COOKIES
(3 *dozen*)

These were a great favorite with my men customers at Neiman-Marcus.

2 cups flour	1 cup water
2 cups sugar	2 eggs, beaten
½ teaspoon salt	½ cup buttermilk
1 cup butter or margarine	1 teaspoon soda
3 tablespoons powdered cocoa	1 teaspoon vanilla

Sift together flour, sugar and salt. Set aside. Mix butter, cocoa and water. Bring to a boil, pour over flour mixture. Add well-beaten eggs, buttermilk, soda and vanilla. Pour into two buttered shallow cake pans approximately 9 x 9-inch. Bake at 375° for 30 minutes.

Topping:

Mix and bring to a boil ½ cup butter, 6 tablespoons half-and-half, 3 tablespoons cocoa. Add mixture to 2 cups powdered sugar, ½ teaspoon vanilla, 1 cup shredded coconut, 1 cup chopped nuts. Mix and spread over cookies as they come from oven. Cut in squares. This is a good picnic cookie — and a nice change from brownies.

SUMMER SOUP
(*for 8 to 12*)

4 cups sour cream	3 tablespoons finely chopped green onion
2 cups ice water	½ teaspoon dried dill
2 cups finely chopped fresh spinach (raw)	Salt and pepper

Mix together and chill. Season to taste. When ready to serve add:

½ cup chopped, peeled and seeded tomato	½ cup chopped, seeded cucumber
	A dash of cayenne pepper

MELBA GRAPEFRUIT SECTIONS

Section grapefruit, cover with puréed and strained fresh raspberries and refrigerate overnight. Both the color and flavor will make them the center of attraction.

COCONUT POUND CAKE

2¼ cups cake flour	¼ teaspoon ground mace (you
1 teaspoon baking powder	may omit)
½ teaspoon salt	1⅓ cups Angel Flake coconut (or
1 cup butter	1 cup fine-grated coconut)
1¼ cups granulated sugar	4 eggs
1¼ teaspoons vanilla or lemon extract	⅓ cup milk

Sift flour and measure. Add baking powder and salt, and sift together. Set aside. Cream butter until very soft and fluffy. Add sugar, 2 tablespoons at a time, creaming thoroughly after each addition. Add vanilla and mace, blending well. Add coconut. Beat in eggs, one at a time, beating thoroughly after each is added. Add flour mixture alternately with milk, beginning and ending with flour and beating after each addition until smooth. Pour batter into a greased bundt pan or a 9-inch tube pan which has been lined on bottom with wax paper. Bake in a slow oven (325°) for 1 hour and 10 to 15 minutes. Cool about 15 minutes in pan. Then turn out, remove paper and turn right side up to cool thoroughly. Sprinkle with confectioners' sugar or a Sugar Glaze.

SUGAR GLAZE
(⅓ cup)

1 cup sifted confectioners' sugar
1 tablespoon hot milk (approximately)

Place sugar in small bowl. Add milk gradually, blending well until mixture is thin enough to spread over cake.

ORANGE PECANS

1¼ cups sugar   ⅛ teaspoon cream of tartar
Grated rind and juice of 1 orange   Pecans

Cook sugar, orange juice and rind and cream of tartar to soft ball stage, remove from heat and beat until creamy. Dip pecans into the mixture, forming into small clusters, or coating singly if they are large. Keep mixture in pan of warm water while dipping.

SHERRY FRAPPE

1 bottle dry sherry   2 tablespoons lemon juice
2 cups apple juice

Mix and put in your freezer compartment. When ready to serve, put in blender and beat to frappé consistency. Pour into stemmed glasses. Decorate with a sprig of mint and serve with a short soda straw.

CROQUE MONSIEUR
(for 24 triangles)

Softened butter   6 slices baked or boiled ham,
Dijon mustard   thinly cut
12 thin slices bread   ½ cup dry sauterne
6 slices Gruyère cheese, thinly cut

Trim the crusts from the bread. Spread softened butter on both sides of bread. Spread mustard thinly on each of 6 slices, place 1 slice ham, 1 slice cheese on each. Top with remaining bread. Sprinkle with the dry sauterne. Place in a 350° oven until sandwich is a light brown. Cut in triangles and decorate, if you wish, with a slice of olive and parsley. Don't forget the wine!

You can make any filling go much further in a small cream puff than in a sandwich — and for some reason guests think fewer calories.

CREAM PUFFS

1 cup boiling water	½ teaspoon salt
½ cup butter	4 eggs
1 cup flour	

Put water in a saucepan, and as it boils add butter. Continue heating until butter is melted. Add flour and salt all at once. Stir until dough forms a ball. Remove from heat. Add 1 egg, beat, let stand 5 minutes. Add remaining eggs one egg at a time, beating after each addition. Let stand 10 minutes. Drop on ungreased baking sheet by level teaspoonfuls for small puffs — 2 inches apart. Bake at 375° 20 to 25 minutes. The surest way to test is to remove one, and if it collapses, it is not done. When cold, split and fill with salad, or cottage cheese and red caviar is delicious too. Dip stuffed edge into chopped parsley.

CHOCOLATE FRUIT BARS
(*about 2 dozen*)

½ cup brown sugar	½ teaspoon baking soda
¼ cup butter	1 cup pecan halves
½ teaspoon salt	1 cup candied pineapple
2 eggs	1 cup candied cherries
¼ cup milk	1 6-ounce package semi-sweet
1 cup flour	chocolate bits
½ teaspoon baking powder	

Cream sugar, butter and salt until fluffy. Blend in eggs, one at a time; add milk. Stir together flour, baking powder and soda; combine with butter mixture. Fold in remaining ingredients. Spread in greased 11 x 8-inch pan. Bake in 350° oven for approximately 25 minutes. Serve as is or dribble lemon juice and powdered sugar icing over the top.

2

Brunches

TIME HAS BROUGHT many changes in the way we entertain. The informality of modern living makes entertaining easier. I agree that gone forever are the days of spending hours in the kitchen. But with all the freedom we cooks do have, it may be only a little imagination that is needed. We can combine the so-called convenience foods and ways of serving and still be traditional in our gracious entertaining.

For daytime entertaining — and it becomes more popular each year — brunches offer great flexibility. Elevenish 'til one as for time, it may be come and go, seated or not, tables or "walk around," expensive or less so. For women, for debutantes, for introducing an author or a favorite politician and various women's club affairs — even men enjoy them. And it is an uncomplicated time of day to entertain.

You may omit a first course or a dessert and no one will talk about you. In fact, very few hostesses today really go through the soup-to-nuts routine.

Buffet

Thinly sliced navel oranges with slices of preserved ginger
Swiss Cheese Soufflé pie with julienne ham in Mustard Cream
Sautéed whole mushrooms with shallots
Cold marinated sweet red and green peppers
Whole-wheat hot biscuits with black raspberry jelly
If you do not wish a dessert, you might pass a tray of good
candy (I am partial to Blum's Almondettes or Almond
Roca myself) or fruit cake, cut in squares with one,
only one, edge dipped in powdered sugar
Border Buttermilk and Kir (Both are mild, as
drinks should be at brunch time.)

Curry of Smoked Turkey on sautéed peach halves
(I use canned cling or Elberta if fresh are not available)
Five various sambals: fresh grated coconut, chutney, quarters of
fresh limes, sliced candied ginger, toasted cashews
Cold cooked salad shrimp (the Greenland frozen or
West Coast variety I prefer)
Papadoms or Puri
Thinly sliced ham sandwiches
Lightly tossed fine Cole Slaw
Fresh Lime Cream Sherbet

I like cole slaw with curry. I usually hear the same comment too. Cole slaw? Fancy that! But it is always gobbled up. Veta Davis from Houston days gave me that tip. This menu could also be used for a supper or dinner buffet. It is also a good way to use smoked turkey. I usually have a smoked turkey on hand at Christmas-time, or I watch for the late August specials in the market and keep one or two in my deep freeze. I save the skin and carcass for soup — later!

Tureen of tomato bouillon (good at any time of the day
with hot buttered beaten biscuits)
Sautéed Sweetbreads with Marrons and Canadian bacon
Molded Eggs and Shrimp
Cucumbers in sour cream with chives
Watercress and endive salad with Sherry French Dressing
Lemon Floating Island on fresh blueberries or strawberries

The joy of color often gives the impression of elegance and hospitality.
I like to use crystal with fruits for this reason.

Crystal bowl of fresh whole berries mixed in cold canned
apricot nectar with scoops of lemon ice (It can be used as a
dessert or a walk-around something while chatting.
Guests like to take or leave dessert today)
Cold Ham Mousse with Parsley Sauce
Hot crisp Rice Cakes with melted butter (to add if desired)
Marinated canned asparagus, sprinkled with capers
Small Gingerbread or Orange Muffins
Pitchers of Rosé wine for individual pouring (I find that more
and more people do not like alcohol at noontime)

Cranberry and apple juice, frappéed
Turkey Loaf served with Mushroom Fondue
Slivered Green Beans, Bean Sprouts and Water Chestnuts,
Flavored with Soy Sauce
Thin slices of French bread spread with mashed avocado
Flan with grated orange peel in the caramel

Slices of ripe papaya with lime dressing
Spinach Pudding Ring (*Helen Corbitt's Cookbook*, page 185) filled in
the center with julienne
fresh vegetables in Newburg Sauce
Thin slices of ham or Swiss cheese rolled around Rice Salad
that has been tossed with peas and chutney
Toasted golden puffs (you buy — Jacob's Golden Puffs)
Orange Chiffon Cake with Coffee Butter Cream Icing
and Slivers of Semi-Sweet Chocolate

Chilled white Catawba grape juice
Crêpes filled with Ratatouille, browned with Parmesan cheese
Peas in Aspic with Minted Carrots
Thinly sliced cucumber sandwiches
Thinly sliced Italian bread and butter sandwiches
A bowl each of stewed prunes, peeled apricots, and the canned
pear quarters with toasted sesame seeds served with a
pitcher of pouring cream
Espresso Coffee and Hot Milk

Salmon Timbales with Asparagus Sauce
Jellied cucumber ring filled with sliced Egg and Celery Salad
Marinated diced raw vegetables
Toasted rolled cheese sandwiches
Apple Baklava

Hot bouillon spiked with dry Burgundy or sherry
Pastry barques filled with mushrooms and peas in curried cream
Cold tomato half piled high with date and celery salad
Hot sausage bread
Peaches à l'Orange

SWISS CHEESE SOUFFLE
(for 8 to 10)

½ cup butter or margarine
6 tablespoons flour
2 cups milk
2 cups grated Swiss cheese (I find French Emmental especially good for a soufflé)
8 egg yolks (use eggs left at room temperature overnight)

1½ teaspoons dry mustard or 1 tablespoon Dijon mustard
⅛ teaspoon cayenne pepper
1 teaspoon salt
8 egg whites (add 4 more for a lighter soufflé)
Parmesan cheese (may be omitted)

Melt the butter, add the flour and cook slowly until mixture foams. Do not brown. Add the milk and bring to a boil; use low heat to ensure the flour and milk being thoroughly cooked. The sauce should be smooth and thick. Remove from heat. Add the cheese and stir until blended. Cool slightly. Beat the egg yolks and add to the mixture. Add the mustard, cayenne and salt. Let mixture cool until you can place your hand on the bottom of the container without feeling any heat. Beat the egg whites until stiff but not dry. (Tip the bowl and if the whites do not slide out, they are ready.) Stir gently about one third of the egg whites into the mixture, then fold in remaining egg whites until well distributed. Pour into a 2½- or 3-quart buttered soufflé dish sprinkled lightly with Parmesan cheese or into two 1½-quart ones. Bake in a 350° oven for 30 minutes if you are going to eat at once, or place in a pan of hot water and bake 1 hour, and it will hold awhile.

You may substitute grated Cheddar, Gruyère or any other hard cheese. I do think Swiss or Gruyère makes a better soufflé.

There are many things you may do with a soufflé besides baking it in a soufflé dish. I like to pour it into a partially baked pie crust for a cheese soufflé pie and bake at 350° until set, about 30 minutes. Use it as a carrier for any creamed food, or you may serve it simply as a soufflé pie. It is delicious topped with broiled mushrooms or broiled shrimp for a less caloric item. You may bake a soufflé in individual casseroles for a seated luncheon. Use your basic soufflé recipe and put on the bottom a layer of one of the following: sliced sautéed mushrooms, sautéed thinly sliced onions, shrimp, or a layer of spinach or ham soufflé and bake together. Use the new see-through glass soufflé dishes and watch your soufflé come to life with the added color. Before cooking, ring the dish with buttered bakers' sheet paper for a higher soufflé (do not use foil). Bake in a shallow casserole for a buffet and cut in serving portions. Use a soufflé in place of a vegetable. Serve it with cold boiled salmon, and pass the melted sweet butter, as the Danish do. With cold baked ham it is divine. Use the leftovers in an omelette, in macaroni and cheese, in an oven-toasted cheese sandwich. Just use soufflés for they are delicious.

I do not think anyone can really enjoy the flavor of mustard in a sauce if a Dijon mustard is not used. Personally, I think the Maille mustard the best. It is found in good food shops and if you do not have it in your area, keep asking. I like Mustard Creams for carrying various foods:

ham, seafood, leftover roast beef, artichoke hearts, green beans, carrots —
oh, many things — and especially to serve over a Cheese Soufflé Pie.

MUSTARD CREAM
(2 *cups*)

4 tablespoons butter or margarine   2 cups half-and-half
2 shallots or green onions, finely   ½ teaspoon salt
   minced   2 tablespoons Dijon mustard
3 tablespoons flour   2 tablespoons dry white wine

Melt the butter, add the shallots or onion. Cook until yellow. Add the
flour; stir and cook until bubbly. Pour in the half-and-half. Cook and
stir with a French whip over low heat until smooth and thickened. Add
salt, mustard and wine. Cook about 5 minutes more. For a thinner
sauce, add a little more half-and-half or chicken broth. To the sauce I
add 1½ cups of slivered ham, chicken, sliced shrimp or crabmeat. Cut
the soufflé pie, then spoon over the sauce. This method may be used as
a basis for making any sauce, i.e., in place of mustard, add capers, parsley,
chives, mixed herbs, slivered vegetables, chopped eggs, seafood — you
name it.

BORDER BUTTERMILK

1 6-ounce can frozen lemonade concentrate
1 lemonade can Tequila

Put in blender. Fill with crushed ice. Blend at high speed until smooth
and frothy and milky looking.

KIR

⅓ ounce Crème de Cassis   3 or 4 ounces Chablis or a dry
white wine

Mix and serve very cold in a stemmed glass.
   This drink, invented by Père Kir of Dijon in the late twenties or early
thirties, has become a most popular aperitif.

CURRY OF SMOKED TURKEY
(for 8 to 12)

½ cup butter
½ cup minced onion
1 clove garlic, crushed
3 to 4 tablespoons curry powder,
 heated in a skillet before using
8 tablespoons flour

4 cups milk, half-and-half or
 chicken consommé
3 to 4 pounds smoked turkey,
 cut in large dice
Salt and cayenne pepper
¼ cup sherry

Melt butter, add onion and garlic and cook until yellow, but not brown. Add curry powder, cook 2 minutes; add flour, cook until foamy. Remove garlic. Pour in milk, cook and stir with a wire whip until thickened. Add the smoked turkey, heat and then season with salt and cayenne pepper. The turkey is salted, so do not salt the sauce before adding the turkey. Add sherry. Keep hot over hot water or cool and reheat.

Use the same basic sauce for seafood or whatever curry. However, when I curry shrimp, I start with raw shrimp and sauté with the onion and garlic, then remove to add later. They will have much more flavor. Sometimes I heat the milk with 2 cups of coconut, cool and strain, discard the coconut.

We have a tendency to serve curry on rice because we first heard of it served on rice. I like to use fresh, frozen or canned cling peach halves, in that order. Dust the peaches lightly with flour and sauté in butter until a lacy brown. Serve curry over them or use corn bread in place of rice — the Creole Corn Bread (*Helen Corbitt's Cookbook*, page 227) still better.

You can use any condiment for the sambals. Your guests will be more impressed if you call them sambals rather than relishes or condiments. These may also be added to the cold shrimp to make a different kind of salad.

I usually fill a large scallop shell with plain cold cooked shrimp as an idea for guests to add a new taste to curry. Tell your guests to sprinkle shrimp with coconut and lime juice to give the curry a flavor sparkle.

Buy the papadoms in packages and deep fry. Papadoms are an Indian bread, similar to the Mexican tortilla and easily mistaken for one. One of the most satisfying moments in my career was when I corrected a noted gourmet of such an error. Papadoms are good as a carrier for curried seafood or curried chicken.

Papadoms, sometimes spelled Pappodums (a trade name) are not always available, but you may make an Indian bread that is similar called Puri. This recipe is from Anil K. Aggarwal, a graduate student at Rice University in Houston, Texas, who plans to stay in this country to teach.

PURI

¾ teaspoon salt	2 cups self-rising flour
½ teaspoon whole cumins	½ cup buttermilk
½ teaspoon baking powder	Cold water

Mix salt, cumins, baking powder and flour. Add buttermilk and mix into a stiff (tough) dough — adding water if necessary to form it. Let stand for ½ hour. Knead it and make 20 small round balls out of it. Roll out flat, very thin and round. Fry in hot deep cooking oil (375°). Be sure oil is hot or the Puri will not puff.

COLE SLAW

To 1 head cabbage, shredded very fine, add 1 teaspoon salt and cover with boiling water. Let stand 5 minutes. Drain and aerate (toss in the air with two forks).
  Mix:

¾ cup cider vinegar	¼ cup salad oil
3 tablespoons finely diced onion	1 teaspoon cracked pepper
2 teaspoons sugar	¼ cup chopped parsley

Toss with the cabbage. Season to taste. Fork lift into serving dish. Use this any time in place of a green salad. 'Tis good!

FRESH LIME CREAM SHERBET
(*1 gallon*)

2 fresh limes	4 cups whipping cream
⅓ cup fresh lime juice	2 cups milk
2 cups sugar	Few drops green food coloring

Trim off ends of 2 limes. Slice fruit into paper thin slices, removing any seeds. Chop fine. Mix with juice and sugar. Cover and refrigerate overnight. Mix 2 cups of the cream and all the milk. Add to the lime mixture. Stir well; mixture will thicken. Add coloring. Freeze in an ice cream freezer until sherbet is partially frozen (6 parts ice to 1 part ice cream salt). Whip the remaining cream and add. Continue freezing until solid. Pack to ripen (8 parts ice to 1 part ice cream salt).

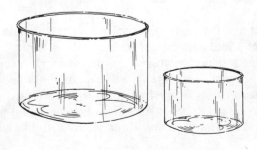

SAUTEED SWEETBREADS WITH MARRONS
(for 6)

3 pairs trimmed calves' sweetbreads
Flour, salt
¼ cup butter
1 tablespoon finely minced shallots or onion

¼ cup Madeira
1 cup chicken stock
12 preserved marrons
12 thin slices Canadian bacon

If possible, obtain the heart sweetbread which is round in shape. Soak
and precook as in recipe for Casserole Sweetbreads. Remove all connec-
tive tissue and membranes. Slice thin and sprinkle with flour and salt.
Melt the butter, add the shallots and cook until yellow. Add sweetbreads, cook 1 minute, turn and cook 1 minute more. Pour in wine and
stock. Simmer at low heat about 10 minutes. Add marrons and continue
cooking until marrons are hot. Correct seasonings. Place sweetbreads
on a serving platter or in a chafing dish layered with lightly sautéed
Canadian bacon. Pour over the marrons and juices. I sometimes serve
them on sautéed pineapple rings. All the ingredients have an affinity for
pineapple. I find this a good buffet supper dish also as the sweetbreads
hold up well on a buffet.

MOLDED EGGS AND SHRIMP
(for 6 to 8)

4½ teaspoons unflavored gelatin
(1½ envelopes)
⅓ cup dry white wine or cold
water
2½ cups seasoned chicken broth

6 hard-cooked eggs, peeled and
sliced thin
2 pounds cooked shrimp, sliced if
large
1 truffle or large black olives

Soften the gelatin in the white wine, or cold water if you do not want the
wine flavor. Set aside. Heat the chicken broth to boiling, remove from
heat and add the softened gelatin. Cool until syrupy in texture. Pour a
thin layer of the gelatin mixture in a 1½-quart mold and one layer of
the sliced eggs and slivers of the truffle, black olives or any other decoration you might prefer. Refrigerate. When firm, fill mold with alternate
layers of the shrimp and eggs, and the remaining truffles. Pour the rest

of the syrupy mixture over, cover with wax paper or foil and refrigerate for several hours. Use this as a quick method for molding seafoods, chicken and vegetables. For meats I prefer using beef consommé, but use the white wine for flavor.

If you are just too too about making your own aspic, go ahead.

ASPIC

2 pounds veal, any cut will do   1 large onion, diced
1 or 2 veal bones   1 cup coarse diced celery
2 pounds chicken bones, wings,   1 cup coarse diced carrots
    backs, etc.   Few sprigs parsley
1 gallon cold water   1 tablespoon salt

Put veal, bones and chicken in a pot, add water and bring to a boil. Skim off scum that will form. Add rest of ingredients, and simmer 3 or 4 hours (under boiling). Add more water if necessary, but keep the ingredients covered with the water. Strain through 2 thicknesses of cheesecloth or a clean towel wrung out in cold water. Refrigerate, then skim off the solid fat which will come to the top of the stock. Clarify.

To Clarify Any Stock:

For each quart of cold, fat-free stock add 1 slightly beaten egg white and 1 egg shell. Stir and simmer for 15 minutes. Do not boil. Remove from heat, let stand 30 minutes. Strain through a clean towel or double cheesecloth wrung out in cold water.

Sherry French Dressing (*Helen Corbitt's Cookbook*, page 43) is one you should make and keep on hand. It is a light, mildly flavored dressing that goes well with any greens, fruit or vegetable. It does not fight with whatever wine you may be drinking. I like it especially on sweet red and green peppers.

SHERRY FRENCH DRESSING
(*5 cups*)

1 egg
1 teaspoon sugar
2 teaspoons salt
4 cups salad oil (half olive oil
   makes even better)

½ cup vinegar
½ cup sherry
2 cloves garlic

Mix egg, sugar and salt together; add oil and vinegar alternately until all the oil is added, then drip the sherry in slowly. Add garlic cloves, barely crushed, and store in a Mason jar until ready to use. Toss among any collection of salad greens you may find and your salad will be a success. This dressing has a special affinity for Roquefort cheese too.

LEMON FLOATING ISLAND

4 cups milk
4 eggs, separated
4 tablespoons confectioners' sugar
½ teaspoon lemon juice

½ cup granulated sugar
Pinch of salt
½ teaspoon lemon extract
Grated rind of 1 lemon

Bring milk to a fast boil in a shallow sauce pan or skillet, but the milk should be at least 1 inch deep. Reduce heat to simmer. Beat egg whites stiff, add confectioners' sugar slowly beating each time to stiff again. Add lemon juice and beat about 1 minute. Drop two or three tablespoonfuls into the simmering milk. Cook 1 minute, turn, cook 1 minute more. Do not crowd in the pan as the mixture will expand. Drain on a clean cloth. Repeat until all egg whites are used. Mix the yolks with the sugar and salt. Pour hot milk slowly into the egg mixture, then return to pan and cook about 3 or 4 minutes until custard coats the spoon. Watch it or you will have scrambled eggs. Remove, strain and add lemon extract and rind. Cool. Place fruit — I especially like blueberries or peaches, or both — in a bowl, pour custard over, and float the egg whites on top. Refrigerate. Before serving, thread Caramelized Sugar over the top. Omit the lemon if you wish to substitute any other flavoring. Candied violet dust is pretty sprinkled lightly on top. You may prepare this the day before, except for the Caramelized Sugar. Be sure to cover and refrigerate if you make ahead.

We see baked ham on many buffet tables at all times of the year. As delicious as it can be, why not make an elegant Ham Mousse which artfully served on a handsome tray with parsley sauce can be a masterpiece.

COLD HAM MOUSSE
(for 6 to 8)

1 tablespoon plus 1 teaspoon un-flavored gelatin	¼ cup mayonnaise
	2 teaspoons Dijon mustard
¼ cup dry white wine or water	2½ cups finely diced or ground cooked ham, or more if you
2 tablespoons butter	
1 tablespoon flour	wish
1 cup half-and-half or chicken broth	½ cup whipping cream

Soften gelatin in wine. Set aside. Melt the butter, add the flour and cook until bubbly. Add the half-and-half, mix and stir with a French whip and cook over low heat until thickened. Add the gelatin. Cool. Mix the mayonnaise, mustard and ham, add to the sauce. Chill. As it becomes thickened and cold, fold in the cream, whipped. Correct seasonings. Pour into a 1½-quart mold lightly rubbed with mayonnaise. Chill in refrigerator until firm. Unmold onto a chilled serving tray and serve with:

PARSLEY SAUCE
(*2 cups*)

½ cup mayonnaise
1 cup sour cream
¼ cup finely chopped fresh spinach
   or watercress

¾ cup finely chopped parsley
Few drops onion juice
Salt and white pepper

Mix, season and serve cold with the mousse.

GINGERBREAD MUFFINS
(*3 dozen small muffins*)

2 cups flour
1½ teaspoons soda
1½ teaspoons powdered ginger
½ teaspoon salt
1 cup molasses

⅓ cup butter or margarine
½ cup buttermilk
1 egg
½ cup raisins
½ cup chopped pecans

Sift the flour, soda, ginger and salt. Set aside. Heat the molasses and butter until lukewarm. Pour in the buttermilk and slightly beaten egg. Beat thoroughly. Add the raisins and nuts to flour mixture, and stir in the molasses mixture only until blended. Drop into buttered muffin pans three-quarters full. Sprinkle top with cinnamon and sugar (½ teaspoon cinnamon, ½ cup sugar). Bake at 325° for about 25 minutes.

One usually thinks of Turkey or Chicken Loaf as a leftover, but this recipe was one of the favorite brunch or luncheon entrées in the Zodiac Room at Neiman-Marcus. It was even a welcomed entrée on our Thursday night buffets. By whom? The men. I serve it frequently for a buffet and it is always a request recipe. Bake the Turkey Loaf in a bundt pan or angel food pan. It looks more interesting, as does any loaf.

TURKEY LOAF
(for 8 to 10)

2 pounds raw turkey or chicken meat, ground

4 eggs

1 cup undiluted canned cream of mushroom soup

1½ teaspoons salt

2 tablespoons chopped pimiento

2 tablespoons chopped green pepper, blanched

1 cup white bread crumbs

¼ teaspoon white pepper

¼ teaspoon Worcestershire sauce

American cheese, sliced

Markets are beginning to sell ground turkey meat now. If yours does not, buy the turkey and ask the butcher to grind it for you — or else do it yourself. No skins. It makes a good burger too. Mix all the ingredients except the cheese. Put half in the buttered pan, then a layer of American cheese. Fill pan with rest of the mixture. Cover and bake in a 350° oven for about 1 hour. Turn out and serve with any sauce you like, but I like:

MUSHROOM FONDUE
(3 cups)

½ pound fresh mushrooms	2 cups half-and-half
¼ cup butter	1 pound Gruyère cheese, diced
¼ cup flour	¼ cup dry sauterne or sherry

Wash and dry the mushrooms and cut in fourths, leaving the stems on. Sauté in the butter for five minutes stirring constantly. Add the flour, cook until bubbly. Add the half-and-half and cook over low heat stirring rapidly. No lumps! Add cheese and wine. Keep warm and serve. Any leftover Turkey Loaf makes a good sandwich the following day, and any sauce reheated and poured over makes it doubly so.

I have a vegetable with this menu I find most popular. The green beans I prefer fresh and cooked just under done, then tossed with crisp bean sprouts and water chestnuts. Just a few drops of soy sauce — Kikkoman I like best. It gives them a sparkle of flavor. You could use the kitchen-cut or French-cut frozen beans, but take them out of their pouch and put in a shallow pan. Cover and cook about 5 minutes, shaking the pan while cooking. The fresh beans I cook in a steamette — and if you do not own one, buy one. You'll enjoy all your vegetables cooked in it; they will look better, taste better and have a better texture. There are various kinds, but the Steam Marvel is the best. Prepare your vegetables, put them in the gadget, and place in a pot with ½ inch only of boiling water in the bottom of the pot. Cover tightly and cook. I do green beans about 3 minutes, snow peas 30 seconds, fresh asparagus for 3 minutes. There is no timetable. You find your own time to suit your taste (double the time for frozen vegetables), but it takes so little time, you cannot complain.

For my vegetable combination to serve 6, I use 1 pound fresh green beans, 1 cup bean sprouts, 1 cup sliced water chestnuts, canned as a rule, 3 tablespoons melted butter and about ½ teaspoon Kikkoman soy sauce.

FLAN
(for 6)

3 eggs plus 3 egg yolks	1 teaspoon vanilla
¾ cup sugar	Caramelized sugar
3 cups milk	1 tablespoon grated orange peel

Mix the eggs and sugar and beat until a light yellow. Warm the milk until hot, but do not boil. Add to the egg mixture and continue beating. Add vanilla. Strain through a sieve into a 1½-quart soufflé dish or mold that has been lined with caramelized sugar and the grated orange peel, or you may strain the mixture into individual custard cups. Bake in a 325° oven in a pan of hot water for about 45 minutes or until firm. Chill. When ready to serve, sprinkle with slivered toasted almonds.

This is a pretty dessert if unmolded and surrounded with the melted caramel and whole strawberries dipped in powdered sugar.

CARAMELIZED SUGAR
(½ cup)

Place 1 cup sugar in a sauce pan and cook over medium heat, stirring frequently until it has a wet look. Then stir constantly until a syrup is formed. Add 2 tablespoons of water and continue cooking until syrup is brown, but do not let it burn. Pour this into your soufflé dish, let it harden, sprinkle with the grated orange peel, and then pour in custard.

RICE SALAD
(for 6 to 8)

3 cups chilled cooked rice	1 tablespoon finely chopped onion
1 cup chilled cooked peas	1 tablespoon salad oil
½ cup chopped Major Grey's Chutney	1 tablespoon wine vinegar
½ cup finely chopped celery	⅔ cup mayonnaise or half sour cream
⅓ cup chopped fresh parsley	Salt and white pepper

Combine the first 6 ingredients by tossing lightly with a fork. Add the oil, vinegar and mayonnaise. Season to your taste. Spoon into a 1½-

quart mold lightly rubbed with mayonnaise. Refrigerate for a few hours for a better mingling of flavors. Turn out onto a chilled serving platter or fill thin slices of ham or Swiss cheese with it, and roll up like an enchilada.

ORANGE CHIFFON CAKE

2¼ cups cake flour	5 egg yolks
3 teaspoons baking powder	¾ cup water
1½ cups sugar	2 teaspoons grated orange peel
1 teaspoon salt	1 cup egg whites (7 or 8 eggs)
½ cup salad oil (not olive oil)	½ teaspoon cream of tartar

Sift the dry ingredients together. Pour in the oil, egg yolks, water and orange peel. Beat until smooth (2 minutes with an electric beater). Set aside. Beat together egg whites and cream of tartar until stiff. Pour mixture over egg whites a little at a time, gently folding in with a spatula. Do not beat. Pour into a 10-inch unbuttered tube pan and bake at 325° for 50 minutes. Increase to 350° and bake an additional 15 minutes, or until the top springs back when you dent it with your finger. Turn pan upside down onto platter. Let stand until cold before removing pan. Or use a cake mix if you must.
Cover with:

COFFEE BUTTER CREAM ICING

½ cup butter	1½ teaspoons instant coffee
2 cups confectioners' sugar	½ teaspoon vanilla

Beat the butter until creamy. Add rest of ingredients and beat until light and fluffy.
Cover the iced cake with shaved semi-sweet chocolate.

SHAVED CHOCOLATE

You need a large piece of chocolate to obtain large rolls or shavings of chocolate. The easiest way to get the large piece is to buy it from a bakery supplier, or ask a commercial baker to sell it to you. Otherwise, buy the packages of 1-ounce squares or morsels and melt over hot water, pour into a loaf tin until you have a piece at least 1 inch thick. Refrigerate until it hardens. Remove from the tin and leave at room temperature for at least 1 hour. Take a heavy sharp knife — I use a French knife — place on top of chocolate, press down lightly and pull the knife over the chocolate toward you. The larger the piece of chocolate, the larger the shaving.

CREPES
(24 to 30 crêpes)

I have found I have a consistently more tender crêpe if I use cake flour, but there is no law that says you must. I use the same formula for dessert crêpes but I add more sugar.

2 cups sifted cake flour	½ teaspoon sugar
2 cups milk, whole or skim	10 tablespoons butter or margarine
4 eggs, separated	

Put flour in a bowl, add the milk and stir with a French whip until smooth. Add 4 egg yolks and 2 of the egg whites, unbeaten, and beat until well blended. Add sugar and butter, melted, not hot, just melted. Let batter stand at least 1 hour before cooking. Fold in the 2 remaining egg whites beaten to soft peak stage. Pour about 1 tablespoon butter into a hot crêpe pan. Swish around until pan is completely covered. Pour off excess butter. Add 1½ tablespoons of batter, more or less. Tilt pan until bottom is covered. Cook about ½ minute, turn with a spatula, cook ½ minute. Remove from pan and repeat. You do not need to add more butter to pan. Pile crêpes on top of one another; it is not necessary to put paper in between crêpes.

If you prefer a thinner crêpe, add more milk. If making ahead of time, wrap in clear plastic or foil. Crêpes freeze satisfactorily. To use after freezing, defrost at room temperature. Do not put in a hot oven or they will melt into one big glop. Regardless of what you put into a crêpe, the important thing to remember is to roll it loosely. Both the crêpe and the filling will have better flavor and texture.

RATATOUILLE

This is the most versatile of all vegetable dishes. You may use it hot or cold, as an hors d'oeuvre, salad or main dish; keep it covered in your refrigerator for several days. I like to put Ratatouille in crêpes and use for a luncheon or brunch.

3 medium-sized zucchini	1 cup thin-sliced onion
1 medium-sized eggplant, peeled	¼ cup salad oil or half olive oil
4 tomatoes, peeled	1 clove garlic, finely minced
2 green peppers	Salt and pepper

Slice zucchini and eggplant into ¼-inch slices. Cut tomatoes in medium dice. Seed the peppers, slice thin and blanch. Sauté the onion in the oil until soft; do not brown. Add tomatoes, cook 1 minute. Mix in rest of ingredients, cover and bring to boiling point. Cook 5 minutes. Remove cover and cook at simmer heat until all liquid has evaporated. Correct seasonings; sprinkle with chopped parsley (for added color).

RATATOUILLE IN CREPES

Put ¼ cup of Ratatouille in each Crêpe, roll loosely and place in a buttered shallow casserole. Sprinkle with grated Parmesan or with half Swiss cheese. Place in a 350° oven until hot and run under broiler to brown. Allow 2 Crêpes per person. I serve these as a vegetable with roast beef or lamb, but then I would serve Ratatouille with anything, because my guests think me smarter than I am. No doubt because I can pronounce Ratatouille.

PEAS IN ASPIC
(for 8 to 10)

1 tablespoon plus 1 teaspoon unflavored gelatin
⅓ cup dry white wine or water
2 cups chicken broth

2 cups cooked frozen petite peas
2 tablespoons chopped mint
2 cups cooked julienne carrots
Salt and pepper

Soften gelatin in the wine or water. Heat the chicken broth to boiling point, remove from heat and add gelatin. Correct seasonings. Coat the bottom of a 1½-quart mold with the gelatin mix. Refrigerate. Add the peas and pour in enough gelatin mixture to hold them in place. Refrigerate to set. Chop the mint very fine (no stems), add to the carrots and arrange over the peas. Add rest of gelatin mixture as it begins to congeal. Refrigerate overnight. Unmold and surround with fresh mint leaves on Boston lettuce. Serve with Mint Dressing. If you can only find the peas in butter sauce, defrost and wash thoroughly.

MINT DRESSING
(2 cups)

½ cup vegetable salad oil
¼ cup red wine vinegar
½ cup fresh mint leaves, finely
chopped

1 garlic bud, crushed
½ teaspoon cracked pepper
1 teaspoon salt

Put in a container and shake.

SALMON TIMBALES
(for 6 to 8)

2 pounds skinned and boned salmon, fresh or canned
Approximately 2 cups white wine
or half water
1 teaspoon minced shallots or
onion
2 egg yolks

1 teaspoon lemon juice
1 teaspoon salt
Few grains cayenne pepper
2 teaspoons cornstarch
1⅓ cups milk
½ cup heavy cream, whipped

Place salmon in a shallow skillet one inch deep with half water, half dry white wine. Add shallots. Bring to just below boiling point, reduce heat and cook gently until fish flakes when tried with a fork. Lift out and drain (or use canned salmon, but be sure to remove skin and bones). Grind very fine or put in a blender with the lemon juice and egg yolks until you have a paste. Add the seasonings and cornstarch. Mix thoroughly. Pour in the milk. Cool and add whipped cream. Fill a well-buttered ring mold or individual custard cups. Set in a pan of hot water. Bake at 350° until firm, or cook covered on top of stove in the hot water at low heat. Turn out at once on hot serving tray. Serve with the sauce you prefer. I like to use slivered cooked fresh asparagus added to a Basic Cream Sauce.

EGG AND CELERY SALAD

10 hard-cooked eggs, peeled
1½ cups blanched celery, thinly
sliced on the diagonal
1 tablespoon white wine vinegar

½ cup mayonnaise
1 tablespoon Dijon mustard
2 tablespoons finely chopped
parsley

Slice 8 whole eggs and 2 egg whites. (Reserve 2 extra egg yolks and rice them for garnish.) Blanch the celery for 1 minute in boiling water. Chill. Toss celery and eggs lightly with the vinegar and mayonnaise mixed with the mustard. Sprinkle with riced egg yolks and chopped parsley.

APPLE BAKLAVA

2 apples, peeled, cored and thinly sliced
¼ cup sugar
½ teaspoon cinnamon
About ¼ pound fillo strudel leaves (also called phylo pastry leaves — you buy in a Greek market or restaurant)

½ pound slivered almonds, margarine
½ pound slivered almonds, lightly browned
½ cup water
½ cup sugar
½ teaspoon lemon juice

Mix apples, sugar and cinnamon. Place a sheet of the pastry leaves in baking pan (13" x 9"). Brush with melted butter. Repeat twice. Scatter some of the apples and nuts over. Cover with another sheet of pastry and repeat process until apple and sugar mixture is used. Place 6 sheets of pastry on top, brushing each sheet with butter and sprinkling with nuts. End with pastry. Brush with butter. Cut baklava into size portions you wish to serve. Bake at 350° until apples are tender, about 50 minutes. Bring water and sugar to a boil and cook until a syrup is formed. Add lemon juice. When pastry is done, pour syrup over. When cold, recut. Note: Keep leaves moist by covering with damp towel.

If you cannot find the phylo pastry leaves, you may order from:

Athenian Candy Shop
233 South Halstead Street
Chicago, Illinois

Ask for one-pound package in a roll.

PEACHES A L'ORANGE

8 fresh, frozen or canned peaches
6 tablespoons melted butter
6 tablespoons light brown sugar

Grated rind of 2 oranges
1½ teaspoons lemon juice
2 ounces Cognac

Peel peaches, if fresh, cut in half and remove pits. Place in a shallow casserole or skillet. (I use a crêpe suzette pan.) Sprinkle with the butter, sugar, orange rind and lemon juice. Place under broiler until hot and bubbling. Pour Cognac over and ignite. Serve warm as is, with almond-flavored whipped cream or over ice cream.

3

Luncheons: Seated and Buffet

UNLIKE BRUNCHES luncheons are more precise as to time and more formal. One might slip into comfortable shoes and an old dress for a brunch, but even with today's informality, luncheons still demand a more formal approach to dress, conversation, food and service.

The dining room is one of the last outposts of civilization. Let's keep it like that. As the hostess, you set the tone of your party. I feel that food can be part of the decoration, so in planning a menu you should see the food in your mind's eye. The color, texture and flavor of your menu is what a discriminating guest will notice. If you plan with your taste buds you will have the whole concept of your menu.

The first course, or even a one-dish luncheon, should indicate to your guests that they are having a lovely meal. The following menus are for seated parties, but could easily be converted to a buffet.

Seated Luncheons

Cantaloupe ring surrounded with clusters of fresh fruit,
powdered sugar in center with lime slices as garnish
Hot Buttered Bread Sticks
Chicken Breast Camillo à la Helen on mushroom risotto
Lemon-buttered slivered carrots and green beans
Kiss Meringues in apricot custard

Jellied madrilene with mashed avocado and twist of lime
(Serve it in crystal for color)
Lightly curried crabmeat on broiled large mushrooms
Fresh asparagus with black butter
Icebox Rolls (*Helen Corbitt's Cookbook*, p. 235)
Fresh pineapple slice with pineapple sherbet and
slivered fresh pineapple

Papaya or mango and romaine salad with Poppy Seed Dressing
Cold poached salmon with cucumber sauce
Hot cheese soufflé served with melted sweet butter
Popovers (*Helen Corbitt's Cookbook*, page 241)
Coffee ice cream and orange ice spooned into low dessert compotes

Cold cream of minted fresh pea soup
Cheese Torte with Stuffed Mushrooms in Cream
Mangetouts (snow peas) with special butter
Buttered small hot biscuits (you may buy them at most
frozen food counters today)
Chilled strawberries and sliced melon, sprinkled with Cointreau

If men are present, you might tempt them with

Cold Ratatouille on half of a peeled tomato, oil and vinegar dressing
Thin slices of Veal Picatte
Fettucine with finely chopped fresh spinach stirred in
(What shall I call it?)
Glazed Apples and thin slices of Cherry Nut Cake

This menu wouldn't be unacceptable for a group of women either. Certainly a change.

Somehow chicken finds its way to many a luncheon. I like the recipe in the following menu as it is both delicious and attractive.

Artichoke and celery knob salad with chive dressing
Breast of Chicken à l'Orange with avocado and papaya
Brown Rice
Icebox Cheese Cake

I have a special salad luncheon that everyone likes. It can be prepared ahead of time, refrigerated and assembled in five minutes. Since I have been in the restaurant business for many years, I am tired of seeing lettuce used for luncheon salads go to waste. So I have designed a salad lunch without lettuce and called it a potpourri of salads.

You may use three small coquilles (per guest) or small dessert dishes. The coquilles may be china, foil or the shells you buy from any kitchenware counter. In one coquille I put an assortment of fresh fruit; in another, chicken salad made with capers in the mayonnaise; and in the third, a seafood or a Rice Salad. Sometimes I make a hot Crab Imperial for one coquille while I'm assembling the other dishes. I place the round edge of the coquilles to the outside of the plate so there is room in the center of the plate for a wine glass or parfait glass filled with a citrus ice or sherbet. I like to use pink grapefruit ice. You may tuck sprigs of watercress or parsley in between the coquilles. I usually serve a thin Melba toast or toasted crackers and coffee. Do not forget to pass Poppy Seed Dressing for the fruit. This is such a pretty luncheon with no jumping up for dessert; it is all there. The menu would be a good suggestion if you were entertaining in a club or restaurant too, as it is pretty to look at and uncomplicated for the cook. Sometimes I use large artichoke bottoms to hold the seafood and the chicken salads, and fill a scooped out orange or papaya with the fruit. You may also use an orange shell to hold the sherbet.

For a summertime luncheon, a small cup of cream of corn soup can be served in the room where guests have gathered. I find if I put my cream soups in the blender my guests can drink without a spoon. On the table:

A salad of season-ripened fruits on a small bed of lettuce
with white meat of chicken salad in the center and a good-
sized bunch of watercress for a garnish
Thin Swiss cheese sandwich triangles
Vanilla ice cream with Sauce Lawrence (*Helen Corbitt's
Cookbook*, page 268)

All these dishes may be prepared ahead of time and refrigerated. The soup could be made the day before; the salad fruits may be cut; chicken for salad likewise. Even the watercress, if washed thoroughly and put in a plastic bag overnight, will be more crisp than if prepared the day it is served.

Fresh spinach and orange salad with Sherry French Dressing
Curried sliced eggs and shrimp (Add a little chutney to the
curry sauce) in hot toasted patty shells (You may buy them frozen,
who will know?)
Slivered green beans with coconut
Individual Cold Lemon Soufflés with puréed apricots

Gazpacho (*Helen Corbitt's Potluck*, page 8)
with sliced cucumbers floating
Individual Avocado Mousse rings (*Helen Corbitt's Cookbook*, page 66)
filled with mixed seafood, Sauce Louis and white asparagus
Chilled Fresh Stewed Pears in Caramel Syrup

The color of Gazpacho should be exploited. I serve this soup in crystal, as it gives a glow to my table, especially if I'm using shades of yellow or orange in my linen.

Fresh asparagus with orange butter
Sliced chicken on mushroom soufflé with fondue sauce
(a nice combination of flavors)
Fresh strawberries with Madeleines

I like fresh asparagus and if it isn't available I usually skip it, except for canned to serve cold. I cut fresh asparagus in slantlike pieces too. It is easier to eat, but I like to serve about three whole stalks hot as a first course with grated orange peel in the butter.

This could be a one-plate luncheon with only the dessert to serve:

Half a peeled avocado, filled with lightly curried chicken,
or any shell fish, topped with whipped cream and browned under broiler
Baked chutney peach half, dribbled with cognac
Homemade Melba toast
Very thin lemon cookies

Grapefruit and apple salad with Apple Dressing
Veal Patties Scallopini
Green Noodles
Cake Crumb Pudding (*Helen Corbitt's Cookbook*, page 245)
with Foamy Sauce (*Helen Corbitt's Cookbook*, page 260)

Half a tomato filled with Raw Vegetable Salad
Mustardy French dressing
Chicken shortcake
Curried fruit
Angel Soufflé with lemon custard sauce

Cream of Peanut Soup
Thin peanut butter sandwich triangles
Thin slices of ham rolled around chicken salad
Individual Corn Pudding (*Helen Corbitt's Cookbook*, page 184)
with curried peas spilled over
Melon balls in Orange Sauce

Buffet Luncheons

It isn't always the thought of the hard work involved in entertaining that keeps us from being relaxed, it is the cost. If you have a low budget, you can have just as successful a party as the one next door with unlimited cash. It takes more imagination and more thoughtful planning, but the result can be a delightful experience for hostess and guests alike.

As restaurants, tea rooms and clubs become more crowded with business executives and regular patrons, we turn more and more to entertaining at home, especially for lunch. Buffet luncheons at home can be more informal. You can expect some guests to be late and some will be; some to forget and some may. But don't have a nervous breakdown. Who cares? It is an informal time of day and your friends know that it's fine to bring along an extra guest without calling you. You may have food left over to freeze or you may run out but you are in your home and the atmosphere is warm and your friends are happy to be included.

Fruit, as a rule, is expensive and soup is not. I have used the following menu for both men and women before or after a football game. It worked. They liked:

A quick Sangria made with a half-gallon bottle
of domestic burgundy
Black Bean Soup, homemade and mighty good, in a big tureen,
often the pot it is made in (The soup is cheap and freezes well.)
Eggs poached in the hot soup are served floating in it
Warm peasant bread cut in thick slices spread with
farmer's cheese and sweet butter
Tossed salad greens with spinach, cherry tomatoes and slivered
green onions served with a Warm Lemon Dressing
Delicious apples sautéed in wine and butter, served with
sour cream and hot buttered walnut meats

Incidentally, Black Bean Soup with the egg poached in it is an acceptable quick supper. Raves from men.

Chicken pie (no vegetables) prepared in a shallow casserole
with crisscross pastry top
Hot tomato halves piled high with Ratatouille
Thinly sliced assorted bread and butter sandwiches
Sherry Glazed Apple Cake

Ham Crêpes in a Gruyère cheese sauce
Jellied Asparagus Salad with Green Herb Dressing
Twisted poppy seed rolls
Strawberries Melba

To honor an individual or for a political rally when you feel you should
host a crowd — try these menus:

Champagne and Chablis Cassis
Beef and mushroom pie
Cold Rice Salad
Marinated vegetables
Toasted split and buttered blueberry muffins
Slices of fresh fruit and Frozen Cheese

Cold Squash Soup
Veal à la crème with Mixed Noodles
Mushroom and spinach salad
Icebox Rolls (*Helen Corbitt's Cookbook*, page 235)
Bing Cherry Pie

Did you know that pie is the most popular dessert in America, with ice cream a close second? From a national survey, of course!

Chicken and almond soufflé, served with
pineapple and paprika sauce
Slivered green onions and peas
Relish salad bowl
Oven-toasted bread sticks
Sour Cream Pound Cake

Thinly sliced ham rolled around a deviled egg,
baked in mushroom sauce
Spinach Pudding Ring (*Helen Corbitt's Cookbook*, page 185)
filled with julienne of carrots
Thin bread and butter sandwiches
Cut fresh fruit over lemon sherbet
Brandy Snaps (*Helen Corbitt's Cookbook*, page 306)

Sandwich Luncheons

Sandwiches may be a delight or a bore. The bread should be fresh and thinly sliced, but the fillings should be thick. Sandwiches may be made ahead of time, wrapped and either refrigerated or frozen. Leftover sandwiches — and there seldom are — can be wrapped and frozen in small packages for a quick snack. When I was responsible for the sandwich bar at Neiman-Marcus, some of the young bachelors would buy our assorted sandwich points to freeze and use for the nights they were not invited out.

One of the most popular sandwiches I have ever served was called the Duke of Windsor sandwich. It was club style with one slice of buttered toast spread with a soft sharp Cheddar cheese, and then a good chutney slathered on; covered with the second slice of buttered toast and sliced turkey or chicken, hot broiled pineapple and a piece of soft lettuce of Boston texture; covered with the third slice of buttered toast. It was cut in wedges. This could be an acceptable luncheon with a green salad and a thin soup at any time. Men adore it.

Chilled Mushroom and Chive Bisque
Hot toasted crabmeat salad and cheese sandwich roll
Oranges Cognac

Hot Swedish Meat Balls (*Helen Corbitt's Cookbook*, page 129)
over sour cream potato salad on pumpernickel bread
Sauerkraut Relish
Apple torte

Curried Seafood Stew served with an assortment of sandwiches:
sliced deviled egg and fresh spinach on white bread with
Green Goddess Dressing (*Helen Corbitt's Cookbook,* page 52);
Toasted rolled asparagus sandwich; chicken salad and
Roquefort cheese on whole-wheat bread
Cold canned apricot halves with sour cream and toasted almonds

Oyster and Spinach Soup
Trays of sandwiches: perhaps tongue salad on dark rye bread
with horseradish butter; sharp soft Cheddar cheese, chutney
and sliced turkey on white bread, cut in quarters; thinly sliced
barbecued fresh pork and pepper relish piled in split
small buttered rolls
Raw relishes in a punch bowl, sprinkled with ice: old stand-bys —
carrot sticks, radishes, cherry tomatoes, fingers of raw
zucchini and yellow squash, asparagus, slices of unpeeled
Jerusalem artichokes, Brussels sprouts, black olives
and pickled corn on the cob
Small assorted tarts: chocolate with cinnamon whipped cream,
fresh strawberry and pumpkin

CHICKEN BREAST CAMILLO A LA HELEN
(for 4)

4 6- to 8-ounce chicken breasts, boneless or from a 1½-pound broiler
¼ cup flour
1 teaspoon salt
¼ cup plus 2 tablespoons butter

½ cup dry white wine
½ cup chicken consommé
1 jigger of brandy
White truffles (you may omit)
Shredded Mozzarella cheese

Remove skin from chicken, flatten with palm of your hand or roll out with a rolling pin. Dust lightly with the flour and salt. Shake off all excess. Melt the ¼ cup butter, add the chicken and sauté about 6 minutes on each side at medium heat. Turn only once. Pour in wine and chicken consommé. Cook slowly uncovered until the liquid is reduced, leaving only enough in the pan to keep the chicken from sticking. Add brandy and ignite. Add 2 tablespoons butter and allow to melt (do not continue cooking). Add 1 slice white truffle to each breast. Serve over rice cooked with chicken bouillon and saffron or over mushroom risotto. Pour the butter and juices left in skillet over the chicken. Sprinkle lavishly with cheese and run under broiler to brown.

I cannot get by without Poppy Seed Dressing though I'm personally tired of it. Why wouldn't I be? Years and years of watching it consumed by customers. Everyone likes this dressing on practically every kind of a fresh salad. I recommend it for fruit. With all their wonderful fruits I do not understand why Poppy Seed Dressing is not served on the West Coast.

POPPY SEED DRESSING
(3½ cups)

1½ cups sugar
2 teaspoons dry mustard
2 teaspoons salt
⅔ cup vinegar

3 tablespoons onion juice
2 cups salad oil, not olive oil
3 tablespoons poppy seeds

Mix sugar, mustard, salt and vinegar. Add onion juice and stir in thoroughly. Slowly add oil, beating constantly, and continue to beat until thick. When you think the mixture is thick enough, beat 5 minutes longer. Add poppy seeds and beat for a few minutes. Store in a cool place or in the refrigerator, but not near the freezing coil.

This dressing is easier and better to make with an electric mixer or blender, using medium speed, but if your endurance is good you may make it by hand with a rotary beater. The onion juice is obtained by grating a large white onion on the fine side of a grater, or putting a medium onion in an electric blender, then straining. (Prepare to weep in either case.) If the dressing separates, pour off the clear part and beat again, adding the poppy seed mixture slowly, but it will not separate unless it becomes too cold or too hot.

CHEESE TORTE

6 egg yolks	¼ teaspoon salt
2¼ cups half-and-half or milk	Pinch of nutmeg
2¼ cups grated Swiss cheese	6 egg whites, stiffly beaten

Beat egg yolks with the half-and-half, add cheese, salt and nutmeg. Mix thoroughly. Fold in egg whites. Pour into an unbaked 10-inch pie shell or pastry-lined torte pan (preferably one with a removable bottom). Bake at 350° until custard is set. Leftovers reheat successfully — but do not freeze.

This is a good entrée as is, but may be dressed up with stuffed mushrooms, broiled mushrooms, or any seafood or chicken in a light cream sauce.

STUFFED MUSHROOMS IN CREAM

16 large mushroom caps and
    chopped stems
½ cup butter
1 cup pine nuts (omit if not
    available)

¼ cup finely diced onion
1½ cups bread crumbs
1 cup half-and-half

Sauté washed mushroom caps in the butter for 1 minute. Remove; add the stems and the onions and cook until onions are soft. Add nuts and crumbs and stir. Stuff caps with the mixture. Place in a buttered serving casserole. Pour over the cream and bake at 350° for 20 minutes.

VEAL PICCATE

2 pounds thinly sliced veal cutlets
1 cup flour
1 tablespoon salt
½ cup butter
¼ cup olive oil

1 cup chicken broth
¼ cup lemon juice
2 lemons, sliced very thin
½ cup finely chopped parsley

Place cutlets between two pieces of foil and pound until they are thin, but not torn. Dredge in the flour and salt; shake off all excess flour. Heat the butter and oil and sauté the veal about 5 minutes over medium heat, turning the meat only once. If skillet is not large enough, as soon as first slices are done, pile on a plate and keep warm. Then return all veal to the skillet, add the chicken broth. Simmer until the liquid is reduced by one-half. Add the lemon juice and the thin slices of lemon. Heat only until lemons are hot. Correct seasonings. Add parsley at the last minute. Serve with the sauce poured over and garnish with the hot lemon slices.

GLAZED APPLES

6 Winesap or similar winter apples
3 cups sugar

1½ cups water
⅛ teaspoon cinnamon

Pare and core apples. Cut into quarters. Mix sugar and water and boil 10 minutes. Add cinnamon and drop apple pieces into syrup. Cook slowly until transparent. Place in a buttered casserole and keep warm. Keep any syrup left for another time. There will be.

CHERRY NUT CAKE

2 cups butter or margarine	¼ pound candied pineapple
2 cups sugar	5 cups broken nutmeats, pecans
6 egg yolks	or walnuts
3 cups cake flour	2 tablespoons lemon extract
¾ pound candied cherries	6 egg whites

Cream butter, add sugar and mix until smooth and light. Beat egg yolks and blend into butter mixture. Sift the flour over the fruit and nuts, and toss together until well coated. Stir into the butter and egg mixture. Add lemon extract. Beat egg whites until stiff but not dry and fold into batter. Pour into a well-buttered 10-inch tube or bundt pan and bake at 300° for 1¾ hours. Let cake cool on a rack for 10 minutes. Remove from pan and cool completely before slicing. When wrapped, this cake keeps for days and freezes well. No icing is necessary. Sometimes I pour over the top a lemon juice and sugar glaze.

BREAST OF CHICKEN A L'ORANGE

8 chicken breasts	2 cups orange juice (or half orange
½ cup flour	juice and half dry white wine)
2 teaspoons salt	Garnish of toasted nuts, avocado,
1 teaspoon paprika	papaya, mushrooms, orange or
½ cup butter or margarine	grapefruit slices (you may omit)

Remove bones yourself if you wish, but try to buy boneless chicken breasts if possible. Remove skin, dust lightly with mixture of flour, salt and paprika. Sauté in the butter at medium heat until a golden brown. Add orange juice, cover and simmer for 15 minutes. Baste once or twice. Uncover, reduce liquid, if necessary, to a slightly thickened sauce. When serving I like to mound whatever I'm serving it with — rice or noodles or vegetables — in the center of my serving tray, and stand the breasts up around it. Pour the sauce over the chicken. Garnish with slices of avocado or papaya, or both, and nuts or mushrooms. If avocado or papaya are not available, use orange and grapefruit sections.

ICEBOX CHEESE CAKE

For the crust, mix:

1½ cups graham cracker crumbs	1 tablespoon sugar
¼ cup melted butter	1 teaspoon cinnamon

Press onto the bottom and sides of a well-buttered 9-inch spring form pan. Bake at 400° for 10 minutes. Cool and chill.

3 egg yolks, beaten	2 8-ounce packages cream cheese
½ cup sugar	½ teaspoon grated lemon peel
½ cup hot water	1 teaspoon lemon juice
1 tablespoon plus 1 teaspoon un-flavored gelatin	4 egg whites
¼ cup cold water	1 cup whipping cream

Mix egg yolks with sugar, add hot water and cook in a double boiler over boiling water for 3 minutes, stirring constantly. Add the gelatin softened in the cold water. Stir in the cream cheese softened at room temperature. Mix thoroughly and strain. Add lemon peel and juice. Fold in stiffly beaten egg whites and cream, whipped. Pour into cold shell and refrigerate for several hours. A dash of Cointreau won't hurt it either.

CRAB IMPERIAL

¼ cup butter
1 tablespoon finely chopped
  shallots or onion
1 cup sliced mushrooms
¼ cup flour
1½ cups milk

½ cup sherry
1 teaspoon salt
2 teaspoons Dijon mustard
1 pound crabmeat, fresh, frozen
  or canned
2 tablespoons mayonnaise

Melt butter, add shallots or onion, sauté 1 minute. Add mushrooms and sauté until limp. Add flour and cook until foamy. Pour in milk, stirring constantly until mixture is thick. Mix in the sherry and seasonings. Cook until thickened again. Add crabmeat, cool and stir in mayonnaise. Correct seasonings. Spoon into lightly buttered coquilles or a 1½-quart shallow casserole. Return to oven at 300° to heat. Run under broiler to brown. May be prepared ahead of time.

COLD LEMON SOUFFLE

1 tablespoon plus 1 teaspoon unflavored gelatin
¼ cup cold water
4 egg yolks
½ cup lemon juice
¼ teaspoon salt
1 cup sugar

1 teaspoon grated lemon peel
¼ teaspoon lemon extract
4 egg whites
1 cup whipping cream
1 cup canned peeled apricots (no
  pits)

Soften gelatin in cold water. Set aside. Mix egg yolks, lemon juice, salt and ½ cup sugar. Cook in double boiler until thickened. Stir in gelatin, lemon peel and lemon extract. Cool. Beat egg whites until soft peaks form. Gradually beat in rest of sugar, and beat until stiff. Whip the cream. Fold egg whites into custard as it begins to congeal, then the whipped cream. Pour into custard cups and refrigerate. Unmold and serve with sauce of apricots puréed in the blender and sweetened to taste. Or pour into a 1½-quart soufflé dish or mold. I like to put a collar of foil around a 1-quart soufflé dish, tie securely, then remove before bringing to the table. This is a delicious soufflé to serve cold with any fruit and flavored whipped cream, if you wish.

You may use the same base for Cold Orange Soufflé, using ½ cup orange juice and 1 tablespoon grated orange peel and omitting the lemon extract.

SAUCE LOUIS
(3½ cups)

2 cups mayonnaise
½ cup chili sauce
2 tablespoons lemon juice (1 lemon normally yields 3 tablespoons of juice)

6 drops Angostura bitters (you may omit)
½ cup whipping cream

Mix mayonnaise, chili sauce, lemon juice and bitters. Whip cream and fold into the mixture. Chill. Good with any kind of seafood.

FRESH STEWED PEARS

1½ cups sugar
3 cups water
Pinch of salt

1 lemon, sliced, or juice of 1 lemon
8 whole fresh pears, peeled and cored

Mix sugar, water, salt and sliced lemon and bring to a boil. Add pears, cover and simmer slowly about 30 minutes until pears are tender. Remove pears. Use syrup pears were cooked in or make a Caramel Syrup and pour over. Serve chilled or warm.

CARAMEL SYRUP
(1 cup)

1 cup sugar   1 cup hot water
½ teaspoon vanilla extract

Melt sugar in a heavy skillet over low heat. Stir constantly until melted and a light brown. Remove from heat and add hot water. It will be lumpy. Return to heat and cook until lumps are dissolved. Cool; add vanilla.

MADELEINES
(for 24)

A very popular French sweet. Madeleine shell pans are sold in gourmet shops.

4 eggs   1 cup flour
¼ teaspoon salt   ½ cup melted butter, cooled
⅔ cup sugar
2 teaspoons grated fresh lemon
   peel

Beat the eggs with the salt until frothy. Gradually beat in the sugar until very thick and lemon-colored. (Use your mixer.) Add the lemon peel. Fold the flour into the egg mixture a little at a time. Fold in the melted butter. Fill buttered and floured shell tins three-quarters full. Bake 8 to 10 minutes at 400°. Remove at once and cool. You may add a few drops of food coloring to tint them if you wish.

   If you dislike grating lemons and oranges as you need them, do a bunch some day and freeze.

APPLE DRESSING
(1 cup)

1 cup apple juice   1 egg, beaten
¼ cup sugar   1 3-ounce package cream cheese
2 tablespoons arrowroot   ¼ teaspoon salt
Juice of 1 lemon

Mix juice, sugar, arrowroot and lemon juice. Cook in double boiler until thick. Pour a little of the hot apple juice mixture into the egg and then add to the remaining hot liquid. Cook 5 minutes over low heat, stirring constantly. Remove, add cream cheese and salt. Stir until completely dissolved. Good on any fruit combination.

Over the years my cooks have greeted me with "What do we scallopini today?" Since I like the flavor, I really do scallopini almost every cut of meat and poultry. These have been among my most popular luncheon entrées.

VEAL PATTIES SCALLOPINI
(for 16, 2-ounce patties)

2 pounds ground veal or stew meat	½ cup flour
	½ cup grated Parmesan cheese
½ cup finely minced onion	½ cup butter
1 small clove garlic, finely minced	¼ cup olive oil
2 teaspoons salt	1 cup Marsala wine
½ teaspoon white pepper	½ cup chicken broth
2 eggs	

Mix the first 6 ingredients and form into patties, 2 inches in diameter. Flatten with palm of your hand. Dust lightly with mixture of flour and Parmesan. Let stand at least 1 hour. Sauté in butter and olive oil until brown. Remove from pan. Add Marsala and chicken broth to pan. Cook until slightly thickened. Correct seasonings. Pour over patties. Allow at least two patties for each serving.

GREEN NOODLES

1 8-ounce package green noodles	1 teaspoon salt
1 cup sour cream	Cracked pepper

Cook noodles in boiling water (with a little olive oil added to keep the noodles from boiling over) until tender. Drain, but do not wash. Add 1 cup sour cream and toss with seasonings until well blended.

RAW VEGETABLE SALAD

1 cup bean sprouts, fresh or canned

½ cup sliced raw mushrooms (you may omit)

1 cup raw cauliflower buds

½ cup thinly sliced water chestnuts

½ cup crisp sliced Brussels sprouts or cabbage

¼ cup slivered green onions

Wash sprouts thoroughly and drain. Combine with rest of vegetables. For the dressing, I use:

½ cup red wine vinegar

1½ tablespoons Dijon mustard

½ cup olive oil

½ cup salad oil

1 teaspoon salt

Cracked pepper

Mix well and serve on raw vegetables atop soft lettuce or tomato halves.

ANGEL SOUFFLE

6 egg whites

Pinch of salt

Pinch of cream of tartar

1½ cups sugar

1 teaspoon lemon juice

1 teaspoon vanilla

Beat egg whites with the salt and cream of tartar until stiff. Add sugar gradually and continue to beat until stiff peaks are formed. Add lemon juice and vanilla. Pour into a buttered square 9-inch cake pan or into a ring mold. Bake at 325° for 45 minutes. Cool, slice and serve with a soft custard, flavored as you wish, and/or with any fresh fruit.

CREAM OF PEANUT SOUP

1 tablespoon butter

2 tablespoons finely chopped onion

1 tablespoon flour

1 quart milk

½ cup peanut butter

¼ teaspoon celery seed

½ cup finely chopped dry roasted peanuts (you may omit)

Melt butter, add onion, sauté until soft but not brown. Add flour and cook until foamy. Add milk, peanut butter and celery seed. Cook over hot water until creamy. Strain through a fine sieve. Add peanuts, correct seasonings.

ORANGE SAUCE FOR FRUIT

1½ cups orange juice ¾ cup melted currant jelly
⅓ cup Kirsch

Mix, pour over cold melon balls or cubes. Garnish with a twist of lemon and fresh mint.

BLACK BEAN SOUP
(for 12)

4 cups dried black beans	1 bay leaf
4 quarts cold water	2 carrots
1 cup sliced onion	Few sprigs parsley
2 cloves garlic, chopped	A ham bone or ½-pound salt pork
4 stalks celery, chopped	or leftover ham scraps
8 peppercorns	Salt and pepper

Cover beans with the water, bring to the boiling point and simmer for 10 minutes. Cool. Add remaining ingredients and cook about 4 hours below the boiling point until beans are soft. Add more water if necessary. Remove ham bone or salt pork, and put beans and vegetables through a Foley mill or purée in your blender. Correct seasonings. If you like, add sherry or Burgundy to taste. Sometimes I add rice, bits of avocado, sour cream, lemon or eggs poached in the soup. You may add the ham scraps too if you wish.

No time? Use canned Black Bean Soup as label directs and sherry or Burgundy will help it.

I like to use this very simple dressing on spinach and green salads if I'm not using Sherry French:

WARM LEMON DRESSING
(½ cup)

⅔ cup salad oil ·	⅓ cup lemon juice
2 tablespoons sliced scallions	Salt and cracked pepper
1 clove garlic, crushed	

Heat the oil and sauté the scallions and garlic for 1 minute. Add lemon juice, remove garlic and pour over salad. Season with salt and pepper.

SHERRY GLAZED APPLE CAKE

1 cup butter	1 teaspoon cinnamon
2 cups sugar	⅛ teaspoon nutmeg
3 eggs	3 cups peeled and chopped apples
3 cups sifted flour	2 cups chopped nutmeats,
1½ teaspoons soda	walnuts or pecans
½ teaspoon salt	2 teaspoons vanilla

Cream butter and sugar until well blended. Add the eggs, one at a time, beating after each addition. Mix dry ingredients and add gradually. Add the apples, nuts and vanilla. Pour into a greased and floured 10-inch tube pan or bundt pan. Bake at 325° about 1½ hours or until a cake tester inserted in center of cake comes out clean. Let stand 15 minutes and turn out.

Glaze: 1½ cups sugar   ½ cup sherry

Mix and stir over low heat constantly until syrup. Pour over cake. This would be a great neighborhood gift at Christmas-time — or any other time for that matter.

ANOTHER APPLE CAKE

Mix together:

2 cups sugar	2 eggs, beaten
1½ cups vegetable oil	Juice of ½ lemon
2 teaspoons vanilla	1 teaspoon salt

Mix 3 cups flour, 1½ teaspoons soda and add to liquids. Add:

3 cups chopped peeled apples   1½ cups broken pecans

Pour into buttered bundt or angel food tin. Bake at 375° for 1 hour or until cake tester comes out clean. Serve plain or with lemon glaze.

Glaze: 1 cup sugar   ¼ cup lemon juice

Bring to a boil.

HAM CREPES

16 thin crêpes	4 cups milk or half-and-half
16 thin slices baked or canned ham or Prosciutto	¼ cup Cognac
16 thin slices Gruyère cheese	Salt and white pepper
4 tablespoons butter	Grated Parmesan cheese
4 tablespoons flour	Paprika

Place a slice of ham and cheese the same length on each crêpe and roll. Place crêpes in a shallow casserole. Melt butter, add flour and cook 1 minute. Pour in milk; cook until thickened. Heat Cognac, ignite, add to sauce and cook 5 minutes. Season to your taste. Pour sauce over crêpes. Sprinkle with Parmesan cheese and paprika. Bake at 350° until brown. You may prepare the day before and reheat, or freeze for a few days. A thin slice of chicken may also be added to the crêpes. Substitute sour cream for the sauce sometime!

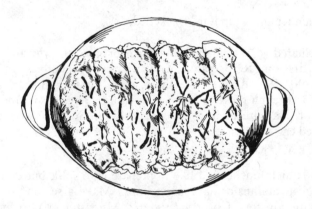

JELLIED ASPARAGUS SALAD

4 cups green asparagus spears	6 tablespoons lemon juice
1 tablespoon unflavored gelatin	1 teaspoon salt
¼ cup cold water	½ cup chopped celery
2 cups liquid from asparagus cans, plus water	½ cup sliced stuffed olives
1 teaspoon sugar	½ cup slivered blanched almonds
	¼ cup chopped parsley

Drain asparagus, reserving the juice. Soften gelatin in the cold water.

Heat the juice from the asparagus, adding enough water to make 2 cups of liquid. Add the softened gelatin to it. Remove from heat, add sugar, lemon juice and salt. When partially set add celery, olives, almonds and parsley. Arrange asparagus standing around sides of a ring mold or bundt pan. (I'll admit I use bundt pans a lot.) Cut up remaining asparagus and add to mixture. Pour into mold and refrigerate for several hours. Unmold on a bed of watercress. Serve with Green Herb Dressing.

GREEN HERB DRESSING
(1½ cups)

½ cup parsley leaves	1 teaspoon Worcestershire sauce
½ cup watercress leaves	2 egg yolks
8 peeled shallots or scallions	1 cup salad oil
2 teaspoons dry mustard	⅓ cup tarragon vinegar
1 teaspoon horseradish	1 teaspoon mixed dried herbs

Put in a blender and whip until thickened.

I find marinated vegetables can fill a need for salad or vegetable without much preparation. Refrigerate cans of whatever vegetables you wish to use overnight. The day you use them, open, drain and marinate with a good basic French dressing an hour or more. Then drain and arrange on a bed of salad greens in a bouquet fashion. Sprinkle with chopped hard-cooked egg and parsley.

One of the quick luncheons I like to prepare is to split, butter and toast either English muffins or hamburger buns. Make a seafood or chicken salad and pile on top. Cover with grated Muenster or Gruyère cheese and run under the broiler to brown.

FROZEN CHEESE

1 8-ounce package cream cheese	½ teaspoon vanilla
½ cup whipping cream	¼ cup confectioners' sugar
2 egg yolks	2 egg whites

Beat cheese and whipping cream until light and fluffy. Add egg yolks, vanilla and sugar. Stir until well blended. Beat egg whites until stiff and fold into the cheese mixture. Pour into a 1-pint mold and freeze. Serve with fresh fruit or preserved ginger.

COLD SQUASH SOUP

¼ cup butter
1½ cups finely chopped onion
1 quart small summer squash, sliced
2 cups chicken broth

¼ teaspoon sugar
2 cups whipping cream
Salt and white pepper
Pinch of nutmeg
Chopped parsley or chives

Melt the butter, add the onion and cook at low heat until soft but not brown. Add the squash and chicken broth. Cook until squash is tender. Add the sugar. Put mixture through a sieve or purée in the blender. Cool, add the cream and season with salt, pepper and a pinch of nutmeg. Chill, serve very cold sprinkled with chopped parsley or chives — good!

VEAL A LA CREME

2 teaspoons sugar
½ cup thinly sliced onion
4 pounds lean veal stew meat
3 cups chicken broth
1 tablespoon butter
1 tablespoon flour

1 cup whipping cream
Salt and white pepper
1 teaspoon grated lemon peel
1 tablespoon slivered lemon peel
Chopped parsley

Put the sugar and onion in a heavy skillet and cook slowly until the onions are glazed and soft. Add the veal and chicken broth. Cover and simmer until the veal is tender (approximately 1 hour). Mix the butter and flour together and blend with some of the liquid — then add to the rest of it. Cook until thickened. Add the cream, seasonings and grated lemon peel. Turn off the heat and let stand for at least one hour. Then reheat and serve with the slivered lemon peel and parsley sprinkled on top if you like. If prepared ahead, this dish has more flavor. It freezes well. I like to serve it with brown rice or Mixed Noodles.

MIXED NOODLES

1 8-ounce package fine noodles   ¼ cup grated Swiss cheese
5 tablespoons butter   Salt and cracked pepper
¼ cup half-and-half   1 cup uncooked fine noodles

Cook the 8 ounces of noodles in boiling salted water until tender. Drain, but do not wash. Add 2 tablespoons butter, half-and-half, cheese, season to your taste. Fry the other uncooked noodles in 3 tablespoons butter until brown. Toss with the hot cooked noodles.

BING CHERRY PIE

This is a divine pie — a great favorite with non-dieters.

1½ cups pecans, coarsely chopped   Red food coloring
5½ cups drained bing cherries,   1½ cups whipping cream
    pitted   1 Graham Cracker Crust
2 15-ounce cans condensed milk   (9-inch)
Juice of 6 lemons

Mix the pecans, whole cherries, milk and lemon juice, and a few drops of red food coloring. Whip and fold in the cream. Pour into prebaked Graham Cracker Crust. Chill. (Keep about 1 cup of mixture out of crust to pile in center after other mixture is set, if you want a high pie.) Cover with a thin layer of sour or whipped cream before serving, if you wish.

Graham Cracker Crust:

30 graham crackers   ¼ cup sugar
½ cup butter softened, not melted

Roll crackers into coarse crumbs. Mix with the sugar and butter and pat into well-buttered 9-inch pie tin. Bake at 375° for 5 minutes. Remove and cool. Always bake a graham cracker or cookie crumb shell before filling.

SOUR CREAM POUND CAKE

1 cup butter	½ teaspoon salt
1½ cups sugar	¾ cup currants
4 eggs	½ cup sour cream
2 cups flour	1 tablespoon Cointreau
¾ teaspoon soda	

Cream butter, add sugar and mix thoroughly. Add eggs and beat mixture until light. Sift flour, soda and salt together, add currants. Stir into the egg mixture alternately with the sour cream. Add the Cointreau and pour into a buttered and lightly floured angel food or bundt pan. Bake at 350° for 1 hour or until cake tester comes out clean. Turn out and while cake is warm pour over a lemon juice and sugar glaze.

MUSHROOM AND CHIVE BISQUE

½ cup butter	2 cups chicken broth
2 cups finely chopped mushrooms	2 cups half-and-half
(I use stems, too.)	¼ cup sherry
4 tablespoons flour	¼ cup finely chopped chives
¼ teaspoon dry mustard	¼ cup whipping cream
1 teaspoon salt	

Melt butter, add mushrooms and sauté until soft. Add flour, mustard and salt; cook 1 minute. Pour in chicken broth and cook until thickened. Add half-and-half, sherry and chives. Heat thoroughly and let stand over hot water until ready to serve. Whip the cream and float on top of soup. If serving cold, I put everything but the whipped cream in the blender, and chill.

ORANGES COGNAC

A few years ago, Marjorie Nyrop, an advertising woman from the West Coast, and I perfected this recipe for the Sunkist people. I use it often, and find both men and women enjoy it.

Peel and section navel oranges and stand each section around a compote-style dessert dish. Pile confectioners' sugar in the center. Serve with a liqueur glass of Cognac. You may dip the orange first into the Cognac, then the sugar or vice versa — or eat the oranges and drink the Cognac! At any rate, you have a delightful dessert with little effort. As a variation, I also melt brown sugar and butter with enough rum to make a syrup. Keep warm in a chafing dish and have a bowl of orange sections for guests to dunk with.

I use this recipe for cocktail parties, morning coffees and such, and vary the fruit: chunks of pineapple, bananas and whole strawberries.

SAUERKRAUT RELISH

4 cups canned sauerkraut, drained	1 cup chopped pimiento
2 red onions, sliced very thin	1½ cups sugar
1 large green pepper, chopped	1¾ cups apple cider vinegar
1½ cups celery, thinly sliced on the bias	1 teaspoon turmeric

Mix well. Store tightly covered. Chill for 48 hours. It will keep indefinitely in a cool place.

CURRIED SEAFOOD STEW

¼ cup butter
2 tablespoons onion, chopped fine
2 teaspoons curry powder
½ pound uncooked shrimp, sliced
¼ pound diced sea scallops

½ pound crabmeat, fresh frozen or canned, or filet of sole
3 cups milk
2 cups half-and-half
2 tablespoons sherry
6 or 8 saltines

Melt butter, add onion and cook until soft. Add curry and cook 1 minute. Mix in the shrimp and scallops and cook 2 minutes. Pour in other seafood, milk and cream. Bring to a boil, then remove from heat. Add the sherry and let stand over hot water until ready to serve. Crush the saltines and add just before serving. Correct seasonings. If you are not calorie-conscious, dollops of whipped cream.

OYSTER AND SPINACH SOUP

4 tablespoons butter
¼ cup finely chopped onion
1 clove garlic, minced
1 pint oysters, chopped
4 tablespoons flour
3 cups half-and-half or milk

1 cup chicken broth
¾ cup spinach purée (made in blender from fresh or frozen uncooked spinach)
Salt and pepper

Melt the butter, add the onion and garlic. Sauté at low heat until soft. Add oysters and cook until they curl. Push aside, add flour and cook until foamy. Add half-and-half, cook until thickened. Mix in chicken broth and spinach. Bring to a boil. Remove from heat. Correct seasonings and serve.

4

Making Friends
with Foreign Kitchens

THE FOREIGN FORTNIGHTS were inaugurated by Neiman-Marcus in 1957 and have since received worldwide attention. They represent a co-operative effort with a specific foreign country and its industries, with appropriate decorations, art, food, and merchandise being featured throughout the store. There is community participation in the two-week celebration in the form of special concerts, art, film, theater and lectures based on, or originating in the country being honored. The Fortnights have been a great inspiration to me as each one necessitated a thorough study of one country's particular history and culture. My special province was, of course, the cuisine of the country and directing the preparation of that country's unique native foods. I am a flag-waving American, but all our American cuisine stemmed from other sections of the world. In fact, I would say that every country's cuisine has been influenced by her next door neighbors to some extent.

A lively television situation comedy could be written about my contact with French cooking. I could cuss in French Canadian (which helped at times) and from high school French I could order a meal with no embarrassment. Papion, Master Chef of the French Line, arrived in Dallas with four assistants and a Liaison Chef from New York. They chose and prepared one entrée each day for lunch and one dinner for the Confrerie des Chevaliers du Tastevin and one dinner for customers. They asked for and received everything they wanted except the skin from a sheep's belly (I didn't know any sheep) and women (I took a full five minutes to interpret that one, but didn't know the right kind).

Papion was the king of his domain. I, the queen of mine. I finally decided that silence was golden. I found that the Frenchmen understood every word I said. Papion and I made peace. He also liked my Poppy Seed Dressing. He showed me and my cooks techniques that we incorporated into our daily culinary routine. I also invited his entire crew to my home for dinner — très gay, très American. They all ate with gusto and Papion arose at the slightest provocation to sing operatic arias. When I was sent to Europe by Stanley Marcus, as a "thank you," I chose the French ship Liberté, because of Papion and their delightful Irish passenger agent, and I had the most fascinating gastronomical binge one could imagine.

The Zodiac Room at Neiman-Marcus was decorated to resemble Maxim's in Paris, and it did. Monsieur Carrère of Maxim's came to keep me in line. He was a dear little man but very opinionated. So was I. He arrived two days before the Monday night French dinner I was to serve, and demanded pressed duck. I said "non." He said "non?" I said "non." As far as I knew, I was the only one in Dallas at that time who knew how to make pressed duck, and I wasn't going to do it.

What a night the Ambassador's dinner was! We borrowed Robert Gourdin from "21" in New York for the wine service during the entire two weeks, and especially for the Ambassador's dinner. We sent for the table lights from the Waldorf; linen from Heaven-knows-where; everything perfect — until the chairs arrived: brown tin. I said "no." The Display Department said "yes." Carrère arrived and jumped six feet off the floor in indignation. When I stomped my feet and demanded their removal, he picked me up, swung me around, kissed and hugged me. That was no mean feat as I weighed 185 pounds then. Needless to say the non-appearance of pressed duck was forgotten, and we became kissin' kin. The dinner was a success! Me? I collapsed in tears with a bunch of red roses and Stanley Marcus patting me on the head and saying: "I'll never ask you to do it again." We both knew he would — God love him.

One thing we learned about the Fortnight, as far as the customers were concerned, was that they didn't give a hoot about foreign chefs. They were more interested in what my staff might do. From then on I researched and experimented with the classic recipes of each country, but recipes from the people. I adapted food to Texans' taste, or at least thought I did, and my cooks were excited and performed beyond the call of duty. With each country we learned the national cooking techniques and added them to our own repertoire of recipes.

I went to England to research our second Fortnight. Oh me! I must have succeeded because Harry Lawrence of the Purdy Gun Works of London said if I opened a stand on Piccadilly Square and served bubble and squeek as we had cooked it, I would be a millionaire in a year's time.

The Ambassador's dinner — all men — went off without a hitch, because what man would not be happy with real prime beef. But my hashed brown potatoes with sour cream, hardly British, took the prize. Every Englishman there wanted the recipe.

The third year our menus shifted to South America. A representative from a South American airline was supposed to help me as health and budget prevented me from making the long trip. He came to visit; I gave him a list of what I wanted. I never saw or heard of him again until thirty minutes after our dining room, decorated as the Grand Azul in Lima, opened. When he bounced in and asked what he could do, I said: "Get out of my kitchen."

We had fun with the South American Fortnight. Later at Edward Marcus' Black Mark Ranch we duplicated a South American Asada, even to the metal cross-like holders for the barbecued beef, lamb and chicken, but added a touch of Texas with sourdough biscuits.

For the Fortnight, we flew naranjas juice from South America to Wil Wright in Los Angeles (we couldn't import the oranges themselves) to make the most refreshing ice I ever tasted, sort of an orange-like pink cloud. I bugged the Dallas produce people so much for yellow potatoes that one of them colored some by hypodermic and doubled the price. (He didn't get away with it.) We became ardent fans of the banana and plantains. Our most popular luncheon entrée was a charcoal broiled sweetbread, kidney, tenderloin and lamb chop served on its own individual broiler to each customer. We featured desserts using coffee, chocolate and caramelized sugar, what else? We also served various South American coffees free to customers all day at a coffee bar, all furnished by Chase and Sanborn. I remember them in my prayers every night! I adapted their brazil nut torte and named it Chantilly Torte. It has graced many a festive meal ever since. I even sent some to New York City for a special dinner given by Adele Simpson. Also our gracious head waiter to serve it.

Then we honored Italy and I spent two weeks in Northern Italian kitchens learning their cuisine. I had a lovely Italian girl, Kitty, as an interpreter. She was as fascinated in learning to cook Italian as I was, so I was constantly shaking her saying, "What did they say?" Those beautiful blue eyes of the Italian cooks also intrigued me. They all looked Irish to me. I really got into the fundamentals of food preparation, and I will have a soft spot in my heart for the Italians evermore. I went early in the morning to a little restaurant to learn about the dessert orange for which they were famous. At Donini's in Florence I went down into the bowels of the earth to learn about the fantastic Cake St. Honoré. The baking room had dirt walls, ceiling and floor and was hotter than the hinges of Hell. I watched from start to finish — three hours. I know I lost three pounds.

At Pappagallo's in Bologna I learned how to prepare pasta. What a day! I think the cooks were as intrigued with my enthusiasm as I was with them. What an antiquated kitchen, but what pasta! In this country can you imagine puréeing spinach through a sheep's belly? But what happy cooks they were. In Venice I stayed at the Ciprioni Hotel (in a broom closet) to learn about their suppa de pesco. They liked me because they had just received an American mixer and didn't know how to operate it. I showed them! At the Bunch of Grapes restaurant I tasted $40.00 worth of antipasto, and I mean tasted. I also downed a half tumbler of Grappa to please the owner.

The proprietor at Camillo's in Florence taught me how to prepare breast of chicken with wine and cheese, the best I ever ate. In Milan I learned to savor good Italian cooking in out-of-the-tourist-trade restaurants. The one observation I made about Italy was that people eat with relish. No dieting there! I should add that I washed everything down with much vino, and began for the first time to appreciate that nonsense about the marriage of wine and food. *I didn't gain an ounce of weight; in fact I lost.*

Rome began to take on the spicy flavor of southern Italy, and since Rome I have become quite a fettucini artist, with variations. I call it "mama food." This dish soothes me and others gastronomically and spiritually. I loved the Roman idea of serving fresh fruits in cold water. And of course, no one has lived until he has eaten fried artichokes.

I came back to Neiman-Marcus and for the first time in our Fortnights served an all-Italian menu. I guess the customers liked it, as they stood in line for hours to get in. The antipasto table was the highlight, and the high loss. Texans loved that antipasto and I had anticipated only samplings of all twenty-seven items. Instead, they filled their plates and went back for more. *Questo é il mundo.*

To honor the Italian Ambassador we took our dinner to the Sheraton Hotel, as the popularity of the Fortnights had increased. Willie Rossel, a Swiss chef, and I hit it off from the start. He did a magnificent dinner for some 1200 people. When I demanded different wine glasses for different wines it took the hotel manager, Randall Davis, to bring about the revolution and the beginning of a new and superior wine service in Dallas.

You know someone once said of me that it was easier to give me what I asked for than to listen to me. I am neither deflated nor flattered by this remark, but if you don't ask you don't receive. Even the Bible teaches you that.

Learning to cook for the Oriental Fortnight took me to the East and West Coasts to study with anyone who could help me. Those store budgets don't always make room for lesser lights like food directors. The late John Kan of Kan's Chinese Restaurant in San Francisco, the sexiest restaurant owner I ever knew, gave me the most help without me getting into his kitchen to work. He was a friend for whom I wish many stars in his crown. By researching, tasting and talking to many chefs we turned out some acceptable and interesting Oriental menus. I enlisted the help of Spice Islands for exotic spices. We researched the foods of the many countries of the area and our menus were exhilarating. We were open on Thursday night for dinner, so the first night I served a Chinese country dinner with Helen Corbitt flourishes; John Kan arranged for the thirteen-layer buns to arrive minutes before we needed them. I had the Almond Eye liquor that he had made into a famous drink made into a delightful taste-teasing ice.

A week later we had an all-Indian dinner that was a smash-aroo, including Helen Corbitt dashing around in a beautiful blue sari.

To honor all the Ambassadors and their wives we turned the entire store over to a benefit. (The dinners for Fortnight openings benefit various cultural activities in the city: the Dallas Symphony, the Ballet, the Civic Opera, et cetera.) We had open bars, Oriental dancers, sword swallowers, Japanese wrestlers, and beautiful merchandise on display. Our Zodiac Room became a set from *The King and I*. There were three buffets: Indian, Chinese and Japanese. The idea, of course, was to choose one. The guests did, all three! Who says the life of a food director is glamorous? The only glamorous thing about me that night was being authentically Chinese: robe, hair and makeup. I went through the receiving line and eagle-eyed Stanley Marcus didn't recognize me until I laughed. I was bent double, not from the obi, but the shoes — and too many guests. At five A.M. I tried to check into a downtown hotel *sans* baggage and with my right name. Well, that's another story.

The next year we were suffering poor foreign relations, so we settled for an American Fortnight. It was both fun and economically sound. Mr. Stanley hired Tony Duquette to decorate the Zodiac Room. He did! The Zodiac Room was transformed into a collage of the Pilgrims floating into a jungle, not Plymouth Rock but the *Santa Maria* filled with orchids floating in space to the Fountain of Youth in Florida. I divided the country into twelve areas and served foods indigenous to each. Every day I passed something extra that bespoke the region: Boston baked beans (yellow eyes), Hoppin' John, gumbo, Mid-Western casseroles (they are noted for them), flapjacks with blackberry syrup from the Northwest, and Shoofly pie from Pennsylvania. One drawback:

I received letters from people years later asking for recipes for some of the casseroles, and I hadn't the foggiest idea because most of them I had invented myself. You see, I like to cook!

For night openings — dinner! One night we served an old-fashioned church supper. What is more American than a church supper with all the tables together and everyone helping himself? There were lasting friendships formed that night by total strangers. I was fully convinced it was real Americana when a gentleman stopped and said, "Helen, it is authentic; the woman passing me the cole slaw licked her thumb which she had imbedded in the salad." I had a fish pond on the way out: homemade bread and chicken pies to buy.

The second night, a county fair with barbecue and beans, hot biscuits and fried chicken with all the fixings. Pot holders, pickles and jellies without labels, cakes and pies to buy as guests left if they wished, and they did. I can safely say without contradiction that from then on the Zodiac Room became a focal point of the entire Fortnight picture, and I give the church supper and county fair full credit.

The next year I went to Switzerland with Thelma Malloy to research their foods. While the Swiss are noted for their great restaurant and hotel schools, you find the native foods in small tucked-away places. I came back with a great respect for veal, cheese and their classic preparations. Again I adapted the meals to Texas palates. The crowds were amazing.

One opening night I served a formal Swiss dinner: reservations only, white gloves, the whole bit. We had so many requests for reservations and no available space because there were only two sittings scheduled. I had forgotten, really I had, that Neiman-Marcus did not belong to me, and I took a third sitting. More elevator men, more air-conditioning, more security, and no one dared object until the next day. Then I caught it, but from then on we planned for three sittings and a Monday night opening besides. I had had such fun in a beer hall in Lausanne that the second night opening I again put the tables together and served family style. On the tables I had draught beer in pitchers, all the cold food and pounds of butter for a help-yourself. Hot food was passed. To this day I have never convinced my customers that it was Swift and Company butter.

The Danish Fortnight took me to that charming country with its high-calorie foods. The open-faced sandwiches had so much butter on them you could hardly taste the variety of things the Danes put on top. I went to a luncheon put on by the Department of Agriculture, and if I could have eaten it all I would never have made it home. I had a delightful young man with me as an interpreter who took me to his home for a Danish tea party — seven flights up — no elevator, but what pastries!

Our Fortnight featured pastries prepared by a Danish baker sent to us from the Danish Pavilion at the World's Fair. Magnificent, except the days he had celebrated too much the nights before. The Danish meat balls were quite different from their Swedish neighbors', and in Denmark I really began to like red cabbage. Our night openings were smorgasbord and again we were amazed at their popularity. Of course we featured the wonderful Danish hams, duck and Cherry Heering.

And then Austria. I was disappointed in Vienna. There were no chandeliers in the streets and the Blue Danube did not flow through my hotel room. But Salzburg gave me my inspiration for the Fortnight food. I stayed at the Goldener Hirsh. Its owner, the Countess Wallendorf, invited me for dinner, served me many of the national dishes and told me how to prepare them. I learned more Austrian cuisine at the Peterskeller. I also gained ten pounds. I must say I like my version of sacher torte better than the Sacher Hotel's. My trip to the Sacher Hotel pastry kitchen is best described briefly because the head of the food service was addressed as "Doktor" and was born without a sense of humor. We had two formal Austrian dinners in the Zodiac Room which was divided into three rooms: the Imperial, the Sacher and the Hellenskeller and you guess why. Tafelpilze, sausage and desserts mit Schlag.

Then we started our Fortnights all over again, each year different from the previous one. The Zodiac Room became a French street scene one year; Watney's beer was featured for Great Britain with a mad Englishman drawing the beer. I do not know whether top management ever knew that both the Zodiac Room and our Espresso Bar were termed Helen's Saloons all over the city. Italy brought both Ferrara pastry and charming men from New York for me to work with. I'm not sure that Alfred Lepore will ever like cappuccino again. He offered to make it for everyone one night — 850 guests! But I tossed the fettucini! And so on and on.

In researching food for the Neiman-Marcus Fortnight, I used typical family recipes and adapted them to my customers' tastes and what was available in the local markets. These menus and recipes are based on this information.

Everyone who cooks as a hobby is sure they are French inspired.

French Dinner

Terrine Pâté
Rack of veal, roasted with cinnamon and lemon
Eggplant Provençale
Flageolets Panaches
Watercress salad
Brie
Baguettes with sweet butter
Hot Lemon Soufflé

Generally speaking, England has exerted its influence more than any other country on our food and eating habits. But I think we have improved upon it, again generally speaking.

It is interesting to note that only in the middle of the 18th century did individual water glasses appear on our tables, while table linen and knives appeared during Queen Anne's reign. Crude forks and fingers before this.

I like the storybook names of English foods: clippingtime pudding, syllabub, huckle my buff (eggnog with brandy), maids of honor: the latter was named by Henry VIII who observed Queen Anne Boleyn's maid of honor eating this pastry. (And I think only the English and Irish make a perfect cup of tea. Strictly personal.)

English Dinner

Cock-A-Leekie
English biscuits
Roast saddle of lamb with fresh mint sauce
Boiled Irish potatoes and peas
Green Cabbage with Bacon and Parsley
Trifle
Stilton cheese and wheatmeal biscuits

Simply put, there is Northern and Southern Italian food. I have always been addicted to Northern Italian cooking; my love affair began when I first started my career in Manhattan. Very seldom do I miss going to the San Marino Restaurant in New York to visit Tony, who started my love for this style of cooking.

Italian Dinner

Garlic Broiled Shrimp
Breast of Chicken Pappagallo
Spinach and White Beans
Peperoni Salad
Italian bread
Cake St. Honoré

I'm sure Cake St. Honoré is not a typical Italian dessert, but I learned to make it in Florence.

Denmark is noted for its open-sandwiches or Smorrebrød. The Danes believe in an abundance of food, so the sandwiches are numerous, all put on very thin slices of bread heavily buttered, and decorated to reflect their refreshing independence.

Danish Buffet Supper

Gravlax
Danish rye bread
Frikadeller
Pickled beets, boiled potatoes
Braised Red Cabbage
Cucumber salad
Danish Layer Cake

A pick-up supper of open-sandwiches would be all advance preparation and uncomplicated service. I arrange them on wooden trays (Danish), wrap and refrigerate. When ready to serve, unwrap and there you are. Just about anything goes on these sandwiches, and different flavors and textures are encouraged. For example, try thin slices of turkey and Danish cheese, sweet gherkins and fresh strawberry garnish. It is an excellent way to clean out your refrigerator.

The food of Switzerland is influenced by the countries that surround it, but I found the Swiss were dedicated to perfection in their cooking.

Swiss Dinner

Vol-au-vent Venetian Shrimp
Lamb Chops Suisse
Rösti
Green beans Hollandaise
Mushroom salad
Fruit Soufflé Glacé

Austria likes its sweets, and no one will argue that whipped cream detracts from tortes, cakes and coffee. There is a formality about everything in Austria that is refreshing.

Austrian Dinner

Chicken and caraway soup
Röstbraten (rib-eye steak with onions)
Chestnuts with Prunes
Spinach pudding
Cucumber and onion salad with horseradish dressing
Chocolate Torte with Schlag

South America is noted for its Asadas — outdoor barbecues — their favorite way to entertain visitors. They might prepare a meal like this.

South American Dinner

Ceviche
Pit-barbecued lamb legs and shoulders butterflied, lamb kidneys
and hearts, beef butts and briskets
Fruit Barbecued Chicken
Brown beans
Mixed green salad with Red Wine Dressing
Peasant Bread
Brazil Nut Torte

You should not mix the national dishes of the Orient and call it Oriental food. Sukiyaki is different from Peking duck, and both are different from Indian cookery. They all date back countless centuries and are a combination of the cooking of many cultures: Greek, Phoenician, Chinese, Muslim, Portuguese and others. Oriental cooking has been influenced by climate, health, religion and taste.

Both Chinese and Japanese cooking take hours of preparation and must be eaten immediately. They are really too difficult for a hostess to cook, serve and smile over without help. The Chinese custom of having the number of dishes equal the number of guests is too much for most Americans. I never attempt more than four courses.

All Indian dinners would be no less intriguing for the taste buds.

Indian Dinner

Pimms Cup
Mushroom curry   Curry of chicken   Curry of lamb, all of them
Rice
5 or 7 Sambals
Stuffed squash
Dhal (lentils)
Papadoms
Mango ice cream sprinkled with rose petals

Dinner with a Chinese Flavor

Velvet Asparagus Soup
Sliced Beef with Leeks
Special Chicken with Almonds
Stir-Fried Shrimp with Snow Peas
Spinach with mushrooms
Fried rice
Chilled peach halves with burnt sugar threads
Tea

All Oriental cooking stresses different flavors and textures to make a dinner more enjoyable in any language. The actual cooking takes little time and each dish should be eaten as soon as possible.

Terrines and pâtés are a part of the French gastronomical scene. Basically this pâté is a mixture of pork, veal, fowl, game and liver baked in a terrine or casserole lined with pork fat. If it is baked in a crust, it is called a pâté; if it is made of all fowl or birds of any kind, and boiled or steamed, it is a galantine.

TERRINE PATE

1 pound chicken livers	¼ cup sherry
¼ teaspoon salt	Dash of salt and pepper
⅛ teaspoon poultry seasoning	¼ pound salt pork, sliced paper
1 tablespoon Cognac	thin
½ pound fresh pork	1 egg, well beaten
½ pound veal	1 bay leaf

Dice half of the livers. Add the salt, poultry seasoning and Cognac. Refrigerate for a few hours. Put the rest of the livers, the pork and veal through your meat grinder. Add the sherry, salt, egg, pepper and mix well. Line the bottom and sides of the terrine or casserole with pork. Put a layer of the ground mixture, then a few pieces of diced liver. Repeat until terrine is filled, ending with mixture layer. Top with the salt pork. Place a bay leaf on top. Cover the terrine and seal the edges with foil. Place in a pan of hot water and bake at 375° for 2½ hours. Remove cover and bay leaf, and refrigerate 24 hours. You may add truffles if you feel extravagant. Slice and serve on soft lettuce or watercress with or without Melba toast.

EGGPLANT PROVENÇALE

1 large peeled eggplant, cut into 8 one-inch circles	2 cups peeled, seeded and chopped tomatoes
1 teaspoon salt	Pinch of thyme
½ teaspoon white pepper	Salt and white pepper
3 tablespoons salad oil	¼ cup chopped parsley
3 tablespoons butter	½ cup white bread crumbs
1 cup chopped onion	1 cup grated Swiss or Gruyère
2 cloves minced garlic	cheese

As the eggplant slices change in circumference, trim so that they are all the same size. Place in a shallow oiled pan. Sprinkle with the salt and pepper. Broil 5 minutes. Heat the oil and butter, add onion and garlic. Cook until yellow. Add tomatoes and trimmings of eggplant; cook until thick. Stir in seasonings and bread crumbs. Correct seasonings. Pile on the broiled eggplant. Cover with the cheese. Bake at 350° until cheese is melted. Good cold, too, as an hors d'oeuvre or salad.

FLAGEOLETS PANACHES

2 15-ounce cans flageolets	½ cup finely chopped onion
1 pound snipped green beans, cooked 3 minutes	¼ cup finely chopped parsley
	1 cup whipping cream
3 tablespoons butter	Salt and pepper

Drain and wash the flageolets. Combine with the green beans. Melt butter, add onion, cook until yellow. Add to beans with parsley and cream. Correct seasonings. Put in a casserole, cover and cook at 350° for 20 minutes, or in a covered skillet on top of the stove.

HOT LEMON SOUFFLE

2 tablespoons butter	4 tablespoons sugar
1½ tablespoons flour	Grated rind of 1 lemon
½ cup hot milk	1½ tablespoons lemon juice
5 egg yolks	6 egg whites

Melt the butter, add the flour and cook until foamy. Add milk and cook until thick. Remove from heat, add egg yolks beaten with 3 tablespoons of sugar. Let mixture cool, add grated rind and lemon juice. Beat egg whites until stiff but not dry, add the last tablespoon of sugar and beat again until stiff. Fold into the egg mixture. Pour into a buttered and slightly sugared 1-quart soufflé dish and bake at 400° for about 20 minutes, or until puffed and lightly browned. Serve at once. This dessert could bake while dinner is being served. If you wish to have the soufflé cook slower, put in a hot water bath, and lower temperature to 350°.

COCK-A-LEEKIE

1 4- to 5-pound chicken or wings
  and backs
3 quarts water or chicken broth
2 bunches of leeks, washed and
  thinly sliced

10 to 12 cooked prunes, sliced
Salt and white pepper
Finely minced parsley

Cook the chicken (and giblets) in the water or broth. When tender remove and add the leeks. Cook until leeks are soft. Add the prunes, some of the chicken and giblets cut in julienne pieces. If you wish to use this as a main dish, cut the chicken in serving pieces. Correct seasonings and add the parsley.

Cock-a-Leekie appears in cookbooks pertaining to the British Isles. No doubt its origin is Scotch, or Irish or whatever. Who cares? You find it everywhere the sun sets on British soil. Texans liked it!

GREEN CABBAGE WITH BACON AND PARSLEY

1 large head green cabbage, cored
Cold water
3 tablespoons sugar
3 tablespoons salt
2 cups boiling water

¼ cup butter
4 slices bacon, finely diced and
  cooked crisp
¼ cup chopped parsley
Salt and white pepper

Cut cabbage in 2-inch pieces. Cover with cold water; add the sugar and salt. Let stand several hours in the refrigerator. Drain. Put in a pot with the boiling water; cover and cook 8 minutes. Drain, add butter, crisp bacon and parsley. Correct seasonings. A variation is to add ¼ cup of pine nuts, which are good added to any vegetable.

TRIFLE

This is Anne Courtin's recipe for Trifle. She is English through and through, and her Trifle is super.

2 dozen lady fingers, split
1 cup black raspberry jam
2 cups sliced fresh or frozen
    peaches or canned Elberta
2 or 3 bananas, sliced
1 pint fresh strawberries, cut in
    half

½ cup sherry (or more if you like)
2 cups hot milk
4 eggs
¼ cup sugar
1 teaspoon vanilla
1 cup frozen raspberries, drained
1 cup whipping cream

Line the serving bowl with one layer of lady fingers. Cover with the jam. Layer the remaining lady fingers, peaches, bananas and strawberries. Add sherry to each layer of lady fingers. Refrigerate. Prepare a soft custard: add the hot milk to the eggs beaten with the sugar and cook over hot water until thickened. Cool and add vanilla. Pour over the prepared fruit and lady fingers. Add raspberries. Whip the cream and cover the Trifle. My mother made this dessert with lady fingers, a layer of macaroon crumbs, currant jelly and fresh raspberries, or other fruit in season, but she was Irish.

GARLIC BROILED SHRIMP

Peel 2 pounds uncooked medium shrimp (15- to 20-count to the pound). Split, remove intestinal vein. Wash well, put in a pan and cover with:

4 tablespoons finely minced
    parsley
4 cloves of garlic, minced

1 cup salad oil (olive oil is better
    but it is expensive)
Salt and pepper

Leave in refrigerator all day — and night, too, if you have the time. When ready to serve, place on a shallow pan with the oil that clings to them and broil 3 minutes on each side. Salt lightly. Be sure you do not overcook or they will be tough and stringy. Sprinkle with freshly ground black pepper. Good, too, to charcoal broil out-of-doors. They are still better if you split, wash and leave the shells on, but you would need to serve finger bowls.

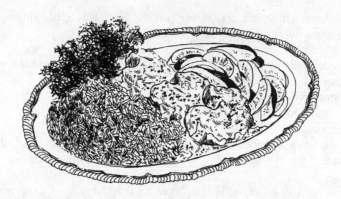

BREAST OF CHICKEN PAPPAGALLO

8 6- or 8-ounce boneless chicken
breasts
⅓ cup flour, 1 teaspoon salt, ⅛
teaspoon white pepper
¼ cup butter
2 tablespoons olive oil

1½ cups champagne
¼ cup sliced white truffles, with
juice
1 cup whipping cream
Salt and white pepper

Remove skin and flatten chicken with palm of your hand. Dust lightly
with the seasoned flour. Melt butter and olive oil. Add chicken with
full side down, sauté at medium heat 5 minutes, shaking pan to prevent sticking. Turn. Add the champagne and continue cooking for 12
or 15 minutes, until the chicken is done and the champagne is reduced
by one-half. Add the truffles and the cream. Cook until sauce is thickened. Correct seasonings and serve. You may prepare this dish ahead,
as it freezes well.

SPINACH AND WHITE BEANS

2 pounds fresh spinach
4 tablespoons butter
½ cup finely diced cooked ham
2 cups cooked white navy beans

2 tablespoons whipping cream
Salt and pepper
Whiff of nutmeg

Wash spinach and cut away heavy stems. Cook 1 minute in a covered container. Drain and put in your blender until finely chopped. Melt the butter in a large skillet. Add the spinach, ham and beans. Stir in cream and cook until the consistency of mashed potatoes. Correct seasonings and add just a whiff of nutmeg. This is a good way to get your children to eat spinach.

PEPERONI SALAD

8 large bell peppers, red and
   green, or all green
1 clove garlic, minced
½ cup olive oil or half salad oil

1 teaspoon salt
¼ teaspoon fresh ground pepper
Juice of ½ lemon

Put peppers under broiler or in a hot oven until skins are black. Turn frequently. Remove, rub off the skin, and extract the seeds. Rinse peppers in cold water. Cut in strips and add the garlic and olive oil, salt, pepper and lemon juice. Marinate for 30 minutes and serve as a salad or as an appetizer. I find American tastes prefer half salad, half olive oil.

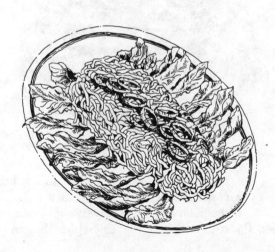

This dessert is not as difficult as you may think.

CAKE ST. HONORE

1 9-inch sweet pastry crust or thin layer of white cake

Pastry Crust:

¾ cup flour   Pinch of salt
2 tablespoons confectioners' sugar   2 tablespoons cold water or milk
¼ cup butter

Mix flour and sugar. Cut in the butter until mixture resembles cornmeal. Add salt and water to make a dough. Roll out on a floured board and fit into a 9-inch cake pan. Place another pan inside to prevent blistering. Bake at 350° for 30 minutes.
   Make about 3 dozen small Cream Puffs.

Pastry Cream:

1 cup sugar   8 egg yolks, lightly beaten
½ cup cornstarch   2 teaspoons vanilla
⅛ teaspoon salt   4 tablespoons unflavored gelatin
4¼ cups milk   8 egg whites, beaten stiff

Mix sugar, cornstarch and salt. Add ¼ cup of milk and mix. Heat 4 cups of milk and add gradually to the sugar mixture. Cook over low heat until thick. Add egg yolks gradually. Stir with French whip. Continue cooking until thick. Add vanilla. Remove and add gelatin softened in ¼ cup cold milk. When the gelatin is cold and beginning to congeal, fold in the egg whites.

Caramelize 2 cups of granulated sugar. Dip the flat side of the cream puffs in the syrup and attach to the edge of the sugar crust making a ring of puffs. Repeat with the second row on top of the first row. Using a pastry tube, fill the puffs with the Pastry Cream. Pour rest into the center of the ring.

Topping:

1 cup whipping cream	½ teaspoon instant coffee
½ teaspoon vanilla	Shaved chocolate

Whip cream until stiff. Fold in vanilla and coffee. Spread over top of filling and cover with shaved chocolate.

GRAVLAX

3 to 3½ pounds fresh salmon, center cut, cleaned and scaled	¼ cup sugar
1 large bunch dill	2 tablespoons white or black peppercorns, crushed
¼ cup coarse (kosher) salt, or if unavailable, substitute regular salt	

Ask the fish dealer to cut the salmon in half lengthwise and to filet it. Place half of the fish, skin side down, into a deep glass, enamel or stainless steel baking dish or casserole. Wash and then shake dry the dill and place on the fish. (If the dill is of the hothouse variety and not very pungent, chop the herb coarsely to release its flavor and sprinkle over the fish.) In a separate bowl, combine the salt, sugar and crushed peppercorns. Sprinkle this mixture evenly over the dill. Top with the other half of the fish, skin side up. Cover the fish with aluminum foil, a heavy platter slightly larger than the salmon and a weight of about 5 pounds on top. Refrigerate for 48 hours (or up to 3 days). Turn the fish over every 12 hours, basting with the liquid marinade that accumulates and separating the halves a little to baste the salmon inside. Replace the platter and weights each time. When completed, remove the fish from its marinade, scrape away the dill and seasonings and pat it dry with paper towels. Place the separated halves skin side down on a carving board and slice the salmon halves thinly on the diagonal, detaching each slice from the skin. Serve with Mustard Sauce.

FRIKADELLER

1 pound ground veal or beef	2 eggs, well beaten
1 pound ground pork	2 teaspoons salt
1 onion, coarsely chopped (½ cup)	½ teaspoon white pepper
2 cups sifted white bread crumbs	6 tablespoons butter
3 cups club soda	

Put veal, pork, and onions together through meat grinder. Stir in the bread crumbs. Beat in soda water a little at a time. Beat in eggs, salt and pepper. Cover and refrigerate for at least 1 hour (over night still better). Shape into oblong patties about 4 inches long (smaller for hors d'oeuvres). Fry in butter a few at a time. Do not crowd in the pan. Cook about 6 minutes, turn only once and cook 6 minutes longer. These are usually served with Red Cabbage.

RED CABBAGE

1 3-pound red cabbage	½ cup vinegar
3 tablespoons butter	½ cup currant jelly
1 tablespoon sugar	1 teaspoon salt

Remove tough outer leaves and core of cabbage. Wash and drain. Slice very fine. Melt the butter in a deep skillet, add the cabbage, sugar and vinegar. Cover and cook 30 minutes or until tender. Stir frequently. Add jelly and salt, blend. Cook 10 minutes longer.

DANISH LAYER CAKE

The man in charge of the Danish Pavilion at the World's Fair in New York told me how to prepare this dessert.

3 thin 9-inch layers of a yellow or
   sponge cake
2 layers of macaroon crumbs
Currant jelly

Chocolate Mousse
Whipped cream
Shaved semi-sweet chocolate

Place a layer of yellow cake on cake plate, spread with a thin layer of currant jelly, then a layer of macaroon crumbs. Repeat with layer of cake on top. Spread the sides and top amply with Chocolate Mousse. Cover top with whipped cream and shaved chocolate. Refrigerate several hours. It is good, but why shouldn't it be?

VOL-AU-VENT VENETIAN SHRIMP

½ cup butter
2 pounds shrimp, P.D.Q.
2 teaspoons capers
2 tablespoons brandy
1½ cups whipping cream
2 peeled, seeded and chopped
   tomatoes

2 teaspoons tomato paste (you
   may omit)
Salt and pepper
Patty shells

Melt butter, add the shrimp and sauté for 3 minutes at medium heat. Stir in capers. Add brandy and ignite. Mix in cream and tomatoes; cook at low heat until cream reduces a little. Add tomato paste, seasonings and heat.

    Vol-au-Vent is a patty shell filled with a creamed mixture, seafood or fowl as a rule, and covered with the pastry lid. Literally means "windward flight," so be sure the patty shells are light and be sure to heat them.

LAMB CHOPS SUISSE

8 double loin lamb chops	¼ cup butter, melted
2 teaspoons salt	½ cup sherry
½ teaspoon pepper	16 very thin slices Swiss cheese
2 cups coarsely chopped mush-	
rooms (use stems)	

Broil chops 8 minutes, turn and broil 8 minutes or longer if you like well-done lamb. Sprinkle with salt and pepper. Sauté the mushrooms in the melted butter. Add the sherry and cook until sherry is reduced. Pile on chops, cover with the cheese and bake at 350° for 10 minutes.

ROSTI

3 pounds potatoes	½ teaspoon salt
1 tablespoon shortening, not	2 tablespoons hot water
butter	¼ cup cooked bacon or ham, diced
4 tablespoons butter, melted	

Boil potatoes in their skins. Cool and peel. Shred on large side of shredder. Heat the shortening in a heavy skillet or griddle. Sprinkle potatoes over evenly. Cook 1 minute; add butter. Add salt and hot water and cover. Cook about 10 minutes, or until potatoes are crusty on bottom, at medium heat. Shake frequently to prevent sticking. Add bacon and turn out on a serving platter, brown side up.

FRUIT SOUFFLE GLACE

I had this dessert every time I saw it on a menu when I was in Switzerland. Willie Rossel, then chef at the Sheraton Hotel, made it for 1200 guests. If you go to Zurich, you'll discover the Dolder Grand Hotel prepares this dessert very well. So can you.

1 cup water	8 tablespoons Grand Marnier
1 cup sugar	1 teaspoon grated orange rind
8 egg yolks, beaten	Pinch of salt
2 cups whipping cream	Violet Dust
½ cup candied fruit, finely diced	

Boil water and sugar together 8 minutes. Pour the hot sugar mixture over the eggs slowly. Stirring with a French whip, cook over hot water until thick. Remove and put saucepan with the egg mix over a bowl of ice to cool. Stir until cold. Whip the cream until stiff and fold into the cold egg mixture. Stir in the candied fruit, Grand Marnier, orange rind and salt. Pour into individual soufflé dishes or dessert dishes and freeze. Sprinkle top with Violet Dust.

VIOLET DUST

You may purchase candied violets in candy or gourmet shops. Roll out between two sheets of foil until you obtain a fine dust. Keeps indefinitely in a covered container.

Using this recipe, rib-eye steaks take on a special flavor done with a Viennese touch.

ROSTBRATEN

8 8-ounce rib-eye steaks	Salt and pepper
¼ cup butter	12 slices bacon, diced and fried
2 cups very thinly sliced onion	crisp
rings	32 sprigs, or more, of parsley

Broil steak to your taste. Melt butter, sauté onion rings until soft. Place steaks on top of onions. Sprinkle with salt and pepper and the crumbled bacon. Fry the parsley and put on top. This is a pretty platter to pass.

I like this dish with almost anything, especially roast turkey.

CHESTNUTS WITH PRUNES

¼ cup butter	1 cup raisins, cooked in beef con-
2 cups chestnuts, canned and	sommé until plump
drained or fresh roasted	Salt and white pepper
1 cup pitted stewed prunes	

Melt butter, add rest of ingredients and toss lightly. Season and serve hot.

CHOCOLATE TORTE WITH SCHLAG

4 egg whites	½ cup finely chopped pecans or
¼ teaspoon cream of tartar	almonds
1 cup sugar	½ teaspoon vanilla
¼ cup cocoa	Pinch of salt

Beat egg whites with cream of tartar until stiff. Gradually beat in ½ cup sugar. Mix the remaining sugar with the cocoa and fold into the egg white mixture. Add the nuts, vanilla and salt. Pour into a lightly buttered 9 x 9-inch glass casserole or cake tin. Bake at 325° for 45 minutes. Cool, remove from pan to a serving tray and cover with 2 cups whipped cream mixed with ¼ cup sugar, ½ teaspoon cocoa and ¼ teaspoon instant coffee.

I think this is the best Barbecue Sauce for chicken. Prepare it ahead and keep in your deep freeze.

FRUIT BARBECUE SAUCE
(for 1 quart)

2 cups onion, chopped	1 teaspoon dried tarragon
2 cloves garlic, minced	1 teaspoon dried rosemary
4 cups catsup	2 teaspoons dried marjoram
½ cup vinegar	¾ cup brown sugar
1 tablespoon plus 1 teaspoon dry mustard	1 tablespoon plus 1 teaspoon salt
2⅔ cups butter	Juice of 2 lemons
2 cups raisins, chopped	1 cup dry Burgundy
2 teaspoons dried basil	2 cups seedless grapes (you may omit)

Mix all the ingredients together except the wine and grapes. Bring to a boil and simmer 45 minutes. Add wine and cook 10 minutes longer. Add the grapes as garnish when ready to serve.

When barbecuing the chicken, either broil or cook over charcoal. Thin the sauce to your liking. Place cooked chicken (allow ½ chicken per person) in a shallow pan. Pour grapes and sauce over. Cover and bake at 325° for 45 minutes. Baste frequently. Run under the broiler before serving.

BRAZIL NUT TORTE

6 egg yolks	6 egg whites, beaten stiff
1½ cups sugar	Cocoa
2½ tablespoons flour	3 cups whipping cream
1 teaspoon baking powder	1 teaspoon instant coffee
3 cups ground Brazil nuts or	1 teaspoon vanilla
pecans	White chocolate

Beat egg yolks, add sugar and beat for 15 minutes. Gradually add flour and baking powder to egg mixture. Add nuts and fold in the egg whites. Bake in two or three buttered 9-inch cake pans lightly dusted with cocoa at 350° for 30 minutes. Cool. Whip the cream until stiff. Add instant coffee and vanilla. Fill layers, top and sides of cake. Completely cover with shaved white chocolate. You can buy the chocolate at any Sears store or some gourmet shops.

VELVET ASPARAGUS SOUP

1 10-ounce can white asparagus	2 tablespoons cornstarch
1 6-ounce breast of chicken,	Cold water
uncooked	Salt to taste
1 quart cold chicken broth	¼ cup slivered ham
1 egg white	

Using a sharp knife, slice asparagus open and scrape out the delicate portions of the stem and tip. Mash to a pulp and mix with ½ cup of the juice the asparagus was canned in. Set aside. Mince the chicken and pound to a pulp with the blunt end of a cleaver, or edge of a heavy plate. Mix with ½ cup of the cold chicken broth and beat until light, removing any sinews. Beat the egg white until frothy and add to chicken mix. Dissolve the cornstarch in a little cold water. Bring broth to a boil; add asparagus pulp and slowly stir in the cornstarch mix. Simmer for 15 minutes. Add salt to taste and beat in the chicken and egg white. Remove from heat and allow chicken to cook in the heat of the soup. Sprinkle with the ham as served.

A wok is not necessary for Chinese frying, but if you like to talk about it, by all means use one. A heavy-bottomed skillet will do as well, but be sure it is clean and dry.

SLICED BEEF WITH LEEKS

4 tablespoons salad oil (I like peanut oil)
1 cup leeks, white part only, thinly
  sliced diagonally
1 pound thin beef slices, tenderloin, sirloin or flank

1 tablespoon soy sauce
Sesame oil
1 tablespoon sherry

Preheat skillet or wok to a very high temperature. Add the oil, and the leeks at once. Cook 1 minute, stirring constantly. Remove from skillet and keep warm. Rub skillet with paper towels. Add remaining 2 table-spoons of oil and the sliced beef. Cook 2 minutes stirring constantly. Add the leeks and the soy sauce. Cook 1 minute more. Add a few drops of sesame oil and sherry just before removing from heat.

SPECIAL CHICKEN WITH ALMONDS

3 6-ounce chicken breasts, boned
  and skinned
Salt
½ cup flour
½ cup cornstarch
½ teaspoon soda
1 teaspoon baking powder
1 cup water

½ cup saltines rolled into fine
  crumbs
½ cup flour or water chestnut
  flour
Peanut oil
1 head iceberg lettuce, shredded
¾ cup slivered toasted almonds,
  chopped

Sprinkle chicken with salt and set aside. Mix next 5 ingredients and dip breasts in the batter, then in a mixture of the flour and saltine crumbs. Fry in deep fat at 375° until a light brown. Remove, let cool and refry at 400° until golden brown. Remove, cut crosswise into ½-inch pieces. Pile on the shredded lettuce and pour over either Lemon Sauce or Foo Yung Sauce and sprinkle with nuts.

LEMON SAUCE

½ cup chicken broth   1 teaspoon finely grated lemon peel
1 teaspoon lemon juice   2 teaspoons cornstarch
½ teaspoon lemon extract   2 teaspoons cold water

Mix and cook until thickened.

FOO YUNG SAUCE

1 tablespoon cornstarch   ¾ cup bouillon or water
1 tablespoon soy sauce   ¼ teaspoon sugar

Mix and cook until thickened.

STIR-FRIED SHRIMP WITH SNOW PEAS

1 pound raw shrimp, fresh or frozen
2 teaspoons cornstarch
1 egg white
1 teaspoon soy sauce
1 tablespoon dry sherry

½ pound snow peas (mange-touts)
2 tablespoons salad oil
2 scallions, slivered
1 tablespoon fresh ginger root, slivered

Remove the black or white intestinal vein of the shrimp by making a shallow slit down the round side of the shrimp. Wash in cold water and dry on paper towels. Split in half lengthwise. Mix with the cornstarch and add egg white, soy and sherry. Wash and sliver the snow peas. Pour boiling water over and drain. Heat the oil in a hot heavy skillet or wok. Add the scallions and ginger root. Stir-fry for 1 minute, then remove from oil. Drain shrimp, reserving liquid, and stir-fry for 1 minute. Add snow peas and stir-fry for 30 seconds. Add leftover cornstarch mixture. Stir and cover for 30 seconds. Serve at once.

The Chinese cuisine does not, I think, include refreshing desserts. I like to end a dinner with very cold peach halves, stewed or canned. Serve in shallow dessert bowls and pour thin threads of caramelized sugar over. In fact it is a delightful ending for any occasion.

5

Dinners: Seated and Buffet

THERE ARE so many aspects of preparation and day-after work to giving a dinner party that both novice and seasoned hostess learn to allow time for all of these tasks. Actually, it is wise to have some menu alternates in mind if the vegetable or fruit you had planned on is not available in the market. Then there is the advance work of getting the linen, the china and the freshly polished silver all together. Once the dinner party is over there is putting the materials away, and that is much more pleasant if you can reflect on memorable food, wine and conversation.

I try to plan my entertaining so that I might do a dinner two nights in a row and a luncheon or supper the third day. It really is easier in the long run. You have only one assembling of incidentals for the three functions. You can use the same flowers and do some of the advance preparation for all parties at one time. You may feel like collapsing at the end of the days of concentrated entertaining, but you can relax until the next bout.

Since I have always favored allowing my taste buds to anticipate dinner, I have never been a devotee of hors d'oeuvres unless they take the place of a first course. Escoffier thought so too. Sometimes if the cocktail hour is going to be long I will put out bowls of iced crudités or a piece of Brie cheese with unsalted crackers for nibbling. But that is all.

However, I do like to serve the first course in the living room, the den or wherever my guests are gathered. If I am without domestic help, it is easier for me to serve; if I have help, it gives them time for other food preparation tasks. This is an informal and pleasant way to have the first course served while the small conversational groups are still intact.

Before dinner I like to serve soup (my Yankee upbringing). Usually I have cold or jellied soups in a crystal bowl or a pitcher. Hot soup I serve either from a tureen or pour in the kitchen and pass. I have made it a hard and fast rule not to divulge the kind of soup until the guests start talking about it, especially if I am serving a yogurt soup, which I do frequently. You and I both know someone who would say "I hate yogurt" and it might be a catching thought.

If you think you must serve hors d'oeuvres before dinner, here are some that might interest you.

Chicken Sates on bamboo skewers
Smoked sturgeon or salmon on dark rye bread and butter, with thin slices of cucumber or capers
Steak Tartare
Mushrooms filled with crab Gruyère, sausage or mushroom salad
Cold Ratatouille on strips of buttered rye bread
Snails in pasta shells
Pâté de fois gras (bought or make your own)
Tiropetes (cheese triangles) — Greek origin, found at frozen food counters today
Cold fresh artichokes with chive dressing
Fresh figs or melon wrapped in prosciutto or Belgian ham
Broiled bacon-wrapped Brazil nuts
Various small quiches: onion, mushroom, Brie, seafood, Lorraine
Toasted mushroom triangles or rolled sandwiches
Avocado butter served with assorted crackers
Scallops Ramaki (I like these better than Ramaki made with chicken livers)
Iced caviar with hot flageolets or with small baked potatoes and sour cream
Chicken liver turnovers
Coquilles of Crabmeat Imperial
Tempura with mustard dip
Fried eggplant rings with sour cream and caviar
Boursault, Boursin or Brie with unsalted crackers

I have been interested in the current trend away from whiskey drinks and toward an imaginative assortment of wines, very cold vodka in an ice case and Champagne. Many have cultivated tastes for Campari, Punt de Mes, Lillet (an orange-flavored Vermouth) and Chablis Cassis which I find especially popular with the younger crowd.

A soup offered along with the drinks cuts down on the amount of all alcoholic beverages consumed before dinner and at cocktail parties. I'm all for it, as the food tastes better and the subtleties of the flavors, textures and colors of a carefully designed and prepared meal are appreciated.

Formal seated dinners are lovely, but you need plenty of help in the kitchen and dining room, and lots of time to prepare. But once in a while it is good for your soul to have a dinner party, even if your wallet is very badly bent.

Formal Seated Dinners

Jellied Consommé Helennaise
Sour cream and toasted unsalted crackers
Brochette of Lobster and Chicken with Escalloped Cucumbers
Fresh Pear Ice laced with pear brandy
Roast Loin of Veal with Shallots and Mushrooms
Salsify Persillade and Snipped Green Beans
Belgian endive salad with lemon dressing
Brie cheese
Hard rolls and sweet butter
Raspberry Mousse with raspberry purée and whipped cream
Demitasse

Cream of fresh mushroom soup with Toasted Mushroom Triangles
Breast of duckling in wine aspic with pâté de fois gras
Roasted rack and loin of lamb, Cumberland
Potatoes Anna
Fresh asparagus with Maltaise Sauce
Watercress salad, oil and vinegar dressing with Roquefort Mousse
Toasted buttered hard rolls
Hot Bourbon Peaches with English Custard and warm macaroons
Demitasse

Brie Quiche with caviar
Quenelles of Sole with king crab in grenadine
Lemon ice laced with Cognac
Tenderloin of Beef with Pâté de Fois Gras
Bearnaise Sauce in artichoke bottoms
Green beans and mushrooms Chinese style
Boston and Romaine lettuce with grapefruit segments and
Sherry French Dressing
Toasted rolled bread and butter sandwiches
Crème Brulé
Demitasse

Between dishes of great richness such as a fish or fowl course and a meat course, a formal dinner could include a small sorbet of ice with or without brandy or just a small liqueur glass of Calvados to clear the palate and to help make room for the rest of the dinner. Another good rule to remember in planning a dinner is not to have fish follow fish or cream sauce follow cream sauce.

It is said that a true gourmet has bread with every meal. Well, whether I am a gourmet or not — and I care less — I do like bread of some kind with my meal. We as a nation have become so conscious of the slim race horse kind of figure, we have a tendency to cut out serving bread. While I agree that fashion has made us better looking and the medical profession has made us more conscious of the dangers of too much weight, let's cut out something else. But either serve good bread, or forget it. Best of all — make it.

For dinner I always serve hot bread with the salad (I still like salad after the entrée). If I can avoid the need of a bread and butter plate, I'm for it. One less dish to wash. I like to serve thin sandwiches too in place of bread — especially if I'm the cook — and I find guests like them. If I buy bread, I find it tastes more freshly made if I heat it, slice and butter, then form it back in the loaf, foil wrap and heat. *No garlic*. I buy frozen baking powder biscuits and keep quiet when they are complimented.

Just Seated Dinners

Hot or Cold Senegalese (*Helen Corbitt's Cookbook*, page 33)
with slivers of white meat of chicken
Homemade Melba toast
Crown Roast of Lamb filled with Mushroom Soufflé
Fresh asparagus with Lemon Cheese Butter
Fresh Snow Pea Salad
Icebox Rolls (*Helen Corbitt's Cookbook*, page 235)
My French Apple Pie

Jellied madrilene (you buy) with chunks of crabmeat,
sour cream spooned over and capers passed
(Do not force added calories, but do pass toasted Bremner crackers.)
Sliced broiled Double Sirloin Steak (32 ounce) with Fried Parsley
Braised Celery
Fried Tomatoes with Spinach and Peas
Marinated Leek Salad
Warm buttered pumpernickel bread
Caramel Soufflé with English Custard

Marinated Fresh Artichokes (finger bowls after these
or else a warm damp serviette, Oriental style)
Squab in White Wine with Wild Rice and Apples
Squash Soufflé (*Helen Corbitt's Cookbook,* page 174)
Belgian Endive and Mushroom Salad
Hard rolls
Coffee Crème Pie

Quick Mushroom Consommé
Roast Pork Loin in mustard and white wine
Rhubarb crisp
Green Beans with Flageolets
Crudités Salad
Popovers (*Helen Corbitt's Cookbook,* page 241)
Mocha Orange Ice Cream

Fresh spinach, grapefruit and orange salad with Poppy Seed Dressing
Leg of Lamb, Muslim Style
Rice with pine nuts
Zucchini fans, persillade
Warm buttered French bread
Chocolate angel food cake frosted with
cinnamon-flavored whipped cream

Chlodnik
Rye Melba toast
Roast Duckling au Naturel
Rice with Curried Fruit
Chinese Style Green Beans and Celery
Spoom
Rolled Wafers

Iced Spinach Soup
Beef and mushroom pan pie with Parmesan crust
Sugar-buttered fresh carrot and potato fingers
Warm bread sticks, rolled in melted butter,
lightly dusted with oregano
Warm baked apple quarters with lemon-flavored whipped cream

Molded Gazpacho Salad
Celery and Mayonnaise Dressing
Breast of Chicken Piquante
Feather Rice (*Helen Corbitt's Cookbook*, page 207)
White Turnips and Peas in Cream
Orange Shell Glacé

Curried Cream Cheese Soup
Poached Red Snapper with Cucumber Sauce
Lemon Steamed Potatoes
Stir-Fried Spinach with shredded beets
Raw relish tray
Stained Glass Window Dessert

Buffet Dinners

I like to serve two meat dishes or one meat and one seafood for a buffet dinner, one of them as a cold item at times.

Sautéed Sliced Beef Tenderloin
Rice Soufflé
Zucchini Fans with Michael Sauce
Oriental Chicken Salad with snow peas
Belgian endive and beet salad, Lemon Dressing
Small brioches
Gourmandise cheese with slices of fresh melon
Almond Cream Cake

Breast of Chicken with Chanterelles
Wild Rice with Grapes
Fresh artichoke bottoms filled with green bean purée
and Hollandaise
Tenderloin of beef en gelée
Ice box rolls, buttered
Crudités Salad bowl
Fresh Blueberry Tartelettes

Roast Veal with Morels in Cream
Shrimp Bel Paese
Slivered carrots with chervil
Pease
Buffet salad bowl
Crusty hard rolls
Cold Italian Meringue with preserved marrons in soft custard

Oriental Roasted Chicken
Fried Rice
Filet of Sole Soufflé with Shrimp Sauce
Stir-Fried Spinach with toasted sesame seed
An assortment of fresh fruit
Cream Cheese and Ginger Dressing
Crêpes Brazil

Braised Beef, Poivre Vert
Eggplant Romanoff
Lyonnaise green beans
Cabbage slaw with beer dressing
Warm buttered French bread
Fresh strawberries with Grand Marnier Sauce

Buffet Ham Madeira
Chicken and Green Chiles Casserole
Escalloped Cucumbers
Tomato and Guacamole Salad (*Helen Corbitt's Cookbook*, pages 12–13)
Hot tortillas and sweet butter
Orange and almond flan

Stuffed Turkey Breast
Baked Acorn Squash
Bouquet of marinated canned vegetables: baby beets, carrots and
rat tail green beans (#1 sieve)
Peasant bread
Blueberry Pancake Stack with Lemon Butter

Meat loaf baked in an angel food tin with a
center of sautéed apples and horseradish
My Favorite Noodles
Everything green salad with blue cheese dressing
Marinated green and red peppers
Thin rye bread and butter sandwiches
Hot orange meringue with cold Foamy Sauce
(*Helen Corbitt's Cookbook*, page 260)

Herbed Leg of Lamb, natural gravy
Crespolini
Cauliflower with browned sesame seed butter
Cold thick tomato slices piled with Ratatouille
Beer muffins
Cluster of small cream puffs filled with vanilla ice cream
and Hot Fudge Sauce (*Helen Corbitt's Cookbook*, page 264)

JELLIED CONSOMME HELENNAISE

4 cups canned jellied beef
consommé
1 cup seeded cucumber, finely
diced
2 cups seeded tomatoes, finely
diced and peeled

½ cup thinly sliced green onion
1 cup finely diced celery
½ cup diced avocado
1 tablespoon olive oil
2 tablespoons red wine vinegar

Mix together lightly all ingredients and refrigerate. Serve from a punch bowl or in individual soup cups. You may serve with or without sour cream. Caviar is a nice addition, but expensive. I sometimes add diced cooked shrimp, chicken or roast beef.

BROCHETTE OF LOBSTER AND CHICKEN

2 8- to 10-ounce lobster tails
2 8-ounce boneless chicken breasts
1 cup sherry wine

½ cup melted butter
Salt and white pepper

Cut lobster tails lengthwise. Place your thumb under the lobster meat at the large end of the tail and loosen meat. Pull the meat out. It will come out easily. Cut tail meat in ½-inch slices. Remove skin from chicken, cut meat in half lengthwise and slice in ½-inch pieces. Thread alternately with the lobster onto a buttered or oiled skewer. (I use bamboo and throw away.) Place in a shallow pan, pour wine over and refrigerate until ready to cook. Bake at 350° for 10 minutes, then under the broiler about 5 minutes. Baste with the wine and butter. Correct seasonings; serve either on the skewer (I do not like) or slip off but retain shape. A lemon cup filled with red caviar would be a pretty garnish. I like to serve these brochettes and any fish with:

ESCALLOPED CUCUMBERS

6 medium-sized cucumbers
Salt and white pepper
Chopped parsley

1½ cups buttered white bread
crumbs

Peel and slice cucumbers ¼ inch thick. Sprinkle with salt and pepper.

Place in alternate layers with the buttered crumbs in a buttered shallow casserole, ending with crumbs on top. Bake at 350° until tender but not mushy, approximately 20 minutes. Sprinkle with chopped parsley.

FRESH PEAR ICE
(*1 gallon*)

2 cups sugar	4 cups puréed fresh ripe pears
4 cups water	½ cup lemon juice

Make a syrup of sugar and water over low heat. Peel and slice the pears, put in the blender and add to the syrup immediately to keep them from turning dark. Cool, add the lemon juice and freeze in your ice cream freezer.

LOIN OF VEAL WITH SHALLOTS AND MUSHROOMS

½ cup butter	½ cup dry white wine
1 clove garlic, crushed	6 shallots, finely minced
2 onions, sliced	2 tablespoons butter
2 carrots, sliced	8 mushrooms, sliced
2 3- to 4-pound loins of veal, boned and tied	½ cup sherry or broth
½ cup beef broth	Arrowroot

Melt the butter in meat pan. Add the garlic, onions and carrots. Put in 375° oven for 10 minutes. Place meat on top and roast at 375°, basting with the butter, beef broth and wine, for about 1 hour or until meat thermometer registers 145°. Remove meat to serving tray. In a separate pan sauté the shallots in the butter and cook until soft. Add mushrooms and cook until translucent. Pour sherry into pan drippings and cook, stirring in all the brown bits that cling to the pan. Mix a little arrowroot (1 teaspoon for each cup of liquid) and cook until clear. Strain, add mushrooms and shallots and serve over the meat. For variety substitute red wine for white or omit wine entirely. Use same recipe for rack or leg of veal.

SALSIFY PERSILLADE AND SNIPPED GREEN BEANS

It is difficult to find fresh salsify in most markets, so use the canned. I drain and wash the salsify and sauté quickly in very little butter. Add enough heavy cream to "stick them." Season with salt and pepper and sprinkle with parsley. Or I use the same preparation as for the Braised Celery. I like to make a ring of salsify on my serving tray and fill the center with very finely snipped cut-on-the-bias green beans, cooked about five minutes, and dressed with sweet butter, salt and pepper. These two vegetables compliment each other.

RASPBERRY MOUSSE

1 cup milk
4 egg yolks
3 tablespoons sugar
1½ tablespoons unflavored gelatin, softened in ¼ cup cold milk

½ teaspoon vanilla
2 cups frozen raspberries (sugared)
2 cups cream, whipped
4 egg whites, beaten stiff

Mix milk, egg yolks and sugar. Cook over hot water until a custard is formed. Remove, add gelatin and vanilla. Chill. Put berries in blender, then strain. Add to the custard. Taste for sweetness; add more sugar if needed. (Some raspberries are not sweet enough.) Return to refrigerator. When mixture begins to thicken, fold in whipped cream and egg whites. Pour into a 2-quart soufflé dish or ring mold. Refrigerate overnight. Serve with puréed strawberries or raspberries and whipped cream. Decorate with fresh berries if available, or with:

COLD ZABAGLIONE SAUCE
(1 cup)

4 egg yolks   3 tablespoons sugar
¼ cup Marsala or sherry

Put egg yolks in top of double boiler, beat until lemon-colored. Beat in the sugar. Heat the wine and add gradually. Place over hot water and cook until thick, beating constantly. Do not overcook. Chill.

POTATOES ANNA

6 cups thinly sliced, peeled russet potatoes, blanched for 5 minutes and dried (never Idaho)

½ cup butter
1 teaspoon salt
White pepper

Butter generously bottom and sides of a 2-inch-deep 8-inch casserole, or use a heavy copper Potatoes Anna pan. Arrange the potato slices slightly overlapping around sides and bottom of casserole. Fill center no more than 1¾ inches deep. Sprinkle with salt and pepper. Melt the butter until it becomes light brown. Pour over the potatoes. Bake at 425° for 40 to 45 minutes or until potatoes are tender in center. Turn over on a serving platter, run under broiler to brown. High in calories, but delicious.

MALTAISE SAUCE

I like Maltaise sauce with salmon. You simply whip 2 tablespoons of orange juice plus ½ teaspoon grated orange rind into ½ cup Hollandaise.

The fresh green taste of asparagus can be ruined with overcooking and overdressing with Hollandaise and other sauces. I find too that men and children hesitate to take asparagus when passed to them. They wonder: "Is it or is it not a finger food, and what will I do if the fork doesn't cut it?" It is hard to judge how much asparagus to buy. You can plan on three or four stalks per serving and sure enough, someone will take eight. By slivering asparagus you have no problem and you use fewer stalks. I sliver the asparagus in 1- or 2-inch pieces, cook about 3 minutes in a steamette and lightly toss with drawn butter, *beurre noir* or lemon cheese butter. (I might add that my converts to this way of eating asparagus are many.)

BOURBON PEACHES

½ cup butter	2 teaspoons lemon juice
8 fresh peaches, halved	4 tablespoons light brown sugar
1½ tablespoons grated orange peel	4 ounces bourbon

Melt butter, add peaches and sauté until lacy brown. Add orange peel, lemon juice and sugar. Cook until thoroughly melted. Add bourbon and ignite. Serve hot or with ice cream. This is an excellent dessert when served with English Custard.

CARAMEL SOUFFLE

2 pounds granulated sugar   12 egg whites
Butter for coating pan

Place 1½ cups of the sugar in a skillet. Heat over medium heat until a brown syrup. Do not let it burn. Pour into a 3-quart casserole or bundt pan, coating the sides and bottom. Cool. Rub the entire pan and coating with butter. Beat egg whites until stiff. Add 1 pound of sugar gradually to the egg whites, beating constantly. Put the remaining sugar in a skillet and brown to a syrup. Add a little water and cook until the syrup forms a thread. Pour into the egg whites and beat at medium speed on your mixer. Increase to high speed and beat for 12 minutes. Pour into the buttered container and bake at 300° in a hot water bath for 1 hour or until firm but light. Turn out onto a serving tray at once. If you wish to prepare the soufflé early in the day, leave in pan and return to a 350° oven for about 20 minutes. It must be hot or warm to come out of the pan. Some of the caramel syrup will stay in the pan. Serve with English Custard. Men adore this dessert.

ENGLISH CUSTARD
(for 10 to 12)

¾ cup sugar	12 egg yolks, beaten until lemon
3 cups milk	yellow
2 tablespoons butter	1 teaspoon vanilla
1 cup heavy cream (you may omit)	

Cook sugar and milk together in double boiler. When hot, add butter and egg yolks. Stir vigorously and cook until thickened. Remove from stove to cool. Add vanilla and cream, either whipped or unwhipped.

The first time I served this was at a Confrerie des Chevaliers du Tastevin. After submitting the menu to "the committee" I was notified that
all was approved except the dessert, which was too feminine, and what
was I going to do about it. I said: "Serve it." Every man present had
two helpings. It is a divine dessert and can be used with any kind of
entrée. I sometimes serve lightly broiled sugared strawberries with it.
You may halve the recipe, but why? Regardless of how few guests you
have, it will all be eaten. It is one dessert of which seconds are always
accepted with glee.

BRIE QUICHE

4 egg yolks	⅛ teaspoon salt
1½ cups half-and-half	4 egg whites
1 pound Brie cheese (mashed)	8-inch pie crust

Beat the egg yolks with the cream, add the cheese and salt. Mix thoroughly. Beat the egg whites until stiff, stir one-third into the mixture,
fold in the rest. Pour into an 8-inch torte pan lined with partially baked
pie crust (10 minutes). Bake at 350° for 30 minutes or until custard is
set. Cut in eighths or less and serve as is or with caviar. It may also be
put into barque or tart shells for a cocktail party tidbit. I like to eat it as
a dessert with a cold Delicious apple. Try it.

QUENELLES OF SOLE

1 pound filet of sole	Pinch of nutmeg
1 cup cold heavy cream sauce (3	½ teaspoon salt
tablespoons butter, 3 table-	1 egg white, beaten stiff
spoons flour, 1 cup milk)	

Put the filet of sole through the finest blade of your food chopper twice.
Mix with cream sauce, nutmeg and salt. Put through a sieve. Stir in
egg white. The mixture should be light and airy. Using two tablespoons,
shape into 16 ovals. Put on a buttered pan and refrigerate several hours.
Poach in hot water over low heat, not boiling, for 10 minutes. Remove
with a slotted spoon and dry on paper towels. You may serve with any
cream sauce, but the one I like I call grenadine. In the strict sense of the
word it isn't, but as this is a request recipe, here it is:

GRENADINE SAUCE

2 tablespoons butter	2 cups whipping cream
1 tablespoon paprika	Salt and white pepper
2 tablespoons flour	2 ounces brandy

Melt butter, add paprika and cook 1 minute. Add flour. Cook until bubbly. Add cream and cook until thickened, stirring with your French whip. Season to your taste. Heat the brandy, ignite and pour into the sauce. As a rule two quenelles are served with the sauce poured over.

I sometimes add Greenland shrimp or Alaskan king crabmeat to the sauce. You may use fish, especially pike, for the quenelles, or raw chicken or veal, free of fat and skin.

TENDERLOIN OF BEEF WITH PATE DE FOIS GRAS

1 trimmed 4- to 5-pound tenderloin of beef	Salt and white pepper
	Chopped truffles
½ cup dry Burgundy	1 ounce Cognac
4 ounces pâté de fois gras	

Place the meat in a 450° oven and roast for 25 minutes. Baste with the wine. Remove, save juices; let meat rest about 5 minutes and slice in the size slice you wish. Place on your serving tray. Between each filet slice spread the fois gras, pushing the pieces together again. Run under the broiler; baste with wine if you wish. Cover with chopped truffles. (You can buy truffle peelings which are good for this recipe and less expensive.) Add 1 ounce warm Cognac, ignite. Serve with Béarnaise Sauce. I usually put the sauce in either fresh or canned artichoke bottoms and surround the meat with them. It then serves as a garnish as well as a sauce for both meat and artichokes.

BEARNAISE SAUCE
(½ cup)

1 cup tarragon vinegar
1 tablespoon dried or a few sprigs
   of fresh tarragon
1 slice of onion

6 egg yolks
1 cup butter
Dash of cayenne

Boil the vinegar, tarragon and onion until reduced to ⅓ of a cup. Strain into top of a double boiler over hot water. Do not let water boil. Add egg yolks to this mixture, beating with a French whip. Melt the butter and pour slowly into the egg mixture, beating constantly. When thick, remove and place in a pan of cold water to stop the cooking. Add the cayenne and keep at room temperature until ready to serve. Béarnaise Sauce complements any vegetable, poached fish and beef. I like it on Eggs Benedict in place of the traditional Hollandaise.

The elegant look of a Crown Roast of Lamb can never be lauded enough. Fill the center with a Mushroom Soufflé and your taste buds and your eyes will love this entrée.

CROWN ROAST OF LAMB

1 crown roast of lamb, consisting
   of 16 well-tied chops

Salt, pepper
1 clove garlic, slivered

Sprinkle lamb inside and out with salt and pepper. Trim all fat. Insert garlic here and there. Place an empty can in center to make a smooth well to hold the Mushroom Soufflé. Cover the chop ends with foil. Roast at 400° for 20 minutes. Remove from oven. Remove can. Pour off all fat. Cut out a circle of foil to cover bottom of roast and place the roast on it. Fill the center with Mushroom Soufflé.

MUSHROOM SOUFFLE

1½ pounds fresh mushrooms	1½ cups hot milk
¼ cup finely diced onion	8 egg yolks, beaten
1 teaspoon salt	8 egg whites, beaten stiff
Pinch of thyme	2 tablespoons grated Parmesan
6 tablespoons butter	cheese
4 tablespoons flour	

Wash, dry and chop the mushrooms fine. Sauté with the onion, salt and thyme in the butter until the onions are soft. Add the flour and cook until foamy. Cook 1 minute more. Add hot milk and cook until thickened, stirring constantly for about 5 minutes. Cool slightly and add the beaten egg yolks. Cool and stir in one third of the beaten egg whites. Fold in the rest, and pour into the lamb roast cavity. Sprinkle with Parmesan cheese. Return to oven and bake at 350° for 40 minutes. Remove to a heated platter, remove foil and strings.

The following sauce may be passed with the Lamb and Soufflé: Add 1 cup beef consommé to roasting pan, and cook for 5 minutes. Add 1 tablespoon currant jelly, 1 tablespoon red wine vinegar. Cook until jelly is melted. Carve 1 double chop for each guest, including some of the Soufflé. Pass sauce. There will be more than enough Soufflé to fill the lamb; put the rest in a buttered soufflé dish and bake along with the lamb.

This is a good way to use up mushroom stems also. And use this recipe any time, lamb or no.

LEMON CHEESE BUTTER

¼ cup butter	1 teaspoon cracked pepper
Grated rind of 2 lemons	¼ cup chopped parsley
1 teaspoon coarse salt	¼ cup grated Gruyère cheese
(Kosher salt)	

Soften butter, add rest of ingredients. Toss into hot cooked vegetables.

SNOW PEA SALAD

1 large head iceberg lettuce,   1 pound snow peas, steamed 30
   shredded fine   seconds
½ cup chopped parsley

Toss lightly with:

SESAME SEED DRESSING

¼ cup sesame seeds, lightly   2 tablespoons vinegar
   browned in oven   2 tablespoons sugar
⅔ cup salad oil   1 clove garlic, crushed
2 tablespoons lemon juice   1½ teaspoons salt

Put all ingredients in a blender except sesame seeds and mix well. Add
seeds. This dressing will store well. I like to lightly pile this salad on red
lettuce leaves, if only for color.

MY FRENCH APPLE PIE

1 cup butter   ¼ teaspoon cinnamon
2 cups sugar   2 teaspoons lemon juice
4 pounds green apples, Winesaps   Pie dough
   or McIntosh   1 cup sugar

Spread a 10-inch pie tin with ½ cup of the butter, about ¼ inch deep.
Pour ½ cup sugar over. Peel and slice thin the apples; mix with 1½ cups
of the remaining sugar. Pile into the pie tin; it will be high with apples.
Dot with remaining butter and sprinkle with cinnamon and lemon juice.
Roll out pie dough and cover the apples, pressing loosely on the sides
of the pie tin. Put in a 450° oven and bake 20 minutes. Reduce heat
to 350° and bake until apples are soft. Remove, cool slightly. Place
a serving plate on top of the pie and invert. Cool. Caramelize 1 cup
sugar and pour over apples. Serve whipped unsweetened cream if you
wish. I don't.

    This is really my version of Tarte Tatin and I like it better than the
original. Funny thing, M. Carrére of the famed Maxim's did too.

DOUBLE SIRLOIN STEAK

2 32-ounce sirloin strip steaks   1 clove garlic, chopped fine (you
   (no bone)   may omit)
Salt, freshly ground pepper   ¼ cup sweet butter, melted
                      2 ounces brandy

Rub meat on both sides with the salt, pepper and garlic. Broil steak 10 minutes on each side. Turn off heat and leave in oven for 15 minutes. Remove to serving platter. Pour sweet butter over and add about 2 ounces of flaming brandy. Slice and serve with juices. One steak will serve 4. Increase broiling time if you like your meat well done. I don't. More vitamins remain if you cook the steak rare.

FRIED PARSLEY

Wash and drain 2 bunches of curly parsley and trim the stems short. Form into small bouquets and put in a frying basket or strainer, a few at a time, and fry in hot deep oil at 380° until crisp, about 2 seconds. Drain on paper towels and lightly salt.

BRAISED CELERY

4 bunches celery	2 cups canned beef consommé
2 tablespoons butter	Chopped parsley
½ cup finely chopped onion	

Cut off tops of celery and tough outer stalks. Split the bunches lengthwise, cover with boiling water and cook for 5 minutes. Remove and cool
with cold running water. Melt the butter and sauté the onion until soft
and yellow. Fold the celery over to make a serving about 4 inches long.
Place in a buttered shallow casserole. Sprinkle with the sautéed onion and
pour over the consommé. Cover and bake at 375° for 1 hour or until celery
is tender. Remove celery to serving platter or tray (keep warm) and continue cooking the liquid until reduced to about ¾ cup. Pour over celery
and sprinkle with chopped parsley. If you use canned celery hearts for a
quicker preparation, reduce baking time to 30 minutes and proceed.

FRIED TOMATOES WITH SPINACH AND PEAS

4 medium tomatoes	¼ cup butter, melted
¼ cup flour, ¼ teaspoon salt and pinch of white pepper	

Cut tomatoes in half, dip in flour and seasonings. Sauté in butter.

1 pound fresh spinach	1 cup cooked peas, chopped
2 tablespoons butter	(frozen or fresh)
3 tablespoons chopped onion	⅓ cup half-and-half
Salt and pepper	

Wash spinach, cook in a covered pot with no added water for 1 minute.
Drain and chop. Melt the butter, add the onion, sauté until soft, not
brown. Add the spinach and peas with the cream. Blend well. Correct
seasonings and pile on the tomatoes. Put in 350° oven for 5 minutes.
You may use the spinach-pea combination without the tomato.

MARINATED LEEK SALAD

8 leeks (usually 3 or 4 bunches)
¼ cup chopped parsley
1 clove garlic, finely minced
¼ cup salad oil
¼ cup olive oil
3 tablespoons vinegar

Salt and white pepper
¼ cup thinly sliced green onion
2 tablespoons green peppercorns
2 tablespoons chopped pimiento or sweet red pepper

Cut away green tops of leeks. Wash well. Slice thin and steam until tender, about 4 minutes. Cool. Mix rest of ingredients and toss with leeks. Serve on watercress or fresh spinach.

MARINATED FRESH ARTICHOKES

I like to serve these as a cocktail tidbit. They are low in calories and light enough not to interfere with the main course.

8 fresh artichokes
½ lemon, sliced

Few slices onion
2 tablespoons olive oil

Wash artichokes in cold salted water, drain and snip off the sharp tips of the leaves with scissors. Stand in a kettle and cover with fresh cold salted water, lemon, onion slices and olive oil. Cover and boil until leaves pull away easily. Remove, turn upside down and drain. Cool. Turn right side up and pour marinade over. Refrigerate for several hours or overnight.

Marinade:

½ cup salad oil
½ cup olive oil
Juice of 2 lemons
  2 tablespoons chopped chives or green onions

¼ cup chopped parsley
¾ teaspoon dry mustard
1½ teaspoons each salt and cracked pepper

Mix thoroughly all ingredients and pour over artichokes. Lift the artichokes onto plates and pour over a little of the marinade.

SQUAB IN WHITE WINE

¾ cup butter
8 squab, split down the middle
Salt and white pepper
6 tablespoons chopped shallots

1 clove garlic, chopped fine
1½ cups plus 1 cup Sauterne or Chablis
6 tablespoons chopped parsley

Melt butter in a skillet and lightly brown the squab. Put in a shallow pan or casserole, split side up, sprinkle with salt and white pepper. Add chopped shallots, garlic and 1½ cups wine. Bake at 425° for 30 minutes, or until tender, basting frequently. (Test for doneness by moving leg.) Remove pan from oven, add chopped parsley and rest of wine. Cook on top of stove until sauce is reduced to desired thickness, but do not thicken.

This is an excellent preparation for Rock Cornish hen and a good picnic item also. Lots of flavor.

WILD RICE AND APPLES

1½ cups wild rice, washed thoroughly
3 cups hot beef or chicken consommé
1½ cups dry white wine

3 Delicious apples, peeled and sliced thin
⅓ cup butter
2 tablespoons brandy

Put rice, consommé and wine in a buttered 1½-quart casserole. Cover and bake at 400° for 1 hour or until rice is tender. Sauté the apples in the butter until soft but not mushy. Fork stir into the rice; add lighted brandy and serve. You may substitute grapes, toasted almonds, mushrooms, cooked peas, anything your heart and stomach desire for the apples. The apple combination is especially delicious with duck, too.

BELGIAN ENDIVE AND MUSHROOM SALAD

4 Belgian endive
8 large fresh mushrooms
Juice of 2 lemons
2 cups slivered celery, blanched 1
minute, drained and cooled
1 teaspoon salt

1 tablespoon chopped chives
¼ teaspoon dried *fines herbes*
¼ cup olive oil
¼ cup salad oil
Cracked pepper
1 bunch watercress

Cut the endive lengthwise in as thin slices as possible. Place in ice water and refrigerate for several hours. Wash and dry mushrooms. Slice very thin. Pour lemon juice over. Toss drained endive with the celery. Add the mushrooms with the lemon juice. Add rest of ingredients except watercress. Toss lightly. Correct seasonings. Sprinkle with cracked pepper and pile on salad plates. Garnish with watercress or parsley.

COFFEE CREME PIE
(*a 10-inch pie*)

½ cup sugar
¼ teaspoon salt
2 egg whites, beaten stiff

½ cup pecans, chopped fine
1 10-inch buttered pie tin

Gradually add sugar and salt to the egg whites, beating as added. Fold in the pecans. Press into the pie tin. Prick with a fork. Bake at 250° for 1 hour. Cool.

Filling:

2 tablespoons instant coffee
½ cup boiling water
½ pound marshmallows, cut in half

2 egg yolks, beaten
2 cups whipping cream
½ teaspoon almond extract

Mix coffee, water and marshmallows. Add beaten egg yolks. Cook 3 minutes stirring constantly. Cool. Fold in whipped cream and almond extract. Reserving a cup of the mixture, pour rest into the meringue pie shell. As the filling begins to congeal, add the cupful to the center. This will make the center of the pie higher. Refrigerate overnight. Cover with shaved chocolate or more whipped cream and toasted sliced almonds. The filling could also be poured into a lightly buttered 1½-quart mold and used as a mousse.

QUICK MUSHROOM CONSOMME

10 cups canned beef consommé　　1 cup water
1 cup thinly sliced fresh　　½ cup sherry or Burgundy
　　mushrooms　　Few slices raw mushrooms

Put first 3 ingredients in a saucepan and simmer for 10 minutes. Add dry sherry or red Burgundy, bring to a rapid boil. Remove and serve with floating slices of raw mushrooms.

PORK LOIN

Marinate a 5-pound boned pork loin in 2 cups dry white wine overnight with fresh herbs. I like a bit of thyme, rosemary and tarragon. Remove the herbs, save marinade. Rub pork on either side with 2 tablespoons salt, 2 tablespoons Dijon mustard and 4 tablespoons brown sugar. Place in roasting pan with clove of garlic, 1 stalk celery, 1 onion, 1 carrot. Bake at 450° covered for 30 minutes. Remove cover, baste with marinade, reduce heat to 350°. Roast uncovered and baste frequently, about 2 hours. Remove meat and pour off excess fat. Add 1 tablespoon flour mixed with 1 tablespoon butter. Cook until brown. Add juices and half water, half beef consommé, to make 1 cup for this amount of flour. Season with more salt and white pepper, if necessary. I like to add a little apple or currant jelly, about 1 tablespoon for each cup of sauce.

The easiest way to remove fat is to pour all the drippings into a glass. The fat comes to the top so you can see it. Spoon off as much as you wish.

GREEN BEANS WITH FLAGEOLETS

2 tablespoons butter　　2½ cups canned flageolets,
2 tablespoons finely chopped　　　drained
　　onion　　¼ cup finely chopped parsley
1 pound snipped green beans,　　Half-and-half
　　cooked　　Salt and pepper

Melt the butter, add onion and sauté until yellow. Add beans, flageolets, parsley and cream enough to just hold all ingredients together. Correct seasonings and serve, or place in a buttered shallow casserole. If you like, sprinkle with buttered bread crumbs and run under broiler to brown.

CRUDITES SALAD

When the first traveler who was served a green salad in Europe came home with the recipe, America shouted "hallelujah." It was grabbed onto like a log by a drowning man. Every restaurant, every hostess, everybody thought they must have a green salad. A green salad is wonderful if made with fresh crisp salad greens — no cabbage, radishes and such — but that doesn't mean you have to serve it every time you entertain. I like to make a salad from crudités — refreshing and good for you.

6 stalks fresh asparagus	1 small cucumber, sliced thin
½ cup raw cauliflower flowerettes	¼ cup sliced green onions
½ cup slivered celery	A few sliced radishes or cherry
1 small zucchini, sliced thin	tomatoes
½ cup fresh Brussels sprouts, cut in half	Sherry French Dressing
½ cup sliced raw mushrooms	8 onion brushes
2 Belgian endive, sliced	Chopped parsley

Cut asparagus on the diagonal, put in a large strainer. Add the cauliflower, celery, zucchini, Brussels sprouts. Pour boiling water over. Drain and cool. Toss with the mushrooms, endive, cucumbers, green onions and radishes. Pour dressing over and refrigerate for at least 1 hour. Drain off the dressing. Serve on very cold salad plates and decorate with the onion brushes and sprinkle with chopped parsley. No lettuce. The salad leftovers are good the following day. You may substitute slivered snow peas, yellow squash, very thin sliced carrots. What I have listed is merely a guide. This is a great buffet salad, especially for a walk-around supper.

MOCHA ORANGE ICE CREAM

4 tablespoons instant coffee   2 cups whipping cream
¾ cup sugar   1 tablespoon grated orange peel
2 cups scalded milk   2 tablespoons Grand Marnier
4 egg yolks, beaten

Add coffee and sugar to the milk and bring to a boil. Add a little of the
liquid to the egg yolks and stir, before adding to the hot liquid. Cook to
a soft custard consistency. Strain and cool. Add the cream, orange peel
and Grand Marnier. Freeze in an ice cream freezer, 6 parts of ice to 1
part of salt. Remove dasher and serve. I make up the mixture and
freeze while my guests are gathering. Leftovers I pack in a container and
deep freeze. I like to sliver some of the orange peel (peel with a potato
peeler) and heat in simple syrup (½ cup water, 1 cup sugar) until it is
glazed and sprinkle on top of each serving. Sometimes I pack the ice
cream in a mold that has been rinsed in cold water and freeze it. Then
unmold and sprinkle the glazed orange peel on top and surround with
Ferrara brand rum babas.

Keep 1 cup of the cream aside, whip and add to frozen mixture about
5 minutes before it is finished. You will have a creamier ice cream. This
is a good idea for all ice creams.

LEG OF LAMB, MUSLIM STYLE

2 tablespoons grated fresh
  ginger
3 cloves garlic, crushed
1 cup yogurt
1½ teaspoons salt
¼ teaspoon black pepper
Juice of 2 limes

1 4- to 5-pound leg of lamb
1 tablespoon ground coriander
½ teaspoon cayenne pepper
½ teaspoon ground cinnamon
½ teaspoon ground cloves
½ teaspoon ground cardamom

Mix ginger, garlic, yogurt, salt, pepper and lime juice. Make several gashes in the lamb and spread mixture over the surface. Marinate overnight. Mix spices and put into a small skillet on medium heat. Cool, sprinkle over lamb. Roast at 450° for 15 minutes. Reduce heat to 350°, and roast for 40 minutes longer, for medium rare (150° on your meat thermometer), longer if you wish it well done (165° on your thermometer). Remove, let rest. Slice thin and serve with strained juices from roasting pan.

At large cocktail parties I like to serve Chlodnik in the living room in a crystal bowl and let my guests help themselves. The color is divine.

CHLODNIK

1 pint chopped cooked beets
1 cup chopped shrimp
1 hard-cooked egg, chopped fine
½ medium cucumber, chopped
  fine
2 tablespoons chopped chives or
  green onions
½ teaspoon dill

2 cups sour cream
1 cup beer
Salt and pepper
1 sliced lemon
A few whole shrimp
Ice cubes
Chopped parsley

Mix together first 8 ingredients and chill. Correct seasonings. Serve in individual soup cups or in a crystal bowl with sliced lemon and shrimp and an ice cube. I usually dip the lemon edge in chopped parsley. Leftovers? Add melted gelatin, 1 tablespoon to 1 pint Chlodnik, and make a salad ring to fill with seafood salad.

ROAST DUCKLING AU NATUREL

Depending on how extravagant you are, there are many ways to estimate how many ducks you will need to prepare. If you serve only half of the breast, you will need 4 ducks; if a quarter, using breast and legs, you will need 2.

2 4- to 5-pound ducks (¼ per serving)
2 teaspoons salt
Juice of 1 lemon or lime
1 teaspoon white pepper
1 orange
1 medium-sized onion
Dry white wine or chicken broth
Garlic, if you like (then you would be cooking the ducks Niçoise style)

There are two schools of thought on roasting duck, depending on whether you like the skin crisp or not. (It doesn't really matter to the duck.) Rub the duck with the salt, lemon or lime juice and pepper. Place on a rack in a pan. Put one half each of orange and onion in cavity and roast uncovered at 450° for 20 minutes. Pour off all melted fat. Return to oven, turn down to 325° and baste with a dry white wine or chicken broth. Roast about 1½ hours or until duck is tender. Wiggle the leg bone! Remove duck. If you wish crisp skin, refrigerate duck until cold or overnight, then return to a 375° oven until thoroughly heated. Baste with juices. Pour off the fat from the juices and add, for a plain sauce, enough chicken broth to make 1 cup and 1½ teaspoons arrowroot or cornstarch and cook until thickened and clear. Strain and serve with the duck, or add ¼ cup brandy or Grand Marnier and ignite. I think the sauce should be passed. Most people like to ladle it for themselves. Throw away orange and onion!

There is nothing better than rice with Curried Fruit to serve with duck or any poultry, pork or ham. I do not recommend it for beef. If I do not use this vegetable, I like to serve a favorite sauce: chopped preserved oranges, one to each cup of sauce, added to the plain sauce. You will find the oranges in any gourmet shop. I use them also in ham juices for baked ham or in the Suzette Sauce for crêpes.

RICE WITH CURRIED FRUIT

½ cup chutney, finely chopped
2 cups melon balls (not watermelon)
1 cup diced fresh pineapple
1 banana, sliced
1 cup other fruit such as peaches, pears, grapes, etc.
2 cups chicken broth
2 teaspoons cornstarch

2 tablespoons curry powder or less
¼ cup pistachios
½ cup slivered toasted almonds
¼ cup plumped raisins (cover with warm water and let stand a few hours, then drain)
4 cups cooked rice, hot
Parsley, finely chopped

Mix chutney, melon balls, pineapple and other fruit and chill well. Mix chicken broth with cornstarch and curry powder and simmer until thickened. Add the nuts and raisins to the chicken broth sauce. Place the hot rice on a heated platter and top with the chilled fruit, then cover the fruit and rice with the curry-flavored sauce. Sprinkle with finely chopped parsley.

This dish is to be a contrast of flavors and textures. The rice and sauce should be at the boiling point, whereas the fruit should be chilled so that you get the contrast in the hot and cold ingredients. Unfortunately, this dish is not designed for buffet or leisurely serving — it should be eaten immediately upon preparation.

CHINESE STYLE GREEN BEANS AND CELERY

1 pound fresh green beans, cut diagonally in thin slices
2 cups celery, cut similar to beans
2 tablespoons salad oil, not olive
½ cup chicken broth or water

1 teaspoon cornstarch (mixed with 2 tablespoons cold water)
Salt and pepper
Chopped parsley

Heat oil in a heavy skillet, add beans and sauté 1 minute at high heat. Stir constantly. Add the celery and cook 1 minute, stirring constantly. Add chicken broth. Cover and cook 2 minutes. Add cornstarch and season with salt and pepper. Sprinkle with chopped parsley. Substitute mushrooms for the celery and fresh asparagus for the green beans. Use same method for any vegetable of similar texture.

This may be used as a dessert or with a fish or fowl course. I always serve it in a stemmed glass.

SPOOM

¼ pound sugar	Lemon sherbet
2 tablespoons water	Champagne
6 egg whites	

Boil sugar and water to make a clear syrup. Beat egg whites until stiff. Add hot syrup gradually and beat until cold. Fold together equal parts of meringue and lemon sherbet; lace with champagne.

ROLLED WAFERS
(3 dozen)

½ cup shortening	1 cup sifted flour
½ cup light corn syrup	¼ teaspoon salt
½ cup sugar	1 teaspoon ground cinnamon

Put shortening, syrup and sugar into a small pan and heat until warm. Stir in sifted dry ingredients. Drop from teaspoon 6 inches apart on greased pan. Bake at 350° for 10 to 12 minutes. Remove from pan immediately and roll around the handle of a wooden spoon. Do not try to bake more than six at a time, as the cookie must be warm to roll — and be quick about it. Or you may leave them flat and call them Lace Cookies.

ICED SPINACH SOUP

3 cups sour cream or yogurt	¼ cup chopped, peeled and
2 cups chopped raw spinach	seeded tomatoes
3 tablespoons finely chopped	8 ice cubes
onion	Salt and pepper
½ cup finely diced cucumber	Dash of Tabasco

Mix and chill. Good for dip too, just leave out the ice cubes. Keeps well for several days in a covered container.

MOLDED GAZPACHO SALAD
(for 8 or 10)

6 large ripe tomatoes, peeled and seeded
1 cucumber, peeled
⅓ cup green pepper, chopped and blanched
1 tablespoon plus 1 teaspoon un-flavored gelatin, dissolved in ¼ cup cold water

1½ cups hot tomato juice
⅛ teaspoon Tabasco
4 tablespoons olive oil
1½ tablespoons wine vinegar
1 teaspoon salt
¼ teaspoon white pepper
1 tablespoon chopped green onion

Chop the tomatoes and cucumber fine. Add the green pepper and sea-sonings. When the gelatin is partially congealed, add the rest of the in-gredients. Pour into individual molds lightly rubbed with mayonnaise. Chill until firm. Turn out on salad greens and serve with: ½ cup mayonnaise mixed with ½ cup sour cream and 1 cup finely diced celery.

This salad is such a nice change from tomato aspic. I really think it is worth the effort to chop the fresh vegetables by hand, but if you don't, use your blender.

BREAST OF CHICKEN PIQUANTE

8 whole chicken breasts, 6- or 8-ounce
1 cup flour, 2 teaspoons salt, ¼ teaspoon white pepper
⅔ cup butter or margarine

2 tablespoons salad oil
1 teaspoon minced shallots
2 garlic cloves, minced
Juice of 4 lemons
½ cup finely chopped parsley

Remove bone from chicken or buy boneless. Remove skin and flatten chicken with the heel of your hand. Lightly dust with flour and season-ings. Heat butter and oil with the shallots and garlic and add breasts, full side down. Sauté lightly, about 6 minutes. Turn once. Continue cooking. Remove to a platter or casserole and keep warm. Add lemon juice to pan and dissolve any cooked brown particles. Boil 1 minute. Correct seasonings, add parsley and pour over chicken. Serve at once. This is excellent for a low-cholesterol diet.

TURNIPS AND PEAS IN CREAM

8 small white turnips, peeled and
   sliced paper thin
2 tablespoons minced onion
3 tablespoons butter
½ teaspoon sugar

½ cup whipping cream
1 cup freshly cooked green peas
Salt and pepper
Chopped parsley

Cook the turnips in a steamette or in boiling water until tender. Drain. Sauté the onion with the butter and sugar for 1 minute. Add turnips and cook only until hot. Add cream and peas and simmer until cream is reduced. Correct seasonings. Sprinkle with chopped parsley.

I have used this recipe for the cooking schools I have taught and the increase in the sale of turnips has been fantastic. The secret is to thin-slice the turnips and cook underdone. You may use rutabagas the same way, but these I like to cut in julienne strips.

ORANGE SHELL GLACE

8 large navel oranges
1 quart vanilla ice cream
1 tablespoon grated orange peel

½ cup slivered preserved or candied ginger
Freshly grated coconut and slivered
   almonds

Cut the blossom end of the orange ¼ inch deep in wide scallops. Put the point of a sharp paring knife about halfway through the orange, then cut in a zigzag scallop or notch until you meet the point where you started. Pull the top and bottom of the orange apart. Cut along the inside of the orange with a sharp knife to loosen the pulp and lift out the fruit with a dessert spoon. Mix the ice cream with orange peel and ginger and pack into the empty shells. Wrap in clear plastic and deep freeze. When ready to serve, cover with the coconut and almonds.

It is a refreshing dessert, because after you eat the ice cream you eat any frozen orange left in the shell. When I use this dessert in an Oriental dinner, I stick a paper parasol in the orange top or sometimes I fasten on a fresh flower with a plastic toothpick.

CURRIED CREAM CHEESE SOUP

4 3-ounce packages cream cheese   ½ medium garlic clove
2 cups canned beef consommé   Salt and pepper
¾ teaspoon curry powder

Put in blender and purée on full speed until smooth. Correct seasonings. Refrigerate and serve very cold. I add shrimp, slivered chicken or, if I'm feeling extravagant, fresh caviar. It is divine.

POACHED RED SNAPPER

For one 6-pound red snapper:

Salt and white pepper   ¼ sliced carrot
1 bay leaf   Few sprigs of parsley
½ sliced onion   Few slices of lemon
1 stalk celery

Sprinkle fish cavity with salt and pepper and fill with rest of ingredients. Wrap in foil, shiny side in, with foil overlapping on top. Place in a roasting pan on a rack. Pour boiling water over until top of rack is reached. Cover and steam for 30 minutes; water should simmer. Test with a fork for fish to flake. (That is why you have the foil overlapping on top of fish.) Remove fish to serving platter, and slip foil out. Remove vegetables and with a sharp knife strip off the skin from the gills to the base of the tail. When serving, cut in portions to the backbone, then remove bone and cut lower half. Use the same method for poaching whole salmon — that is if you do not have a fish poacher. I personally like a cold sauce with the hot fish — this one especially:

CUCUMBER SAUCE

3 cups chopped cucumbers,   1½ cups sour cream
   peeled and seeded   2 tablespoons mayonnaise
⅓ cup chopped green onion   Few drops Worcestershire sauce
1½ teaspoons lemon juice   Salt and white pepper

Mix and season to taste.

A sauce less expensive than Hollandaise or Maltaise, which are both elegant but expensive, is:

LEMON SAUCE

2 egg yolks
1 tablespoon flour
1 cup liquid from fish poaching or
chicken broth

1 tablespoon fresh lemon juice
2 tablespoons chopped parsley
Salt and white pepper

Mix egg yolks with the flour, add liquid and stir with your French whip until thick. Add lemon juice and parsley and correct seasonings. Add more lemon juice if you desire.

LEMON STEAMED POTATOES

½ cup butter
16 small, peeled new potatoes
2 teaspoons grated lemon peel

1 tablespoon lemon juice
Coarse salt and cracked pepper

Melt butter in a heavy skillet. Add potatoes, lemon peel and juice. Cover and cook until tender, shaking frequently. Sprinkle with coarse salt and cracked pepper. Toss again before serving.

STIR-FRIED SPINACH

2 pounds fresh spinach   ⅓ cup butter or margarine
Salt and pepper

Wash spinach and remove any heavy stems. Melt the butter in a large skillet. Add the spinach and cook over high heat stirring constantly with a long fork. You may add very thinly sliced onion or mushrooms. Cook only 1 minute; then add seasonings. No water is used in cooking, only the water that remains on the spinach from washing. Add brown butter if you wish, toasted sesame seeds, a little grated raw beet or carrot for color; I like to toss in a few capers. Of course the old standby: grated hard-cooked eggs, but why?

STAINED GLASS WINDOW DESSERT

Why the name? Because this dessert looks like one. At any rate, it doesn't look like fruit gelatin, which it is. But it is fresh tasting and low in calories. It is your imagination that makes it a beautiful dessert.

Serve this on a flat 12-inch round silver or crystal tray.

1 tablespoon unflavored gelatin, dissolved in ¼ cup cold water
1½ cups fresh orange juice
1 tablespoon lemon juice
1 tablespoon sugar
1 orange, unpeeled
4 fresh peaches

1 small cantaloupe, sliced in bite-sized pieces
2 dozen honeydew melon balls
1 dozen large strawberries
½ cup white grapes
½ cup blue grapes, seeded, cut in half

I might choose any other fruit with the exception
of fresh pineapple

Melt the dissolved gelatin over hot water and add to the fresh orange juice with the lemon juice and sugar. Cut the orange in half lengthwise and slice in thin slices. Use these to form a scallop around rim of tray. Pour enough of the gelatin mixture to hold the orange slices in place. Refrigerate until set. Place one-half of a freshly peeled peach or plum in center of tray with enough gelatin to hold it. Let it set also; then make a design of the fruit using slices of peaches and cantaloupe, the melon balls and strawberries cut in half and the grapes in a cartwheel fashion. Pour gelatin mixture over, but do not cover the fruit. In season I sprinkle blueberries or raspberries here and there. Refrigerate for several hours until set. Bring to the table and cut like a pie. Pass whipped cream or sour cream sweetened with brown sugar. It is a delightful dessert.

Lazy? Use any flavored gelatin. I use canned pear juice sometimes in place of the orange juice. You may use any fruits.

SAUTEED SLICED BEEF TENDERLOIN

4 pounds tenderloin or sirloin, sliced ¼ inch thick	1 cup dry red wine
1 teaspoon salt	1 cup beef broth
Freshly ground pepper	¼ cup butter, melted
4 tablespoons flour	¼ cup olive oil

Be sure all fat is removed from meat. Mix the salt, pepper and flour on a flat pan and dust each slice of meat lightly. Shake off any excess. Pour one-half the butter and oil into a 10- or 12-inch frying pan and set over high heat. When the pan is hot, add half the meat. Sauté no longer than 2 to 3 minutes. Add a little red wine and let it evaporate. Turn into a warm serving dish and repeat with remaining steak in the same pan. Remove and keep meat warm. Pour the beef broth into the pan. Bring to a boil, scrape and stir constantly to dissolve all the dark particles. Add rest of wine and boil about 3 minutes. Add the cooked meat only to heat, but do not cook further. If you wish your sauce thicker, add a little arrowroot dissolved in ½ teaspoon lemon juice. You may add thinly sliced onions and mushrooms. I sometimes dip each piece of meat in half Kikkoman soy sauce and half sherry or bourbon, sauté quickly, but serve no sauce with it.

I prepare this recipe in my dining room in electric skillets and usually some of my men guests say "Let me" — and I do. I always feel a party a success if someone else gets into the act.

MICHAEL SAUCE FOR ZUCCHINI FANS
(1 cup)

¾ cup sour cream
2 teaspoons tarragon vinegar
2 egg yolks

½ teaspoon paprika
8 small zucchini

Cook all ingredients except zucchini over hot water, not boiling, until thick and smooth. You must stir constantly.

Choose small zucchini about 4 inches long, allowing two per person. I find one zucchini never enough. Slice lengthwise almost to end in as thin slices as you can. The more slices, the prettier the fan. Cook in your steamette or in very little water until tender, about 6 minutes. Drain and arrange on a serving dish in fan shapes. Pour sauce over, sprinkle lightly with salt and run under the broiler for 1 minute.

ORIENTAL CHICKEN SALAD

2 cups fried Chinese rice noodles
6 8-ounce chicken breasts, boned
  and skin removed
Soy sauce to cover plus 2 teaspoons
4 tablespoons butter
4 tablespoons cooking oil

2 heads iceberg lettuce, shredded
  as fine as possible and crisped
2 tablespoons peanut oil
2 tablespoons vinegar
mayonnaise
Chopped parsley

The rice noodles may be purchased in any Chinese-type grocery store and are prepared by frying a few seconds in deep hot oil. Remove as soon as they puff and before they take on any brown color. Marinate chicken breasts in soy sauce for 20 minutes. Then sauté in butter and cooking oil, 5 minutes on each side. Keep warm. Cut chicken into thin strips and toss with the shredded lettuce, soy sauce, peanut oil, vinegar and fried noodles. Add just enough mayonnaise to blend and season to taste with salt. Garnish with chopped parsley and a few additional fried noodles. I like to surround the salad with snow peas, steamed 60 seconds, and dressed with Sesame Dressing.

If you cook your chicken ahead of time, keep at room temperature or reheat. The flavor is much better than if the chicken is cold.

ALMOND CREAM CAKE

1 cup whipping cream	1 cup sugar
2 eggs	2 teaspoons baking powder
¼ teaspoon almond extract	⅛ teaspoon salt
1½ cups sifted flour	

Whip cream until soft peaks form. Add eggs, one at a time, beating well after each addition. Stir in the almond extract. Sift together the flour, sugar, baking powder and salt. Add to the cream mixture and stir only until blended. Pour into a buttered and floured 8-inch spring form pan. Bake at 350° for 45 minutes until lightly browned on top and toothpick inserted in center comes out clean. During the last 10 minutes of baking time prepare the topping:

2 tablespoons butter or margarine	1 tablespoon whipping cream
⅓ cup sugar	1 tablespoon flour
¼ cup blanched, slivered almonds	

Mix all ingredients together and stir over low heat until well blended. Pour over cake and bake 10 minutes at 350°. Serve as is or with whipped cream. I sometimes bake this cake in a 9-inch pie tin and serve warm.

When men ask for a chicken recipe to serve when they entertain, I rate the following a good one. I have cooked it for all my cooking classes. It is easy to prepare and may be made ahead; it freezes well.

BREAST OF CHICKEN WITH CHANTERELLES

8 4- or 6-ounce whole chicken breasts, boned and skin removed	1½ cups chanterelles or thinly sliced mushrooms
½ cup flour	4 tablespoons flour
1½ teaspoons salt	½ cup dry sherry
¼ teaspoon paprika	3 cups half-and-half
⅔ cup butter	½ cup grated Gruyère cheese

Flatten chicken with heel of your hand and lightly dust the chicken in the flour, salt and paprika. Melt butter and sauté 5 minutes full side down. Turn and cook 5 minutes more. Remove and keep warm. Add chanterelles and cook 1 minute. Add flour, cook 1 minute. Pour in sherry and cream; cook until thickened. Use your French whip and stir constantly to avoid lumps. Add cheese. Return chicken to skillet and heat thoroughly. Correct seasonings, place in a casserole and pour sauce over. Heat in a 350° oven. You may omit cheese, but the cheese makes it creamier. Sometimes I add slivered cooked ham, about 1 cup for this amount.

For a brunch or supper I cut the uncooked chicken in thin strips and proceed as above, but sauté the chicken only 5 minutes, stirring constantly. I serve the chicken in crêpes (sprinkled with half Parmesan and half Gruyère cheese and heat) or spooned into pastry shells or over Spoon Bread (*Helen Corbitt's Cookbook*, page 230) or whatever suits my fancy at the moment.

Chanterelles are an edible yellow field mushroom with a very short stem. The canned ones from Europe are not too expensive, so you can be as extravagant as you wish in using them. (Be sure to examine them for sticks and stones.) They have a distinct flavor that is especially good with chicken or veal. I like them tossed in a green salad also.

WILD RICE WITH GRAPES

2 cups wild rice, washed thoroughly	2 cups canned seedless grapes or fresh grapes, peeled and seeded
4 cups hot chicken broth	½ cup sherry
1 cup white wine	4 tablespoons chopped parsley
½ cup butter	

Put the rice, broth and wine in a covered casserole and bake at 400° until tender, about 1 hour. Melt the butter, add the grapes and sauté 1 minute. Add the sherry and bring to a boil. Toss into the rice, add the parsley, fork stir and serve. Or make a ring out of the rice, and put the grapes with the wine and butter in the center.

FRESH BLUEBERRY TARTELETTES

2 cups sifted flour   1 egg, slightly beaten
1 teaspoon salt   2 tablespoons cold water
⅔ cup vegetable shortening   2 teaspoons lemon juice

Sift flour with salt into mixing bowl. Cut in shortening with a pastry blender or two knives. Mix egg, water and lemon juice. Sprinkle over flour mixture, toss and stir until mixture is moist enough to hold together. You may need to add a little more cold water. Sprinkle flour on board to roll pastry on. Rub rolling pin with flour. Do not press down too hard on dough, but roll until dough is smooth and thin. Fit crust tightly into tart tin, fit a second tin into it to hold it firmly in place. Bake at 350° until golden brown. You can buy frozen tart shells or use commercial pastry sticks.

Line the shells with the following cream cheese mixture:

1 8-ounce package cream cheese   3 tablespoons sugar
                3 tablespoons lemon juice

Mix until consistency of whipped cream and spread generously inside the tart shells. Fill with fresh blueberries. Cover with blueberry sauce:

1 cup fresh blueberries   2 tablespoons sugar or more
2 tablespoons Crème de Cassis (you may omit)

Crush berries in blender. Add sugar and Cassis. Pour over berries. Serve plain or with sour or whipped cream.

ROAST VEAL WITH MORELS IN CREAM

1 6-pound boned and tied loin or   Few sprigs parsley
  leg of veal   1 clove garlic (you may omit)
½ cup thinly sliced onion   Salt and white pepper
¼ cup small-diced carrots   1 cup dry white wine
¼ cup small-diced celery

Place veal in a shallow pan, uncovered, large enough to hold the veal. Put in a 450° oven for 15 minutes. Remove from oven and put vegetables around the veal. Sprinkle with salt and white pepper; return to oven turned to 350°. Pour some of the wine around the veal after 15 minutes. Baste frequently with the rest of wine and drippings. Roast about 1 hour if a loin roast, about 1 hour and 20 minutes if cut from the leg. The temperature on a meat thermometer should be 170°. Do not overcook. Remove strings and transfer to a warm serving platter or tray. Serve with the juices and:

Morels in Cream:

| ½ pound dried morels | 1 tablespoon flour |
| 3 tablespoons butter | 1 cup whipping or sour cream |

Rinse morels thoroughly many times until all sand is removed and let soak for several hours in cold water.

Melt butter, add drained morels and sauté until they are shiny. Add flour and cook 1 minute. Add cream and simmer for 5 minutes. You may use canned morels, chanterelles or fresh mushrooms in place of morels.

Morels are edible wild mushrooms with spongy oval caps. They must be carefully cleaned and cooked for a long time if fresh or dried. Very expensive, but worth it at times, I think.

SHRIMP BEL PAESE

32 raw shrimp 8 to 10 count, peeled, deveined and quick frozen (P.D.Q.)

Cover with cold water, a cup of clam juice, a few slices of lemon, a piece of crushed garlic and a few slices of onion. Bring to a boil only. Drain. Split shrimps lengthwise and flatten. Put in a shallow buttered casserole and sprinkle with ⅔ cup sherry. Cover with grated Bel Paese cheese and run under broiler to lightly brown. I substitute Parmesan when I'm counting calories. Muenster cheese is a pretty good substitute for Bel Paese and not as expensive.

I find as the variety of vegetables is nil at times, I fall back on peas and green beans, but purée them in my blender or put them through a food mill. Peas are peas, but when you purée them and top them with Hollandaise they are:

PEASE

3 packages frozen peas   ⅓ cup whipping cream
2 tablespoons butter, melted   Salt and white pepper

Defrost peas and put in blender just long enough to smash. Pour into a skillet with the melted butter and cream. Cook 2 minutes, after the mixture begins to boil. Season to your taste. Place in serving dish and cover with Hollandaise.

HOLLANDAISE

½ cup butter or margarine   1 tablespoon lemon juice
2 egg yolks, slightly beaten   A dash of cayenne

Divide butter in two and put one-half in top of double boiler with the egg yolks and lemon juice. Stir constantly over boiling water. To prevent curdling, do not let boiling water touch the bottom of pan until butter is melted. Add remaining butter and stir until thick. Remove, place in cold water to stop the cooking. Add cayenne.

You may purée any vegetable, and you may name it. I like peas and beans especially, also onions, and — oh yes — white turnips.

COLD ITALIAN MERINGUE

2 cups sugar   ⅛ teaspoon salt
½ teaspoon cream of tartar   6 egg whites
½ cup water   1 teaspoon vanilla

Mix the sugar and cream of tartar in a 2-quart saucepan. Add the water. Cook slowly until the sugar is dissolved and water begins to boil. Cover and fast boil 3 minutes. Remove cover and boil without stirring to 242° on a candy thermometer or until syrup spins a thread. Add the salt to the egg whites and beat until stiff. Gradually beat in the hot syrup. Add the vanilla and continue beating until very stiff. Pile into a crystal bowl, refrigerate and serve on crystal plates with soft custard and store-bought preserved marrons.

I like Oriental food, especially Cantonese. I had the great privilege of knowing John Kan of Kan's Restaurant in Chinatown, San Francisco. He put on several ceremonial dinners for me, and always came to my table with something extra special when I dropped in for lunch. I had always wished I could work in his kitchen to learn a few authentic techniques. Finally the day came. Danny Kaye and I are, or were at that time, the only non-Orientals who were allowed that privilege. If you haven't been to Kan's, make it a must on your next trip to San Francisco. Don Sid is the charming assistant; tell him you are a friend of mine. He will seat you sooner, perhaps?

In Oriental cooking, the advance preparation is something, but the results are always worth the effort. I like to use Oriental cooking combined with other food, but keeping the Oriental taste. This chicken recipe does just that.

ORIENTAL ROASTED CHICKEN

2 cups soy sauce	3 tablespoons shredded ginger
¼ cup gin	root
3 tablespoons honey	2 teaspoons salt
8 cloves garlic, crushed	3 2½-pound roasting chickens or 4
2 bunches scallions, chopped	1¾-pound

Mix all the ingredients and rub the chickens inside and out with some of the mixture; then pour rest of the marinade over the chickens. Cover and marinate several hours or overnight, but turn the chickens occasionally. If you like a lighter flavor, marinate 45 minutes. Roast at 350° for 1 hour or until the fleshy part of the leg feels soft. Or you may fry in vegetable oil as the Orientals do. Disjoint and serve with any of the remaining hot marinade.

P.S. Don't get up in the middle of the night to turn the chickens. Anytime in the morning will do.

A word about ginger root. It is the part of the ginger plant that delights the world. Since it is native to the tropics and semi-tropics, there are only a few places on earth that have suitable soil and climate conditions to produce the aroma, taste and tenderness found in high-grade ginger. It is available at all fresh vegetable counters.

I have heard repeatedly that men like only meat, potatoes and a green salad. I can disprove that statement many times over. When I have a fish soufflé on my buffet table, the men come back for a heaping second helping.

FILET OF SOLE SOUFFLE

3 tablespoons butter	¼ teaspoon Worcestershire sauce
3 tablespoons flour	1 pound cooked, flaked filet of
1 cup milk	sole
1 egg yolk	6 egg whites
¼ teaspoon dry mustard	⅛ teaspoon cream of tartar
1 teaspoon salt	2 tablespoons Parmesan cheese
2 teaspoons lemon juice	

Melt the butter, add the flour and cook 1 minute. Add the milk and cook until thick. Use your French whip to stir in the egg yolk, mustard, salt, lemon juice and Worcestershire. Remove from stove; add flaked fish. Cool until you can put your hand on the bottom of the pot; then beat the egg whites with the cream of tartar until stiff. Stir one third of the egg whites into the mixture and fold in the rest. Pour into a 2-quart buttered shallow casserole. Sprinkle with the Parmesan. Bake in a 375° oven for 30 minutes or until puffed and lightly browned. As a variation, put soufflé into individual custard cups or coquilles and use as a first course or luncheon entrée.

SHRIMP SAUCE

3 tablespoons butter	½ cup clam juice
1 cup chopped raw shrimp	1 teaspoon lemon juice
¼ teaspoon dry mustard	1 teaspoon chopped chives or dill
3 tablespoons flour	Salt and white pepper
1½ cups milk	

Melt the butter, add the shrimp and mustard. Cook 1 minute. Add flour, cook until bubbly. Pour in milk and clam juice; cook until thickened. Mix in lemon juice and seasonings.

I use this sauce on poached salmon or red snapper, filet of sole roulades or any seafood soufflé; sometimes on an individual cheese or mushroom soufflé; for a luncheon entrée; seafood crêpes, too, although I add some whole shrimp to the sauce.

CREPES BRAZIL

When I had Crêpes Brazil on my dessert menu in the Zodiac Room, everything else took second place. This is not the classic recipe but my version.

16 thin dessert crêpes	2 cups Caramel Syrup
1 quart Butter Pecan Ice Cream	1 cup whipping cream

You may buy the ice cream and the caramel sauce, but why?

BUTTER PECAN ICE CREAM

1 cup coarsely chopped pecans	¼ cup dark brown sugar
6 tablespoons butter	2 cups milk
3 tablespoons cornstarch	2 teaspoons vanilla
1 cup sugar	2 cups whipping cream

Toast the pecans in butter in the oven. Mix cornstarch and sugars in a heavy skillet, add milk and cook until thick, stirring constantly. Remove from heat, add vanilla and chill. Add cream and freeze in your freezer until partially done. Add pecans and resume freezing. Or whip the cream until stiff, fold in sugar mixture and pecans, pour into freezing trays and put in your deep freeze.

Use the Caramel Syrup recipe in Chapter 3 and cook longer until the syrup is a thicker consistency.

Heat the crêpes, spoon the ice cream into each, fold once. Put a dollop of whipped cream on top, and pour the sauce over, letting your conscience be your guide.

BRAISED BEEF, POIVRE VERT

1 5-pound boneless chuck, top
  butt or bottom round of beef
Salt and pepper
3 tablespoons cooking oil
2 cups dry red wine
1 cup beef bouillon

2 teaspoons brown sugar
¼ cup very finely chopped onion
1 clove very finely minced garlic
Dash of nutmeg, pinch of thyme
2 tablespoons green peppercorns
4 tablespoons chopped parsley

Rub meat with salt and pepper, using at least ½ teaspoon salt per pound of meat. Brown meat on all sides in cooking oil. When browned, transfer to a baking dish, adding all other ingredients with the exception of the green peppercorns and the chopped parsley. Bake at 350° for approximately 2 hours, basting frequently with the pan liquid. Turn meat twice to insure even cooking. Remove meat and reduce the pan liquid over high heat until slightly thickened. Add green peppercorns to the sauce. Carve the roast into very thin slices and arrange in serving dish. Pour sauce over all and sprinkle chopped parsley on top, or slice at the buffet table and add sauce as served.

This eggplant dish goes well with beef or with any other meat, and could be used for a main dish supper. I first tasted this recipe in Mexico.

EGGPLANT ROMANOFF

1 large peeled eggplant, cut in 1-
  inch slices
Flour, salad oil
1 teaspoon salt
4 tablespoons melted butter

2 tablespoons flour
2 cups sour cream
Parmesan cheese
Paprika

Dip the eggplant in flour and sauté in oil until golden brown and dry. Remove from pan. Sprinkle with salt. Heat the butter, add flour and cook 1 minute. Add the sour cream and blend. Place one layer of the eggplant in a buttered casserole and cover with some of the sour cream. Repeat, with the sour cream last. Sprinkle with grated Parmesan and paprika. Keep warm until ready to serve; then run under broiler to brown.

GRAND MARNIER SAUCE

1 cup whipping cream	6 tablespoons Grand Marnier
½ cup sugar	1 teaspoon grated orange peel
3 teaspoons lemon juice	

Whip cream until soft peaks are formed. Fold in sugar and rest of ingredients. Spoon over any fresh fruit, but this is especially good on strawberries.

BUFFET HAM MADEIRA

1 10- to 12-pound boneless banquet style ham	2 tomatoes, chopped
½ cup chopped onion	¼ teaspoon oregano
	3 cups Madeira wine

Place ham on bed of onion and tomatoes. Sprinkle with the oregano. Bake at 350° until the ham is tender, about 2 hours, basting frequently with the wine. Strain the juices and serve with the ham as it is sliced.

CHICKEN AND GREEN CHILES CASSEROLE

1 4-pound chicken or 2 2½-pound frying chickens,
or 2 pounds canned chicken, boned

Cover chicken with water plus 1 tablespoon salt. Cook until tender. Cool, and remove chicken from bones. Cut in large pieces.

4 tablespoons butter or chicken fat	½ 10-ounce can Rotel tomatoes with green chiles (you may omit)
1 cup coarsely chopped onion	10 or 12 tortillas, torn into small pieces
3 tablespoons flour	
2 cups milk	1½ teaspoons salt
1 cup chicken broth	1 or ¾ pound grated sharp Cheddar cheese (4 cups)
1 4-ounce can green chiles, seeded and cut in strips	

Melt the butter or chicken fat. Add the onion and sauté 1 minute. Add flour, cook until bubbly. Pour in milk and broth and cook until thickened, stirring with a French whip. Mix green chiles with the sauce, add the Rotel tomatoes. Place a layer of chicken in the bottom of a buttered shallow 3-quart casserole, then a layer of tortillas, cheese, then sauce. Repeat, with cheese on top. Bake at 375° until bubbling. This may be prepared ahead and frozen. For myself I make individual casseroles and freeze to have when I crave a touch of Mexico.

If you like this recipe hotter, add 2 tablespoons slivered jalapeño peppers.

Even if you do not have an expert carver around, I think you can use a whole turkey breast to great advantage. It is available frozen the year-round in all supermarkets today. There are fewer leftovers, if you are as allergic to them as I am. This preparation is excellent for a buffet.

STUFFED TURKEY BREAST

¼ cup butter
½ cup finely chopped onion
½ cup finely chopped celery
2 tablespoons chopped green pepper, blanched
2 cups cooked rice
1½ teaspoons poultry seasoning

1 egg
¼ cup chopped parsley
½ cup chopped nutmeats or raisins (you may omit)
1 8- to 10-pound turkey breast
Salt and white pepper
Dry white wine

Melt the butter. Add the onion, celery and green pepper. Cook 1 minute; add rice, poultry seasoning and egg. Mix thoroughly; add parsley and nuts. Season to taste. Cut the turkey in thick slices from the breast bone to the rib cage, keeping the slices attached to the bone. Stuff the rice mixture into the slits. Sprinkle with salt and pepper and wrap in one layer of cheesecloth to hold the rice stuffing intact. Place in roasting pan and roast at 350°, basting frequently with dry white wine or chicken broth. If browning too quickly, lay a piece of foil over the top. When finished cooking, remove from the oven, and take off the cheesecloth at once or it will stick to the turkey. Let rest for at least 30 minutes before carving. You may prepare this recipe ahead of time and reheat. It is good cold, too. Serve with the juices left in the pan. I like to surround it with:

BAKED ACORN SQUASH

4 acorn squash   ½ cup chutney
Salt and pepper   ½ cup grated coconut
½ cup butter

Wash and cut squash in half. Remove seeds, place in a shallow pan, cover tightly with foil and bake at 350° until soft, about 1 hour. Remove, sprinkle each half with salt and pepper; add 1 tablespoon butter or less depending on size of squash. Add the chutney and coconut. Return to oven and bake until bubbly.

PANCAKE STACK

Traditionally speaking, pancakes are served at breakfast, but one may use them just about any time of the day. The young-fry, the debutantes, adore them, and as far as I know everyone else does too.

If you do not have a nonsticking electric griddle, you should invest in one, as you may use it for other things, such as hash brown potatoes, hamburgers, grilled sandwiches. It is well worth the investment.

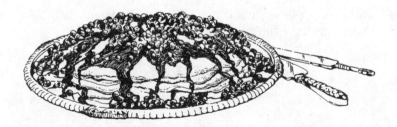

I use pancake stacks for brunches and for desserts and never have any leftovers. The blueberry stack for all occasions. It is an impressive dessert to pass after a seated dinner, and so good. You make your basic griddle or pancake mixture, thin it with milk to a thin consistency, then pour the size you wish. I do a 12- or 14-inch one, and use 10 to 12 cakes for a stack. You can make ahead and pile them on top of each other with wax paper between, and cover with a towel to keep from drying. When ready to assemble, spread your tray with lemon cream butter, then top with one pancake. Spread it with lemon cream butter and a little of the hot blueberry sauce. Repeat until you have as high a stack as you wish. Pour more blueberry sauce over all and a goodly dollop of the lemon cream butter. Put in a 350° oven for 3 minutes. Cut in narrow pie-shaped portions and pass.

For 10 or 12 thin pancakes:

2½ cups milk (about)	4 teaspoons baking powder
4 tablespoons melted butter	4 tablespoons sugar
2 eggs, separated	1 teaspoon salt
2 cups flour	

Mix milk, melted butter and egg yolks. Stir in the rest of ingredients and the egg whites, stiffly beaten. Add more milk if necessary to make the pancakes thin. Cook and stack.

LEMON CREAM BUTTER
(for 1 stack)

½ cup butter	3 tablespoons lemon juice
2½ cups confectioners' sugar	Grated rind of 1 lemon

Cream butter, add sugar and beat. Stir in the lemon juice and grated rind. Beat until the consistency of whipped cream.

BLUEBERRY SAUCE
(for 1 stack)

4 10-ounce packages quick-frozen blueberries	3 tablespoons cornstarch
	6 tablespoons sugar
1 cup cold water	2 tablespoons lemon juice

Defrost berries and strain, reserving juices. Combine water and juices, and add the cornstarch and sugar. Cook over low heat until clear and thickened. Add berries and cook 5 minutes. Remove from heat and add lemon juice.

If using fresh berries, mix 3 cups sugar with 3 tablespoons cornstarch; add 1½ cups boiling water. Bring to a boil and let cook for 5 minutes.

Add 3 cups fresh blueberries, 1 tablespoon lemon juice. Add more sugar if necessary.

During my days at Neiman-Marcus the Thursday night buffets became very popular and the pancake stacks were asked for time after time. We made them with various accompaniments; lingonberries and sour cream with beef, orange butter with chicken, maple syrup and ham juices with chicken and ham, cinnamon butter, whatever came to mind, always cut like a pie. The blueberry pancake was used with everything. I have pancake parties at home and have a variety of stacks and only thin-sliced ham or Canadian bacon and creamy cole slaw, but I need someone to help. You would too, unless your guests want to help.

Turkey is no longer only a Thanksgiving and Christmas dinner bird. Economically, turkey is a good buy and an easy main course to prepare. You may find markets that promote ground turkey meat, turkey sliced for steaks, and thinly sliced for dishes like scallopini. If markets do not carry turkey steaks and such, buy a whole one and do your own.

SCALLOPINI OF TURKEY

4 pounds thin-sliced white meat
   of turkey
Salt and white pepper
¾ cup flour
¼ cup olive oil

3 tablespoons butter
¾ cup dry Marsala or Madeira
¾ cup chicken or beef broth
¼ cup finely chopped parsley
¼ cup softened butter, not melted

Put the sliced turkey between two sheets of wax paper or foil and pound firmly with a cleaver or rolling pin, but do not pound hard enough to break it up. Lightly sprinkling with salt and white pepper, dip each slice of turkey into the flour, shaking off any excess. There should be only a faint coating of flour. Heat the olive oil and butter in a large skillet. Lay the turkey in one layer deep and not overlapping and cook at medium heat for 2 minutes on each side. The slices should show streaks of light brown. Remove to serving dish. Pour off excess fat, so that you have about ¼ cup left in pan. Add the Marsala and broth. Cook at high heat until it comes to a boil, scraping all the brown particles in the pan into the liquid. Boil 1 minute, add the cooked turkey and cook about 10 minutes at low heat. Test to see if tender enough. Place in a

serving dish and cover with chopped parsley. Put the soft butter in the
pan, bring to a foamy state and pour over the turkey. Add sliced mushrooms if you wish. You may substitute sherry for the Marsala. It all depends on your taste and budget. I usually serve it with green noodles
tossed with cream, butter and Parmesan cheese and leftover minced ham.
Scallopini freezes well.

These are good for buffets because they hold well and leftovers may be
frozen and reheated. I freeze them in small packages if left over.

MY FAVORITE NOODLES

2 cups thinly sliced white or yellow onions
½ cup butter
2 cups sliced fresh or canned
mushrooms

1½ cups heavy cream
1 1-pound package noodles, fine
or fettucine
Salt and cracked pepper

Sauté onions in the butter until yellow, not brown. Add mushrooms
and, if fresh, cook until translucent. Add cream and bring to a boil.
Cook the noodles in salted water (1 tablespoon salt to 1 gallon water)
al dente. Combine with the cream mixture. Season with salt and pepper. You may cut down on the cream if you wish a dryer noodle but
I don't.

HERBED LEG OF LAMB

1 5- to 6-pound boned leg of
lamb, trimmed for the oven
1 clove garlic
1 teaspoon salt
½ teaspoon dried oregano
¼ teaspoon thyme

¼ teaspoon ginger
½ teaspoon white pepper
8 canned Elberta peach halves
1 cup dry red wine
2 tablespoons currant jelly

Cut a slit at base of roast, near the bone, and place the garlic clove in it.
Mix the dry ingredients and rub thoroughly over the meat. Place lamb
in a roasting pan on a rack and roast uncovered in a 300° oven about 2
hours (165° on a meat thermometer) for well done, less for medium

rare. Surround lamb with canned Elberta peach halves the last 20 minutes. Baste frequently with the cooking juices and the wine. Remove lamb and peaches to a serving platter. Remove garlic bud and let lamb stand a few minutes before carving. Strain the fat from the juices, add the jelly and heat until melted. Serve jelly with the thinly sliced lamb. The taste of both roast lamb and veal are improved with thin slicing and lamb should always be hot or cold, but never warm. Flame with a jigger of gin, if you like to show off.

CRESPOLINI

1 pound fresh or frozen spinach
1 cup Ricotta cheese or dry cottage cheese
2 eggs, lightly beaten
½ cup grated Parmesan cheese

16 thin crêpes
1 cup thin cream sauce (1 tablespoon butter, 1 tablespoon floor, 1 cup milk)
1 cup grated Muenster cheese

Cook the spinach 1 minute if fresh, or defrost the frozen. Drain dry. Put in the blender and purée. Mix with the Ricotta cheese, eggs and the Parmesan cheese. Put 2 tablespoonfuls in each crêpe. Roll and place in a buttered shallow casserole. Cover lightly with the cream sauce and sprinkle with the grated Muenster cheese and a few dots of butter. Bake at 375° until bubbling. Run under broiler to lightly brown. Do ahead? Yes!

ICE CREAM BOMBE

3 quarts vanilla ice cream
2 cups cool Fudge Sauce (*Helen Corbitt's Cookbook*, page 264)

1 very cold 3-quart melon mold or 2 1½-quart size

Coat the molds with vanilla ice cream about 1½ inches thick. Pack firmly and quickly. Do not let ice cream melt. Fill center with fudge sauce and cover with more ice cream. Cover with wax paper and press on the lid. Place in freezer overnight. When ready to serve, run a wet knife around the edge of the mold. Place a hot towel over for a minute, then turn upside down on a chilled serving dish. Cut in slices at the table and serve with whipped cream and Crème de Cacao. Use same method for any flavored bombe.

CARAMELIZED BREAD PUDDING

Put in top of double boiler:

> 2 cups brown sugar
> 8 slices of white bread, buttered and cut in cubes

Combine:

> 6 eggs, lightly beaten   2 teaspoons vanilla
> 4 cups milk   ½ teaspoon salt

Pour liquid mixture over bread and sugar. DO NOT STIR. Cook over boiling water 1 hour or until custard is formed. Serve warm. The brown sugar in bottom forms sauce. I find men like this and always ask for more. You may put the ingredients in a see-through soufflé dish and proceed as directed.

I like to serve this when I serve an entrée that has a sharp flavor, like the Chicken Piquante, Oriental Roasted Chicken or when I do not want to spend too much time and money on a dessert. It can look elegant and expensive too!

CUCUMBER COLE SLAW

1 head cabbage, shredded fine

Wash, put in a covered container and chill in refrigerator early in the day. Mix and cook until thick:

> 2 eggs   1 tablespoon sugar
> ½ cup vinegar   2 teaspoons dry mustard
> 1 tablespoon salt   ¼ teaspoon white pepper

Cool and add 2 cups sour cream. Add 2 cups shredded cucumbers and ¼ cup sliced green onion to the cold crisp cabbage — and as much dressing as you wish. The dressing is wonderful for potato salad too.

6

Sunday Entertaining

A GOOD TIME to entertain in an unhurried manner is Sunday, early noon! I think people like to be entertained with a buffet this time of day. Guests may make it their one meal of the day and have more leisure for other things. They can take their time and eat when and all they wish, or nothing. The hostess will not notice. Men like it too . . . no yard cutting that day, no counting calories either. The hostess can be more relaxed as she knows her guests have no definite regime to follow as they do during the week. She can do more advance preparation, include more delectable dishes and serve lower in cost food.

To me there is something Victorian about a Sunday Brunch and I like it. The buffet table, whether simple or elaborate, is always inviting me to hurry and sample, because I guess I am hungrier this time of day. Too, whether they are there or not, I see covered silver casseroles, liveried servants and pink hunting jackets. Oh well, I can dream, can't I?

People are usually happy this time of day, and milk punches, Bull Shots, Bloody Marys, Alexanders, Champagne and Sangria are excellent unless you prefer an open bar. If you do not want liquor, then serve pitchers of freshly squeezed orange and grapefruit juices, mixed half-and-half, vegetable juices, even a hot soup, and hot coffee. If you have space for tables, fine; if not, food can be what I call walk-around and guests will find places to sit, even on the floor.

The menu that follows I chose for friends of the bride. It was easy because most of the food could be prepared ahead. It was walk-around food, and guests sat all over the place, even up and down the entrance stairway.

Bloody Marys and milk punch poured from pitchers into stemmed
glasses. I'm hooked on stemmed glasses. They look elegant!
Slices of ripe melon with a pipkin of fresh lime
and mint syrup to pour over
Thin slices of white meat of turkey in lightly curried cream
and covered with slices of crisp bacon
Grits Soufflé (*Helen Corbitt's Cookbook*, page 86)
Blueberry Drop Biscuits
Slices of toasted buttered pound cake

It doesn't take long to slice the melon, and the mint syrup is made the day before. The turkey has been sliced, wrapped with the sauce and brushed with butter to keep from crusting and refrigerated for reheating. I measure out the ingredients for the grits and biscuits the day before to be ready for combining. I buy the pound cake if I'm going to toast it.

For a complete change in pace, this menu has met with kudos.

Bull Shots and Bloody Marys
French goose basket (used for centerpiece also) filled
with fresh strawberries, bowls of raspberry and strawberry purée
to spoon over
King crab in cream over poached eggs on Parmesan cheese toast
Sherried chicken livers, apples and almonds
(*Helen Corbitt's Potluck Cookbook*, page 28)
Thick slices of cold ripe tomatoes
Slivered fresh asparagus, cooked Chinese style
Hot biscuits, whipped butter, lime marmalade
Various cookies

Or Sangria makes the world brighter too and it is easier to prepare than other drinks. Let your guests pour their own.

Omelettes are always good for Sunday entertaining. Each guest comes to the kitchen to pick up his omelette as it is made, because no omelette is good if it sits around waiting to be eaten. You can make the omelettes, or else have someone like a kind husband or friend do it. The omelette mixture can be made up in advance if you like. A side buffet with trays of sliced spring onions, diced crisp bacon, creamed mushrooms, bowls of red caviar, sour cream and halves of strawberries lightly sugared, bar le duc and Crema Dania cheese or any other soft cheese could tempt your guests to try all of them, and of course, a 2- or 3-egg omelette for everyone. Serve buttered and toasted French bread, Lahvash (you buy), apple and almond kuchen, or apple strudel, if you think you need it — and of course guests may always go back for more.

By the way, once you conquer the omelette, and it really is not difficult, you can use it for many occasions. My friends Muriel and Don Seldin entertain easily with an omelette brunch. She is a busy person, keeping a house, teaching French and working on an advanced degree. She makes her kitchen part of the entertainment. Don is Chairman of the Department of Internal Medicine at Southwestern Medical School and travels all over the globe. When she can catch him, he makes the omelettes with great concentration and precision. They entertain hundreds of guests on New Year's Eve with omelettes and champagne at midnight — quite a coup.

To invite out-of-staters for a Texas country brunch will give them memories and a little extra weight for a few days!

Bourbon milk punch, strong coffee and iced tea
Pink grapefruit
Ham Steak with Onion Gravy
Fried chicken livers and giblets
Grits casserole, black-eyed peas
Texas toast, white bread cut thick, buttered and oven-toasted
Pear preserves, red pepper jelly
Crumb Coffee Cake, oatmeal cookies

Weather permitting, serve out-of-doors: fresh air will make everyone hungry.

My Sunday-Before-Christmas brunch I enjoy. The fireplace is filled with poinsettias, fresh evergreens fill the rooms with their fragrance, and small Christmas bouquets in red ribbons hang from my chandelier in place of a table decoration. I set a polished table and let the reflections of the silver and copper I use give off a warm glow to the heavily laden table. I serve bourbon milk punches and Chablis cassis. I think eggnog is not good with food even at this time of year.

Julienne Breast of Chicken and Chanterelles in brandied cream
Spoon Bread, and lots of it
Piperade
Pear halves baked with lemon marmalade and toasted almonds
Baked whole boneless ham, sliced thin at the table
12-inch round Pancake Stack, with butter, real maple syrup
and the juices from the ham poured over (my mother's trick)
then cut like a pie
A molded cream and ricotta cheese
with black cherry preserves spilled over
Hot biscuits and Melba toast
Rum cake, apple cake and Bananas Foster, believe it or not
Coffee

Needless to say, I have help for serving and making the piperade and pancakes.

One of the most successful Sunday morning hostesses I know is Sharon Simons of Dallas. She often has a crowd before or after something exciting going on in town — maybe a special symphony concert, a football game or an outstanding lecturer. Nothing is more exciting than her Sunday morning parties. Her menu is good, satisfies all ages and is pretty to look at.

She sets tables up on the terrace and front porch with bright cloths and pots of growing flowers (she grows them herself, so they are always different). There is an open bar, and trays are passed with Bloody Marys and other drinks. Guests wander, chat and then each picks up his own silver, napkin and plate, and selects from the excellent variety of food on the buffet table. An iced champagne bottle is placed on each table if the party is especially festive. Sharon is a perfectly relaxed hostess because her guests are well fed and happy. A combo plays danceable music for those who do and many do. I might add that she doesn't do her own cooking, but she plans every detail of the menu and the service.

On a table away from the brunch buffet, a tureen of hot soup, such as French onion laced with port, is served with Parmesan toast or thin Swiss cheese sandwiches. If the weather is warm, Gazpacho, icy cold, with cheese straws, or thin cucumber sandwiches. Sharon also has a liking for fresh crab bisque laced with sherry.

On the buffet:

Large trays of season ripened fruits with Poppy Seed Dressing
Elegante Chicken Hash
Grits Soufflé (*Helen Corbitt's Cookbook*, page 86)
Broiled little pig sausages and chicken livers sautéed
in sweet butter and sherry
Hot buttermilk biscuits and black cherry preserves
Imported cheeses and Lahvash
Butterscotch Brownies and other cookies
Coffee, mixed with Espresso

Do you wonder her guests go home happy? There is nothing like good food for good thoughts about your hostess.

The Sunday brunch given at the home of Stanley Marcus honoring Prince Rainier and Princess Grace of Monaco had a menu which is one of my favorites.

Yogurt soup served in demitasse cups
Wine or Bloody Marys

On the buffet:

Calves' sweetbreads sautéed with chanterelles in sweet butter
and Madeira, julienne of prosciutto ham tossed in lightly
A crystal compote filled with lump crabmeat, framed with watercress,
Remoulade and cocktail sauce to spoon over
Cold marinated cooked vegetables in a bouquet: julienne of
carrots, baby beets, white cauliflower and crisp snow peas,
lightly dusted with chopped parsley
A round sandwich loaf filled with an assortment of
sandwich points
Pancake Stack with Lemon Butter and Blueberry Sauce
Slices of Casaba and Spanish melon with twists of lime
Kirsch Meringue Torte
Coffee

The tables were set with white linen patterned with sprigs of green, and brightly blooming cacti were the table decorations. A chilled Chablis was poured too.

HOW TO PREPARE AN OMELETTE

It really isn't difficult. If you have an omelette pan reserved for omelettes, fine, if not, any 8- or 9-inch skillet will do. Be sure it is very clean and dry. Two or 3 eggs make a better omelette than 1. Melt 2 tablespoons butter in the pan, swivel it around so that the bottom and sides are completely covered. Beat the eggs lightly with ½ teaspoon salt and 1 tablespoon cold water or milk, pour into the hot pan. Butter should be sizzling. Cook at high heat. As the omelette begins to cook, swirl it and pull edges of the mixture toward center of pan. The liquid part will fill the space. Repeat until all of the egg is cooked, but soft. With a spatula fold toward center of pan. Lift pan so omelette slides out. Lift pan up to edge of plate and turn out. If you wish to add anything to the omelette such as jelly, sour cream, strawberries, cheese, mushrooms, add just before you fold. Don't let your omelette stand around.

Then there is the Fluffy or Angel Omelette. You separate the eggs, beat the whites until stiff. Beat the egg yolks with 1 tablespoon of cream and fold into the whites. Pour into the pan coated with melted butter. Cook 1 minute at medium heat. Fold in half gently and put in a 375° oven for about 4 minutes. I usually sprinkle a little Parmesan cheese on top before putting it in the oven.

BLUEBERRY DROP BISCUITS

This recipe is typically Yankee. Serve these biscuits hot and dripping with butter.

2 cups flour	1 cup milk
3 teaspoons baking powder	1 cup blueberries, fresh or drained,
1 teaspoon salt	if frozen
4 tablespoons butter	

Sift flour twice, add baking powder and salt. Sift again and work in the butter with a fork or pastry blender. Add the milk and berries and drop by tablespoonfuls onto a greased baking sheet. Bake at 375° for about 12 minutes.

HAM STEAK WITH ONION GRAVY

6 tablespoons butter	2 cups thinly sliced onion
8 6-ounce ham steaks, horseshoe-cut ½ inch thick	1 tablespoon flour
¼ cup hot coffee	1 cup sour cream

Melt the butter in a skillet, add ham steaks and pan fry at medium heat until lightly browned. Baste with the coffee. Remove and keep warm on serving platter. Add the onion to the pan and sauté at low heat until soft and yellow. Add the flour and cook until bubbly. Add the sour cream, and thoroughly heat. Pour over the ham steaks; run under broiler for a few seconds.

CRUMB COFFEE CAKE

½ cup butter
2 cups brown sugar
2 cups flour

1 teaspoon cinnamon
1 teaspoon salt

Mix until crumbly. Reserve 1 cup, then add to the rest:

1 cup buttermilk
1 teaspoon soda
1 egg

¼ teaspoon powdered cloves
⅛ teaspoon grated nutmeg
½ teaspoon baking powder

Spread mixture in a buttered 8 x 12-inch shallow casserole. Sprinkle the cup of crumbs over the top. Bake at 350° for 35 to 40 minutes.

And do guests gobble up:

JULIENNE BREAST OF CHICKEN AND CHANTERELLES

8 chicken breasts, boned and skin removed
¼ cup flour
1 teaspoon salt
⅛ teaspoon paprika
½ cup butter

2 cups canned chanterelles
2 tablespoons flour
4 cups half-and-half
¼ cup Gruyère cheese
⅓ cup Cognac or brandy
Salt and pepper

Cut chicken breasts in strips about ¾ inch wide and 2 inches long. Lightly dredge in ¼ cup flour, salt and paprika. Melt the butter. Stir in the chicken and sauté 2 minutes, fork stirring. Remove and keep warm. Add the chanterelles; sauté 1 minute. Add the remaining flour and cook until bubbly. Mix in the cream, cook until thickened and add the chicken and the cheese. Pour over the brandy and ignite. Stir until thoroughly mixed and hot. Correct seasonings.

SPOON BREAD

4 cups milk	1 teaspoon sugar
1 cup cornmeal	4 tablespoons melted butter
2 teaspoons salt	6 eggs, separated
1 teaspoon baking powder	

Scald milk, add the cornmeal and cook until thick. Add the salt, baking powder, sugar and butter. Beat the egg yolks and add to the cornmeal mixture. Beat the egg whites until soft peaks form and fold into the batter. Pour into a well-buttered 3-quart casserole and bake uncovered in a 375° oven for 25 to 30 minutes. Grits may be substituted for the cornmeal.

Piperade is a wonderful egg dish, but as someone once said, never before 10 A.M. unless you are addicted to garlic. It does disappear like magic on a brunch buffet.

PIPERADE

2 tablespoons butter	4 ripe peeled tomatoes, chopped
1 tablespoon olive oil (you may omit)	1 tablespoon plus 1 teaspoon salt
	⅛ teaspoon white pepper
2 cloves garlic, crushed	¼ cup chopped parsley
½ cup thinly sliced onion	12 eggs
2 green peppers, slivered and blanched	Cracked pepper
	Chopped chives or parsley

Melt the butter, add the olive oil, sauté the garlic, onion and green peppers 1 minute. Add tomatoes and slowly cook until all the liquid from the tomatoes has evaporated. Add 1 tablespoon salt and rest of seasonings and parsley. Beat the eggs lightly with 1 teaspoon salt and stir gently into the tomato mixture. Let them cook over low heat until set. They should never be hard-cooked. Slide onto a heated platter or serve in the skillet. Sprinkle with cracked pepper and chives. For a large group as I usually have, I soft-scramble the eggs and pile on top of the tomato mixture. Eat as soon as possible in either case. Anchovies are a nice addition for supper, but not for breakfast. I use smoked sausage frequently.

This is a good preparation to serve in crêpes. You can prepare ahead of time and freeze. Add the brandy as you reheat.

ELEGANTE CHICKEN HASH

1 quart diced cooked chicken or turkey
1 cup half-and-half
6 tablespoons butter
4 tablespoons flour
2 cups milk
3 egg yolks, lightly beaten

½ teaspoon salt
White pepper
1 teaspoon grated onion
½ cup grated Swiss cheese
1 cup sliced mushrooms, canned or fresh

Simmer the chicken in the cream at low heat. Melt the butter in a skillet. Add the flour and cook until bubbly. Pour in milk and cook until thick and smooth. Add the egg yolks and cook over low heat. Mix half the sauce with the chicken and cream mixture; heat thoroughly. Season with salt and pepper. Pour into a shallow buttered 2-quart casserole. Add the onion and half the cheese to the rest of the sauce. Correct seasonings. Cook until blended. Put mushrooms on top of chicken, pour the rest of the sauce over. Sprinkle with the remaining cheese and run under broiler to brown.

One can usually eat a chocolate brownie and rest his conscience, but a butterscotch one — no — you always want one more.

BUTTERSCOTCH BROWNIES

4 tablespoons melted butter
1 cup dark brown sugar
1 egg
½ teaspoon salt
¾ cup flour

1 teaspoon baking powder
½ teaspoon vanilla
¼ cup coconut
½ cup broken nutmeats

Mix and spread in a buttered 8 x 8-inch square pan. Bake at 350° for 25 minutes. Cool and spread with:

CARAMEL ICING

½ cup butter
½ cup brown sugar
¼ cup milk or half-and-half

1¾ to 2 cups confectioners' sugar
1 teaspoon maple extract or
vanilla

Melt butter until brown, add sugar and cook, stirring until sugar is completely melted. Pour in milk and stir. Cool. Add sugar and extract; beat until thick enough to spread.

KIRSCH MERINGUE TORTE WITH BING CHERRIES

4 egg whites at room temperature
⅛ teaspoon cream of tartar
½ teaspoon salt
1 cup sugar
1 teaspoon vanilla

2 cups whipping cream
2½ cups canned bing cherries,
drained and pitted
2 tablespoons Kirsch
Confectioners' sugar

Beat egg whites with the cream of tartar and salt until they form soft peaks. Beat in sugar a little at a time until all the sugar is added and the meringue holds very firm peaks. Add vanilla and fold in thoroughly. Draw three 8-inch circles (use an 8-inch cake tin for a guide) on brown paper or foil, shiny side up. Spread meringue within the circles. Bake at 250° for 1 hour. Turn oven off and leave layers in to dry. You may make these days ahead of time. Whip the cream, add the bing cherries and Kirsch. Sift confectioners' sugar over each meringue crust and put together with the whipped cream mixture. If you like the flavor of nuts, you could add ½ cup grated almonds to the meringue before baking. Use the same procedure for a meringue torte of any kind without the Kirsch. I use it with fresh peaches, fresh strawberries, layers of cream fillings — let your imagination take over.

Sunday Night Entertaining

Sunday night entertaining should be early as one must face the new week bright-eyed and cheerful. Somehow I do not like to spend much time in my kitchen on Sunday unless it is cold and rainy, so I plan simply prepared suppers or ones with advance preparation.

Buffet — who has help on Sunday?

Cold boiled salmon with cucumber sauce
Spoon bread with melted sweet butter to spoon over,
lots of both
Rolled ham and chicken crêpes à la Swiss
Spinach salad with Sherry Dressing,
Roquefort mold and red caviar
Crescent rolls
Oranges Cognac and Pistachio Cookies dipped in chocolate

Lobster and Chicken
à la Crème
Pastry barques or patty shells spread with pâté de fois gras
Cold sliced rare Rib-Eye en Gelée
Tomatoes filled with Emerald Rice
Romaine and hearts of palm salad, oil and vinegar dressing
Warm buttered hard rolls
(Hard rolls get harder if you get them too hot)
Nesselrode Sponge Roll

Tournedos of Beef, in artichoke bottoms
Green Enchiladas with sour cream
Cold lobster and king crab on rings of papaya with curried mayonnaise
Flageolet Salad
Hot bread sticks
Glazed Strawberries

Cassoulet
Wilted Spinach and Mushroom Salad
French bread
Raspberry bombe
Brandy Almond Cake

London broil with red wine butter
(Don't pass this by) Mushrooms au Cresson in Crêpes
Molded asparagus salad
Cheesed Bread
Fudge Cake iced with Strawberry Whip

Chicken and Artichoke Hearts in Newburg Sauce
in hot patty shells filled with grated Gruyère cheese
Ham salad in parsley aspic
Avocado with Shrimp Mayonnaise
Oven-toasted buttered rolls
Fresh strawberries with rum-flavored Soft Custard and
Mokka Sticks (you buy, Verkade brand)

I like to serve all sauces separately. Some like a lot; some, not any.

Shrimp or Chicken Pudding
Tomato Medley Salad filled with Russian Salad
Watercress or soft lettuce sandwiches
Frozen Cake Crumb Tortoni

Sweet and Sour Pork
White rice
Oriental Vegetable Salad
Cheese biscuits and plum jam
Pineapple ice and almond cookies

Curry of Lamb on crisp cornbread
Three-boy relishes: chutney, riced egg and chives,
chopped dry roasted peanuts
Green beans with sautéed onion rings and coconut
Thin-sliced orange bread
Fresh Fruit with Gingered Cream and unsalted crackers

German Beef Stew
Potato Pudding
Thick slices of tomato piled high with Cottage Cheese Scramble
Hot buttered French bread
Chocolate Toffee Pie

Sunday night is a good time for a gumbo supper, and you can make it as inexpensive as you wish.

Seafood Gumbo
White rice
Salad of everything green with bits of feta cheese
and oil and vinegar dressing
Homemade ice cream and Praline Cookies

And for a hearty meal:

Baked Bean Bash
Buffet Salad Bowl
Cold Salmon Mousse with cucumbers in sour cream
Thin brown bread and sweet butter sandwiches
Clusters of raisins and red Delicious apples

PISTACHIO COOKIES
(2 dozen)

½ cup butter
⅓ cup sugar
1 egg yolk
½ teaspoon almond extract
¼ teaspoon salt

1 tablespoon grated lemon rind
1 tablespoon grated orange rind
1 cup flour
1 egg white
Pistachio nuts

Cream the butter, add sugar, egg yolk, extract, salt, lemon and orange rinds. Mix thoroughly until creamy. Add flour and mix. Shape into small balls. Roll each ball in unbeaten egg white, and then in chopped pistachio nuts. Make indentation in top of cookie with your thumb. Bake on greased cookie sheet at 350° for 12 to 15 minutes.

LOBSTER AND CHICKEN A LA CREME

½ cup butter
1 tablespoon minced shallots
2 cups uncooked lobster meat,
   cut in large dice
¼ cup sherry
4 tablespoons flour

3 cups half-and-half
4 cups cooked breast of chicken,
   cut in large dice
Salt and white pepper
Chopped truffles

Melt the butter, add the shallots and sauté 1 minute. Add lobster and sauté 2 minutes, fork stirring. Pour in sherry, cover, cook until liquid is reduced. Add flour, cook until bubbly; add cream and cook until thickened. Mix in chicken and heat thoroughly. Correct seasonings. Sprinkle with chopped truffles.

Any time you add foie gras (goose liver pâté) to a meat preparation you will enrich the dish, so save your pennies and have a tin of pâté hidden away for special occasions. Take the same attitude about truffles. Both give meats and poultry a flavor you will enjoy.

RIB-EYE EN GELEE

1 whole rib-eye of beef, well
   trimmed
2 cloves garlic, crushed
Salt and pepper

2 tablespoons unflavored gelatin
3 10½-ounce cans beef
   consommé
½ cup dry white wine

Rub the rib-eye of beef with the garlic, salt and pepper. Roast at 450° for 30 minutes. Reduce heat to 350° and cook 20 minutes longer. Do this the day before serving. Dissolve the gelatin in ½ cup of the consommé. Bring the rest of the consommé to a fast boil. Remove from heat. Add the gelatin and wine. Pour a thin layer in a shallow pan or platter. Chill until almost set. Slice beef in thin slices and place overlapping on top of aspic. Pour a thin layer of the gelatin mixture over and chill again. Decorate with thin-sliced canned mushrooms, tiny carrots, julienne of tongue or ham, artichoke hearts, whatever suits your fancy. Pour more aspic over all and chill again. Repeat, but be sure you have a thin layer of the aspic each time. Pour leftover aspic in pan. Let set until firm, overnight. Take a long spatula and remove the meat to your serving tray. Cut aspic left in pan in small cubes and use as decoration on the tray.

You may prepare a tenderloin of beef the same way, only roast for 25 minutes at 450°. If you wish your meat well done, increase the roasting time. Or a baked boneless ham may be done the same way, adding 1 cup of finely chopped parsley to the gelatin mixture. Leftover ham may be diced, put into a loaf pan and covered with the gelatin. Leftover roasted veal combined with the ham in the parslied aspic is delicious.

EMERALD RICE

4 egg yolks	⅓ cup grated Parmesan cheese
4 cups cooked rice	½ teaspoon paprika
1 cup raw spinach, minced	1 teaspoon salt
½ cup green pepper, minced	4 egg whites
¼ cup onion, minced	Sour cream
1 cup whipped cream	Chives

Beat egg yolks, add rice, spinach, green pepper, onion, whipped cream, grated cheese, paprika and salt. Mix thoroughly, fold in stiffly beaten egg whites. Pour into 1½-quart mold. Place in a pan of hot water and bake at 350° for 45 minutes. A variation is to scoop out tomatoes, fill with rice mixture and bake until puffed and lightly browned. Serve either preparation with sour cream and chives on top.

NESSELRODE SPONGE ROLL
(2 rolls)

1 cup cake flour	¼ cup plus ¾ cup sugar
1¼ teaspoons baking powder	1 teaspoon vanilla
¼ teaspoon salt	1½ tablespoons cold water
4 eggs, separated	1½ tablespoons lemon juice

Mix the flour, baking powder and salt. Beat the egg whites until stiff and beat in the ¼ cup of sugar. Beat the yolks until thick and beat in the vanilla, water, lemon juice and ¾ cup sugar. Fold into the egg whites, then fold in the flour mixture. With heavy wax paper line the bottom of a shallow pan, about 8 x 12-inches. Butter the paper and pour in half of the mixture. Spread evenly. Bake 12 minutes at 350°. Turn out on a towel or foil sprinkled with confectioners' sugar. Pull off paper quickly. Cut edges off so cake will roll easily. Roll in the towel and let stand for a few minutes. Repeat with rest of batter. Unroll and spread with:

Nesselrode Filling:

1 cup sugar	2 eggs, slightly beaten
6 tablespoons flour	2 teaspoons unflavored gelatin, dis-
2 cups milk	solved in 2 tablespoons cold milk

Mix sugar and flour. Stir in milk. Cook over low heat until thick. Add eggs and cook about 3 minutes longer. Remove from stove and add gelatin. Cool and fold in:

½ cup Nesselrode Sauce, or more   1 teaspoon vanilla
½ cup whipping cream, whipped

Roll cake and wrap in wax paper and refrigerate. When ready to use, spread outside with whipped cream, as thick as you like, flavored with rum and slightly sweetened. Decorate with shaved chocolate and slivered almonds.

You may buy Nesselrode Sauce in good grocery stores or gourmet shops. Raffetto brand is good.

This same rolled cake could be filled with any flavored custard or ice cream and frozen. Try filling with whipped cream and fresh fruit.

Tenderloin of Beef

By buying a whole tenderloin of beef (a tender), you can obtain better meat and save money. To prepare the whole tender, strip off the darkened fat, the yellowish gristle-like cord and the thin sinewy sheath between the fat cover and the meat itself. Below is sketched the whole tender with notations describing the various cuts that can be obtained:

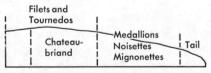

Filet Mignon:	1½ to 2 inches thick
Tournedos:	1 inch thick
Chateaubriand:	3 to 4 inches thick and by weight, 13 ounces.

TOURNEDOS

Tournedos are for informal suppers. For a seated dinner you need a larger filet mignon, 6 to 10 ounces. These are tournedo preparations you could use.

1. Halve lengthwise one clove of garlic and brown in a small amount of olive oil, salad oil, or oil and butter, about 1 tablespoon for each tournedo. Add the meat and brown both sides quickly, turning only once. Add 1 tablespoon sherry for each tournedo and stir the skillet to incorporate all the brown bits of oil and meat. Remove meat and let the sherry reduce a little. Pour the liquid over the meat and serve. I like to rest tournedos in a freshly cooked artichoke bottom.

2. After cooking meat deglaze skillet with pale dry Madeira. Spoon over meat.

3. Deglaze with brandy, igniting same to burn off the raw taste of the brandy, then add ½ teaspoon of Dijon mustard and ¼ cup sour cream for each tournedo. Heat, but do not boil, then pour over meat.

4. Deglaze with red burgundy wine, place a thin layer of Roquefort cheese on top of meat. Spoon sauce over.

5. Deglaze with Madeira, place a slice of pâté de fois gras on top of each tournedo and pour over sauce (called Rossini).

6. Serve with Béarnaise Sauce.

CHATEAUBRIAND

This particular steak was created in 1812 by the Champeaux Restaurant in the Place de la Bourse in Paris. The dish honors François René de Chateaubriand after the publication of his book, *Itineraire de Paris à Jérusalem.*

Sprinkle both sides of meat with salt and white pepper and spread with softened butter. Broil 6 to 8 minutes on each side. Allow to rest in the hot oven for approximately 10 minutes for easier carving. If you wish more butter, add a small amount when finished cooking.

If the Chateaubriand is very thick, you may wish to start it in a 375° oven and then finish under the broiler. This steak is always served sliced.

GREEN ENCHILADAS

This delicious recipe is from Lola Hunt of Mexico and Dallas. The day before serving prepare the following:

Sauce:

1 large white onion
2 4-ounce cans green chiles
½ cup parsley sprigs or raw spinach
2 chicken bouillon cubes
1 can mushroom soup

1 green tomato, if available
    (otherwise omit)
2 cups whipping cream
Salt and pepper

Put onion, chiles, parsley, bouillon cubes, soup and tomato in blender. When blended, add the cream. Season with salt and pepper.

½ cup salad oil, not olive oil
16 soft tortillas or crêpes
1 pound Swiss cheese, grated

Meat from a 3-pound roasted
    chicken, shredded

Have 2 small skillets ready. In one heat the oil, in the other ¾ cup of the sauce. Dip each tortilla into the hot oil quickly and drain. Dip into the sauce and stack. When all are ready put 1 tablespoon of the cheese and some of the chicken on each tortilla and roll. Place in an 8 x 12-inch casserole. Mix rest of sauce with rest of cheese and any of the sauce left from dipping. Pour over the enchiladas. Bake at 350° until hot. When serving, top with sour cream. For a luncheon entrée you could use individual casseroles, serving two enchiladas per person.

FLAGEOLET SALAD

6 cups canned flageolets, drained,
    or cooked dried flageolets
¾ cup finely chopped parsley
½ cup thinly sliced green onion

1 clove garlic, finely minced
6 tablespoons olive oil
4 tablespoons vinegar
Salt and cracked pepper

Mix and marinate overnight. Serve with or without salad greens.

This recipe should be prepared on a dry day and not over 3 hours before serving.

GLAZED STRAWBERRIES

2 cups sugar	⅛ teaspoon cream of tartar
⅔ cup water	Pinch of salt

Mix and place in small saucepan. Bring to a boil and cook at high heat until boiling point is reached. Reduce heat to medium temperature and cook until 310° by a candy thermometer or the syrup threads in cold water. Remove and place in cold water to stop cooking, then place over hot water, not boiling. This prevents the syrup from hardening.

Dip dry, chilled fruit quickly in the syrup, drain and place not touching on a tray covered with foil, shiny side up. Use the same syrup for glazing nuts or any fruit. Strawberries are especially pretty, as are cherries with stems, orange sections, small bunches of grapes.

While I was growing up in Northern New York I had what my mother called Saturday night bean and meat dish. It wasn't until I began to be what I thought was sophisticated that it turned out to be:

CASSOULET

3 pounds dried white beans	2 tablespoons chopped parsley
1 large carrot	1 pound lamb cut in 1-inch pieces
1 large onion, studded with	(leftover roast is fine, or use
2 cloves	lamb stew meat and braise)
3 cloves garlic, crushed	1 pound fresh pork, cooked, cut
1 bay leaf	in 1-inch pieces
⅛ teaspoon thyme	½ pound mild pork sausage,
1 tablespoon salt	cooked
½ pound salt pork	1 roasted 4- to 5-pound duck or
¼ cup butter	goose, cut in pieces, no bones
2 cups thinly sliced onion	1 cup dry white wine
½ cup peeled, diced and seeded	¼ cup chopped parsley
tomato	Dry white bread crumbs, buttered

Soak beans overnight. Drain, cover with fresh water. Add the carrot,

onion with cloves, garlic, bay leaf, thyme, salt and salt pork. Cook slowly until beans are soft, about 1 hour. In another pan melt the butter, add the onions and cook until soft, not brown. Add the tomatoes, half the parsley and cook 5 minutes. Remove salt pork from beans, dice and brown in a skillet. Drain the beans (reserving liquid) and remove the carrot, onion and bay leaf. Place some of the browned salt pork in the bottom of a large heavy casserole. Add a layer of the cooked beans, then a layer of onion mixture, a layer of meats; repeat until casserole is full. Add the wine and enough of the liquid from beans to cover. Spread the top with the bread crumbs and rest of parsley. Bake at 375° until crust forms. Take a large spoon and gently turn the top under. Repeat three times. If you have any juices left from cooking the meats, add to the beans before topping with the crumbs.

Leftovers freeze well.

WILTED SPINACH AND MUSHROOM SALAD

½ pound bacon, diced
½ cup sliced scallions
4 tablespoons lemon juice
2 tablespoons salad oil, not olive

1 pound washed and trimmed
spinach
1 pound thinly sliced fresh
mushrooms

Salt and pepper

Cook bacon until crisp. Remove, add scallions and sauté until soft. Add lemon juice and salad oil. Pour over spinach and mushrooms. Toss in bacon and correct seasonings. I sometimes add 1 cup diced avocado for this amount and a few cherry tomatoes or sliced pickled beets and sliced hard-cooked eggs. This is a good basic salad using spinach as the greens.

BRANDY ALMOND CAKE

1 cup butter	Grated rind of 1 lemon
1½ cups sugar	2 cups flour
4 eggs, separated	2 teaspoons baking powder
3 tablespoons coffee cream	1 cup slivered untoasted almonds
½ cup brandy	Sifted confectioners' sugar
2 tablespoons lemon juice	

Cream butter and sugar, add egg yolks beaten until light. Add cream, brandy, lemon juice and rind and flour sifted with the baking powder, then the almonds. Fold in egg whites, beaten stiff. Bake at 325° for 1 hour, 15 minutes longer in a greased tube pan. Cover with brown paper while baking. If you are unsure of your oven temperatures, put a layer of brown paper in bottom of a pie tin and put tube pan on it. In other words, the cake should be a very light brown when finished. Sprinkle with sifted confectioners' sugar while warm. This is a great, not too sweet, cake for the holidays (especially with eggnog).

MUSHROOMS AU CRESSON IN CREPES

2 pounds mushrooms, fresh or canned, browned in butter	2 cups sour cream
½ cup butter	3 cups watercress leaves, not minced but leaves removed from stems, about 2 bunches
½ cup finely chopped onion	
½ teaspoon salt	½ teaspoon Worcestershire sauce
2 tablespoons flour	16 thin crêpes
½ cup dry white wine	

Wash and slice the mushrooms. Sauté in the butter with the onion and salt. Add the flour, cook until bubbly. Pour in the wine and cook until thickened. Add the sour cream, watercress and Worcestershire sauce and heat only. Correct seasonings. Put 2 tablespoons in each crêpe, roll and place in a shallow 8 x 12-inch casserole or in a crêpe suzette pan. Bake at 350° until hot. Run under broiler to brown. Without the crêpes this is a good hot cocktail dip for steak bits or meat balls. Sometimes I add a tablespoon of Dijon mustard to the mixture. This is also a good first course for a seated dinner.

CHEESED BREAD

1 loaf unsliced French or Italian bread
1 cup grated Cheddar or Muenster cheese

¼ cup butter
½ teaspoon Worcestershire sauce

Cut the bread in 1-inch slices to the lower crust. Mix the cheese, butter and Worcestershire sauce and spread on each slice. Push the bread together and wrap in foil. Heat in a 350° oven until cheese and butter have completely melted.

This cake recipe was sent to me by Mabel McKellar from Michigan, who made a name for herself and supported her family with it.

DEVIL'S FOOD CAKE OR FUDGE CAKE

½ cup water
1½ teaspoons soda
½ cup cocoa
1¾ cups sugar
⅔ cup butter

2 eggs
2½ cups sifted flour
¾ cup buttermilk
½ teaspoon salt
1 teaspoon vanilla

Mix the first three ingredients and set aside. Cream sugar and butter together until fluffy. Add eggs one at a time and beat well. Sift flour, measure and add alternately with buttermilk. Add salt and vanilla. Add the cocoa mixture and blend in thoroughly. Turn into two buttered 9-inch layer cake pans and bake at 325° to 350°, 30 to 45 minutes.

Chocolate has an affinity for strawberries, so mash a few and fold into whipped cream to ice this cake. Or, a chocolate pudding between layers with or without the addition of nuts will insure the cake's freshness, and then ice cake with Fudge Icing (*Helen Corbitt's Cookbook*, page 253) or Colonnade Icing (*Helen Corbitt's Cookbook*, page 252).

CHICKEN AND ARTICHOKE HEARTS IN NEWBURG SAUCE

6 tablespoons butter	1 tablespoon plus 1 teaspoon
6 cups cooked chicken, cut in	lemon juice
2-inch pieces	½ teaspoon salt
3 tablespoons sherry	⅛ teaspoon white pepper
1½ cups half-and-half	2½ cups canned artichoke hearts
4 egg yolks, well beaten	

Melt 3 tablespoons of the butter, add the chicken and heat. Add sherry and ¾ cup of the cream. Let come to a boil. Add rest of cream mixed with beaten egg yolks, stirring all the time. Add lemon juice, salt and pepper and rest of the butter. Add the artichoke hearts and heat until thickened at low heat. *Do not boil.* This sauce is not as thick as a cream sauce and will take 10 minutes to cook after eggs are added. If you make ahead of time, reheat over hot water.

AVOCADOS WITH SHRIMP MAYONNAISE

Avocados cut in large dice, dipped in Fruit Fresh (you buy in the markets) or in lemon juice to keep their color, arranged around a bowl of shrimp mayonnaise, adds both color and interest to your table. I find I can count on about 18 pieces to a large avocado. Be sure it is ripe, but not soft. Sometimes I mix it with chunks of cantaloupe. The dressing, good for both, is made merely by adding cooked shrimp, chopped fine (buy the broken pieces), to homemade mayonnaise (1 cup shrimp to ½ cup mayonnaise), a little onion juice, lemon juice, Tabasco and a bit of anchovy paste.

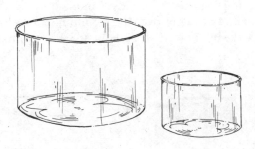

A jar of Soft Custard in your refrigerator is your answer to making a quick and strictly your own concoction of a dessert. If one is ill, it is perfect as a custard. You may combine it with fruit, pour it over ice cream, puddings, soufflés or freeze it for a custard ice cream.

SOFT CUSTARD
(*4 cups*)

6 eggs
½ cup sugar
¼ teaspoon salt
4 cups scalded milk or half-and-half

1 teaspoon flavoring: vanilla, lemon, almond extract, sherry or brandy to taste

Beat eggs, add sugar and salt; stir in milk and cook over very low heat, or in a double boiler over hot, not boiling water, until custard coats a spoon. If you have a candy thermometer, cook to 175°. Cool and add flavoring. If you cook it too long or too quickly and it curdles, beat with an egg beater and strain. You may use skim milk and artificial sweetener if you wish to cut calories.

SHRIMP OR CHICKEN PUDDING

1 teaspoon dry mustard
6 tablespoons butter
10 slices white bread, crusts removed
2 pounds cooked shrimp or chicken

4 cups grated American cheese
5 eggs, beaten
1 quart milk
1 teaspoon salt
Paprika

Mix mustard and butter. Spread on the bread and cut into cubes. Arrange bread, shrimp and cheese in layers in a 2-quart shallow casserole. Mix eggs, milk and salt. Pour over the shrimp mixture. Sprinkle with a little paprika. Bake in hot water for 1 hour at 350° or until set.

TOMATO MEDLEY SALAD

3 tablespoons unflavored gelatin
3 cups diced, peeled and seeded tomatoes, drained and added to enough tomato juice to make 5 cupfuls
3 tablespoons red wine vinegar
2 tablespoons horseradish sauce
Few drops Tabasco
1 tomato, sliced

2½ cups canned artichoke hearts, cut in half
1 cup thinly sliced green pepper, blanched
1 cup thinly sliced celery, cut on diagonal, blanched
½ cup green onion, sliced thin
1 cup thinly sliced cucumber, well scrubbed and skin left on

Salad greens

Dissolve gelatin in ½ cup of the tomato juice. Heat the rest of the juice and add the gelatin mixture. Add seasonings. Alternate a slice of tomato with an artichoke half in bottom of a 2-quart ring mold that has been rubbed lightly with mayonnaise. Cover with a thin layer of the gelatin mixture. Refrigerate until set. Layer the rest of vegetables to fill the mold. Pour remaining gelatin mixture in as it begins to congeal. I like to blanch celery and green pepper in boiling water for 1 minute. The color is better. Refrigerate for several hours. Turn out onto salad greens and fill center with Russian Salad or Cottage Cheese Scramble. Sliced canned tomatoes may be used successfully.

RUSSIAN SALAD

1 cup cooked green beans, cut in small pieces
1 cup cooked diced carrots
1 cup cooked peas
1 cup cooked diced potatoes

½ cup cooked diced celery
¾ cup mayonnaise
Salt and pepper
2 hard-cooked eggs, chopped fine
½ cup cooked diced beets

Combine the first 6 ingredients. Season with salt and pepper. Cover with chopped eggs and beets.

CAKE CRUMB TORTONI

2 cups whipping cream
½ cup plus 4 tablespoons sugar
2 tablespoons instant coffee
2 teaspoons vanilla

Few drops lemon extract
2 egg whites
2 cups cake crumbs

Whip cream, fold in ½ cup sugar, coffee and flavorings. Beat egg whites until stiff. Add 4 tablespoons sugar and beat until stiff. Fold the crumbs into the egg whites and whipped cream. Put into 1½-quart mold. Freeze. Serve with or without a sauce. I use as a sauce puréed and strained frozen raspberries or strawberries.

SWEET AND SOUR PORK

2 pounds boneless pork loin
2 tablespoons sherry or rice wine
4 tablespoons soy sauce

4 tablespoons flour
2 tablespoons cornstarch
Peanut oil

Cut pork in 1-inch cubes. Flatten with palm of your hand. Mix with sherry and soy sauce. Roll in the flour mixed with cornstarch. Fry in peanut oil at 375° until brown and crisp, about 5 minutes.

Bring to a boil:

¾ cup sugar
½ cup soy sauce
2 tablespoons sherry or rice wine
4 tablespoons vinegar

4 tablespoons tomato purée (canned)
4 tablespoons catsup

Add:

2 tablespoons cornstarch 1½ cups water

Cook until clear.

Heat in a large skillet or wok:

4 tablespoons oil

Add:

4 slices canned pineapple, quartered
2 green peppers, cut into chunks

Cook at high heat for 2 minutes, stirring constantly. Add the pork and the sauce, cover. Cook at medium heat for 2 or 3 minutes. Serve on hot white rice. Sounds complicated? It isn't.

ORIENTAL VEGETABLE SALAD

4 cucumbers	1 bunch radishes, sliced
3 green peppers	2½ cups canned bean sprouts,
1 sweet red pepper	washed and drained, or fresh

Dressing:

6 tablespoons salad oil	½ teaspoon salt
1 tablespoon sugar	2 heads Boston lettuce (you may
4 tablespoons vinegar	omit)
1 teaspoon soy sauce	

Slice cucumbers very thin. Remove seeds from peppers and slice thin. Toss with the radish slices and bean sprouts. Chill. When ready to serve, toss with the dressing and put into a salad bowl with lettuce.

CURRY OF LAMB

¼ cup butter	1 teaspoon chopped mint, fresh
¾ cup diced onion	or flakes
1 teaspoon sugar	1 tablespoon flour
1 teaspoon salt	2 cups chicken broth
3 pounds lean lamb, cut in 1-inch	1 cup plus ½ cup half-and-half
pieces	¼ cup shredded coconut
¼ cup diced preserved ginger	2 tablespoons lime juice
2 tablespoons curry powder	

Melt the butter, add the onion, sugar and salt. Sauté until yellow. Add the lamb and cook at medium heat until lamb is tender. Add ginger, curry powder and mint. Cook 1 minute. Add flour and cook 1 minute. Pour in chicken broth and cook until liquid is reduced by one-half. Stir in 1 cup half-and-half and coconut. Cook until thickened. Add lime juice and rest of half-and-half. Heat thoroughly, but do not boil. You may prepare ahead and freeze.

We are prone to serve curry on rice, but it is more interesting served on cornbread, sautéed peaches or on small crisp croutons.

FRESH FRUIT WITH GINGERED CREAM

Gingered Cream:

2 3-ounce packages cream cheese
1 tablespoon lemon juice
2 cups whipping cream
1 teaspoon sugar

3 tablespoons chopped candied
ginger
1 tablespoon grated orange rind

Put all ingredients into a mixing bowl and whip until creamy. Serve on or pass with slices of fresh fruit. Sprinkle with chopped pistachio nuts for added color.

I always make this stew the day before, as the flavor is better the second day. I freeze it too.

GERMAN BEEF STEW

Mix, put in a bowl, cover and marinate overnight:

3 pounds beef stew meat
⅔ cup water
⅔ cup vinegar

1 clove garlic, slivered
1 bay leaf
4 whole cloves

Then prepare the following:

1 cup sliced onion
½ cup chopped parsley
1 cup sliced carrots
½ cup slivered celery
1 cup peeled diced tomatoes

4 cups beef broth
½ cup gingersnap crumbs
1 tablespoon vinegar
Salt and pepper

Remove meat from marinade, put into a heavy saucepan and brown with the onion. Add the parsley, carrots, celery, tomatoes and beef broth. Cook uncovered at medium heat until meat is tender (approximately 1½ hours). Skim off any fat; add the gingersnaps and vinegar. Cook until sauce is thickened. If during the cooking the meat becomes dry, add more broth or water. Season with salt and pepper.

POTATO PUDDING

6 medium baking potatoes,   1 teaspoon salt
  peeled and grated   1 cup hot milk
¼ cup grated onion   ¼ teaspoon pepper
3 eggs, beaten

Drain grated potatoes thoroughly. Add rest of ingredients. Pour into a buttered shallow 1½-quart casserole and bake in a 350° oven for 1 hour or until potatoes are tender.

COTTAGE CHEESE SCRAMBLE

4 cups cottage cheese   1 cup diced water chestnuts
½ cup diced, peeled and seeded   ¼ cup chopped chives or green
  tomato   onions
½ cup diced cucumber   ½ cup sour cream
½ cup diced celery   Salt and pepper
½ cup thinly sliced radishes

Mix, season and refrigerate until ready to serve. This is also a good low-calorie lunch.

CHOCOLATE TOFFEE PIE

1 9-inch pie shell, baked   ½ cup chopped walnuts

Fill with:

1 cup butter   5 eggs
1½ cups sugar   2 teaspoons unflavored gelatin dis-
2 squares bitter chocolate,   solved in 2 tablespoons cold
  melted   water
4 teaspoons instant coffee

Cover with:

1 cup cream, whipped   1 teaspoon instant coffee
1 tablespoon confectioners' sugar

Cream butter, add sugar, beat until fluffy. Stir in chocolate and coffee.

Add eggs one at a time and beat after each addition until mixture is fluffy. Melt the gelatin over hot water and add. Pour into baked pie shell sprinkled with the nutmeats. Chill. Cover with whipped cream mixed with instant coffee and confectioners' sugar. Refrigerate.

SEAFOOD GUMBO

¼ pound bacon, diced
¼ cup diced onion
¼ cup diced green pepper
1 cup diced celery
¼ cup chopped parsley
1 clove garlic
2 cups peeled, diced tomatoes, fresh or canned

4 cups fish or chicken stock
2 cups okra
2 cups raw cleaned shrimp
2 cups crabmeat or fish, fresh or frozen
1 cup oysters
Gumbo filé

In the pot you plan to prepare the soup, sauté the bacon until limp. Add the onion, green pepper and celery and sauté until onion is yellow, but not brown. Add parsley, garlic, tomatoes and stock. Cook at low heat until vegetables are soft. Add the okra, cover and cook 5 minutes. Add the seafood, cook 5 minutes more. When ready to serve, add gumbo filé to your taste, and salt and pepper. Do not boil after this step. Never put the filé in before you are ready to serve as it becomes stringy. You might have extra filé available for those who like more. Serve from a tureen or the soup pot over rice. You may vary this by adding ham or chicken or both in place of the crabmeat or use all three.

PRALINE COOKIES
(about 2 dozen)

1½ cups sifted flour	½ teaspoon lemon extract
½ teaspoon salt	½ teaspoon grated lemon peel
¼ teaspoon cinnamon	¼ cup confectioners' sugar
½ cup butter	¼ teaspoon cinnamon
¾ cup sugar	2 egg whites, slightly beaten
2 eggs yolks, beaten	⅓ cup chopped blanched almonds
2 tablespoons milk	

Sift together dry ingredients. Cream butter, add sugar gradually and continue creaming until light. Combine egg yolks, milk, lemon extract and peel. Add to butter and sugar mixture. Add liquid to dry ingredients and blend thoroughly. Turn into two greased 8-inch square pans. Add confectioners' sugar and cinnamon to egg whites. Spread over surface of dough. Sprinkle nuts on top. Bake in moderate oven (350°) 25 to 30 minutes. Cut in squares while warm.

BAKED BEAN BASH
(for want of a better name)
(for 25)

This is a good inexpensive dish to use any time, especially as a money-making entrée for large groups such as the PTA.

3 pounds ground beef	10 cups canned baked beans
2 teaspoons salt	½ cup dry red wine or beef
½ teaspoon pepper	consommé
2 cans sliced tomatoes	½ cup bread crumbs
2 cups thinly sliced onions	½ cup grated sharp cheese
¼ cup butter	

Brown beef in skillet, season with salt and pepper. Add juice from the tomatoes and cook until liquid has evaporated. Sauté onions in butter until yellow, but not brown. Place a layer of beans, a layer of cooked meat, one of onions and slices of the tomato in a buttered 2-quart shallow casserole. Repeat. Add the red wine; sprinkle the crumbs and cheese over the top. Place foil over top and bake at 350° until brown and bubbling. Make the day before and bake when you serve.

BUFFET SALAD BOWL

1 head red lettuce
2 heads Boston lettuce
1 head Romaine
6 stalks celery, sliced thin in diagonal pieces and blanched
1 small head cauliflower, broken into small pieces and blanched
½ cup sliced green onions
2 hard-cooked eggs, chopped

⅓ cup red vinegar
2 tablespoons lemon juice
⅓ cup olive oil
⅓ cup salad oil
1 tablespoon Dijon mustard
2 tablespoons chopped parsley
½ teaspoon salt
¼ teaspoon fines herbes
Cracked pepper

Wash and break salad greens. Mix with the celery and cauliflower. Cover and refrigerate. Mix rest of ingredients and toss with the greens when ready to serve. Correct seasonings. Sprinkle with cracked pepper. Add other vegetables such as green beans, mushrooms, cherry tomatoes, artichoke hearts, slices of avocado. It is a good clean-out-the-icebox salad.

SALMON MOUSSE

1 tablespoon unflavored gelatin, softened in ¼ cup cold water
1 cup hot sour cream (do not boil)
1 pound canned or 2 cups left-over cooked salmon or fish

¼ cup mayonnaise
1 tablespoon grated onion
¼ cup finely chopped celery
1 cup whipping cream
Salt and white pepper to taste

Add softened gelatin to hot sour cream. Cool. Add the salmon, mayonnaise, onion and celery. When mixture begins to congeal, fold in the cream, whipped. Correct seasonings and pour into a wet mold. Chill. Decorate with slices of pimiento and black olives.

7

Suppers: Early, Late
and Late Late

As AMERICANS, and everyone else for that matter, eat more, they think up more excuses for entertaining, and suppers are gaining in popularity. Come for supper on Sunday, a holiday evening, after the theater or a large cocktail party, or just about any night at all. As to dress, come as you are, depending on where you started from. Serve buffet, of course.

Beef Stew in Burgundy with Parmesan Crust
Cold Poached Trout
Thin-sliced cucumbers and scallions in sour cream
Thin wholewheat bread and butter sandwiches
Clusters of fresh fruit, slices of melon and
a bottle of Kirsch for dousing
Toasted unsalted crackers served with cheese tray:
Brie, Cantal, Cheddar

Paella
Cold Tongue with Mustard Mousse
Leek and spinach salad
Hard rolls and sweet butter
Fresh Peach Compote with lemon sherbet and slivered preserved ginger
Marzipan Cookies

Bouillabaisse Salad with Caviar Dressing
Breast of Chicken in Aspic
White asparagus vinaigrette
Wild Rice Salad
Warm French bread
Chocolate Mousse with Marrons

Lasagne Verde al Forno
Broiled Italian sausages
Caramelized carrots and onions
Piquante Salad
Crusty Italian bread and sweet butter
Stewed Pears in White Wine

Smoked turkey and oysters Rockefeller
Baked Virginia Ham with Natural Gravy
(*Helen Corbitt's Cookbook,* page 143)
Rice Spoon Bread
Cold Ratatouille
Toasted cheese biscuits
Apple and Prune Strudel with Lemon Hard Sauce

Cold pork loin in wine aspic
Stuffed Zucchini
Very fine Cole Slaw with Beer Dressing
Hot blueberry muffins with whipped lemon butter
Sissie Quinlan's Angel Cake

Ham Loaf (*Helen Corbitt's Cookbook*, page 147)
with honey mustard sauce (honey and Dijon mustard mixed together)
Hominy Hashed in Cream
Vegetables in Aspic with Green Mayonnaise
Hot bread sticks
Very cold canned Elberta peaches sprinkled with Cointreau
A bowl of Orange Whipped Cream for those who will

Chicken Pancake Casserole
Marsala carrots
Green bean and red onion salad with oil and red wine vinegar dressing
Thin ham and chutney sandwiches
Baked apples with whipped lemon ice cream

Cheese torte with Frizzled Beef
Oeufs Mollets in Aspic
Layered vegetable salad
Warm French bread
Thin slices of fresh pineapple
Graham Cracker Cookies

Late Late

The all-night coffee shops and restaurants seem to be disappearing from the gastronomical scene, thus giving another reason to entertain between midnight and 4 A.M.

I find parties are more relaxing when guests get into the act. The following menu has all advance preparation and takes only a few minutes to assemble. Then the hostess can put her feet up and relax with the guests.

Stacks of thin crêpes (made ahead of time, refrigerated
and left at room temperature a few hours before using,
otherwise do not refrigerate)
Chafing dishes of creamy chicken hash and soft scrambled eggs
with a whisper of curry in the butter
Bowls of: grated Gruyère cheese, melted butter, cottage
cheese, sour cream, butter pecan ice cream, caramel sauce, orange
marmalade, strawberries, Cognac, orange and strawberry liqueurs
and whipped cream
Crêpe suzette pans over sterno (not alcohol, you might burn
the house down) and allow everyone to do his own. (I find
everyone tries everything.)
Pitchers of cold milk and urns of hot coffee.

Soup parties too:

Tureens of oyster stew or clam stew with sautéed diced
mushrooms to add
Strained onion soup
Thin chicken sandwiches
Ricotta and cream cheese, mixed and molded
Lahvash, Melba toast and guava jelly
Slices of fresh fruit and a pipkin of fresh lime syrup

Eggs in ramekins, ready to slip into the oven while guests
may be having a milk punch or champagne (Put a slice of pâté
de fois gras on top of the eggs before serving sometime.)
Warm baked Canadian bacon to slice
Very cold sliced tomatoes
Cinnamon toast
Chicken livers in paprika sauce
Apple strudel (Make it, it is easy.)
or
Omelette Shortcake with Seafood Sauce
Little pig sausages
Blueberry muffins

When I lived in New York and tripped around in the early-morning hours, my favorite late late was Clam Pie. It does give you a nice gentle feeling. It can be served any time and is always a good second item on a buffet. For a late buffet, serve with bacon finger roll sandwiches and a hot tomato bouillon.

And my very favorite expensive late late: poached egg on toasted English muffin, fresh caviar and hollandaise — and champagne, of course.

BEEF STEW IN BURGUNDY WITH PARMESAN CRUST
(for 8 to 10)

¼ cup salad oil	½ pound diced salt pork, sautéed
4 pounds beef round or	until crisp
tenderloin, cut in 1-inch pieces	20 small white onions, cooked
2 tablespoons flour	20 fresh mushrooms, quartered
3 cloves garlic, minced	and sautéed in butter
3 cups dry red burgundy	Salt and white pepper
2 cups beef broth or water	Pie crust
1 stalk celery	Melted butter
Few sprigs parsley	Parmesan cheese
1 carrot	

Heat the oil in the pot you will cook the stew in. Add the beef and brown on all sides. Drain the oil. Add the flour and cook until foamy. Stir in garlic, wine, broth or water and bring to a boil. Add the celery, parsley and carrot. Cover and simmer about 2 hours or put in a 350° oven to cook until meat is tender. Remove the celery, parsley and carrot. Add the salt pork, onions and mushrooms and simmer until thoroughly hot. Skim off any excess fat from the top. Season with salt and pepper. Transfer to a shallow 2½- or 3-quart casserole. Cover with pie crust, brush with melted butter and sprinkle with Parmesan cheese, freshly grated if possible. Return to oven to bake at 350° until crust is brown. I like to serve this also as a stew over crisp hashed brown potatoes or thin cornbread — but then I like stew.

COLD POACHED TROUT

8 brook trout, 6 or 8 ounces each	1 stalk celery
	1 bay leaf
1½ quarts dry white wine or half wine, half water	Juice of 1 lemon
	12 peppercorns
2 slices onion	1 tablespoon salt
1 carrot	Twists of lemon and truffles
Few sprigs parsley	

Wash the trout. Mix the wine with the next 8 ingredients (court bouillon) and simmer for 30 minutes, covered. Add the trout, cover and poach for 5 minutes. Drain and chill. Cut a line just below the head and above the tail of the trout and remove the skin. Decorate with twists of lemon and truffles. Serve on top of or beside cucumbers and scallions in sour cream.

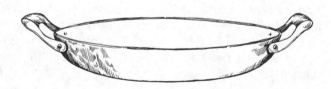

When I want my guests to watch me cook, which isn't often, the watching I mean, I do a Paella. This could be a one-dish supper with salad and bread, and can be made as expensively as you wish or as cheaply. I recommend it to young brides who want to make their party food appear ample. I always recommend it be brought to the table in the pan it was prepared in, preferably a paella pan which can be used for other things. I like to use a patchwork quilt for my table (it looks full already), a whole loaf of bread to slice or hard rolls, and perfect peaches used as a centerpiece. Then I tell my guests peaches are the dessert. I find my guests either eat them or take them home, sometimes both.

PAELLA

3 tablespoons olive oil
1 cup diced onion
1 clove garlic, minced
½ pound fresh lean pork, cut in cubes
1 2-pound broiling chicken uncooked, meat cut from bones, or 1 pound uncooked turkey meat
1 cup white rice, uncooked
1 pound sliced mildly seasoned smoked sausage
1 cup peeled sliced tomato, fresh or canned
3 cups chicken broth
½ cup dry white wine
Pinch of saffron
1 pound uncooked shrimp, peeled
1 uncooked sliced lobster tail
2 dozen mussels in shell or littleneck clams
2 tablespoons pimiento, chopped
Salt and pepper
¼ cup finely chopped parsley

Heat the oil in the paella pan. Add the onion and garlic, cooking them until soft and yellow, not brown. Remove. Add pork and chicken and sauté at medium heat until brown. Remove from pan. Add rice and sausage and stir until lightly toasted. Stir in tomatoes, the cooked chicken, pork, broth, wine and saffron; cook covered about 25 minutes. Add shrimp, lobster and mussels or clams; cook 6 minutes, stirring with a fork. Add pimiento and stir. Correct seasonings. Add parsley and serve at once. Paella is best when eaten immediately. Leftovers freeze well, but the seafood will be soft — sorry! You can use whatever proportions of meat, fish and rice you like, but this recipe is the one I find everyone likes.

TONGUE

1 4-pound fresh beef tongue
2 carrots
2 stalks celery
1 onion
1 bay leaf
Few sprigs parsley
3 cloves
1 clove garlic
½ teaspoon sugar

Place the tongue and rest of ingredients in a large kettle. Cover with cold water and bring to a boil. Skim the froth from the surface and simmer covered for 3 to 4 hours or until tongue is tender. Remove tongue, rinse with cold water and take off the skin. When tongue is cold, slice in ¼-inch slices and re-form as a whole tongue. Garnish with watercress and serve with a sauce or with:

MUSTARD MOUSSE

1 tablespoon unflavored gelatin
2 tablespoons cold water
2 tablespoons dry white wine or champagne
2 cups sour cream or whipped cream

¼ cup chopped chives
¼ cup Dijon mustard
½ teaspoon hot dry mustard
1 tablespoon lemon juice
Few drops Tabasco

Dissolve gelatin in cold water. Heat gelatin mixture and pour in wine; add to sour cream mixed with rest of ingredients. Pour into a 1-pint mold and refrigerate until set. Good also with ham. You may omit the gelatin and use as a sauce.

FRESH PEACH COMPOTE

Select firm ripe fresh peaches, put in a steamer (steamette) for about 6 minutes. Then test to see they are tender, not soft. They will retain their fresh flavor. Remove from steamette, slip the skins off and place in a shallow container. For 8 peaches add enough cold water to the water left from steaming to make 2 cups. Then add 2 cups sugar and 1 thinly sliced lemon. Cook over low heat, stirring frequently until lemon is soft. Add ⅛ teaspoon salt. Turn off heat and cover for 5 minutes. Pour over peaches. Any syrup left may be stored in a closed container for future use.

This is a nice cookie to add to your Christmas baking.

MARZIPAN COOKIES
(*48 cookies*)

½ cup butter
½ cup sugar
¼ cup brown sugar
1 8-ounce can almond paste

1 egg, slightly beaten
1¼ cups flour
½ teaspoon soda
½ teaspoon salt

Mix the butter, sugars and almond paste until light and fluffy. Beat in the egg. Stir in the flour, soda and salt until well blended. Wrap in foil or clear plastic and refrigerate for 15 minutes. Dip a dessert-sized spoon or teaspoon into cold water, fill with the dough and drop with the rounded side up onto a cookie sheet. Bake at 375° for 8 to 10 minutes until lightly brown. Remove and slide cookies onto a rack to cool. When cold, store in a tight container.

BOUILLABAISSE SALAD

2 heads Boston lettuce, washed and crisped
3 heads endive, washed and leaves separated
1 pound fresh crabmeat
1 lobster tail, cooked
1 pound cooked shrimp
½ cup slivered celery, blanched one minute in boiling water

2 peeled ripe tomatoes
2 hard-cooked eggs, finely chopped
1 tablespoon chopped chives
Salt and pepper
¼ cup thinly sliced green onion or small white onion
1 bunch watercress

Line a large shallow salad bowl with lettuce leaves. Add the endive leaves. Arrange seafood, celery and tomatoes on top. Sprinkle with the chopped eggs, chives and seasonings. Heap the onion on top; put a bunch of watercress on either end of bowl. When guests come to the table, toss with:

Caviar Dressing:

> 1 cup sour cream   2 tablespoons horseradish sauce
> 1 cup mayonnaise   ¼ cup caviar, black or red

But do let your guests see the salad before tossing.

BREAST OF CHICKEN IN ASPIC

8 6-ounce boned whole chicken   Pâté de fois gras
  breasts or half breasts   White wine
4 cups chicken broth, consommé   2 tablespoons unflavored gelatin
  or water   Truffles or hard-cooked egg

Poach the chicken breasts in the chicken broth until tender, about 20 minutes. Remove the skin and any fat clinging to the chicken. Clarify the broth (or used canned chicken consommé). For 2 cups of consommé, pour in ½ cup white wine, heat, and add softened gelatin. Pour a thin layer of the consommé in a shallow pan; refrigerate to set. Place the breasts on top and pour over a thin layer of gelatin mixture. Refrigerate. Spread a tablespoon of pâté on top of each breast and again pour over a thin layer of gelatin. Refrigerate until set. Decorate with truffles, sliced hard-cooked egg or both. Repeat with the gelatin mixture. When remaining gelatin becomes syrupy, pour over and chill thoroughly. Remove chicken to a chilled tray, chop the extra aspic and surround the chicken.

There is a Swiss granulated unflavored gelatin called Lucul in gourmet shops. You can use it for all aspic preparations, and I wouldn't be without it — but then maybe I am a bit lazy.

WILD RICE SALAD

1 clove garlic   1 8½-ounce can artichoke hearts,
3 cups cooked wild rice   cut in half
2 tablespoons sliced scallions   ¼ cup Sherry French Dressing
1 cup cooked peas   Chopped parsley
8 cherry tomatoes, cut in half   Salt and pepper

Rub your wooden salad bowl with a clove of garlic. Add the rest of the ingredients and toss lightly. Correct seasonings and serve at room temperature.

CHOCOLATE MOUSSE WITH MARRONS

3 squares (3 ounces) unsweetened chocolate
3 tablespoons water
½ cup sugar
Pinch of salt
2 egg yolks, beaten

1 tablespoon Cognac
3 tablespoons chopped preserved
marrons
1 cup whipping cream, whipped
2 egg whites, beaten stiff

Melt chocolate in the water over low heat. Add sugar and salt; simmer 3 minutes, stirring constantly. Blend a little of the chocolate mixture into the egg yolks, then blend in all of it. Cool. Add Cognac and marrons. Fold in whipped cream and egg whites. Pour into 1½-quart soufflé dish and refrigerate or freeze, if you wish. I use a ring mold and unmold on a silver tray. Fill the center with unsweetened whipped cream and cover the whole thing with shaved semi-sweet chocolate (white chocolate I prefer). Leave out the marrons and Cognac and substitute 1 teaspoon vanilla.

The following recipe was brought to me by my favorite wine merchant, Tony LaBarba, from one of his many trips to Europe. An Italian-American, he recognized its worth.

LASAGNE VERDE AL FORNO

Bolognese Sauce:

½ pound ground salt pork
1½ pounds ground top round of
      beef
½ pound ground lean veal
2 cups thinly sliced onion
2 carrots, thinly sliced
2 stalks celery, diced
2 cloves

2 cups beef consommé
2 tablespoons tomato paste
1 teaspoon salt
Few twists from pepper grinder
1 cup water
½ pound mushrooms, diced
4 chicken livers, diced
1 cup heavy cream

Put salt pork into a deep skillet and fry until brown. Pour off the melted fat. Put in beef and veal, onions, carrots, celery and cloves. Brown over low heat. Add the consommé and cook until it evaporates. Add tomato paste, salt, pepper and water. Cover skillet and cook at low heat for 1 hour. Add mushrooms and chicken livers and cook 15 minutes longer. Just before assembling lasagne add cream and reheat.

Béchamel Sauce:

4 tablespoons butter
3 tablespoons flour
2 tablespoons finely chopped
      onion

2 cups chicken broth or milk
Salt and pepper
¼ cup heavy cream

Melt the butter. Add flour and cook until bubbly. Stir in onion and cook 1 minute. Pour in broth or milk, stirring constantly with a French whip until thickened. Season to taste. Add cream and simmer until thoroughly heated. Strain.
   Next:

1 pound spinach lasagne noodles
      or strips

2 cups grated Parmesan cheese
2 cups grated Gruyère cheese

Cook noodles in boiling salted water until just tender, but not soft. Drain, but do not wash. Place a layer in a shallow 3-quart oblong casserole. Cover with a layer of the meat sauce (Bolognese), then a layer of the Béchamel, then grated cheese. Continue layering in the same order, ending with grated cheese on top. Bake in 375° oven until brown and bubbling. Let stand outside of oven 10 minutes before serving.

Prepare ahead of time, and it freezes well. If you cannot find spinach lasagne noodles, use plain ones.

I also like the meat sauce in *Helen Corbitt's Potluck Cookbook*, page 82, which is for a much lighter lasagne.

PIQUANTE SALAD

2 peeled quartered tomatoes
2 cups cooked snipped green beans
  (cook 3 or 4 minutes, then cover
  with ice)

2 heads Boston lettuce
4 hard-cooked eggs, chopped
¼ cup chopped parsley

Chill all ingredients together thoroughly and just before serving, toss with:

Warm Salad Dressing:

1 cup heavy cream
4 tablespoons olive oil
2 tablespoons prepared mustard

2 tablespoons wine vinegar
1 tablespoon dried tarragon

Mix cream, olive oil and mustard; add vinegar and float tarragon on top. Heat in double boiler until slightly thickened. Then stir until blended. Serve warm over chilled ingredients above. Also excellent on raw spinach.

STEWED PEARS IN WHITE WINE

1½ cups dry white wine
1½ cups sugar
  1 piece cinnamon stick

4 whole cloves
1 lemon, sliced thin
8 whole peeled fresh pears

Mix wine, sugar, cinnamon stick, cloves and lemon. Bring to a boil and cook 5 minutes. Add pears, cover and simmer until tender, about 30 minutes, depending on the pear variety and its ripeness. Cool in the syrup; remove the cinnamon stick and cloves. Serve in a crystal bowl and pass with sour cream.

RICE SPOON BREAD

1 cup boiling water	1 cup milk
1 cup cornmeal	3 tablespoons melted butter
2 cups cooked rice	½ teaspoon salt
2 eggs, separated	½ teaspoon sugar

Pour boiling water over cornmeal. Mix with the rice and egg yolks beaten with the milk. Add melted butter, salt and sugar. Cool. Beat egg whites until stiff and fold in. Pour into a buttered 1-quart casserole and bake at 350° for 45 to 50 minutes.

APPLE AND PRUNE STRUDEL

4 strudel leaves (you buy a package)	½ cup chopped stewed prunes
	1 teaspoon lemon juice
3 large Rome Beauty or Greenings apples, sliced thin	Grated rind of 1 lemon
	⅛ teaspoon cinnamon
½ cup sugar	½ cup melted butter
¼ cup slivered almonds	1 tablespoon sugar

Unfold 4 leaves of strudel dough from package. Mix the apples, ½ cup sugar, almonds, prunes, lemon juice, grated rind and cinnamon. Place 1 leaf of the dough on a piece of foil or a damp towel. Brush with the melted butter. Sprinkle with sugar. Place second leaf on top, and repeat 2 more times. Place apple mixture on top of the leaves and roll like a jelly roll, lengthwise with the aid of the foil or towel. Place on a buttered tin and brush again with butter. Mark with a sharp knife 8 portions. Bake at 350° until golden brown (about 50 minutes). Cut while warm. Serve with:

LEMON HARD SAUCE

½ cup butter	1 teaspoon lemon juice
1 cup granulated or 1½ cups confectioners' sugar	½ teaspoon grated lemon rind

Cream butter, beat in sugar and flavorings.

STUFFED ZUCCHINI

8 medium zucchini
2 eggs, beaten
1 cup cooked rice
2 cups small curd cottage cheese
½ cup chopped onion

2 tablespoons chopped parsley
½ teaspoon salt
Dash Tabasco
Cheese Sauce or slices of American
   or Gruyère cheese

Wash, trim ends and halve zucchini lengthwise. Parboil until tender-crisp, drain. When cool, scoop out center pulp and arrange shells in buttered casserole. Chop pulp; mix with beaten eggs, rice, cottage cheese, onion, parsley, salt and Tabasco. Stuff shells and bake at 375° for 20 minutes. Spoon over hot Cheese Sauce or cheese slices and run under broiler to brown.

COLE SLAW WITH BEER DRESSING

1 head cabbage, medium-size
1 green pepper
½ cup beer
1 cup mayonnaise

1 teaspoon salt
1 teaspoon celery seed
¼ teaspoon Tabasco

Shred cabbage finely. Slice thinly the green pepper after you have seeded it and removed the white ribs. Mix rest of ingredients and toss with the cabbage and green pepper mixture.

This slaw has more character than you would think from the spices and ingredients prepared for the dressing. Use the ingredients given and taste before you decide that more seasonings are needed.

Dressing will not hold more than one day.

SISSIE QUINLAN'S ANGEL CAKE

Bake an angel food cake in a loaf pan. Slice lengthwise 3 times. Cover each slice with the following sauce and stack.

¾ cup sugar
1 tablespoon cornstarch
2 eggs, beaten
Juice of 1 lemon
Juice of 1 orange

2 tablespoons flour
1 cup whipped cream
1 10-ounce package frozen
    raspberries

Mix sugar, cornstarch, eggs, lemon and orange juice and flour; cook in top of double boiler until thick. Cool and mix with the whipped cream. Chill in the refrigerator. Do not freeze. Put the raspberries in blender, strain, add sugar if necessary. Slice cake and pour over the strained raspberry sauce.

HOMINY HASHED IN CREAM

4 cups canned whole hominy
3 tablespoons butter

1 teaspoon salt
1 cup half-and-half

Sauté hominy in butter until brown. Add salt and cream; simmer until thickened.

VEGETABLES IN ASPIC

1 tablespoon unflavored gelatin
2 cups beef or chicken consommé
    or madrilene
½ cup thinly sliced cucumber,
    unpeeled
¼ cup parsley

2 cups cooked mixed vegetables
    such as carrots, peas, green
    beans
½ cup celery, cut in match-like
    pieces
Salad greens

Chill a 1-quart ring mold. Dissolve the gelatin in ¼ cup of the consommé. Heat the remaining liquid and add the dissolved gelatin. When cool, pour a thin layer in bottom of mold. Refrigerate until set. Arrange the cucumbers in a decorative pattern on the aspic. Pour another thin layer of aspic, refrigerate. Mix the rest of the vegetables and add to the mold. When aspic begins to thicken, pour it over the vegetables. Refrigerate for several hours or overnight. Unmold on salad greens and serve with:

GREEN MAYONNAISE
(3 cups)

2 cups mayonnaise	½ cup finely chopped chives
1 cup finely chopped raw spinach	2 tablespoons chopped capers
½ cup finely chopped parsley	Freshly ground pepper

Mix and refrigerate. Good with seafood. If you are dip minded, use as a dip for crudités.

A clear crystal bowl or transparent soufflé dish for a salad of layered vegetables always adds interest to a table. Toss the vegetables for guests to watch. I usually use this combination: thin slices zucchini on the bottom, then slices of radishes, celery, tomatoes, green pepper, cauliflower, unpeeled but scraped cucumber, watercress leaves on top. Pour on an Oil and Vinegar Dressing with Dijon mustard added and toss. You could use this dish as a decoration for the table also.

ORANGE WHIPPED CREAM
(2 cups)

4 egg yolks	1½ tablespoons lemon juice
½ cup sugar	1 cup whipping cream, whipped
⅓ cup orange juice	until stiff

Mix egg yolks and sugar. Add juices and cook over hot water until thick. Cool and fold into cream.

Since America adopted the crêpe, it has been used in every imaginable way. Instead of rolling or folding them with a creamed food, I like to layer them in a casserole with either leftover chicken, turkey or meats done in Hungarian fashion. The following is a great do-ahead casserole and will freeze well.

CHICKEN PANCAKE CASSEROLE

3 tablespoons plus 2 tablespoons
  butter, melted
1 cup sliced fresh mushrooms
2 tablespoons chopped chives
1 teaspoon paprika
2 tablespoons flour

1 tablespoon lemon juice
2½ cups sour cream
6 cups diced white meat of
  chicken
Salt and pepper
16 crêpes

Melt 3 tablespoons butter, add the mushrooms, sauté one minute. Add chives, paprika and flour; cook until bubbly. Stir in lemon juice and sour cream. Add cooked chicken and correct seasonings. Place a layer of crêpes in bottom of shallow buttered 2-quart casserole, cover with layer of chicken mixture. Alternate layers until casserole is filled. Dribble with rest of melted butter and bake at 325° until hot and bubbly.

FRIZZLED BEEF

⅓ cup butter
1 pound fresh mushrooms
2 5-ounce jars dried beef
2 ounces or ⅓ cup sherry

6 tablespoons flour
3 cups milk or half-and-half
Salt and pepper

Melt butter, add mushrooms, sauté 1 minute. Stir in beef and sauté until edges curl. Pour in sherry and cook until evaporated. Add flour, cook until bubbly. Add milk, cook over medium heat until thickened, stirring constantly. Correct seasonings. I sometimes serve this on heavily parslied potato balls.

When is a hard-cooked egg not an egg? When it becomes Oeufs Mollets, pronounced "Moolay" — a tender egg, cooked longer than soft-cooked, but not as long as hard-cooked and served cold in an aspic or hot with anything you can think of.

OEUFS MOLLETS IN ASPIC

Plunge eggs that have been at room temperature (all night is best) in a kettle of boiling water deep enough to cover the eggs with an inch to spare. Cook just below simmering for 6 minutes. Water will cool after eggs are added so count after water begins to boil again. Remove eggs and plunge into cold water to keep from cooking any further. Discard shells. Place eggs in cold water until ready to use.

3 cups chicken or beef bouillon
Few fresh tarragon leaves (you
  may omit)
1 tablespoon plus 1½ teaspoons
  unflavored gelatin
½ cup dry white wine

8 Oeufs Mollets (tender eggs),
  cold
8 thin slices of ham (you may
  omit)
Watercress

Heat bouillon with tarragon, add all the gelatin which has been dissolved in the wine. Strain. Pour a little gelatin mixture into the bottom of a 1½-quart mold or into individual molds and refrigerate until almost set. Stand the tender eggs in the aspic and pour enough aspic to hold them in place. Refrigerate until set. Then pour over rest of aspic until the eggs are covered. Place ham on top and refrigerate until firm. Unmold onto a bed of watercress and serve with or without mayonnaise.

GRAHAM CRACKER COOKIES
(24 cookies)

24 square graham crackers
½ pound butter
1 cup firmly packed brown sugar

1 cup finely chopped walnuts or
pecans

Arrange the crackers on a buttered oblong pan that has edges. Bring butter and sugar to a boil and boil 2 minutes. Add nuts and spread over all the crackers. Bake at 350° for 10 minutes. Cool slightly, cut between each square and remove. Do not use a flat cookie sheet as some of the sugar mixture may slide into your oven.

OMELETTE SHORTCAKE

8 eggs, separated
1 teaspoon salt
⅛ teaspoon white pepper
4 tablespoons flour

2 tablespoons butter
1 shallot, minced
Chopped parsley or truffles

Beat the egg yolks until lemon-colored and smooth. Beat in salt, pepper and flour. Melt the butter, add the shallot and sauté 1 minute. Pour the butter mixture into two 9-inch cake pans and rub over bottoms and sides until completely covered. Beat the egg whites until stiff and fold the egg mixture into them. Spread over pans evenly. Bake at 350° until a cake tester comes out clean — about 15 minutes. Invert one pan on a serving tray, cover with either seafood (see following recipe) or chicken in a wine flavored cream. Cover with second layer and more sauce. Sprinkle with chopped parsley, truffles or sautéed diced mushrooms.

SEAFOOD SAUCE

3 tablespoons butter	½ cup dry white wine
3 tablespoons flour	2 cups cooked seafood or chicken
1 cup half-and-half	Salt and pepper
1 cup chicken broth	

Melt the butter, add the flour and cook until bubbly. Add half-and-half, chicken broth and wine. Cook until thickened, stirring constantly with a French whip. Mix in seafood and correct seasonings. Simmer about 5 minutes at low heat. Keep hot over hot water.

CLAM PIE

Pastry for 9½-inch 2-crust pie	Salt and pepper
2 tablespoons chopped parsley	¼ teaspoon Worcestershire sauce
6 tablespoons butter	4 cups chopped clams (fresh,
⅔ cup chopped onion	canned or frozen)
6 tablespoons flour	1 egg yolk mixed with 1 teaspoon
3 cups half-and-half	water

Line a pie tin with one-half the pie crust rolled thin. (I use a Pyrex pie casserole for this.) Sprinkle bottom with chopped parsley. Melt the butter, add onions and sauté until soft, but not brown. Add flour and cook until bubbly. Pour in half-and-half and cook until thickened. Season with salt, pepper and Worcestershire sauce. In alternate layers put the clams and sauce into the pastry-lined tin. Cover with a top crust thinly rolled. Crimp the edges to seal. Decorate top with pastry cutouts, leaves, flowers or shells. (It depends on how good an artist you are.) Brush with the egg and water and bake in a 425° oven for 35 to 40 minutes. Brush once during baking with the egg wash. Serve very hot.

Kitchen Buffets

Entertain in the kitchen? Why not? Kitchens today often get as much thought and careful decorating as the Victorian parlor used to. And if yours isn't a decorator's dream, so what? It is a delightfully informal place to serve a buffet. Using your range to keep the food hot is a lot easier than getting out chafing dishes or warmers. Pots and pans are attractive enough in color and design to put conventional chafing dishes to shame. You can always hide the lids and extra cooking things. I put mine in one half of my double sink, cover them with an attractive towel and dare my guests to look underneath. Sometimes I fill the other side of the sink with ice to hold my salad bowl or cold soup.

There is a relaxed atmosphere about a kitchen buffet. Guests enjoy it, feeling, I think, that no one is watching them and that they may take what they wish and go back for seconds without urging. I always add a whimsical touch to the range: a skinny vase with one flower, a decorative pepper grinder or candle. There is lots of color on my dining room table with gay linen, bright colors in china and the pitchers of wine to be poured by the guests. Sometimes too I let my guests cook their own entrées — when I know my guests well and know in advance they will relish the chance to cook some. Best of all I ask them to bring their soiled dishes back to the kitchen — not always, but usually when I have no one in to help. Every time I have a kitchen buffet it seems to me that people are enjoying this kind of informality more and more.

These are the dinners I have done — and I always serve the first course in the living room.

Cold Yogurt Soup ladled from a crystal bowl into punch cups
(I serve this frequently as it is refreshing and low in calories.)
Thin homemade whole-wheat Melba toast

From the Range

Beef Carbonnade
Kasha
Green Bean Casserole
Wilted Spinach and Mushroom Salad
French bread
Fresh Peach Dumplings with Hard Sauce

Papaya Oriental

From the Range

Leg of lamb with Cumberland Sauce (*Helen Corbitt's
Cookbook*, page 155) and brandy flamed
Snow peas with peas
Artichoke Soufflé
Celery knob salad
Thin whole-wheat sandwiches
Marron Trifle

The leg of lamb I carve and put back together, pour over the Cumberland Sauce and brandy flame. I do this for a seated dinner also. It looks so good. I find the Texans who think they hate lamb gobble it up and ask for more. I also like to broil a leg of lamb for this kind of party.

Consommé Bellevue with Avocado

From the Range

Ham Steak à la Bourguignonne
Onions and Leeks in Cream
Broiled Potato Slices
Tom Hunt's Spinach Salad with Greek olives
Hot biscuits
Whole strawberries with brown sugar and sour cream
Oatmeal cookies

Pickled eggs and okra

From the Range

Chicken Madeira with croutons
Yellow squash with mint dressing
Red cabbage, avocado and grapefruit salad with Poppy Seed Dressing
Maple Mousse

Spinach Vichyssoise

From the Range

Osso Buco
Mushroom rice
Layered Vegetables
Hard rolls (to sop up the sauce from Osso Buco)
Watercress salad
Sour Cream Apple Pie

Crudités

From the Range

Italian sausages
Fettucine Alfredo
Spinach ring filled with carrots and grapes
Marinated sliced tomatoes and scallions
Italian bread and sweet butter
Petite babas (buy them), split and filled with coffee ice cream,
frozen, then served with hot Caramel Sauce

Demitasse of Cold Tomato Soup

From the Range

Braised Shortribs of Beef with Horseradish Mousse
Champ
Green Cabbage in Cream
Potato Bread with Raisins
Apple and Watercress Salad
Stilton cheese, Wheaten biscuits

Matzo Ball Soup

From the Range

Mixed Seafood in Crêpes
Sliced Brussels sprouts in brown butter
Beer Muffins or Biscuits
Layered Vegetable Salad
Hot poached peaches with chilled sour cream to spoon over

COLD YOGURT SOUP

3 cups yogurt
½ cup half-and-half
1 hard-cooked egg, finely chopped
6 ice cubes
½ cup finely chopped cucumber
¼ cup finely chopped green onion
1 teaspoon salt

½ teaspoon pepper
½ cup raisins, soaked in 1 cup
  cold water
1 tablespoon chopped parsley
1 tablespoon chopped fresh dill
  (or 1 teaspoon dried)

Put yogurt in mixing bowl with the cream, egg, ice cubes, cucumber, onion, salt and pepper. Stir well. Add the drained raisins and cold water. Refrigerate for several hours. Serve with chopped parsley and dill.

BEEF CARBONNADE

I like this because I can put it in the oven and do other things, like getting my hair restyled. It can be prepared the day before or can be frozen for a later meal.

4 pounds lean beef stew, cut in
  2-inch pieces
½ cup flour
½ cup salad oil
2 pounds onions, sliced (about 4
  medium size)
6 garlic cloves, crushed
3 tablespoons brown sugar

1 bay leaf
1 teaspoon dried thyme
½ cup chopped parsley
1 tablespoon salt
2 10½-ounce cans beef
  consommé
3 cups beer
2 tablespoons red wine vinegar

Dredge the meat in the flour and brown in the salad oil on all sides in a skillet. Do only a few pieces at a time. Put in a casserole and add the onions. Brown the garlic in oil left in the skillet. Add to the meat with the brown sugar, bay leaf, thyme, parsley, salt, consommé and beer. Cover and bake at 325° about 2½ hours or until meat is tender. Pour in vinegar and cook on top of stove until bubbling. If you wish a thicker sauce, add a little Arrowroot mixed with cold water. You could use this as a basis for a beef pie or add mushrooms if you wish.

When you ask your guests to have groats, they usually say an embarrassed "no thank you," but Kasha, yes.

KASHA

1 cup butter	2 cups thinly sliced mushrooms
1 cup pine nuts	2 cups groats
1 cup thinly sliced onion	6 cups chicken or beef broth

Melt half of the butter in the casserole you will cook in and sauté the pine nuts until a golden brown. Remove the nuts, add the onions and mushrooms. Sauté until onions are soft, about 1 minute. Stir in the groats and broth; cover and bake for 1 hour. Add rest of butter and nuts, toss lightly. Kasha is so good with beef, lamb and chicken and my men adored it. You may prepare rice the same way as this Kasha recipe.

GREEN BEAN CASSEROLE

3 cups fresh green beans or frozen, kitchen-cut	1 cup sliced water chestnuts
1 cup slivered celery, cut slantwise	½ cup sour cream
	¼ cup mayonnaise
½ cup thinly sliced onion	⅛ teaspoon curry powder
	Salt and pepper

Cook the beans, celery and onion *al dente*. Add water chestnuts. Mix with the sour cream, mayonnaise and curry powder. Season to your taste. Pour into a shallow casserole and bake in a 300° oven until hot. Run under broiler to brown.

FRESH PEACH DUMPLINGS

3 cups flour	1 tablespoon lemon juice
1½ teaspoons salt	10 to 12 tablespoons ice water
1¼ cups shortening	8 fresh peaches

Mix flour and salt. Cut in shortening with a pastry blender or two knives until mixture looks like cornmeal. Add lemon juice and water; mix quickly until mixture is free from the bowl. Add more water if necessary. Roll out on a floured board until thin. Cut in large 6-inch squares. Wrap around a fresh peach, leaving the skin on and stone in. Bake at 425° for about 30 minutes. Cool, make a hole in top large enough to remove stone. It will slip out easily with an iced-tea spoon. The skin disintegrates in the baking. Put back in oven to heat, as they are better hot. Fill cavity with Hard Sauce.

Or, peel and remove stone, keeping peach as whole as possible. For each peach add to cavity:

1 tablespoon sugar   1 tablespoon butter
Pinch of cinnamon

Wrap with 6- or 8-inch square of pastry and bake at 425° for 15 minutes. Lower heat to 350° and bake about 45 minutes, basting frequently with:

Brown Sugar Syrup:

1 cup brown sugar   ½ cup water

Bring to a boil and continue to cook until a thin syrup is formed.

Serve dumplings with whipped cream, flavored with half lemon–half almond extract or:

HARD SAUCE

½ cup butter   1½ cups confectioners' sugar

Blend until smooth and flavor with lemon or almond extract or rum.

PAPAYA ORIENTAL

3 cups cooked tiny shrimp or diced shrimp
2 cups fresh grated coconut or angel flake

2 teaspoons grated fresh ginger
4 papayas, peeled and cut in half
½ cup fresh lime juice
Preserved ginger

Mix the shrimp, coconut and ginger. Pile into papaya cavity. Pour lime juice over. Decorate with thin slices of preserved ginger. Chill. This makes a nice luncheon salad also.

ARTICHOKE SOUFFLE

3 tablespoons butter
3 tablespoons flour
¾ cup milk
2 teaspoons grated onion
1 teaspoon salt

6 egg yolks
2½ cups mashed canned or freshly
  cooked artichoke bottoms
7 egg whites

Melt the butter, add the flour, cook until bubbly. Pour in milk and cook until thick. Remove from heat. Add onion, salt, egg yolks and mashed artichokes. Let mixture cool (until you can put your hand on bottom of pan). Beat egg whites until stiff. Stir in one third of them; fold in the rest. Pour into buttered 2-quart casserole. Bake at 350° for 35 to 40 minutes, or set in a pan of hot water and bake 1 hour, but test with a toothpick or cake tester. Serve as is or with Hollandaise.

MARRON TRIFLE

16 lady fingers, whole
2 tablespoons rum
1 cup whipping cream
2 cups cold Soft Custard

1 cup mashed marrons (preserved
  chestnuts)
Violet dust

Line a 2-quart shallow casserole with 8 of the lady fingers. Sprinkle with rum. Whip the cream and fold 1 cup into the soft custard. Add the marrons. Pour half the mixture over the lady fingers. Repeat. Chill. Top with the remaining whipped cream and sprinkle with violet dust.

CONSOMME BELLEVUE WITH AVOCADO

2 10½-ounce cans chicken
  consommé
2 cups clam juice

2 cups diced avocado
⅓ cup sherry
½ cup whipping cream

Heat consommé and clam juice to a rolling boil. Add avocado and sherry. Pour into cups or an oven-proof tureen. Whip the cream and spoon on top. Run under the broiler to brown.

HAM STEAK A LA BOURGUIGNONNE

I would suggest you buy a whole bone-in ham and have the butcher cut two 2-inch steaks through the center. You can use the rest of the ham for baking or boiling. Rub the steaks with Dijon mustard, cover with honey and dry red wine and marinate for several hours or overnight. Place on your broiling rack and broil for 20 to 30 minutes, 5 inches from heating element, basting frequently with marinade. Slice thinly and serve. You may do ahead of time and reheat. Cover with mushrooms sautéed in butter and red wine. I use the entire mushroom, split in half; allow 3 mushrooms per person. I also like to stuff prunes with sharp Cheddar cheese and marinate with the ham; broil the prunes with the ham the last 5 minutes.

ONIONS AND LEEKS IN CREAM

3 bunches leeks	Salt and pepper
4 medium onions	¾ pound bacon, finely diced
1½ cups whipping cream	Chives (you may omit)

Wash and slice the leeks in thin slices. Peel the onions and slice in paper thin slices. Steam both vegetables or cook in very little water until tender. Mix with the cream and season to your taste. Pour into a shallow 1½-quart casserole. Bake at 350° until hot. Fry bacon until crisp; drain and sprinkle with the chives over the onions. Especially good with beef or turkey.

BROILED POTATO SLICES

My employees at Neiman-Marcus called these Helen's Cottage Fried Potatoes. You may call them whatever you like. It is difficult to judge how many to fix; given the opportunity, some will eat them like potato chips. I usually allow one-half medium-sized Idaho potato per person. Scrub the potatoes and leave the skin on. Slice as thin as you possibly can and no thicker than ⅛ inch. While slicing, drop into cold water to keep from turning dark. When ready to prepare, drain and pour boiling water over for 5 minutes. Drain again and dry the potatoes. Place slices just overlapping, one layer thick in a buttered shallow casserole or skillet. (I use a crêpe suzette pan.) Season with salt, pepper and a dusting of paprika and grated Parmesan cheese. Dribble a little melted butter over. Broil on lowest rack, about 12 inches from heating element, until brown. They will be crisp on top, soft on the bottom. You may also brown them in a 375° oven for 30 minutes. Do with margarine if you are concerned about cholesterol.

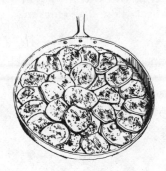

TOM HUNT'S SPINACH SALAD WITH GREEK OLIVES

1 pound fresh spinach
¼ cup thinly sliced green onion
1 clove garlic, finely minced
1 cup sliced Greek olives (in brine)
2 cups slivered blanched celery

2 cups finely grated raw carrot
1 cup diced Feta cheese
2 cups yogurt
2 tablespoons Dijon mustard
1 teaspoon salt
Cracked pepper

Wash spinach, pull out any heavy stems. Put in a plastic bag and refrigerate until crisp. Put into a salad bowl with the onion, garlic, olives, celery, grated carrots and cheese. Mix the yogurt with the mustard and salt and toss with the salad ingredients. Correct seasonings and sprinkle with cracked pepper. Refrigerate for an hour before serving. Use this dressing for other salad greens, cold seafood and on hot vegetables.

CHICKEN MADEIRA

4 2-pound roasting chickens or Rock Cornish hens
½ cup butter
1 tablespoon salt
½ teaspoon white pepper

½ cup Madeira
2 cups tiny crisp croûtons
½ cup grated Parmesan
Lemon peel, cut in thin strips (no white)

Rub chickens inside and out with the butter, salt and pepper. Place in a shallow pan and roast at 375° for 20 minutes. Then baste with wine and continue roasting for 30 minutes, basting frequently. Remove from oven, cut in half, removing the back bone. Cut in quarters. Place chicken on top of croûtons sprinkled with the cheese on serving tray. Add lemon peel to pan juices and heat. Pour over chicken.

This is a Yankee recipe. My brother Michael sends me maple syrup every year from Colton, New York. I've given up pancakes and such for myself, so I make this recipe for dessert and sometimes sprinkle walnut dust over the top of it.

MAPLE MOUSSE

4 egg yolks   ¾ cup maple syrup (real)
2 cups whipping cream, whipped

Beat yolks until light. Heat syrup in top of double boiler. When hot, stir in the egg yolks. Stir and cook until thickened. Cool, fold into the whipped cream. Pour into a wet 1-quart mold and chill, or deep freeze for Maple Glacé.

SPINACH VICHYSSOISE
(makes 1 quart)

¼ cup butter
4 leeks, white part only
¼ cup chopped onion
2 large Idaho potatoes, peeled and sliced

1 carrot, sliced
4 cups chicken broth
1 teaspoon salt
1 pound slightly cooked spinach
2 cups half-and-half or milk

Melt butter; sauté leeks and onions at medium heat until yellow, not brown. Add potatoes, carrot and chicken broth and salt. Cover and simmer until potatoes and carrot are soft. Cool. Put potato mixture in blender with 1 cup of cooked spinach. Add half-and-half, correct seasonings and chill. Purée remaining spinach and season to taste. Serve soup in very cold cups with a spoonful of the puréed spinach swished on top. If potato mixture becomes too dry during cooking, add more chicken stock.

OSSO BUCO

10 pounds veal knuckles (each knuckle could weigh ½ pound, so allow 2 per person)
1 cup flour
1 tablespoon salt
½ teaspoon white pepper
½ cup butter
½ cup olive oil
3 cups sliced onion
4 garlic cloves or more
8 ripe tomatoes, peeled and quartered
2 cups dry white wine
Chicken broth to cover
2 bay leaves
1 cup parsley pieces
12 peppercorns
Rind of 3 lemons

Dredge knuckles in the flour, salt and pepper. Melt the butter in a skillet, add the olive oil and brown each knuckle. Place in a large roasting pan. Add the onion and garlic to skillet and cook until onion is soft. Add to meat with butter left in skillet. Stir in the remaining ingredients and cover. Use foil if you do not have a cover. Simmer at low heat until meat is tender and bone is soft. Add more liquid if necessary. Remove meat, strain the sauce. Correct seasonings. Pour sauce over the meat and let stand in the liquid until ready to serve. Allow about 3 hours for this preparation. You may simmer (covered) in the oven also. Add thin slices of lemon just before serving — and I add boiled little white onions. Serve a cocktail fork along with so the marrow inside the knuckle can be eaten. My men's cooking class sure did like these.

LAYERED VEGETABLES

This is my favorite combination:

Little white onions (fresh boiled, canned or frozen) seasoned with salt and pepper. Sprinkle with sugar and butter, and heat only until sugar begins to caramelize.

Canned celery hearts, heated in consommé.

Kitchen-cut frozen beans, taken out of their pouch and cooked in a covered skillet for 5 minutes. (If fresh, cut slantwise in very small pieces, cooked *al dente*, seasoned and buttered.)

Then assemble. Put the onions on the bottom; the celery in the middle; the green beans on top. Sprinkle finely chopped parsley over all. Help yourself to all three layer as I do.

SOUR CREAM APPLE PIE

A most requested recipe.

5 cups pared, cored and diced apples	1 cup sour cream
1 cup sugar	1 teaspoon vanilla
2 tablespoons flour	¼ teaspoon salt
1 egg, slightly beaten	1 9-inch unbaked pie shell

Topping: ½ cup sugar   5 tablespoons flour
                         ¼ cup butter

Chop apples fine. Mix the sugar and flour. Add the egg, sour cream, vanilla and salt. Beat until smooth. Add the apples and pour into pie shell. Bake at 350° for 30 minutes. Mix the sugar, flour and butter to resemble crumbs. Cover the pie and bake for 15 minutes longer.

COLD TOMATO SOUP

4 large ripe tomatoes, peeled	1 cup sour cream
4 tablespoons ice water	1 teaspoon grated lemon rind
1 tablespoon sugar	2 teaspoons lemon juice
1 slice white onion	Melon balls

Purée tomatoes, water, sugar and onion in blender. Strain; add sour cream. Stir in grated rind and lemon juice just before serving. Float melon balls on top or serve soup in halves of ripe cantaloupe.

BRAISED SHORTRIBS OF BEEF

8 pounds well-trimmed shortribs
1 cup flour
1 tablespoon salt
½ teaspoon white pepper
¼ pound diced salt pork
2 cups diced onion
1 cup diced carrots
1 cup diced celery

3 garlic cloves, minced
3 tablespoons brandy (you may omit)
4 cups red wine or beef con-sommé or half wine (or more)
1 bay leaf
½ cup chopped parsley
⅛ teaspoon thyme

Cut the ribs into serving pieces; dredge in the flour, salt and pepper. Place in an oiled roasting pan and roast uncovered at 450° for 25 minutes. Drain off excess fat. Brown the salt pork until crisp; remove and sauté the vegetables in the remaining fat until yellow. Add to the shortribs. Ignite the brandy and add with the wine, consommé and seasonings. Cover and bake at 350° for about 2 hours or until tender. Remove ribs, skim off excess fat and strain the sauce. Correct seasonings. Return meat to pan, pour over the sauce and add the crisp salt pork just before serving. You can do ahead of time as shortribs freeze well. Use the same recipe for brisket of beef.

HORSERADISH MOUSSE

2 teaspoons unflavored gelatin
¼ cup cold water
1 tablespoon butter
1 tablespoon grated onion
1 tablespoon flour
½ teaspoon dry mustard

1 cup half-and-half
½ cup white horseradish sauce
Few drops Tabasco
Salt and pepper
¾ cup whipping cream

Soften the gelatin in cold water. Melt the butter, add the grated onion and cook 1 minute. Add flour and mustard; cook until bubbly. Pour in half-and-half and cook until thickened. Remove from stove; add gelatin, horseradish sauce and Tabasco. Season with salt and pepper. Cool. Whip the cream and fold into the sauce. Pour into a wet mold and refrigerate until set.

Mashed potatoes with a well of melted butter in the center has graced many a table; perhaps the soul food of Americans. When you make potatoes as the Irish do you call the dish:

CHAMP

2 dozen green onions	mashed potatoes (about 6
2 cups whole milk	cups)
4 pounds freshly cooked hot	½ cup butter
Salt and pepper	

Chop green and white part of the onions; simmer in the milk until soft. Drain, but save the milk. Add onions to the mashed potatoes, half of the butter and enough of the milk to make the potatoes creamy. Season with salt and pepper; put into a serving bowl. Make a well in the center and add the rest of the butter.

GREEN CABBAGE IN CREAM

When I serve Cabbage in Cream, my men guests are ecstatic. I wash the cabbage and dice in large pieces. Cover with boiling water, cover and cook 10 minutes. Drain, put into a skillet with melted butter and just enough cream to "stick" the cabbage. Heat thoroughly, season only with salt and pepper and lots of chopped parsley. My grandmother's recipe. No matter how much I fix, there is never quite enough for seconds and thirds.

POTATO BREAD WITH RAISINS
(2 loaves)

4 to 5 cups flour
½ cup sugar
1 teaspoon salt
2 packages dry yeast
1 cup potato water or water
½ cup butter or margarine

2 eggs
¼ cup mashed potato
1 cup seedless raisins (you may omit)
Melted butter

Mix 1½ cups of flour, the sugar, salt and yeast. Heat potato water and butter until lukewarm and butter is melted. Add to flour mixture gradually and beat 2 minutes at medium speed with your electric mixer. Add eggs, potato and more flour to make a thick batter. Beat at high speed for 2 minutes, scraping sides of bowl. Stir in the raisins and enough flour to make a soft dough. Turn out on a floured board and knead until smooth and elastic. Return to bowl and rub top with melted butter. Cover and let rise in a warm place until double in bulk, about 1 hour. Punch down, turn out on floured board. Shape into loaves; put into greased loaf pans. Cover with a towel and let rise again until doubled in bulk. Bake at 350° for 35 to 40 minutes. Turn out on racks to cool.

APPLE AND WATERCRESS SALAD

2 bunches watercress, washed and crisped
2 heads Belgian endive, thinly sliced
2 unpeeled cored red Delicious apples, thinly sliced
¼ cup salad oil
¼ cup olive oil
4 tablespoons white vinegar

½ teaspoon salt
½ teaspoon sugar
¼ teaspoon dry mustard
Cracked pepper
1 clove garlic
½ cup dry bread crumbs or ¼ cup wheat germ, browned in butter

Aerate the watercress and endive. Toss with the apples, oils, vinegar and seasonings in a salad bowl rubbed with garlic. Sprinkle with the bread crumbs or wheat germ.

MATZO BALL SOUP

2 cups water
3½ tablespoons rendered chicken
 fat or butter
2 cups matzo meal

3 tablespoons finely chopped
 parsley
1 teaspoon salt
4 eggs

Boil water and while it is boiling add the chicken fat or butter, then the meal and parsley. Cook until thick. Cool. Add salt and the eggs beaten until foamy. Refrigerate for several hours. Make into small balls and drop into boiling water. Cook for 20 minutes. Drain, add to:

2 quarts chicken broth   2 cups chopped cooked chicken

You can make the balls, cook and freeze for future use — and you don't have to be Jewish to enjoy this soup.

BEER MUFFINS OR BISCUITS
(makes 12)

2 cups Bisquick   ⅛ teaspoon salt
2 teaspoons sugar   ½ can beer, about

Mix the Bisquick, sugar and salt; add the beer. Stir only until the ingredients are blended. Drop into greased muffin tins and bake in a 450° oven for approximately 10 minutes.

If you plan to roll these and cut them out with a biscuit cutter, decrease the amount of liquid used so that you have a firmer dough.

8

Cocktails and Cocktail Buffets

WHEN I GIVE a cocktail party, I like to prepare for the individual tastes of my guests — those who drink and those who don't; those who watch their weight and others who do not care. For non-drinkers I provide a cold or hot soup. There is nothing worse than spending an evening with a dumb glass of tomato juice or a soft drink in one's hand. I find too that the soup table is usually more popular than the bar. For those who drink, you can no longer provide just whiskey. Wine, beer and champagne are becoming the usual rather than the exception. Too, I think something sweet is a good idea. Some people shudder at the thought of liquor and sweets. Go ahead and shudder. There is never a crumb left. Don't forget coffee, and, of course, plates and forks. No dribbles on the rug.

The cocktail buffet table should look heavily laden whether it is or not; I find a round or oval table helps to create this illusion. Guests today expect food either to hold them over until they go somewhere else for dinner or home for breakfast.

Cocktail food can be tedious to prepare. We have thought it must be bits and pieces of various flavors and textures. Dips are passé — aren't you glad? I always resented dipping. I either had too much or too little on that piece of whatever was provided to dip with. Exception: cold fresh artichoke, with a dip, and who doesn't like to dip into fresh caviar?

These cocktail menus are not too difficult. They can be done beforehand and provide an interesting taste. My opinion — you do not have to agree with me.

Lobster Bisque from a tureen into small cups
Spiced Beef
Small buns kept warm and served with horseradish mustard butter
King Crab à la Helen
French cheese ball covered with caviar
Toasted unsalted crackers
Fresh raw asparagus and black olives in ice
Melon balls and fresh figs wrapped in Belgian or prosciutto ham
Tiny Pecan Tarts
Espresso coffee

Jellied chicken consommé with chopped truffles in a crystal bowl
to spoon into punch cups
Vitello Tonnato
Chicken Sates
Scotched Crayfish in pastry cups with fresh dill
Bacon-wrapped prunes stuffed with sharp Cheddar cheese
Sliced fennel in ice
Canned-in-oil artichoke hearts served in
canned marinated mushroom caps
Rolled watercress sandwiches
Chinese Chews
Coffee and brandy

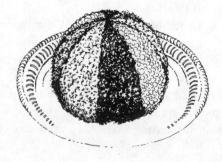

Cold borscht in crystal pitchers to pour into punch cups
with sour cream to add
Broiled Leg of Lamb, basted with gin,
Green Pepper Jelly
Brown Butter French Bread
Lightly Curried Crabmeat in pastry barques
Ham Mousse
Beaten biscuits
Pickled Shrimp (*Helen Corbitt's Cookbook*, page 22)
Decorated Cheese Ball, unsalted crackers
Large-dice red and green peppers in Mustard French Dressing
Glazed walnut halves and cashews
Coffee

Tandoori Turkey to slice for sandwiches in small Onion Rolls
(order from a bake shop or make)
Hot Cheese Croquettes
Crab fingers with red sauce
Flageolet Salad
Iced raw relishes
Florentines
Coffee

Broiled oysters Parmesan
Honey and Mustard Spareribs
Cold Chicken Livers with Mustard Sauce
Garbanzo Salad
Artichoke hearts (canned) filled with red caviar and
sieved hard-cooked eggs
Rich Chocolate Cookies
Coffee

Boiled Beef Brisket with green peppercorns and mustard butter
Salt-rising bread and butter for sandwiches (buy it)
Sausage Balls in Chile Con Queso
Avocado Butter with toasted crackers
Deviled eggs with Green Herb Dressing
(Do several days ahead of time) canned mushrooms marinated with
green chiles in oil and vinegar dressing with garlic
Black Walnut Cookies
Coffee

Lemon Broiled Chicken Drumsticks
Hot Corn on the Cob Rings with Horseradish Butter
Eggplant Caviar with pumpernickel bread
Shrimp Balls with Mustard Sauce
Russian Salad open-face sandwiches (mixed cold cooked vegetables
in mayonnaise)
Bread Crumb Macaroons
Coffee

Curried tuna in pastry cups
Hoomis with Lahvash
Shrimp butter with Pulled Bread
Pickled sausage (you buy)
Cocktail Vegetable Salad
Hush puppies (buy the frozen, or make) with Chili Con Queso
Small cake squares iced all over with coffee rum icing
rolled in grated bitter chocolate
Coffee

Fish balls
Cucumbers in sour cream
Cold Curried Chicken Mousse
Texas caviar (Pickled Black-eyed Peas,
Helen Corbitt's Cookbook, page 13)
Sausage Biscuits
Liptauer Cheese with rye breads (as prepared
in the Viennese restaurant, the "Little White Chimney Sweeper")
and red Delicious apples
Coffee

LOBSTER BISQUE

3 tablespoons butter
3 tablespoons finely minced onion
2 cups chopped lobster meat,
    fresh or frozen

3 tablespoons flour
5 cups half-and-half or milk
1 teaspoon salt
⅓ cup sherry

Melt the butter, add the onion and sauté until soft, but not brown. Add the lobster and cook at low heat until thoroughly heated. Remove the lobster; add the flour, cook until bubbly. Add half-and-half and cook until thickened. Return the lobster, correct seasonings and let stand over hot water until ready to serve. Heat the sherry and float on top. It will mix as the Bisque is ladled out into cups.

A few years ago I suggested that Neiman-Marcus Epicure Shop list a spiced beef in their Christmas catalog for a gift idea. They had to cut off the orders as no one fully anticipated its appeal. I received as many, if not more, requests for the recipe. You can wrap and keep it refrigerated for a long time or freeze. It is worth the effort.

SPICED BEEF

1 pound beef suet
2 ounces ground allspice
2 ounces cayenne pepper
1½ ounces ground pepper
2 ounces ground cloves
2 ounces ground cinnamon

2 ounces ground nutmeg
1 12-pound to 14-pound top butt of beef or sirloin tip roast
4 or 6 jars saltpeter (buy in a drugstore)
Cracked pepper

Melt suet, add spices and heat 5 minutes. Cool slightly. Punch holes through beef and pour mixture into the holes. I use a wooden spoon handle to punch the holes. Tie and wrap beef in cheesecloth. Make a brine of saltpeter and water (enough to float an egg). Soak beef for 2 or 3 weeks refrigerated. Cook on top of stove in fresh water for approximately 2½ hours. Remove and, while still hot, take off cheesecloth and sprinkle the beef heavily with cracked pepper. Rewrap and refrigerate. Serve cold, thinly sliced, with sliced breads or hot biscuits.

KING CRAB A LA HELEN

2 pounds frozen king crab legs, cut in 1-inch chunks
Sherry
1 teaspoon salt

1 cup whipping cream
1 pound Bel Paese or Muenster cheese

Place crab chunks in a lightly buttered shallow casserole or skillet. Sprinkle with sherry and salt. Pour cream over crab to just cover the bottom of the casserole or skillet. (I use my crêpe suzette pan.) Sprinkle heavily with the shredded cheese. Heat until cream is bubbly; then run under the broiler to melt and brown the cheese. Do shrimp and scallops the same — all divine.

DECORATED CHEESE BALL

1 3-pound loaf cream cheese
½ pound Roquefort cheese
½ pound sharp Cheddar cheese, soft
½ cup chopped chives or green onion
1 garlic bud, minced
2 tablespoons red caviar
2 tablespoons black caviar
2 tablespoons chopped green olives
2 tablespoons finely chopped parsley
2 tablespoons chopped capers
2 tablespoons chopped pimiento
2 tablespoons diced bacon, crisped
2 tablespoons chopped black olives

Divide cream cheese into three parts. Mix one part with the Roquefort; one part with the Cheddar; one part wtih the chives and garlic. Pile each part on top of one another and shape into a ball. Mark the ball with a knife into eight sections. Cover each section with one of the following: red caviar, black caviar (whitefish), chopped green olives, finely chopped parsley, chopped capers, chopped pimiento, crisp diced bacon, chopped black olives. Refrigerate.

When you cut into the cheese, you taste the different flavors. This could also serve as the centerpiece for your table. It is a nice neighborly gift too.

I also like to form imported Gourmandise and Port Salut into a ball and cover with red or fresh caviar. I have to feel extravagant when I do this, but I find it very much appreciated.

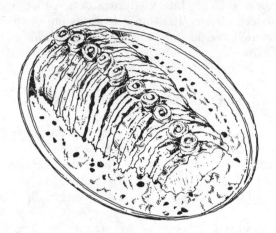

VITELLO TONNATO

There are many recipes for Vitello Tonnato, all equally good and rather complicated. I think this recipe is fairly easy.

½ cup finely chopped onion
3 garlic cloves
¼ cup butter
2 tablespoons olive oil
1 3-pound piece shoulder or leg of veal
1 teaspoon salt
½ teaspoon white pepper
½ teaspoon dried basil
1 bay leaf
1 carrot
1 stalk celery

Few sprigs parsley
1 cup dry white wine
1 cup chicken consommé
1 7-ounce can white meat tuna fish
4 anchovy filets
1 cup olive oil
Juice of 1 lemon
Whipping cream
Capers
Rolled Anchovy Filets

Sauté the onion and cloves in the butter and 2 tablespoons oil until limp. Add the veal, rubbed with the salt, pepper and basil. Brown on all sides. Add bay leaf, carrot, celery, parsley, wine and consommé; simmer slowly (basting often) on top of stove or roast in a 325° oven for about 2 hours or until medium done. Add more chicken broth if necessary. Transfer meat to a platter and refrigerate overnight. Strain juices and chill overnight also. Skim off the fat and mix remaining juices with the tuna and anchovies. Put in blender at slow speed and make a paste. Gradually add 1 cup olive oil and the juice of a lemon. Thin with whipping cream to a smooth medium-thick sauce. Cut the veal in very thin slices and arrange on a platter or in a shallow tureen. Pour over the sauce and refrigerate overnight. Garnish with capers and rolled anchovy filets.

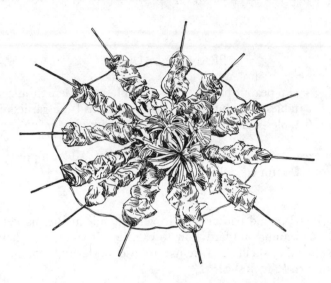

You may put bits and pieces of many foods on bamboo skewers. How much you like to spend determines the kind of food. The morsels should be small, though, as they are eaten off the stick.

CHICKEN SATES
(for 8 to 10 sates)

1 broiler-sized chicken	2 slices fresh ginger
6-inch bamboo skewers (from Oriental or gourmet shops)	2 cloves garlic, mashed
	Fresh ground pepper, a twist or two
1 cup soy sauce	½ cup dry white wine or sake

Remove skin from chicken and cut off all the meat from the carcass. Cut into ½- to 1-inch size pieces and thread 5 or 6 onto the skewers. Place in a shallow pan and cover with the marinade consisting of remaining ingredients. Refrigerate for several hours. Remove from marinade. Place on a shallow pan or rack and broil, about 5 minutes, on each side. Baste with marinade. Serve hot or warm. Beef, lamb, shrimp, scallops, pork — try any of them.

Sometimes I have a Peanut Sauce handy to dip the sates into before eating. Be sure you leave enough space at the end of the skewer to hang onto.

PEANUT SAUCE

⅔ cup peanut butter   2 tablespoons lemon juice
2 tablespoons butter   2 teaspoons fresh garlic juice
6 tablespoons soy sauce   ⅔ cup whipping cream

Cook all except cream over hot water until hot. Add whipping cream. Keep warm. Use for egg rolls and tempura, too.

You can buy 1-pound packages of frozen crayfish in the market today. No fuss, no cleaning and fairly low in calories. If you do not have crayfish, use any other shellfish. I frequently use lobster tails (about 4 large ones), cut into ½-inch slices.

SCOTCHED CRAYFISH
(for 8 to 10)

4 tablespoons sweet butter   2 tablespoons flour
½ pound diced fresh mushrooms   2 tablespoons butter
  (you may omit)   ½ teaspoon salt
2 pounds frozen crayfish   ¼ teaspoon Worcestershire sauce
2 ounces Scotch whiskey   Dash of Tabasco
1½ pints whipping cream

Melt the butter, add the mushrooms and sauté for 1 minute; add crayfish and cook until hot. Pour in the whiskey and ignite. Add cream and stir while heating, but do not boil. Make a paste (beurre manie) of flour, butter and rest of ingredients. Add to the cream mixture. Cook for 5 minutes or until thickened. Serve in pastry cups or on rice as an entrée.

CHINESE CHEWS
(*48 cookies*)

This cookie has many names and when I serve them they disappear like magic. Here is the oft-requested recipe.

1 cup butter (½ pound)   2 cups flour
1 cup light brown sugar

Mix and spread evenly over a 8 x 12-inch pan (approximately). Bake at 350° for 15 minutes. Remove from oven and cool. Mix together:

4 eggs, lightly beaten   2 cups coarsely chopped pecans
¼ cup flour   or walnuts
3 cups dark brown sugar   1 teaspoon salt
1 cup Angelflake coconut   ½ teaspoon vanilla

Spread on baked layer. Bake at 325° for 35 to 40 minutes or until cookie is firm. Dribble over top while cookie is warm:

1 cup powdered sugar mixed with 1 tablespoon orange juice and
½ teaspoon orange rind

When cold, cut in fingers.

Here is another version of the same recipe. Both are good. Take your choice.

½ cup butter   ½ cup dark brown sugar
1 cup flour

Mix and press into a buttered 8 x 8 x 2-inch pan. Spread evenly into the corners. Bake at 350° for 20 minutes. Remove from oven and cool. Mix together:

2 eggs   1 cup chopped pecans or walnuts
1 cup light brown sugar   1 teaspoon vanilla
½ cup shredded coconut mixed   ⅛ teaspoon salt
with 2 tablespoons flour

Beat eggs until frothy; gradually add sugar. Beat until thick. Add rest of ingredients mixed together well. Spread over baked crust. Bake 20 minutes at 350° or until well-browned. Sprinkle with powdered sugar and cut into squares.

I know that many recipes using lamb disguise the flavor, but I find this simple preparation meets approval.

BROILED LEG OF LAMB

1 5- to 6-pound boned leg of lamb, butterflied
2 cloves garlic or more, minced
1 tablespoon salt

¼ cup dried rosemary, crushed
1 cup gin, bourbon or consommé
2 tablespoons butter

Pull off the thin skin that covers the fat of the lamb leg. Rub lamb with garlic, salt and rosemary. Let this rest at room temperature for at least 1 hour. Place fat side up in a buttered pan. Broil for 15 minutes. Remove, pour over half of the gin and ignite. (Do not put it back under the broiler before igniting or you'll burn the house down.) Turn the lamb, and broil 15 minutes more. Remove, pour over rest of gin and ignite. Add the butter. Turn off the broiler and return to stove to keep warm. Slice thin and use juices as a sauce. Well done? Just increase broiling time.

GREEN PEPPER JELLY

A nice change and especially good with lamb. This recipe came from Dallas's Suzy Nash who says it originates from the Higginbotham Family Cookbook called *This Little Higgy Went to Market*. It really does not matter where it comes from. It is divine.

¾ cup green bell peppers (about 4 small), seeded and cut up
¼ cup jalapeño peppers (canned)

1½ cups cider vinegar
6 cups sugar
1 bottle Certo

Put peppers in the blender with ½ cup of vinegar at high speed. Blend well. Pour into a saucepan, rinse blender with remaining vinegar and add to peppers. Add sugar and bring to a rolling boil that you cannot stir down. Remove from heat. Let stand 5 minutes. Skim if necessary.

Pour in Certo. You may add a little green coloring. Pour into 5 sterilized ½-pint containers and seal.

BROWN BUTTER FRENCH BREAD

Cut French bread into thin slices. Melt butter in a heavy skillet until it turns golden brown. Let solidify again and spread the bread lightly. Form the bread loosely into a loaf again. The flavor is especially good with lamb.

CURRIED CRABMEAT
(for 6 to 8)

¼ cup butter	1 pound lump crabmeat
1 tablespoon curry powder	2 tablespoons brandy
2 tablespoons flour	2 cups half-and-half or milk

Melt the butter, add the curry powder and cook 1 minute. Add flour; cook until bubbly. Mix in crabmeat and fork stir; pour in brandy and ignite. Add half-and-half, and cook until thickened. Serve from a chafing dish into small pastry or patty shells. Extend or vary this recipe by adding diced mushrooms, sliced eggs or both.

This is strictly a cocktail item as it has lots of flavor. It freezes well and makes a wonderful canapé, if you are canapé-minded.

HAM MOUSSE

½ pound boiled ham	1 tablespoon Dijon mustard
¼ pound butter	1½ tablespoons unflavored gelatin
1 cup whipping cream	½ cup Madeira
1 tablespoon salt	1 cup chicken broth
1 teaspoon white pepper	¼ cup Cognac

Put ham through the meat grinder, using finest blade. Combine the ham and butter in a bowl, mixing well. Blend in the cream; stir vigorously. Add salt, pepper and mustard. Soften the gelatin in the Madeira. Bring broth to a boil, remove from flame and add gelatin, stirring to dissolve.

Cool, add to the ham. Check seasoning. Mix well with Cognac and pack in 1½-quart soufflé dish or mold. Refrigerate. Unmold and serve with lightly salted toasted crackers or dark bread.

TANDOORI TURKEY

For a cocktail party an 18- to 20-pound turkey should be plenty for 35 to 40 people. After all it is not a dinner party.

1 quart yogurt	1 teaspoon cayenne pepper
1 cup lime juice	1 teaspoon powdered anise (you
12 cloves garlic, crushed	may omit)
2 tablespoons grated fresh ginger	1 18- to 20-pound turkey
2 tablespoons ground coriander	1 orange, cut in half, and 2 onions
1 tablespoon cumin	1 cup melted butter

Mix the yogurt with the lime juice and garlic. Heat all the spices in a skillet and add to the yogurt mixture. Rub turkey inside and out with the marinade, then pour rest of it over the turkey. Put 2 orange halves and 2 onions in cavities of turkey. Cover the bird and marinate 24 to 48 hours, turning the turkey a couple of times. Put in a roasting pan and roast at 375° until the leg is tender. Baste with butter and the marinade. Put a piece of foil over top of turkey, but do not fold over the pan. Serve cold or warm. Leftovers: dice and put in a curry sauce and serve over rice and fried apple rings.

ONION ROLLS
(makes 36 small or 18 large)

1½ cups water	4½ to 5 cups flour
1 tablespoon plus 1 teaspoon sugar	Melted butter
1 tablespoon butter	1 egg yolk
1 teaspoon salt	1 teaspoon water
1 package dry yeast, dissolved in ¼ cup lukewarm water	1 cup finely chopped onion
	2 tablespoons butter
	Coarse (Kosher) salt

Heat the water, 1 tablespoon sugar, butter and salt to lukewarm and until butter is melted. To the dissolved yeast add 1 teaspoon sugar. Add the butter mixture to the yeast and stir in 4 cups of flour. Turn out on a floured board and knead in ½ to 1 cup more flour to make a soft dough. Put back in bowl, brush with melted butter. Cover. Let rise in a warm place until double in bulk. Punch down and turn out on your board. Form into 1-inch flat rolls. Make a deep crease in each roll. Place dough 2 inches apart on a buttered baking sheet. Brush with butter. Let rise again. Brush with egg yolk beaten with the teaspoon of water. Sauté the onion in the 2 tablespoons butter 1 minute. Pile in the crease and on top. Sprinkle with coarse salt. Bake at 350° for 30 minutes or until onion is golden brown.

HOT CHEESE CROQUETTES
(makes 24)

½ pound Mozzarella cheese, grated	¼ teaspoon salt
½ cup flour	Pinch cayenne
1 egg	Flour and cornstarch

Mix first 5 ingredients, shape into balls and roll in mixture of half flour, half cornstarch. Fry in hot oil (375°) until brown.

FLORENTINES
(about 3 dozen)

½ cup whipping cream	¼ pound diced preserved orange peel
3 tablespoons sugar	
¼ cup flour	4 ounces semi-sweet chocolate, melted
⅓ cup slivered almonds, blanched	

Mix first 5 ingredients together. Spread a cookie sheet with unsalted shortening and flour lightly. With a teaspoon drop the batter; allow ample space between each cookie. Bake the cookies in a 350° oven until golden brown, from 8 to 10 minutes. Cool. Spread the cookie bottoms with the semi-sweet chocolate.

HONEY AND MUSTARD SPARERIBS

1 tablespoon dry mustard
1 teaspoon chili powder
1 teaspoon sage
1 tablespoon salt
10 pounds spareribs, cut in 3-inch

pieces (The butcher will do it
for you.)
1 bottle beer
1 cup honey
1 tablespoon lemon juice

Mix the spices and rub on the ribs. Mix the beer, honey and lemon juice. Pour over the ribs and marinate overnight. Roast uncovered at 350° for 2 hours. Baste with the leftover marinade.

COLD CHICKEN LIVERS WITH MUSTARD SAUCE

2 pounds chicken livers
Milk
2 teaspoons salt

⅛ teaspoon pepper
½ cup butter
½ cup sherry

Cover livers with milk for at least 1 hour. Drain and sprinkle with the salt and pepper. Melt the butter and sauté the livers at medium heat about 5 minutes. Add sherry and continue cooking until cooked through, about 5 minutes. Drain on paper towels and cool. Serve with:

Mustard Sauce:

1 cup mayonnaise
4 tablespoons Dijon mustard

Few drops of Tabasco
¼ cup finely chopped parsley

Mix and chill.

GARBANZO SALAD (CHICK PEAS)

5 cups canned chick peas
½ cup olive oil
¼ cup salad oil
¼ cup red wine vinegar
1 teaspoon diced onion or shallots
1 teaspoon sugar

½ teaspoon salt
½ teaspoon cracked pepper
1 garlic clove, finely chopped
⅓ cup chopped parsley
2 tablespoons chopped pimiento

Wash the chick peas. Drain. Mix rest of ingredients and pour over. Let marinate for 24 hours.

These oversized cookies are always the conversation piece of the occasion. You will find your own satisfaction ample payment for any time you spend in preparation.

RICH CHOCOLATE COOKIES
(18 *large cookies*)

1 cup butter	¾ cup cocoa
⅔ cup sugar	¾ cup flour
2 eggs, well beaten	1 teaspoon vanilla

Cream the butter, add sugar gradually, then eggs, cocoa, flour and vanilla. Drop a tablespoonful in center of a buttered round 9-inch cake pan. Dip the blade of a spatula in cold water and spread out dough to about 7 inches. Bake at 375° for 6 minutes. Remove immediately from oven, cool and remove from pan and repeat. They are thin and delicious. Use the same recipe and vary it; for instance, substitute the same amount of flour for the cocoa and use lemon or almond extract. Sprinkle slivered almonds or granulated sugar on top before baking. Even sophisticated men adore them. Of course you may make small ones if you wish — about 5 dozen.

I happen to like boiled brisket of beef, Irish Yankee upbringing perhaps, but it has good flavor and is tender if cooked properly. Make sure you slice it thin. With whipped cream heavily seasoned with horseradish and mustard it makes a cocktail party worth remembering. Or serve with whipped butter mixed with Dijon mustard and green peppercorns:

1 cup butter	2 tablespoons green peppercorns
1 teaspoon Dijon mustard	

BOILED BEEF BRISKET
(for 10 to 12)

1 5- to 6-pound piece of brisket	Few sprigs of parsley
1 large onion stuck with 2 cloves	6 peppercorns
1 bay leaf	1 bottle beer (you may omit)
1 piece celery with leaves	1 tablespoon salt
2 carrots	

Place the beef in a kettle and cover with boiling water. Add rest of ingredients. Bring to a boil, reduce the heat to simmer, and cook for 3 to 4 hours or until meat is tender. Add 1 tablespoon salt after 1 hour's cooking. Do not overcook or meat will be stringy and will not slice properly. Remove, and keep warm. Cut off any excess fat before serving, but leave on while cooking. If you wish brisket for an entrée, strain the juices left from cooking, skim off the fat, and for each cup of liquid, add:

1 cup whipping cream	1 teaspoon chopped chives
¼ cup grated horseradish or horse-radish sauce	½ teaspoon dry mustard
	¼ cup diced apple

Cook until reduced to a thin sauce. Serve over thinly sliced meat.

SAUSAGE BALLS IN CHILE CON QUESO

I find you can take short cuts in many ways, so for Chile con Queso I make or buy a cheese sauce and add canned Rotel (tomatoes and green chiles). If I wish it hotter, I add some chopped jalapeño peppers. A favorite men's cocktail item. Form the sausage balls, bake in the oven, drain on paper towels and cover with the Chile con Queso. You may prepare this the day before; the sauce freezes well. If I have sausage and sauce left, I combine them with slices of eggplant, floured and sautéed in salad oil. It makes a delicious vegetable and can also be used for a supper entrée. I call it "Mamacita's Supper Dish." I also make it when I do not have leftovers. It is not a one-helping dish. 'Tis good!

I keep Avocado Butter in my deep freeze to bring out for a quick cocktail tidbit and find it always fascinates guests. Do some in a crock and give it for a Christmas gift.

AVOCADO BUTTER
(for 1 pound)

1 large ripe avocado	¼ teaspoon ground ginger
2 tablespoons fresh lime juice	Natural almonds or filberts
1 pound sweet butter	

Peel and remove seed from the avocado. Put in blender with lime juice. Beat in the butter and ginger. Form into a ball, roll in chopped nuts. Chill. This is also good to use as a butter for any kind of sandwich, or on steak. I also like it with radishes.

Deviled eggs find their way to many a cocktail party and they look mighty tired after a few minutes. So devil them, stick them together and cover them with whatever dressing you like. I like Green Herb Dressing.

BLACK WALNUT COOKIES

In a bowl beat 1 egg with a pinch of salt until frothy. Add ½ cup brown sugar, a little at a time, and beat the mixture with a whisk until thick and it ribbons when the whisk is withdrawn. Fold in 3 tablespoons sifted flour and ½ cup coarsely chopped black walnuts. Drop the batter by teaspoons onto a buttered and floured baking sheet 2 inches apart. Bake the cookies in a hot oven (400°) for 6 to 8 minutes or until they are well browned. Remove them to a rack and let them cool. In the top of a double boiler melt 3 squares (3 ounces) sweet chocolate and 1 tablespoon butter. Brush the chocolate over the cookies to form a thin glaze and chill.

LEMON BROILED CHICKEN DRUMSTICKS
(for 12)

½ cup vinegar
2 tablespoons cracked pepper
1 teaspoon salt
¼ cup brown sugar

¼ cup lemon juice
2 cups salad oil (I like peanut oil.)
18 chicken drumsticks

Bring the vinegar, pepper, salt and sugar to a boil. Remove from stove; add lemon juice and oil. Marinate drumsticks several hours. Place on a rack over broiler pan and broil, basting with the marinade about 10 minutes on each side. Serve with a container of soy sauce nearby for those who like to use it.

CORN ON THE COB RINGS WITH HORSERADISH BUTTER

Corn on the cob cut in 1-inch rings steamed (or boiled with little water) 5 minutes, dressed with melted butter and lots of horseradish makes a surprisingly popular cocktail bit. I usually attach them with picks onto a head of cauliflower or grapefruit. Plan on your guests eating several.

I find I can use this eggplant concoction on a cocktail table or as a salad with equal success, but I try not to answer questions until it has disappeared.

EGGPLANT CAVIAR

1 eggplant, medium size
½ cup finely chopped onion
1 clove garlic, crushed
1 tomato, peeled, seeded and chopped fine

3 tablespoons olive oil
2 tablespoons vinegar
1 teaspoon sugar
Salt and cracked pepper
4 tablespoons chopped parsley

Bake the eggplant at 400° for 30 minutes. Cool and peel. Chop fine and mix with onion, garlic, tomato, oil, vinegar and sugar. Season with salt and cracked pepper. Cover with chopped parsley and chill several hours. Serve with slices of dark rye bread or Lahvash — or on a thick slice of tomato as a salad.

SHRIMP BALLS WITH MUSTARD SAUCE

1½ pounds cooked shrimp
½ cup finely chopped water
    chestnuts
1½ tablespoons cornstarch
1 tablespoon sherry or sake
1 egg, slightly beaten

Chop the shrimp very fine, almost to a paste. Add rest of ingredients and shape into balls about 1 inch in diameter. Fry in deep fat or oil at 375°. Drain and serve with a hot mustard dip:

½ cup dry mustard   1½ cups boiling water
½ cup boiling pineapple juice

Stir until it becomes a smooth paste. This is a very hot sauce.

BREAD CRUMB MACAROONS
(*about 3 dozen cookies*)

1 cup fine, dry bread crumbs
    (3 bread slices make 1 cup
    crumbs)
1 cup sugar
¼ teaspoon salt
1 cup chopped nuts
2 eggs, beaten
1 teaspoon vanilla extract

Combine bread crumbs, sugar, salt and nuts. Blend eggs and vanilla; stir into bread crumb mixture, mixing well. Drop by teaspoons onto greased baking sheet. Bake in 350° oven 12 to 15 minutes or until lightly browned. Remove from baking sheet to wire rack at once.

Borrowed from the Middle East this is an inexpensive cocktail spread.
Serve with Lahvash or cold relishes.

HOOMIS

3 cups cooked chick peas, puréed   6 cloves garlic, minced
1 cup lemon juice   2 teaspoons salt
1 cup sesame oil   Chopped parsley

Mix the puréed chick peas; slowly add the lemon juice and sesame oil, alternately. It will become a thick and smooth paste. Add the garlic
mixed with the salt. Correct seasonings. Place in a bowl or mold and
cover with the chopped parsley.

PULLED BREAD

Take a fork and pull out chunks of unsliced bread about 2 inches long
and 1 inch wide. Brush with melted butter and sprinkle with salt and
paprika. Bake in a 300° oven until golden brown. A sort of crazy Melba
toast. Before baking I sometimes sprinkle over Parmesan cheese.

COLD CURRIED CHICKEN MOUSSE

1 tablespoon unflavored gelatin   ½ teaspoon salt
1 cup milk   4 cups finely diced chicken
2 tablespoons butter   ½ cup mayonnaise
½ teaspoon curry powder   ½ cup whipping cream, whipped
1 tablespoon flour

Dissolve the gelatin in ¼ cup of the milk. Melt the butter, add the
curry powder, cook 1 minute, then add the flour. Cook until bubbly.
Add ¾ cup milk and cook until sauce is smooth and thickened. Use a
French whip to stir. Add salt and softened gelatin. Stir until gelatin is
dissolved. Cool. When partially congealed, add chicken and mayonnaise, then fold in whipped cream. Pour into a mold rubbed lightly with
mayonnaise. Unmold and garnish with whatever you like. I often use
watercress and onion brushes.

SAUSAGE BISCUITS

1 10-ounce bar extra sharp cheese
1 pound hot sausage (Owens, if available)
3 cups biscuit mix
1 teaspoon salt

Grate cheese and let stand at room temperature. Mix all the ingredients with your hands. Shape into small balls or patties. Bake at 375° for 12 minutes. Serve hot. You may bake and freeze, then put frozen in a 300° oven for 10 minutes.

LIPTAUER CHEESE

3 8-ounce packages cream cheese
1 cup sour cream
Watercress or parsley
¼ cup chopped chives or green onion
2 tablespoons paprika
4 tablespoons chopped capers
2 tablespoons cracked pepper
2 tablespoons salt
¼ cup chopped parsley

Mix cheese and sour cream; form into a ball. Place in center of serving tray. Surround with watercress or parsley. In small piles around the edge, about 1 inch from the ball, make separate piles of each remaining ingredient. Serve with a small flat-bladed knife, and let each person mix whatever seasoning they wish with their cream cheese. Serve with dark bread. This also keeps your guests busy.

I like to host a large cocktail party because I like to see a lot of people. After all, I'm used to people: I would have had to change my profession if I hadn't always enjoyed people.

One of my favorite people in Texas is Mrs. Edward (Anne) Clark from Austin. Her husband was Ambassador to Australia and Anne had her letters to friends and family at home published. I had a Poor Author Open House and chose this menu. I patted myself on the back as I did all the preparations myself and had help in only for service. I placed the food in various rooms of my apartment. One hundred and twenty-five guests is a bunch anywhere except in a ballroom. In the den I placed marinated fresh artichokes for dieters, also a frozen Bleu cheese mousse with thin slices of pumpernickel bread. Then in the dining room on a round table:

> Snails in pasta shells kept hot in a crêpe suzette pan over sterno
> Prunes stuffed with cashew nuts and chutney, marinated 24 hours
> in red wine, wrapped in blanched bacon and broiled
> Meat balls with a mustardy sweet-and-sour sauce
> Chicken liver paté with buttered toast squares
> A crystal vase filled with honeydew melon balls with
> slivers of candied ginger
> For old times' sake, I passed warm slices of baked ham on
> hot buttered biscuits — very Texas!

In one corner of the living room, one-inch squares of Butterscotch Brownies and demitasse were waiting. In the entrance hall, champagne and an open bar.

P.S. Anne sold some books too!

I have always been fortunate in having customers who became good friends, so I decided to have a "thank you for being nice to me" party. In my den I put a big tureen of curried chicken soup and tried to keep it filled all evening. The soup never had time to cool off! I kept a bowl of O.T.C. crackers handy, so Yankee-bred guests could reminisce. You can find these crackers in most fine food stores; if you don't, ask for them. They come from Trenton, New Jersey, and are divine with any soup.

Gingered Rib-eye of Beef with buttered small rolls
Broiled mushrooms filled with sausage patties with chutney
Sautéed Frogs' Legs
Deviled Crabmeat Maryland in clam shells
Smoked turkey breast en gelée with pâté de fois gras
Onion brushes and black olives
Roquefort Mousse with sliced apples
Chantilly Torte
Demitasse

For my Skidmore College Alumnae party I used a bright orange cloth on the dining room table and three brass trays graduated in size, one on top of another. I draped them with ripe peaches and blue grapes. Of course they were eaten — why not? I then filled the table with substantial knick-knacks.

Broiled Leg of Lamb, basted with bourbon
Thin slices of buttered French bread for guests' sandwich-making
and Cumberland Sauce to make it still better
Scallops Ramaki
Hot Shrimp Balls with Mustard Sauce
Eggs deviled with wild rice, put together and covered with
Green Herb Dressing
Molded cheeses with toasted torn rolls
Fresh pineapple chunks with hot rum for dunking

The young men present at another successful cocktail party still stop me when I'm grocery shopping to ask about something I had served. Again hot crab bisque laced with sherry in my den; the dining room table with no decoration except the reflection of the copper and brass on the polished surface. I hung bouquets of flowers from the chandelier to give the guests as they left. I forgot to give them, so had another party the next night.

Barbecued pork tenderloin with hot Mustard Sauce
Hot buttered biscuits to make sandwiches
Brochette of beef tenderloin and lobster tail with
Bearnaise Sauce kept warm in a chafing dish
Oriental Chicken Salad with snow peas and Sesame Dressing
Small patty shells filled with mushroom au gratin
Baked Stuffed Shrimp
Thin dark rye bread and gourmandise cheese sandwiches
Crudités in ice

On a side table: petite lemon chess and grasshopper tarts, apple cake, fresh pineapple dipped in semi-sweet chocolate, rolled wafers and demitasse.

SNAILS IN PASTA SHELLS

Snails I like but not in their shells. (Somehow I feel the snails might resent them.) I like to serve snails in the pasta shells you find in the grocery stores — the sea shell macaroni is best. Drain and wash the snails and for 2 dozen, which is the small can size, sauté in 2 tablespoons butter and 2 cloves of finely chopped garlic for about 5 minutes. Cool and stuff each snail into a cooked macaroni shell. Cover with the following butter mixture: ½ cup butter, 1 teaspoon chopped shallots, 2 tablespoons chopped parsley, 1 clove finely minced garlic, juice of ½ lemon and a few drops of Worcestershire sauce. Let stand several hours, then bake in 350° oven until sizzling. You eat the snail with the pasta and all the butter. I find they disappear like magic. You can prepare these several days ahead and freeze.

GINGERED RIB-EYE OF BEEF

1 8-pound eye of the rib beef roast
1 tablespoon salt
2 tablespoons grated fresh ginger root

½ cup soy sauce
1 cup sliced onion
1 cup sherry or beef consommé

Be sure beef is well trimmed. Rub with salt, ginger and soy sauce. Place in a roasting pan on top of the sliced onions. Roast at 350° allowing 10 minutes per pound for rare. Baste with the sherry or consommé. Let rest at least 10 minutes before slicing.

FROGS' LEGS

8 pairs frogs' legs
2 tablespoons lemon juice
Flour
¼ cup butter
2 tablespoons olive oil

1 clove garlic, crushed
2 tablespoons chopped chives
2 tablespoons dry white wine
Salt and white pepper

Cover the frogs' legs in water mixed with the lemon juice. Dry and dust lightly with flour. Shake off excess. Melt butter, add oil and garlic. Sauté 1 minute. Add chives and frogs' legs. Shake pan while cooking to prevent sticking. Turn once. When golden brown, add wine, season with salt and pepper, and chopped parsley if you wish. Use the same ingredients for shrimp or chicken, especially the wings, which make a good cocktail morsel.

DEVILED CRABMEAT MARYLAND

1 pound fresh white crabmeat
Juice of 1 lemon
⅛ teaspoon Worcestershire sauce
Few drops of Tabasco
1 teaspoon Dijon mustard

2 tablespoons butter
2 tablespoons chopped onion
1 tablespoon flour
1 cup half-and-half
Salt and white pepper to taste

Mix crab, lemon juice and seasonings. Melt butter, add onion and cook 1 minute. Stir in flour, cook until bubbly. Pour in cream, cook until thick. Add to crabmeat mixture. Correct seasonings. Pile into clam shells, toast rounds or artichoke bottoms. Mix ½ cup white bread crumbs with 2 tablespoons melted butter and 2 tablespoons mayonnaise. Crumble on top of crab mixture. Bake at 375° until hot. Run under broiler to brown. Go ahead and refrigerate but do not freeze.

9

Picnics and Outdoor Parties

PIQUE-NIQUE, the French for "pick up a trifle" and which means a picnic for you, can range from the elaborate to a delicatessen sandwich or fried chicken in a bucket. At any rate, it is a pack-up-your-food-and-follow-the-action to roadside parks, a football game, the county fair, the beach, the mountains — just go. It is good for you to relax in fresh air. (You can always find some if you look for it.)

It is easy to have a picnic even though it takes some behind-the-scenes planning. We have picnic hampers today — sophisticated ones — or you can use an egg crate and all kinds of styrofoam containers to carry both hot and cold food. You do need a check list: can opener, eating utensils, a knife for slicing, chopping board, ice container, bottle opener, insect repellent, table cloth and napkins, salt and pepper and such, pot holder, fuel of some kind, matches, paper towels, trash bag, soap, and a bottle of iodine.

I like picnics near a babbling brook, if only for remembering past fun picnics. One beautiful day in Ireland some friends and I sat on a fallen tree trunk and had that wonderful Irish bread with their equally wonderful ham and Blarney cheese. We made our own sandwiches with sweet butter and champagne mustard and had raisin pound cake, as only the Irish can make, fresh cherries and bananas, a white wine cooled in the brook. Simple, but the birds sang, the sun shone and the whole world looked bright and uncomplicated.

I like to be extravagant when I give a picnic — and I liked this one — as did my guests.

Fresh caviar with Hot Flageolets
Leg of Lamb in Pastry
Rice Salad
Romaine with fresh mint in the Sherry Dressing
Salt-rising bread and butter sandwiches
A well-packed freezer of homemade strawberry ice cream
with cones (*Helen Corbitt's Cookbook*, page 289)
Peanut Cookies (take lots)
Chablis in ice
Vacuum jug of coffee

Take a portable grill, and this menu you could do easily.

Cold Roquefort Soup
Marinated skewered Beef Tenderloin
and Chicken Livers to grill
Bean and Eggplant Salad
Hard rolls with Port Salut cheese
Raw vegetables in ice
Fresh peaches to toast on the coals
White chocolate pound cake
Sangria (It goes so very well with the peaches too.)

Cold boiled lobster tail with lemon mayonnaise
Cold tarragon chicken
Vermicelli Salad (*Helen Corbitt's Potluck*, page 39)
A round loaf of bread hollowed out and the center
filled with cucumber and egg salad sandwiches
(This keeps them moist.)
Almond cream cake
Fresh pineapple wedges in ice with brown sugar
A Sancerre or champagne

And perhaps a candelabra, to give it a flair. It goes without saying: no paper plates. And, oh yes, choose a spot away from the noise of moving objects.

A menu with a South of the Border flavor:

Guacamole, corn chips, cherry tomatoes, green onions, and jalapeños
Flank steaks, marinated with dry red wine, olive oil and garlic
(Grill with a few jalapeño peppers here and there.)
Shrimp, marinated in olive oil, garlic and lots of chopped parsley to grill
Rolls to toast
Soft cheeses, guava jelly, or guava shells and thin crackers
Good chocolate candy
A chilled sparkling Rosé

A less expensive menu I use frequently is:

Deviled Rock Cornish Hens cooked in foil
(carried to the picnic in the same foil)
Cold Ratatouille
Texas caviar (Pickled Black-eyed Peas,
Helen Corbitt's Cookbook, page 13)
Loaves of homemade bread with asparagus spears or salami
cooked inside, butter to spread
Margaret Hull's Rum Cake

The hero (also known as spucky, grinder and submarine) sandwich makes a good picnic! You can find a commercial bake shop to make the long sandwich bread for you. Order a three-foot-long (or longer) loaf of French bread. At Neiman-Marcus we made three-, four- and six-foot ones — the six-foot one served thirty people. Slice the long way, butter it and spread with a good mustard. I like the New Orleans type for this. Then fill it with very thin slices of cold meats: ham, salami, liverwurst, beef and thin-sliced Swiss cheese, tomatoes, hard-cooked eggs, soft lettuce and mayonnaise. Add a few anchovies if you like. I don't.

Or fill with chicken or seafood salad. Wrap in clear plastic or foil and keep as cool as possible. Slice as you serve it. Pickled vegetables go well with it; you find all kinds in the grocery stores today. Serve cold watermelon and either beer, red wine, or lemonade. Add a chocolate layer cake with apricot jam filling and chocolate icing.

Fourth of July is a good time for a picnic and American fare.

Hamburgers to grill formed with Roquefort cheese
and butter in the center
Cold roasted chicken, Dijon mustard
Corn on the cob, cooked in the coals
Cucumber sandwiches, squashy ones
French potato salad
Tomatoes and scallions, Vinaigrette Dressing
Peach cobbler
Lemonade, beer and coffee

I like to make the cucumber sandwiches with lots of mayonnaise so they are moist. Everyone calls them squashy ones.

And picnics for small fry, all items put in gaily colored paper bags, tied with bright ribbons and small toys. Let each child pick his own. You might tie the bags to low branches on a tree or hide among bushes for a "picnic" hunt. You cannot stray too far away from the conventional for them, so a Punch and Judy sandwich (peanut butter and jelly), a sliced chicken sandwich, sugar cookies and fresh fruit. To drink serve pink lemonade and chocolate milk (but homemade).

A tin of fresh caviar costs a great deal of money and comes in a very plain package. I like to dress up caviar by putting it in a cabbage to keep cool. I put a medium-sized cabbage in warm water; let it cool and stand in the water all night. Then peel back the outside leaves to form a crown. Cut away the center of the head. Refrigerate in a plastic bag or put in ice water again. When ready to use, drain and set the tin of caviar in the center. This will keep the caviar cold and pretty up the tin. Spoon caviar on:

HOT FLAGEOLETS

⅓ cup sliced green onion
4 tablespoons butter
4 cups canned flageolets
Salt and fresh ground pepper
Chopped parsley

Sauté the onion in the butter 1 minute. Add beans which have been drained. Correct seasonings. Cover and bake at 350° for 20 minutes. Sprinkle with chopped parsley and serve warm. Wrap in foil to carry to a picnic.

Any picnic is elegant with:

LEG OF LAMB IN PASTRY

1 boned leg of lamb, 5- to 6-pound size or smaller
2 cloves garlic
Salt and pepper
2 teaspoons dried or 2 sprigs of fresh rosemary
2 tablespoons melted butter
White wine or consommé
Pie crust
1 egg mixed with 2 tablespoons cold water

Rub leg with garlic, salt and pepper. Cut a few slivers of the garlic and insert into slits here and there in the flesh. Sprinkle with the rosemary and butter. Roast uncovered in a 450° oven for 15 minutes. Reduce the heat to 375° and roast about 10 minutes for each pound or 140° on your meat thermometer. Baste frequently with the wine or consommé. Remove from oven and cool. Shape the meat as well as you can to look like original leg. Roll out pie crust about ⅛ inch thick, large enough to cover the meat; allow 3 inches in length and 2 inches in width to overlap. Place seam side down on an ungreased cookie sheet. Roll out some of the dough and cut into decorative pieces and fashion over the pastry. Bake at 425° for 10 to 15 minutes. Brush with egg and cold water and return to oven. Continue to bake until pastry is brown, brushing once more during baking with the egg wash.

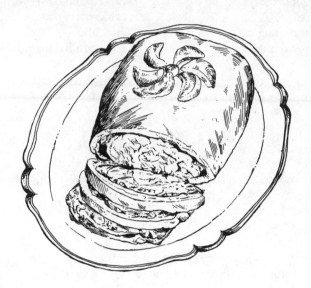

RICE SALAD

4 cups cooked chilled rice (try with Uncle Ben's Wild Rice Mix)
1 cup chopped crab, lobster, shrimp, or crayfish
½ cup slivered ham (Virginia, if available)
1 cup *finely* chopped celery
3 hard-cooked eggs, finely chopped
2 tablespoons chopped chives
⅓ cup chopped parsley
2 tablespoons olive oil
2 tablespoons wine vinegar
½ cup mayonnaise
Salt and freshly ground pepper

Combine by tossing lightly the first 7 ingredients. Sprinkle with oil and vinegar. Add mayonnaise and season. Let stand in refrigerator a few hours for a more tangy flavor. (Better made the day before; however, salt and pepper just before serving.) Try as an entrée with sliced cantaloupe and honeydew.

PEANUT COOKIES
(6 dozen small cookies)

1 cup chopped dry roasted
  peanuts
1 cup shortening
½ cup brown sugar

1 tablespoon corn syrup
1 tablespoon peanut butter
1 cup flour
¼ teaspoon baking powder

Mix, knead and roll out. Cut and bake on a lightly greased cookie sheet at 350° for 20 to 25 minutes.

COLD ROQUEFORT SOUP

2 cups crumbled Roquefort
  cheese (you may use Blue)
16 ice cubes
4 tablespoons chopped parsley

4 tablespoons chopped green
  onions
4 cups sour cream
Salt and pepper

Put cheese, ice cubes, parsley and onions in blender. Whip until smooth. Add sour cream and correct seasonings. Carry to a picnic in a vacuum jug. You will need all of it. For a cup at home, use half the recipe and add red or Romanoff caviar or finely diced shrimp or lobster. Leftovers? Add 1 tablespoon melted unflavored gelatin to 1 pint of soup. Pour into individual molds and refrigerate. A superb salad with beef.

BEEF TENDERLOIN AND CHICKEN LIVERS

2 cloves garlic
¼ cup olive oil
2 tablespoons Dijon mustard
2 pounds beef tenderloin
1 pound chicken livers

8 bamboo skewers
4 slices bacon, cut in 1-inch pieces
Salt and cracked pepper
Brandy

Mince the garlic, mix with the oil and mustard. Cut the tenderloin into ½-inch slices. Separate chicken livers. Place alternately with the bacon on a buttered or oiled bamboo skewer. Rub with the mustard mixture and wrap in foil. When ready to broil, sprinkle with salt and pepper. Broil over charcoal about 5 minutes on each side. Ignite some brandy and pour over. Eat off skewer.

BEAN AND EGGPLANT SALAD
(for 8 or more)

3 cups canned Great Northern
beans, drained
3 cups canned or cooked pinto
beans, drained
3 cups canned red kidney beans,
drained
1 cup minced green onion or
chives
½ cup finely minced parsley

2 garlic cloves, crushed
2 cups eggplant, cut in 1-inch
dice
Flour, salt and pepper
¼ cup olive oil
1 cup diced, peeled and seeded
tomatoes
Mustard French dressing

Mix beans, onion, parsley, and garlic together. Cover with:

Mustard French Dressing:

⅓ cup olive oil
⅓ cup salad oil
⅓ cup wine vinegar

1 tablespoon Dijon mustard
Salt and pepper to taste

Refrigerate for several hours. Lightly dust eggplant with flour, salt and pepper and sauté in the olive oil until a light brown. Drain and cool. Add the eggplant and the tomatoes to the beans a few hours before serving. I serve this salad in an earthenware crock. Sometimes I add broiled, lightly smoked sausage in place of eggplant. Never, never any leftovers.

DEVILED ROCK CORNISH HENS

8 10- to 12-ounce Rock Cornish
hens
Salt and white pepper
½ cup Dijon mustard

⅔ cup white bread crumbs
3 tablespoons minced shallots
½ cup butter
White wine

Rub each bird with salt, pepper and 1 tablespoon of the mustard. Sprinkle with bread crumbs. Place in a square of foil and fold to center. Add 1 teaspoon shallots, 1 tablespoon butter and 3 tablespoons white wine to each package. Fold over the foil tightly and bake at 400° about 50 minutes or until chicken is done. Carry to picnic in the foil.

Good for informal eat-on-the-floor to watch a television show. No knives and forks. Good cold too.

MARGARET HULL'S RUM CAKE

1 box Duncan Hines Yellow Cake
   Mix
1 small package instant vanilla
   pudding
4 eggs

½ cup salad oil
½ cup water
½ cup dark rum
1 cup broken pecans
Granulated sugar

Topping:

1 cup sugar   ¼ cup water
½ cup butter   ¼ cup dark rum

Beat cake and pudding mix with the eggs, salad oil, water and rum for 10 minutes, at medium speed on mixer. Grease and lightly flour a 13 x 9-inch (approximate) pan. Sprinkle over 1 cup nutmeats. Carefully pour in batter. Bake at 325° about 45 minutes or until it tests done. Let cake stand a few minutes to cool, then turn out on a sheet of foil sprinkled with sugar (foil shiny side up). Boil the 1 cup sugar with the butter and water 2 minutes. Remove from heat. Add rum. Stir well and drizzle over cake letting it all soak in.

10

Weddings, Receptions
and Teas

WEDDINGS ARE memorable occasions and food plays an important part in
the proceedings, more so now than in the past. A good rule to follow is
to do only what can be done smoothly and happily whether it be catered
at home, a club or hotel. The food selection should be up to the bride.
It is her day!

Personally I feel the reception that has champagne and punch with
simple thin sandwiches and wedding cakes for both the bride and groom
has a dignity that is fitting. However, the plans of today often mean an
open bar, hot and cold hors d'oeuvres and food of all kinds. If one is
opposed to alcohol, there is no rule that says you must serve it. Fruit
punch, tea and coffee are just as desirable.

The time of day also determines the kind of food and service: inside
or out-of-doors, walk-around or seated.

The groom's cake, his favorite and undecorated, disappears quickly as
he chooses the always popular spice or chocolate cake. A coffee service,
demitasse, of course, is a good gesture to offer with it.

The elaborate bride's wedding cake with the exception of the bride
herself is the focal point of the reception. Out-of-doors it is beautiful if
in an arbor of flowers or greens and spotlighted in the evening. At home,
it should be away from any other food or drink and visible to everyone
entering.

In choosing flowers and food for a reception at home be sure their
respective fragrances do not clash; garlic and orange blossoms simply do
not go together.

I think we must break with tradition at times for the bride who likes the earthy approach to a wedding. After all, if she wants her wedding cake hanging from her favorite tree in the back yard, garden to some, that is her business. If beer and hot dogs are her idea of a greeting to her invited guests, go along with it. Tradition will not suffer.

Reception Ideas

Pass on trays:

Champagne (punch, plain or both)
Trays of thin-sliced smoked turkey on lightly curried buttered thin bread
Virginia ham on cheese bread with sweet butter
Lobster or shrimp salad made open-face on thin slices of cucumber on buttered rounds
Rolled watercress sandwiches
Soft lettuce sandwiches
For one hot sandwich: mushroom-buttered rolls or triangles, toasted, and a touch of thyme added to bring out the flavor of the mushrooms.
Two-inch finger rolls buttered and filled with any of the following:

Pâté with truffles	Brie
Prosciutto ham	Seafood or meat salad
Smoked turkey or ham mousse	Egg salad and chutney
Cream cheese and preserved ginger	

All could be made ahead of time and frozen.

I have recommended a soup served in demitasse cups and found it more popular than the champagne. One mother of the bride took the initiative and served navy bean soup only, her special recipe, no punch or champagne, and everyone thoroughly approved.

Wedding cakes are more or less traditional even for the less traditionally minded bride. But a white cake, white filling, white icing of cardboard consistency can be deadly. When I was the manager of the

Houston Country Club, we did not make wedding cakes. Every time a cake of this kind was served, I remember finding pieces hidden behind the draperies, the furniture and even tossed into light coving.

I think the filling should be flavorful, the icing soft but not sticky. I often used the Colonnade Icing (*Helen Corbitt's Cookbook*, page 252) or else a butter cream. These are some of the combinations of flavors: white cake with a cream filling with Nesselrode or preserved chestnuts, rum or vanilla flavoring or a butter cream mixed with fresh strawberries, coffee or chocolate or both; yellow or white cake with a tart lemon filling, Lady Baltimore or coconut. I liked to use fresh flowers as decoration at times instead of icing, especially for outdoor receptions. My special favorite was angel food cake with Nesselrode filling, then whatever pastel color icing the bride chose. Then we threw shaved white chocolate over all. It looked like white feathers. A container in the top layer held an airy arrangement of flowers to accent the color of the icing. A spring wedding had yellow icing and daisies; a fall wedding had an ice blue with the red, lavender, pink and blue gentian type daisies.

I never have been entranced by the bride-and-groom ornaments on top of a wedding cake. No matter who makes them, they look scared to death. I like either flowers or birds. I use white paper doves, covered with icing, and place two on top taking off, so to speak, on a great adventure.

Let's get back to the menu. An excellent idea is a table holding:

A variety of cheeses, whole or partially cut
(but please not in cubes with picks)
Toasted unsalted crackers
Roquefort Mousse
Slices of melon, apples, ripe pears
Thin-sliced breads
A molded fish or chicken mousse
Whole shrimp with Green Herb Dressing
A whole loaf of pâté de fois gras

This cuts down on any work for the mother of the bride (except to assemble the makings). The idea, however, must be a help-yourself, go sit or stand where you like. Small plates, forks and napkins.

Hot hors d'oeuvres are a gourmet touch but need last-minute supervision, and if one has help in the kitchen, fine.

Any of these:

Crabmeat Lorenzo

Mushrooms filled with crab or lobster Gruyère

(*Helen Corbitt's Cookbook*, page 16)

Stuffed Shrimp

Small patty shells of lobster in vermouth sauce (Newburg)

Small brioche filled with sweetbreads and morelles in cream

Pastry turnovers of: cheese and chutney, chicken liver pâté

or mushrooms in sherried butter

Mushrooms filled with Quiche Lorraine

Miniature Greek pastries (buy from a Greek restaurant)

Chicken livers and shrimp brochettes with Bearnaise Sauce

Butterfly Shrimp

Prunes filled with sharp Cheddar cheese, bacon-wrapped and broiled

Hot cheese balls

Shrimp Balls with peanut dip

Add a mixture of cold hors d'oeuvres:

Mushrooms filled with sour cream and chopped dry roasted

peanuts or with cottage cheese and walnuts

Small cream puffs filled with: Boursin cheese and caviar,

any seafood or meat salad, Cream Cheese Mousse or sliced

sautéed mushrooms in a sharp cheese

Cherry tomatoes filled with Shrimp Butter

Pickled mushrooms, Jerusalem artichokes, tiny eggplants

Cucumber cups filled with Roquefort cheese or shrimp salad

Steak tartare balls

Decorated cheese ball

Vitello Tonnato canapés

Pickled Shrimp (*Helen Corbitt's Cookbook*, page 22)

Buttered pecans

Glazed cashews

The simple expensive reception could be:

Fresh caviar with blinis
Homemade Melba toast squares, and lemon wedges and/or
smoked Irish or Scotch salmon with thin-sliced rye breads,
sour cream and sweet butter

Only a favored few could afford this for a very large reception, not to mention champagne served with the wedding cake to toast the bride and groom.

A less expensive menu could be:

Champagne punch
Thin slices of ham in small hot biscuits
Thin-sliced turkey sandwiches with watercress and butter
Champagne for toasting

An inexpensive menu could be:

Wine punch
Toasted rolled cheese sandwiches or cheese straws
Closed cucumber sandwiches
Egg salad and chive sandwiches
Champagne for toasting

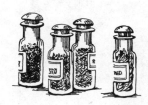

Wedding Breakfast

Champagne
Cheese and anchovy straws

Seated

Melon Boat with hot grenadine to pass
Poached eggs on artichoke bottoms (canned) with lobster
in cream browned with Mousseline Sauce
or
Elegante Chicken Hash in crêpes browned with Gruyère sauce
Small brioche
Lemon Velvet Ice Cream with candied violets
(*Helen Corbitt's Cookbook*, page 288)
Wedding cake
Champagne

Buffet

Slices of melon, fresh figs and papaya, each wrapped
in prosciutto
Lobster Newburg
Mushrooms Fondue in patty shells
Breast of chicken in aspic
Watercress sandwiches, Orange Bread sandwiches
Wedding cake
Champagne

Champagne Punch

Seated

Fresh strawberries with warm honey
Chicken and oysters in cream in patty shells
Corn Soufflé
Rolled asparagus sandwiches
Wedding cake
Champagne

Buffet

An arrangement of fresh fruits with limes and fresh mint
Poached eggs Benedict in artichoke bottoms
Cream cheese loaf rolled in toasted sesame seeds
Popovers and hot biscuits
Strawberry jam and orange marmalade
Wedding cake
Champagne

Wedding Punch

Seated

Broiled half grapefruit with sherry and honey
Deviled eggs on toasted English muffins with chipped beef
in cream spooned over
Apricot bread and butter sandwiches
Beignets Soufflés
Wedding cake
Champagne

Buffet

Broiled sausage patties in peach halves
Soft scrambled eggs
Chicken Hunter Style (small legs)
Toasted cheese triangle sandwiches
Wedding cake
Champagne

Wedding Luncheon

Champagne
Hot hors d'oeuvres of Crabmeat Lorenzo and mushroom ramekins

Seated

Jellied Watercress Soup
Thin buttered Melba toast
Breast of Chicken in Cream and Apples
Fresh asparagus, melted butter
Two-inch Parker House rolls
Orange ice with Grand Marnier
Wedding cake
Champagne

Buffet

Hot poached salmon, orange Hollandaise
Roasted (pink) tenderloin of beef in aspic with truffles and mushrooms
Cold Rice Salad
Cucumber sandwiches
Small finger rolls
Strawberry Melba
Wedding cake
Champagne

Spritzers
Toasted rolled parsley sandwiches

Seated

Cold avocado soup with cinnamon toast croutons
Tarragon Roasted Chicken
Orange Rice
Celery heart salad, Mimosa Dressing
Fresh toasted English muffins
Molded peach ice cream
Wedding cake
Champagne

Buffet

Cheese torte
Whole mushrooms in sherried cream
Chicken salad with minted peas in aspic
Assorted buttered breads
Fresh cut-up fruit in lime syrup
Wedding cake
Champagne

Fresh Fruit Punch

Seated

Cold shrimp soup
Thin-sliced ham and chicken rolled in crêpes
with Gruyère cheese sauce
Fresh fruit salad with Poppy Seed Dressing
Lemon Muffins (*Helen Corbitt's Cookbook*, page 221)
Wedding cake
Champagne

Buffet

Fresh pineapple slices sprinkled with brown sugar,
sour cream and grated orange sauce
Stuffed Macaroni with Spinach and Chicken Livers
Ham and vegetable salad à la Russe
Wedding cake
Champagne

Wedding Dinner

Champagne

Fresh caviar in ice, lemon wedges
Thin toast

Seated

Cream of fresh mushroom soup
Toasted thin mushroom sandwich triangles
Tenderloin of beef with pâté de fois gras
Fresh artichoke bottoms filled with Bearnaise Sauce
Rice Soufflé
Bouquet of vegetables
French vanilla ice cream on whole strawberries
with Almond Soft Custard
Wedding cake
Champagne

Buffet

Baked Virginia ham with Champagne Sauce
Curried thin-sliced Smoked Turkey with chutney baked peaches
Fresh crabmeat salad, marinated in lime juice and
tossed with mayonnaise
Wild rice and mushrooms
Bibb lettuce with Sherry French Dressing
Fresh Pineapple Boat marinated in Kirsch
Wedding cake
Champagne

Golden Spike
Petite cream puffs filled with cream cheese and red caviar
Croque Monsieur

Seated

Consommé Bellevue with slices of avocado
Souffléed Crackers
Breast of Chicken Piquante
Molded rice with Pease
Julienne carrots and grapes
Thin bread and butter sandwiches
Bombe Melba
Wedding cake
Champagne

Buffet

Corned Beef Brisket with Oranges
Galantine of Turkey decorated with slices of melon and grapes
Green bean casserole
Sliced egg and potato salad with caper mayonnaise
Sandwich Loaf with Assorted Sandwiches
Ice cream wedding cake
Petits fours
Champagne

Easy White Sangria
Eggplant caviar and Melba toast

Seated

Oriental chicken soup
Crisp Crackers
Rock Cornish hen roasted in white wine
Rice and Cheese Casserole (to pass, of course)
Orange and watercress salad with Sherry French Dressing
Lahvash and sweet butter
Glazed strawberries
Wedding cake
Champagne

Buffet

Ham steak baked in red wine
Noodles à la Crème
Spinach Ring with Celery and Peanuts
Melon balls in fruit aspic
Wedding cake
Champagne

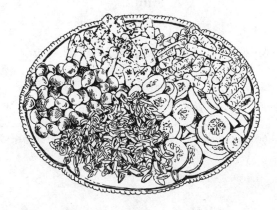

Wedding Supper

Champagne
Small Brie quiche with fresh caviar
Pâté de fois gras on open-face smoked turkey sandwiches

Seated

Breast of Chicken and Lobster en Brochette
Bearnaise or Sweet and Sour Sauce
White rice
Fresh asparagus with truffle butter
Celery heart Victor
Buttermilk Biscuits spread with Smithfield ham
Poached Fresh Peaches with Raspberry Sauce
Wedding cake
Champagne

Buffet

Tournedos Rossini
Breast of duckling in aspic with black cherries
Snipped Green Beans with Chanterelles
Bouillabaisse salad
Assorted cheeses
Hard rolls
Raspberry ice with strawberry purée and slivered almonds
Wedding cake
Champagne

Kir
Open-face avocado sandwiches
Scallops Ramaki

Seated

Boula Boula (*Helen Corbitt's Cookbook*, page 32)
Thin cucumber and chive sandwiches
Braised breast of chicken, Hunter Style
Lightly curried rice
Zucchini fan, Parmesan
Ambrosia
Wedding cake
Pink Champagne

Buffet

Filet of Sole in Pastry with Caper Sauce
Green Peas with Leeks
Tomatoes filled with Ratatouille
Green salad with slivers of ham and Feta cheese, Mustardy Dressing
Hot small rolls
Lemon ice with hot brandied blueberries
Wedding cake
Champagne

Tequila and Kahlua (called a Brave Bull)
Crudités in ice

Seated

Jellied cucumber ring filled with shrimp and egg salad
Hot bread sticks
Sliced Flank Steak with Red Wine Butter
Tomato filled with Spinach Mornay
Three-fruit sherbet
Wedding cake
Champagne

Buffet

Layered crêpes with paprika chicken
Piperade
Cheese Custard
Grapefruit and chicory salad
Sherry French Dressing
French bread and butter sandwiches
Wedding cake
Champagne

Teas

When Sally Marcus of the American Red Cross called me and said, "I want something at a reception for a few thousand. Not tea, not punch," I said, "Okay, how about Gazpacho and cheese straws?" Of course it took all the demitasse cups in the city of Dallas and my baker almost resigned, but it was a welcome change from punch and cookies.

So if you are "the committee," give them something different. If it is an afternoon reception for women where no alcohol is served, why not a crystal cup of fruit ice, such as strawberry or lemon, and some thin chocolate cookies and candied ginger or glazed cashew nuts; or a demitasse cup of a mushroom consommé with thin shrimp butter sandwiches and a toasted rolled asparagus sandwich and small French lemon tarts; or a cup of Senegalese served with small cream puff shells filled with smoked salmon or caviar mousse, and black olives rolled in oil and vinegar dressing and chopped parsley.

I like to serve a Champagne Peach and almond-flavored rich cookies sprinkled with slivered almonds (*Helen Corbitt's Cookbook*, page 303); or sugared orange sections in Lillet (an orange-flavored vermouth); or Coffee Punch and all kinds of little sandwiches. If men are about, I find they will gather around a Coffee Punch table or the soup tables. Of course, if at all possible, I think every reception should have a tea table for those like me who like tea in the afternoon.

I have had tea every afternoon of my life since I was old enough to have "cambric tea"; tea is a great pick-me-up. If you are in hot country, iced tea should be present.

Late receptions can follow the same practice: a hot soup (regardless of its kind, if you put the soup in your blender, you do not need to provide spoons), simple thin bread-and-butter sandwiches, coffee and Sanka. Coffee Punch is good for this time of day too. Thin slices of White Chocolate Cake would make anyone have pleasant dreams.

With the change in our way of living, teas have become more geared to special events. A Christmas Holiday Tea, a debutante tea or one welcoming new members to a woman's club — they can be done with a thought to not serving what our mothers did.

A Christmas Holiday Tea

Strained oyster bisque served from a punch bowl into
demitasse cups
Roquefort cheese straws
Sparkling wine bottles surrounded by ice in a punch bowl,
with stemmed glasses
Open-face white meat chicken salad sandwiches with
orange cranberry relish in center of sandwich
Nut bread with preserved ginger and butter sandwiches
Rolled mushrooms and Muenster cheese sandwiches to toast
Curried crabmeat salad Rollwitches
Warm rum cake
Orange pecans
Melba grapefruit sections
Divinity fudge
Tea and Coffee

The above menu was prepared; then we had a snowstorm. The party
had to be canceled, but everything was frozen and used at a later time.
So life isn't as complicated as it might be.

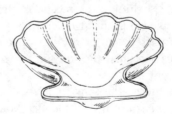

A few years ago I was asked to cater a debutante tea, a high tea.
When we arrived to assemble the party I found that the florist had used
almost the entire table for the centerpiece, a gazebo. What to do? I
dashed home and took all my trays, large and small, that were on bases,
for if we were to use the table everything had to be elevated. The final

effect was lovely and also created the illusion of much more food. Waldo Stewart, do you remember?

A High Tea Menu

Creamed white meat of chicken and lobster in Parmesan
toasted small patty shells (I always dig out the center,
so only the shell remains)
Mushroom ramekins
Honeydew melon balls, rolled in prosciutto
Rolled watercress sandwiches
Open-face chicken salad sandwiches with strawberry halves
(flat side up) on top
Twisted parslied rolls, oven-buttered
Coffee angel food balls rolled in Coffee Butter Icing
with toasted almonds
Little cakes filled with chocolate fudge and the caps iced
in pastel fondant
Pecan Dainties
Tea and Coffee

A New Members Tea

Fresh orange juice with orange ice
Crabmeat and Almonds in Cream for small pastry cups
Avocado balls in Lime French Dressing
Open-face cucumber and Roquefort cheese sandwiches
Small cream puffs filled with Curried Chicken Mousse
Filbert Cookies   Pecan Puffs   Rolled cookies
Tea and Coffee

A Simple Tea for a Few

Golden Spike
Rolled cranberry butter sandwiches
Canned large mushrooms filled with Guacamole
Cucumber cups filled with seafood salad
Small orange brioche
Cake of Many Flavors
Tea and Coffee

STUFFED SHRIMP
(for 36 shrimp)

36 large shrimp in the shell
 4 cups chopped cooked shrimp
 1 teaspoon salt
½ teaspoon white pepper
 1 teaspoon lemon juice
½ tablespoon onion juice
⅔ cup soft white bread crumbs

1 tablespoon chopped parsley
1 cup thick white sauce (3 tablespoons butter, 3 tablespoons
   flour, 1 cup milk)
Pinch of paprika
Buttered crumbs

Wash and remove "feathers" from shrimp. Split down center back, remove intestinal vein, flatten and loosen meat from shell, leaving the tail on. Wash and drain. Mix rest of ingredients and pile on the shrimp. Sprinkle lightly with buttered crumbs. Bake at 350° for 10 minutes.

BUTTERFLY SHRIMP

24 large shrimp, about 2 pounds, shelled and deveined
2 tablespoons soy sauce
2 teaspoons sherry
1 teaspoon salt
½ teaspoon grated ginger

3 eggs, whites beaten separately
3 tablespoons cornstarch
3 tablespoons flour
3 tablespoons cold water
Bowl of ice
Peanut oil

Cut shrimp halfway through on inside curve, spread out to form a butterfly. Pour over the marinade (soy sauce, sherry, salt, ginger). Marinate for 30 minutes. Remove and dry thoroughly on paper towels. Mix a batter with the egg yolks, cornstarch, flour and water. Fold in egg whites. Place in a bowl of ice to keep cold. I add a couple of ice cubes to be sure the batter is cold. Dip the shrimp in the batter and coat well. Heat at least 2 inches of peanut oil to 350°. Fry until golden brown. Serve at once with a Hot Mustard Dip. I make mine by stirring dry mustard into the syrup left from pickled peaches or watermelon.

I also use this batter for the Special Chicken with Almonds recipe.

There is just no way to prepare cream cheese better than a mousse.

CREAM CHEESE MOUSSE

Put 1 6-ounce package cream cheese, ½ cup jellied beef consommé, ¼ teaspoon curry powder, 1 garlic clove in the blender and blend thoroughly. Remove, add 2 tablespoons red caviar and 1 teaspoon lemon juice, 1 tablespoon chopped chives. Use to fill: small cream puffs, cherry tomatoes, or use as a filling for split cooked shrimp (the round side) or for sandwiches or canapés. You may put into a ring mold and serve as a salad. Be sure you do not break the caviar eggs.

MELON BOAT

I think the most beautiful first course is a melon boat. When a guest comes into a dining room and sees this on the table, he is sure the meal to follow will be perfect. You use whatever melon you wish, but honeydew, casaba or Spanish makes a prettier boat than cantaloupe. Remove the seeds. Section the melon in sixths or eighths, depending on the size of the melon. Take a sharp knife and cut the meat of the melon in one whole slice away from the rind, leaving it on the rind; then cut this slice of melon into 1-inch pieces and push out each piece about 1 inch in opposite directions. This forms a wide bed on which to pile other pieces of fruit. Regardless of what kind of fruit you use, cut in definable pieces — halves of large strawberries, sections of oranges or grapefruit, chunks of pineapple, slices of peaches or plums, etc. Pile as high and wide as you wish.

Cover with clear plastic wrap and chill. Place on serving plates; I like crystal. Decorate with fresh mint, a slice of orange, half of a lime, a small cluster of sugared grapes or fresh flowers. Pass Poppy Seed Dressing or Hot Grenadine or both. Even the melon cut as described looks better than a plain section of melon. Looks like more food too.

I have many recipes for orange nut breads, but I find that Derelys Hungarland in Huntsville, Texas, has a better one. It freezes well and can be sliced very thin for sandwiches. Plain sweet butter or cream cheese and preserved ginger makes yummy sandwiches. You can make the sandwiches, wrap in plastic, and either refrigerate or freeze.

ORANGE NUT BREAD
(2 *loaves*)

1 cup water   2 teaspoons soda
Outer peelings from 4 to 5 oranges

Boil until tender, drain and mash. Add:

¾ cup water   1 cup sugar

Cook until consistency of thick apple sauce — almost crystallized. Set aside. Mix:

1 cup sugar	3 teaspoons baking powder
2 eggs, well beaten	2 tablespoons melted butter
1 cup milk	½ teaspoon salt
3¼ cups flour	1 cup broken nutmeats

When mixed thoroughly, combine with the peel mixture. Mix well but do not beat. Pour into two well-buttered loaf tins and bake at 325° for 35 to 40 minutes or until a cake tester comes out clean.

CHAMPAGNE PUNCH
(for 50)

1 quart sauterne   2 quarts champagne
2 cups brandy   1 quart sparkling water

Mix wine and brandy. Pour over block of ice; add champagne and sparkling water. Serve at once.

CORN SOUFFLE

4 packages frozen corn   1 teaspoon salt
1 tablespoon flour   Few drops Tabasco
6 egg yolks   ¼ cup butter, melted
2 cups milk   4 egg whites, beaten stiff
1 tablespoon sugar

Defrost and drain corn. Chop fine or put in blender for 30 seconds. Remove to bowl. Add flour. Beat the egg yolks; add to them the milk, sugar, salt and corn and flour. Mix only. Add Tabasco and the melted butter. Beat the egg whites and fold into the corn mixture. Bake at 350° for 45 to 50 minutes. Serve immediately!

WEDDING OR RECEPTION PUNCH
(for 50)

¾ cup sugar   1½ cups orange juice
Juice of 3 lemons   1½ cups Cointreau
  2 quarts of fresh strawberries or 3   3 bottles champagne, ⅘ quart
    10-ounce packages of frozen   1½ quarts sparkling water
    sliced strawberries

Dissolve the sugar in lemon juice. Slice berries. Add with orange juice and Cointreau to sugar mix. Chill for 1 or 2 hours. Pour into a punch bowl, add champagne and sparkling water.

BEIGNETS SOUFFLES

A light airy pastry that makes an impression on guests, but if you have a crowd, have someone prepare them for you.

1 cup water	4 eggs
½ cup butter	1 teaspoon vanilla or rum
1 teaspoon sugar	Deep fat or oil
¼ teaspoon salt	Confectioners' sugar
1 cup plus 2 tablespoons flour	

Bring water, butter, sugar and salt to a fast boil. Remove from heat and add flour all at once and beat. Cook over low heat until dough leaves side of pan and forms a ball. Remove and add eggs one at a time, beating after each addition. Beat until batter is smooth and glassy-looking. Add flavoring. Heat oil to 365° and drop batter by a teaspoon into the fat; fry until golden brown. Drain on paper towels. Sprinkle with confectioners' sugar. Serve hot or warm, but not cold. You may use as a dessert with a hot Vanilla or Lemon Sauce.

CHICKEN HUNTER STYLE

This preparation I have found to be popular all times of the day, even for breakfast. Men like it, and a confirmed novice cannot fail in its preparation. For a cocktail table you need to serve many pieces. I have used this style for drumsticks, wings and veal cutlets. I also butterfly a leg of lamb and cook it Hunter Style.

¼ cup butter	1 clove garlic, crushed
2 tablespoons olive oil	1 cup fresh mushrooms or canned
8 chicken breasts (whole or halves), 6- or 8-ounce size	1 cup dry sauterne
½ cup flour	1 cup chicken or beef consommé
1 teaspoon salt	1 cup diced peeled and seeded fresh tomatoes
¼ teaspoon white pepper	¼ cup chopped parsley
1 cup sliced spring onions, white part only	Salt and pepper

Melt butter, add olive oil. Remove skin from chicken; dust lightly in flour, salt and white pepper. Shake off any excess. Brown lightly in the butter and oil. Remove. In the same pan, sauté the onions, garlic and mushrooms until soft. Pour in rest of ingredients and the chicken; simmer until sauce is thickened. Correct seasonings. You may put in a casserole and finish in the oven. You may do ahead and reheat. In fact, the chickens have more flavor if you do. They freeze well.

If preparing the lamb, I have the butcher bone and butterfly a leg. I rub the lamb on each side with butter and oil and broil for 15 minutes, then finish on top of the stove basting with the sauce made from rest of ingredients. Slice thin and serve with the sauce.

In using chicken legs and wings, I use 2 dozen with the amounts for 8 — and add more wine or consommé, if needed, as they simmer.

I do shrimp also, only cook the sauce separately and add uncooked shrimp to simmer 6 minutes.

JELLIED WATERCRESS SOUP

The simple way to make jellied watercress soup is to mince the watercress (leaves only) and add to jellied chicken consommé (canned), so why bother any other way? Serve with a twist of lemon.

BREAST OF CHICKEN IN CREAM AND APPLES

8 6- or 8-ounce chicken breasts, or   1½ cups cider
   8 halves of broiling-sized   ½ cup brandy
   chicken, dusted with flour   2 cups whipping cream
8 tablespoons butter   Salt and pepper
4 tablespoons minced onion
8 peeled fresh apple rings, ½ inch
   thick

Sauté the chicken breasts in the butter with the onion over low heat. Poach the apple rings in the cider until soft. Add brandy to the chicken and ignite. (Always light brandy and burn off; you will destroy the raw taste of the brandy.) Add cider left from poaching the apples. Cook at low heat until chicken is tender, about 10 minutes. Add cream and continue cooking until the sauce is thickened. Season to your taste. Place chicken on serving platter, a slice of apple on each piece, and pour sauce over all. Run under broiler to brown.

I served this frequently when I wished to impress guests both at Nei-man-Marcus and at home. Someone always accuses me of being extrava-gant enough to serve pheasant. Why disillusion them? Anyhow you may do pheasant or guinea hen this way with success, but I always marinate these birds in a dry white wine for a few hours or overnight.

STRAWBERRY MELBA

1 quart fresh strawberries	1 cup whipping cream, whipped
½ cup sugar	2 quarts vanilla ice cream

Wash and hull strawberries; mash with sugar. Fold into whipped cream. Put whipped cream mixture over the ice cream. Cover with Strawberry Melba Sauce.

Sauce:

1 tablespoon cornstarch	2 cups frozen raspberries
1 tablespoon sugar	1 pint fresh strawberries, crushed
⅓ cup honey	1 tablespoon lemon juice

Mix cornstarch, sugar and honey. Add raspberries and cook until clear. Cool. Strain, add strawberries and lemon juice.

SPRITZERS

Usually served in a tall glass; they will last longer than champagne. Pour about 6 ounces of California white or Rhine wine over ice, add a lemon peel and fill up with club soda. Or you may serve in a stemmed glass, using lesser amounts of the ingredients. They are cool and especially good for a summer wedding or reception.

This is a favorite buffet dinner recipe because it can be done ahead of time and reheated.

TARRAGON ROASTED CHICKEN

4 2- to 2½-pound chickens or Rock Cornish hens
2 teaspoons salt
½ teaspoon white pepper
8 fresh tarragon sprigs or 2 teaspoons dried tarragon

½ cup butter, melted
1 cup chicken broth
1 cup dry sauterne or broth
1 cup cream (you may omit)

Wash and dry chickens. Rub with salt and pepper inside and out. Place 2 sprigs of tarragon inside each cavity, or if using dried, mix with the salt and pepper. Tie the legs together and pour the butter over each. Place in a 400° oven and roast for about 1 hour, basting frequently with the chicken broth and wine. Remove chickens, let cool enough to handle them, then cut backbone out and disjoint. Reduce liquid left in pan to one-half, add cream and bring to a boil. Strain, correct seasonings and serve over the chicken. If you do not wish the cream, merely strain the liquid left in pan.

FRESH FRUIT PUNCH

Punch comes from a Hindu word meaning "5," so a fruit punch should have at least five ingredients. This is my favorite of the moment.

3½ cups sugar
1 pint hot tea
2 cups lemon juice
3 quarts orange juice (I use frozen, but dilute with pineapple juice in place of water.)
1 quart ginger ale

1 cup shredded fresh pineapple
1 cup sliced fresh fruit: peaches, strawberries, nectarines, orange sections, white grapes, whatever is available.
Fresh mint

Dissolve sugar in hot tea. Cool and add next 5 ingredients. Pour over a block of ice made from the punch recipe. Garnish with mint.

STUFFED MACARONI WITH SPINACH
AND CHICKEN LIVERS

12 No. 20 macaroni shells
3 quarts boiling water
1 teaspoon salt
1 teaspoon salad oil
1 pound spinach, fresh preferred
2 cups dry cottage or Ricotta
  cheese
½ cup grated Parmesan cheese

1 pound chicken livers
2 eggs, lightly beaten
Pinch of nutmeg
Salt and pepper
2 cups thin cream sauce (2 tablespoons butter, 2 tablespoons
  flour, 2 cups milk)
1 cup grated Gruyère cheese

Cook macaroni in the boiling water with salt and oil *al dente,* 15 minutes. Drain, wash and drain again. Wash spinach and put in a covered pot; cook 1 minute only. Drain and put in blender until chopped, but not liquid. Mix with the Parmesan cheese. Sauté the chicken livers in a little butter; slice. Add to the cheese mixture with the eggs and nutmeg. Mix thoroughly. Season to your taste. Stuff the mixture into the cooked macaroni and place in a buttered shallow casserole. Pour over the cream sauce (seasoned with salt and pepper). Sprinkle with the Gruyère cheese and bake. This is a rich delicious pasta, and one shell should be enough. I usually add a few more so the men can have two.

CHAMPAGNE SAUCE FOR HAM

When ham regardless of kind is ready for oven (in a roasting pan), pour 1 bottle champagne over and marinate for several hours (overnight). Bake in a 350° oven and baste with all of the marinade. About 1 hour before finishing, rub ham with either maple syrup or white Karo and continue to baste. Remove, strain fat from the juices and slightly thicken with arrowroot (1 teaspoon to 1 cup of liquid).

CURRIED SMOKED TURKEY

Slice smoked or roast turkey in thin slices; place overlapping in either a casserole or on a serving tray. Then pour either a lightly curried cream sauce or mushroom sauce over. This looks like a much more compli-cated entrée. Somehow when you dice the turkey and add to a sauce, it usually falls into a "oh we had creamed chicken" category.

GOLDEN SPIKE

For a change and good for large occasions. Half fill a blender with crushed ice and pour in 3 jiggers of vodka and 3 jiggers of orange juice. Blend 30 seconds and pour into stemmed glasses. Nice for a morning wedding or any time.

SOUFFLEED CRACKERS

Split Boston common crackers or water crackers. Soak in ice water to cover for 8 minutes. Drain. Dot with butter and bake at 450° until puffed. When nearly brown, reduce heat and bake until dry inside.

CORNED BEEF BRISKET WITH ORANGES

1 4-pound corned beef brisket	¼ cup brown sugar
2 oranges, sliced	1 tablespoon pickling spices
1 lemon, sliced	Brown sugar
2 peeled onions, sliced	

Cover beef with cold water, bring to a boil and skim. Add rest of ingredients. Simmer at medium heat until tender, about 4 hours. Remove, sprinkle with brown sugar and bake at 350° until sugar melts. Slice thin and serve hot or cold.

GALANTINE OF TURKEY
(for 8 to 12)

1 12- to 16-pound turkey	⅛ teaspoon mace
Meat from legs and wings	2 teaspoons salt
1 pound lean veal	¼ teaspoon thyme
1 pound lean pork	Chicken broth
½ pound cooked smoked tongue or ham, slivered	1 carrot
½ cup pistachio nuts	1 onion
1 truffle, diced	Few sprigs parsley

Have the butcher bone the turkey. (He will for a smile.) Lay the turkey out flat on a double thickness of cheesecloth. Remove the meat from the legs and cut off the wings, leaving enough skin to cover the openings. Grind this meat with the veal and pork. Mix with the tongue, nuts, truffle and seasonings. Spread the mixture onto the boned turkey. Roll up and fasten together with toothpicks or sew with a heavy thread. Place in a kettle and cover with chicken broth and vegetables. Simmer at low heat for 2 hours. Remove. Refrigerate, weighing it down with a heavy plate. Let stand overnight. Strain the broth and proceed with any aspic, if you wish it in aspic. (You could ask your best hotel or club chef to do the whole bit for you, but why?) Anyhow, regardless of who does it, slice and form back into the original shape. Decorate with slices of fresh fruit. I like it sliced, no aspic, and with melon and bunches of sugared grapes.

SANDWICH LOAF

A sophisticated approach to the sandwich business is to buy a 10- or 12-inch round loaf of bread. Cut the top off about 1 inch from the edge of the loaf. Then scoop out all the bread inside, leaving only the shell. (Make Caramel Bread Pudding out of it or crumbs to freeze.) Prepare your small sandwiches and pile into the empty bread shell. Cover with the top, plastic wrap and refrigerate or freeze. When you serve put the whole loaf on the table. This method keeps the sandwiches moist. I usually stand the top against the side and put it back on if there is a lull in service. You can keep the bread shell and freeze for future use, and it is always a conversation piece. Make two — you will need for refills.

EASY WHITE SANGRIA

1 whole orange	1 quart sparkling water
1 whole lemon	Vodka (you may omit)
½ cup sugar	
2 bottles white Burgundy wine,	
⅘ quart	

Slice the orange and lemon in very thin slices. Remove seeds. Add sugar and crush together. Pour in wine and chill several hours. Strain; pour over ice and add sparkling water. Add 1 cup vodka if you wish.

CRISP CRACKERS

Split water crackers or saltines in half. Spread generously with butter and
bake at 450° until delicately browned.

RICE AND CHEESE CASSEROLE

3 cups sour cream
1 4-ounce can green chile peppers,
  sliced and chopped, no seeds

4 cups cooked rice, packed
Salt and pepper
¾-pound Cheddar cheese, grated

Mix sour cream and peppers. Season rice with salt and pepper. Put a
layer of rice in bottom of a 1½-quart casserole, then a layer of sour cream
and a layer of cheese. Repeat with cheese on top. Bake at 350° until
bubbly. Make ahead of time, refrigerate and bake when ready to serve.

NOODLES A LA CREME

1 pound vermicelli noodles,
  cooked and drained
½ pound bacon, cooked crisp and
  crumbled
3 cups creamy cottage cheese
3 cups sour cream
2 cloves garlic, crushed

2 cups finely chopped onion
1 tablespoon Worcestershire
  sauce
2 teaspoons salt
3 tablespoons horseradish
½ cup grated Parmesan cheese

Mix all the ingredients except the Parmesan cheese. Put into a buttered
3-quart casserole. Cover with Parmesan cheese and bake at 350° for 40
minutes or until hot and bubbly.

SPINACH RING WITH CELERY AND PEANUTS

2 quarts chopped raw spinach,
  about 3 pounds
2 10-ounce cans cream of
  mushroom soup

4 eggs
Pinch of nutmeg
Salt and pepper

Chop spinach fine and mix with the soup, beaten eggs and nutmeg.

Season with salt and pepper. Pour into a greased 2½-quart ring mold. Bake at 325° until firm. Turn out on serving tray and fill center with:

Celery and Peanuts:

2 tablespoons butter	2 cups peanuts, dry roasted
2 tablespoons flour	6 cups slivered celery, steamed
2 cups half-and-half or milk	Chopped parsley

Melt the butter, add flour, cook until bubbly. Pour in half-and-half, cook until thick. Add peanuts and celery. Season and sprinkle with chopped parsley. Especially good with any ham preparation and strictly Southern, ma'am.

BUTTERMILK BISCUITS
(*makes 12 large or 24 small biscuits*)

2 cups sifted flour	¼ cup cold shortening
½ teaspoon baking soda	1 cup cold buttermilk or sour
2 teaspoons baking powder	milk
1 teaspoon salt	

Sift dry ingredients together and cut in shortening until mealy. Add milk and mix quickly. Knead very lightly on a floured board. Pat to ½-inch thickness and cut with floured biscuit cutter. Place in greased pan close together for crust on top and bottom only; put far apart if crust is desired on sides also. Bake at once in 450° oven for 12 minutes or until brown.

SCALLOPS RAMAKI

Boiling water	24 whole water chestnuts
12 slices bacon	2 tablespoons soy sauce
24 sea scallops	½ cup dry white wine

Pour boiling water over bacon and let stand 5 minutes; drain and dry. Stretch the bacon as long as you can and then cut each slice in half. Wrap around a scallop and a water chestnut and secure with a toothpick. Cover with the soy sauce and wine in a shallow pan. Marinate for several hours. Remove and put in a 350° oven until bacon has cooked.

Remove toothpicks and replace with fresh or plastic ones. Serve hot. These are better than the old stand-by of bacon and chestnuts with chicken livers.

The Bakery restaurant in Chicago does a filet of sole in pastry that is superb. Louis Szathmary is an old friend of mine but he would not give me the recipe. Here is my interpretation. I have made it into either individual servings for a fish course or an entrée or into a large serving, sliced and served with either a Seafood or Caper Sauce (depending on my budget).

So with apologies to Louis:

FILET OF SOLE IN PASTRY

2 pounds cooked filets of sole or any white fish	Homemade mayonnaise
	Salt and pepper
1 cup finely diced celery	Pastry for 2-crust pie
½ cup finely chopped parsley	1 egg yolk
¼ cup finely minced onion	2 tablespoons cold water

Flake the fish and mix with the celery, parsley, onion and enough mayonnaise only to hold together. Season with salt and pepper. Roll out pie crust on a floured board or foil. Form the fish mixture into the shape of a fish in the center of the pastry (swimming, not sleeping), overlapping the pastry on top of the shaped fish. With the scraps of pastry fashion a tail and fins and fasten to the fish by moistening with cold water and pressing into the pastry. Press with a fork to resemble the ridges in the fins and tails. Snip the pastry here and there with manicure scissors to resemble scales. Place on a slightly greased baking sheet and bake at 400° for 20 minutes. Brush with the egg-water mixture and return to oven to bake an additional 10 minutes or until pie crust is done.

GREEN PEAS WITH LEEKS

6 leeks	¼ cup plus 2 tablespoons butter
4 cups green peas (about 3 pounds fresh or 3 packages frozen)	⅓ cup boiling water
	Salt and pepper

Trim the roots of leeks and cut off the tops, leaving 1 inch of the leaves.

Wash thoroughly under cold running water many times. Slice thin and steam in your steamette 5 minutes or cook covered in very little water about 8 to 10 minutes. Put the peas in a shallow skillet with the ¼ cup butter until butter is melted and peas are covered. Add boiling water. Cover the peas and cook 10 minutes, shaking frequently to keep them moving. If you cook them in your steamette for about 8 minutes, add the butter only at the end. Put peas in serving container and pile the leeks in the center, or around the peas, but do not mix. Do the same with green beans in place of peas.

BRAVE BULL

Mix equal parts of Tequila and Kahlua and pour over ice. Add a few twists of lemon peel and stir well. Pour into old-fashioned glasses with an ice cube.

SENEGALESE

3 tablespoons butter	1 cup finely slivered cooked
3 teaspoons curry powder	white meat of chicken
3 tablespoons flour	Salt and pepper
4½ cups chicken broth	1 tablespoon chives
1½ cups whipping cream	

Melt butter, add curry powder and cook 1 minute. Stir in flour; cook until bubbly. Pour in broth. Cook until thickened, stirring with a French whip. Add cream and heat, but do not boil. Add chicken and chill. Season when cold.

CHAMPAGNE PEACH
(1 for each guest)

1 ripe Freestone peach, peeled
Crushed ice   Champagne, chilled

I like to use a whole peach, but you could slice and use less. Pile into a saucer wine glass. Cover with crushed ice and pour the champagne over. Or half fill a punch bowl with sliced peaches and proceed. The peaches must be sweet and the champagne not too dry.

I recommend this coffee punch for all occasions: cocktail parties, weddings, teas, receptions. High calorie, but you will find men will sometimes like it better than whiskey.

COFFEE PUNCH
(for 50)

2 gallons strong coffee (I add 2
tablespoons instant Espresso to
the coffee), cooled
2 gallons vanilla ice cream

1 pint half-and-half
Sugar to taste
2 bottles Cognac or brandy, ⅘
quarts

Freeze 1 quart of the coffee in a ring mold. Pour the rest into a punch bowl. Add ice cream, cream, sugar and frozen coffee. Stir well and add Cognac.

Mrs. John Yeazel from Omaha, Nebraska, sent me this recipe for which I will be eternally grateful.

WHITE CHOCOLATE CAKE

1 cup butter
2 cups sugar
4 eggs
¼ pound white chocolate melted
in ½ cup boiling water

2½ cups cake flour
1 teaspoon soda
1 cup buttermilk
1 teaspoon vanilla

Cream butter and sugar. Add eggs one at a time, beating well after each addition. Cool the melted chocolate in the water and add to the egg mixture. Add the flour, soda and buttermilk alternately to the chocolate mixture. Stir in the vanilla. Pour into well-buttered layer cake pans and bake 40 minutes at 350° or until done. You may vary this recipe by the following:

Add only egg yolks to butter and sugar. Use baking powder in place of soda. Then add beaten egg whites to mixture just before vanilla. Fold in 1 cup finely chopped pecans and 1 cup coconut. Bake in 2 layers. Frost with Colonnade Icing (*Helen Corbitt's Cookbook*, page 252) or Chocolate Fudge Icing.

ROLLWITCHES
(for want of a better name)

For this hors d'oeuvres I use canned biscuits. I split each in half, press my thumb in the middle to make an indentation and fill with crabmeat, lobster, tuna fish, shrimp, chicken or ham salad with a little curry powder added to the mayonnaise (especially if I am using seafood). I then cover generously with grated Gruyère cheese and bake according to directions on package. These are good! I know that when I have them on a cocktail buffet, as I do when I'm in a hurry, I need lots — and someone to keep them coming out of the oven.

CRABMEAT AND ALMONDS IN CREAM

3 tablespoons butter	2 tablespoons flour
½ cup slivered toasted almonds	1½ cups half-and-half
1 cup crabmeat	Salt and white pepper

Melt the butter, add almonds and brown. Add the crabmeat and sauté 1 minute, fork stirring. Stir in flour, cook 1 minute. Add half-and-half and cook until thickened, fork stirring so you will not mash the crabmeat. Season with salt and pepper. Keep heated over hot water. For variations: substitute chicken for the crabmeat; add ½ teaspoon curry powder to the butter; pour in 2 tablespoons sherry if you wish the flavor of wine.

Tom Hunt, one of my cooking school angels, brings me these for Christmas. I do not give a single one away, but keep them all for me.

FILBERT COOKIES

1 pound shelled filberts, not blanched, but coarsely ground (2 pounds filberts in shell will equal 1 pound shelled filberts)	1 pound light brown sugar 4 egg whites, stiffly beaten 1 teaspoon vanilla Granulated sugar

Mix ground filberts and brown sugar thoroughly. Add beaten egg whites and vanilla; mix very well. The batter should be stiff enough to leave side of bowl clean; if not, add a small amount of ground pecans or English walnuts. Shape into marble-sized balls, roll in granulated sugar, and bake on greased cookie sheets 15 minutes in 350° oven. These will brown very slightly with the top showing lots of cracking.

PECAN PUFFS

½ cup butter
4 tablespoons granulated sugar
1 teaspoon vanilla

1 cup pecans, ground
1 cup sifted cake flour
Confectioners' sugar

Cream butter and granulated sugar; add vanilla. Mix together pecans and flour and add to butter mixture. Roll into small balls and bake on cookie sheet in 350° oven for 12 to 15 minutes. While still hot roll in confectioners' sugar.

CAKE OF MANY FLAVORS

Use your favorite white cake recipe or mix and prepare six or seven thin layers. Make a Butter Cream Icing and flavor lightly with Jamaica rum. On the first layer sprinkle Crème de Cacao, then ice with the Butter Cream. Repeat layers with a different liqueur sprinkled on each. Cover the entire cake with the Butter Cream Icing. It depends on how many liqueurs you have and how heavy your hand is for the flavors of the cake, but it is one you will enjoy — but not for children. A nice cake for celebrations.

Holidays: Christmas, Fourth of July, St. Patrick's and Others

NEW YEAR'S EVE is a happy wind-up of a season — what with Bowl Games, many parties, a hectic week of putting away the trappings of the holidays, and the optimistic beginning of a new year. Your entertaining could be a seated dinner or an informal pick-up supper to kick the gong around.

New Year's Eve Dinner

Beef and mushroom pie
Cauliflower and snipped green beans
Hearts of palm and avocado salad, Oil and Lemon Juice Dressing
Cheeses and hard rolls
Champagne Mousse with puréed strawberries
Champagne

New Year's Eve Supper

Split pea soup made with smoked turkey
Corn Bread (*Helen Corbitt's Cookbook*, page 237)
Roast loin of pork stuffed with prunes and apples
Escalloped Oysters and Eggplant
(*Helen Corbitt's Cookbook*, page 171)
Raw relishes in ice
Fresh fruit bowl

And if you are superstitious you should have black-eyed peas (Texas caviar) as an extra vegetable and a can of them to give each departing guest. They will bring good luck for the coming year.

My favorite holiday to celebrate is March 17, Saint Patrick's Day. Ireland is a country that has such soft-spoken people even though they have fiery political differences. March 17 is usually a fun-filled day for everyone, Gaelic or not. I think everyone feels the Irish have a secret. They do.

This is my usual celebration supper that begins and ends with the supper on the table; my guests eat all evening.

Saint Patrick's Day Supper

Cream of corn soup
Smoked salmon (if I have a few extra dollars around,
if not a cold salmon mousse)
Hot corned beef
Hot horseradish apples
Creamy cole slaw
Blarney cheese
Wheat and rye breads
Trifle
Irish Coffee

Easter Sunday Dinner

Fresh pineapple boat with lime syrup
Rack of Lamb Dijon
Rice with pine nuts
Minted scallions and peas
Crescent rolls
Lemon Custard Pie

It really is spring during the month of May. The joy of color is never so true as in May. Perhaps a

May Day Luncheon

Avocado halves filled with cold fruit soup
Crabmeat Chantilly
Mushroom crumbed asparagus
Bowknot parslied rolls
Lemon Soufflé with almond-flavored
English Custard

Fourth of July

Why not an old-fashioned celebration for neighbors and relatives? Out of doors, games and songs — a picnic supper.

Fresh vegetables kept cold in a wheelbarrow
filled with ice
Charcoal broiled flank steaks and hamburgers
Potato salad
French bread and buns to toast
Old-fashioned Strawberry Shortcake
Fresh peach ice cream cones

Labor Day

A back-to-school patio supper for all ages.

Barbecued chicken
Marinated shrimp (to charcoal broil)
Beef tacos
Corn-on-the-cob with Horseradish Butter
Green bean salad
Peasant Bread (see Chapter 13)
Cream Cheese Pears with Hot Fudge Sauce
Cookies

Halloween

My debut as a hostess was a Halloween party for my first grade friends. Along with cream of tomato soup and little sandwiches were served Jack-o-lantern pies: pumpkin pies made in saucers with a Jack-o-lantern face. I remember to this day the excitement of each of us having his own Jack-o-lantern. So impressed was I that I have served them every Halloween Day since: in hospitals, the Houston Country Club, the Zodiac room at Neiman-Marcus, everywhere I've been — and the results are always the same — complete delight regardless of my guests' ages.

Thanksgiving dinner is still evidenced by a plentiful food table even if it means sharing with a televised football game. Although turkey is a year-around bird, you ought to serve it on Thanksgiving if only to keep alive a tradition.

Thanksgiving Dinner

Pink grapefruit and shrimp cocktail with Green Herb Dressing
Roast turkey with Cornbread Dressing
(*Helen Corbitt's Cookbook*, page 101)
Cranberry sauce
Hot kumquats
Scalloped Onions and Almonds (*Helen Corbitt's
Cookbook*, page 191)
Brussels sprouts with brown butter
Knob celery salad
Parker House rolls
Sour Cream Pumpkin Pie
Ambrosia (*Helen Corbitt's Cookbook*, page 343)

As many hosts have become discouraged with fighting the battle between

Thanksgiving football games and dinner, why not try a buffet where everyone can eat, watch, and come and go as they please?

Baked ham with preserved orange sauce
Lobster Tail au Gratin
A super sandwich of: cold sliced turkey with molded cranberry sauce,
thin bread and butter, homemade mayonnaise, pepper and salt
A variety of cheeses with apples and pears
Caramel Soufflé with English Custard
White Chocolate Pound Cake with pecans and coconut

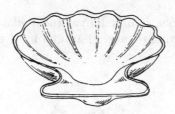

Christmas dinner no longer leaves one gasping for breath from over-indulgence in the great abundance of food. In fact Christmas Eve has become more popular as family and friends are asked to join in a come-and-go evening. The dining should be traditional as to the flavor of the holidays but you do not necessarily have to serve Christmas goose. This menu could be used any time during the holidays; much of the food could be prepared ahead.

Christmas Eve Buffet

Mushroom Consommé
Roast Round of Veal
Scalloped Oysters (*Helen Corbitt's Cookbook*, page 115)
Spinach Crêpes Veronique
Spiced cranberries, sherried prunes and other preserves
Sally Lunn
Fresh pineapple fingers, dusted with chopped pistachios
Pots de Crème

Christmas breakfast was and is more important to me than any other meal of the day. Opening Christmas stockings, filled with small gifts practical or not, makes the day more joyful and should be encouraged.

Christmas Breakfast

Baked apples
Eggs in ramekins
Sausage patties cooked in beer
Spoon Bread
Toasted Stöllen

Serve late-ish. No one is in a hurry, and I like to serve on trays for everyone to help themselves and sit around for lively conversation.

Christmas Day Supper

Jellied madrilene with chives and salted sour cream
Breast of chicken sautéed in curry butter with mushrooms
in sherried cream
Asparagus with grated orange peel
Watercress, julienne beets and celery, Mustardy French Dressing
Chocolate Mousse with Marrons
Christmas cookies
Eggnog (*Helen Corbitt's Cookbook*, page 296)

Very Special Days

Parties for children are indeed fun and gratifying; when children clasp their little hands together and smile their secret smiles, you forget the work involved.

Mindy Is Three

Chicken salad sandwich quarters with animal crackers riding on top
Carrot sticks
Little Princess Sundae

Mindy Is Five

Have a circus party with paper hats and flowers,
serpentine and noise makers
Clown Salads
Grilled cheese sandwiches
Ice Cream Clowns
Clown birthday cake
Pink lemonade

Mindy Is Eight

Box lunch party (Boxes wrapped with gaily colored papers
and decorated with a toy for each guest to take home.)
Small finger rolls filled with peanut butter
Rolls filled with cream cheese and raisins
Cup of red jello cubes
Happy birthday cup cakes
Ice cream served from an ice cream freezer
Chocolate milk

Anniversary Dinner

Gazpacho,
diced cucumbers, chives, tiny croutons to add
Mushroom and watercress crêpes
Sliced double sirloin steak flamed with Cognac
Yellow Squash Soufflé (*Helen Corbitt's Cookbook,* page 174)
Bibb lettuce with Oil and Vinegar Dressing
Pâté de foie gras
Fresh strawberry water ice
Raspberry sauce
Chocolate Thin Cookies

Strange things may happen at a dinner party. I served this menu in my home on an antique table that seated twelve. It was a gay with color and pretty table which slowly sank to the floor as the dinner progressed. We just made it through the dessert before the table gave up and went down completely. The Moral: Be sure of your antiques.

Kentucky Derby Breakfast

Gingered glazed apples
Pot Roasted Quail
Baked country ham with red-eye gravy
Hominy grits soufflé
Fried Green Tomatoes
Hot biscuits and bran muffins
Jams and jellies

Supper on Your Boat

Hot fried chicken (in thermelene containers)
Cold boiled shrimp with lemon mayonnaise and capers
Cold rice salad with peas and chutney
Thin ham sandwiches
Peaches with pear brandy
Orange Marmalade Cookies

Game Dinner

Petite marmite
Chukars with bread dressing
Roast Loin or Rack of Venison
Barley Casserole
Baked acorn squash with chutney
Celery and black olives
Pancake Stack with Lingonberries and Sour Cream

For a change of pace in entertaining, try a Many Mini-Dinner. This is a number of hors d'oeuvres served buffet style with a dessert. For a meal of this type you should allow three of each item for every guest.

I entertained the board of directors and their wives of the National Club Managers Association. I chose to prepare a Mini-Dinner because these guests were all strangers to me and I wished to keep the meal informal. Their reaction was favorable. For a group of strangers in your home, I think it a good kind of dinner to serve, as it keeps everyone busy tasting.

A punch bowl of yogurt soup
Barbecued pork tenderloin with small buttered rolls
Swiss Cheese Ramekins
Shrimp Balls with Hot Mustard Sauce
Ham-Stuffed Mushrooms
King Crab à la Helen
Chicken Yaki-Tori

The dessert table

The Seven Deadly Sins
Hot bourbon peaches

While you might think this would be a lot of work, there is very little actual preparation; what there is can be done ahead of time and finished quickly. I find myself turning to this kind of menu frequently.

CHAMPAGNE MOUSSE

1 cup sugar
3 egg yolks
1 cup pink champagne
1 tablespoon unflavored gelatin

¼ cup champagne
1 cup whipping cream, whipped
3 egg whites

Mix sugar and egg yolks until frothy. Heat the pink champagne and pour into the sugar mixture slowly, beating with a French whip. Cook over hot water until thickened. Dissolve the gelatin in the ¼ cup of champagne and add to the hot mixture. Blend and cool. As the champagne mixture begins to thicken, fold in the whipped cream; beat the egg whites until stiff and fold in last. Pour into a 1½-quart mold and refrigerate or freeze. Serve with puréed and strained fresh or frozen berries of any kind.

SUGAR SYRUP

2 cups boiling water   2 cups granulated sugar

Cook for 15 minutes. Cool and pour into jars to use when needed. Add 2 tablespoons lemon or lime juice to each cup of syrup to use over fruit.

LAMB DIJON

3 tablespoons Dijon mustard
3 teaspoons salt
2 cloves garlic, minced
⅓ cup olive oil

3 single racks of lamb, trimmed
for the oven
1½ cups dry red wine
2 tablespoons honey

Mix mustard, salt, garlic and oil. Rub over the racks and let stand for several hours. Roast at 375° for 40 minutes, basting with the wine and honey. Serve with juices. Cook longer for well done, but I think you will enjoy lamb pink — at least give it a try.

LEMON CUSTARD PIE
(for a 9-inch pie)

The very best pie I ever ate. I made it for a crusty friend who said, "It was so good I'd fight my Daddy for it."

4 large eggs	Grated rind and juice of 1 lemon
1 cup sugar	4 teaspoons butter, just softened
2 teaspoons flour	1 9-inch unbaked pie shell
1 cup Karo (white)	

Beat the eggs, add sugar mixed with the flour. Add rest of ingredients. Pour into shell and bake at 350° for 60 minutes or until knife test shows it is done. Do not refrigerate.

CRABMEAT CHANTILLY

3 tablespoons butter	5 egg whites
3 tablespoons flour	¾ cup mayonnaise
1½ cups milk	¼ cup grated Parmesan cheese
1½ pounds white crabmeat or 3	
7½-ounce cans king crab	

Melt butter, add flour and cook until bubbly. Pour in milk; cook until thick, stirring with a French whip. Add crabmeat and fork stir so as not to mash the crabmeat. Place in a buttered shallow 1½-quart casserole. Beat the egg whites until stiff and fold in the mayonnaise; cover the crabmeat with egg white mixture. Sprinkle with the Parmesan cheese. Place in a 350° oven until hot and run under the broiler to brown.

You may use any white fish, flaked, or lobster. It is a lovely seafood dish. You could extend it with a layer of rice, white or wild, in the casserole before putting in the seafood mixture. I use the same recipe and use creamed sweetbreads and mushrooms over wild rice in place of the seafood. Men like both, but then if food is good, they like everything. (It is their mothers and wives who don't like something or other.)

There is nothing better than a good shortcake, and strawberry or peach is best. I like to make individual ones and serve on 12-inch crystal plates.

OLD-FASHIONED STRAWBERRY SHORTCAKE

2 cups flour
4 teaspoons baking powder
¾ teaspoon salt
⅓ cup sugar
½ cup shortening

½ cup whipping cream or
   half-and-half
¼ cup water
Sugared strawberries

Mix the flour, baking powder, salt and sugar. Cut the shortening in with a blender or two knives. Mix cream and water and stir in quickly. Do not over mix. Dump out on a floured board and pat about 1 inch thick. Cut with a 3- or 3½-inch cutter and put on ungreased cookie sheet about 2 inches apart or drop by heaping tablespoons. Bake at 450° for 15 minutes. Split and butter. Cover first layer with sugared strawberries slightly mashed. Cover with other half and repeat with strawberries. Either be generous with the berries or peaches or don't make it. Serve with whipped or pouring cream. I like this dessert with lemon ice cream between the halves with the berries.

CREAM CHEESE PEARS WITH HOT FUDGE SAUCE

Two canned pear halves filled with softened cream cheese and put together and frozen is an easy dessert. Serve frozen standing upright, with hot fudge sauce over, or any other sauce for that matter, but fudge sauce is best. You may also substitute ice cream for the cheese.

SOUR CREAM PUMPKIN PIE

12 ounces (4 3-ounce packages)
   cream cheese
¾ cup sugar
1½ tablespoons flour
1 teaspoon grated orange peel
½ teaspoon grated lemon peel

2 eggs plus 2 egg yolks
1 cup cooked or canned pumpkin
⅛ teaspoon cinnamon
1 9-inch graham cracker crust,
   unbaked

Blend in your electric mixer the cheese, sugar, flour and grated peels. Add eggs and egg yolks; beat at medium speed until smooth. Mix in pumpkin and cinnamon; continue beating until light and smooth. Pour into prepared crust. Bake at 350° for 40 minutes or until custard is set. Remove and spread with the following mixture:

> 2 cups sour cream   3 tablespoons sugar
> 1 teaspoon vanilla

Bake 10 minutes longer. Remove from oven, cool and spread with a thin layer of cold sour cream.

LOBSTER TAIL AU GRATIN

4 8-ounce lobster tails	Salt and pepper
4 tablespoons butter	¼ cup grated Parmesan cheese
½ pound fresh mushrooms or	2½ cups canned artichoke hearts,
1 cup sliced canned	drained
3 tablespoons flour	1 cup grated Swiss cheese
2 cups milk or half-and-half	Paprika

Boil lobster tails 12 minutes. Remove, cool and split. Remove meat by running your thumb under thick end to loosen, then pull and slice. Melt the butter, add the mushrooms and sauté at medium heat for 5 minutes. Remove mushrooms and add the flour. Cook until bubbly. Add milk and cook until thick, stirring constantly. Season with salt and pepper. Add mushrooms. Spread bottom of a buttered shallow 1½- or 2-quart casserole with half the grated Parmesan. Add lobster, artichokes and Swiss cheese in layers. Cover with mushroom mixture. Sprinkle with remaining Parmesan mixed with a little paprika. Bake at 350° for 30 minutes or until hot and bubbling. Substitute any vegetable for the artichokes and any seafood, chicken, veal or ham for the lobster.

ROAST ROUND OF VEAL

1 10- or 12-pound veal round, *rump and shank off, be sure*	Few sprigs of parsley
	Grated rind and juice of 4 lemons
2 teaspoons white pepper	1 quart dry white wine or water
2 tablespoons salt	¼ cup butter
2 teaspoons ground cinnamon	Arrowroot
3 medium-sized onions	1 lemon, sliced thin
2 carrots	¼ cup finely chopped parsley

Place meat in a roasting pan. Mix together the pepper, salt and cinnamon and heat in a skillet. Pat over the veal. Add the onions, carrots and parsley to the pan. Roast uncovered at 350° for 1 hour. Add lemon peel and juice. Baste frequently with wine or water and juices. Roast until a fork comes out easily when tested (185° on meat thermometer). Strain juices and serve plain or slightly thickened with arrowroot and very thin slices of lemon and the parsley. Let meat rest at least 30 minutes before carving. This is an especially good preparation for a buffet.

Vegetables can be used to greater advantage than we think and with little preparation. I like to put some, like spinach, in crêpes.

SPINACH CREPES VERONIQUE

First, prepare the

Blender Hollandaise:

6 egg yolks	⅛ teaspoon salt
2 tablespoons lemon juice	1 cup melted butter

Warm the blender container with hot water or put in a 250° oven. Put egg yolks in the container with the lemon juice and salt. Cover and set blender on high for 3 seconds. Remove cover and add the melted butter in a steady stream while blender is on high speed; turn off as soon as all the butter has been added.

2 pounds fresh spinach	16 crêpes (2 per person)
¼ cup plus 1 cup whipping cream	1 cup Blender Hollandaise
2 tablespoons butter	2 cups peeled and seeded grapes
Salt and pepper	or canned white grapes
Pinch of nutmeg	

Wash spinach and trim heavy stems. Cook covered without any added water for 1 minute only. Drain and put in blender at medium speed until thoroughly puréed. Put into a skillet with the ¼ cup cream and butter; cook until well blended. Season with salt, pepper and a tiny pinch of nutmeg. Put about 2 tablespoons of spinach mixture into each crêpe and roll loosely. Place in a buttered shallow casserole. Cover with the grapes and the 1 cup cream (whipped) folded into the Hollandaise. Put in a 350° oven for 10 minutes. Run under broiler to brown. The combination of whipped cream and Hollandaise is called Mousseline Sauce.

The easiest dessert to prepare ahead and serve is:

POTS DE CREME
(for 8 except someone always wants 2)

3 cups half-and-half	¼ teaspoon salt
9 egg yolks	1½ teaspoons vanilla
¾ cup sugar	Light brown sugar

Heat the half-and-half. Beat egg yolks with sugar and salt. Beat in the hot half-and-half gradually with a French whip. Add vanilla. Strain and pour into pots de crème cups. Cover the pots and put in a pan of hot water 1-inch deep. Bake at 325° for 30 minutes or until a knife when inserted comes out clean. Remove pots and chill. Place a teaspoon of brown sugar on top of each dessert and run under the broiler to melt; cover and serve. Use the same recipe but change the flavoring; omit the brown sugar (brulée). Add 6 ounces semi-sweet chocolate to the hot milk for Pots de Crème au Chocolat.

STOLLEN (A Christmas Bread)

1 cup raisins	½ cup lightly toasted slivered
½ cup currants	almonds
1 cup mixed candied fruit	1 Basic Bread Recipe (2 loaves)
Cognac	

Cover raisins, currants and fruit with Cognac for at least 1 hour. Drain, mix with nuts and knead into bread dough. Cut dough in half; roll each piece into an oval about ½ inch thick. Fold over almost in half, so that bottom edge extends beyond the top. Lightly roll to set. Place on a buttered baking sheet; allow to rise until puffy. Brush with melted butter. Bake at 375° about 45 minutes until loaves are golden brown. Brush again with melted butter while loaves are warm. Decorate with sugar icing, whole toasted almonds or pecan halves and candied fruit. Wrap in clear plastic until needed or freeze.

LITTLE PRINCESS SUNDAE

Place a ball of ice cream in a meringue shell or on a round of white cake to anchor the ice cream to the plate. Place a tiny doll head (found in variety stores) in the top of the ball. Dribble whipped cream from a pastry tube or an ice tea spoon to make the ice cream ball look like a bouffant skirt. Sprinkle with silver dragees and candied flowers (buy also). You may deep freeze. Place a paper parasol over the head when you serve. Little girls from 3 to 80 love them.

CLOWN SALADS

Use a canned peach or pear half for the body and face; decorate with Maraschino cherries and raisins for a face and buttons. Form the legs, arms and hat with cream cheese.

ICE CREAM CLOWNS

Anchor a ball of ice cream to the plate you serve on with a round of cake or a meringue shell. Put an ice cream cone upside down on top of ball for the hat. Make a face with cherries, pecan halves for the ears, and whipped cream rosettes on the hat.

I find that small decorated birthday cakes appeal to children more than a large one. I usually put the candle in a little wooden or ceramic holder for each guest to take home. Children like to carry away something from a party — either decorations or small gifts make them happier than leaving empty-handed.

POT ROASTED QUAIL

16 or more quail (1 for each guest
   is not enough)
Salt and paprika
½ cup butter, melted
 2 tablespoons salad oil
½ cup sherry

Juice of 2 lemons
2 teaspoons Worcestershire sauce
3 tablespoons flour.
3 cups half-and-half or whipping
   cream

Wash quail and remove any shot if possible. Sprinkle the bird with salt and paprika. Tie with string. Sauté in the butter and oil until brown on all sides. Cover and simmer slowly for 1 hour. Add sherry, lemon juice and Worcestershire. Cook until evaporated. Remove birds and add flour. Cook until bubbly. Add half-and-half; cook until sauce becomes thick. Add quail and reheat.

FRIED GREEN TOMATOES

I was always amazed when customers sent for me to ask if I knew my cook had prepared green tomatoes — even when I had listed this vegetable as green on the menu. Oh well! Anyhow, wash tomatoes, cut in 1-inch-thick slices, dip in flour seasoned with salt and pepper and sauté in melted butter.

ORANGE MARMALADE COOKIES
(*10 dozen medium-sized cookies*)

½ cup butter	½ teaspoon soda
1 cup sugar	½ teaspoon salt
2 eggs, well beaten	1 cup thick orange marmalade
3 cups sifted flour	

Cream shortening, add sugar and cream until light and fluffy. Mix in eggs. Mix flour, soda and salt and stir into egg mixture. Add marmalade and blend. Drop by teaspoonfuls 1 inch apart on well-buttered cookie sheet. For small cookies, a half-teaspoon. Bake at 350° for 12 to 13 minutes. Remove and cool. If you wish, cover with:

ORANGE ICING

¼ cup orange juice	3 tablespoons soft butter
1 teaspoon lemon juice	3 cups confectioners' sugar
2 teaspoons grated orange peel	⅛ teaspoon salt
1 teaspoon grated lemon peel	

Mix juices and grated peels. Cream butter and sugar. Blend with juices. Add salt and mix until smooth.

These cookies keep well in a covered container but disappear quickly.

CHUKARS

8 chukars (Hungarian partridge)	1 egg, slightly beaten
2 cups white bread crumbs	1 clove garlic, minced (if you like)
Grated rind and juice of ½ lemon	Salt and white pepper to taste
⅓ cup melted butter	

Wash and dry chukars. Mix rest of ingredients and stuff lightly into the body cavity and between the skin and the breast. Never pack, but always stuff any bird lightly. Tie with string and roast covered at 325° about 45 minutes. I use my electric skillet for these. Remove and deglaze pan with sherry or brandy. Serve chukars whole with juices.

ROAST LOIN OR RACK OF VENISON

2 loins or racks of venison　　　8 sprigs of parsley
Red wine or half wine and half　½ cup melted butter
　water　　　　　　　　　　　Salt and pepper
2 bay leaves　　　　　　　　　1 cup red wine
2 onions, sliced　　　　　　　　1 cup currant jelly
A few juniper berries　　　　　2 tablespoons arrowroot
8 peppercorns

Cover meat with the red wine; add bay leaves, onions, berries, peppercorns and parsley. Cover and refrigerate for at least 24 hours. Remove,
drain and dry. Sprinkle with salt and pepper and roast uncovered in a
400° oven for 45 minutes. Baste with the strained marinade and butter.
Use a meat thermometer and cook until medium rare (140°). Remove
meat and let rest. Add 1 cup wine and the jelly to juices to make 1 pint
or more of sauce. Add the arrowroot mixed with a little cold water to
make a paste and heat until thickened. Slice meat in thin slices and
serve with sauce, unstrained.

BARLEY CASSEROLE

6 tablespoons butter　　　　　4 cups chicken broth
2 cups barley, not quick-cooking　Toasted chopped almonds or pine
2 cups diced onion　　　　　　　nuts
1 cup diced mushrooms, fresh or
　canned

Melt butter, add barley and brown, stirring constantly. Spoon into a
2½- to 3-quart casserole. Sauté the onion until soft in the butter, and
add. In the same skillet, sauté the mushrooms and add to the barley.
Pour in 2 cups of chicken broth and bake covered at 350° for 45 to 60
minutes. Stir, add rest of broth and continue cooking until liquid is
absorbed and barley is soft. Stir again and if not soft, and it is dry, add
more broth and continue cooking. Just before serving add almonds or
pine nuts.

SWISS CHEESE RAMEKINS
(for 24)

2 eggs
1 cup half-and-half
¼ teaspoon salt
2 cups grated Swiss cheese

¼ teaspoon dry mustard
Pinch of cayenne pepper
Pie crust

Beat eggs, add next 5 ingredients and mix. Pour into ramekin tins lined with pie crust. Bake at 400° for 15 minutes. Lift out of tin with a pointed knife. These are good to serve with cocktails.

HAM-STUFFED MUSHROOMS
(for 24)

½ pound ground cooked ham
1 clove finely minced garlic
1 cup finely minced parsley
1 cup finely minced mushroom
   stems
½ cup fine white bread crumbs

½ cup grated Parmesan cheese
Salt and pepper
24 medium-sized mushrooms
Pine nuts
½ cup butter, melted

Mix ham, garlic, parsley, stems, crumbs and cheese. Taste for more salt and pepper if needed. Stuff the mushrooms (you have removed the stems for mincing). Decorate with the pine nuts. Place in a buttered casserole, pour butter over and bake at 375° for 25 minutes.

CHICKEN YAKI-TORI

6 chicken breasts, 4- or 6-ounce
   size

Sansho pepper
Dry white wine

Remove skin and bone from chicken. Cut white meat into small pieces and thread on bamboo skewers. Sprinkle with the pepper and cover with the wine. Marinate overnight. You may add soy sauce if you wish. Broil about 4 minutes on each side. Sansho is a Japanese pepper and can be found in oriental food shops.

1 2

Luncheons and Dinners
Unobtrusively Low-Calorie

LOW-CALORIE MENUS are not difficult if you remember to omit an excess of butter, cream, high fat foods and starches. The menus can be made interesting in flavor by using whipped butter, fresh or dried herbs, citrus juices and peels, and wine, if you cook with it. Do not drink it!

A sense of humor is necessary — accept your fate! For instance, a heavily decorated table in a room with too many flowers is not compatible with lower-in-calorie foods — and most of all, either keep quiet about dieting or else tell everyone. I prefer the former and find that my guests enjoy themselves. Remember: it isn't always what you eat but how much.

Alcohol is taboo if you are really serious about dieting. The calories count, but most of all your resistance to eating too much is lowered. Conversation and sober elbow lifting can be amazing, given a chance.

BLOODY MARY
(serve in an Old Fashioned glass)

1 stalk celery	Ice cubes
1 finger cucumber	Dash of Worcestershire sauce
1 slice green pepper	Dash of Tabasco
1 scallion	½ cup cold tomato juice

Stand the vegetables up in the glass. Put in 2 or 3 ice cubes, fill up glass with tomato juice. Follow the same procedure with beef consommé and call it the "Virtuous Bull." Use half sauerkraut or clam juice with tomato juice, but serve with the vegetables. For one thing, these drinks keep everyone busy!

Any fresh fruit put into a blender with ice, artificial sweetener and a bit of lemon juice and frappéed, poured into stemmed wine glasses decorated with mint, is refreshing. But serve only one glass, as it does have calories. Unsweetened fruit juices may be treated the same way.

Luncheons

Broiled Danish lobster tails with lemon and chive butter
Fresh spinach soufflé ring filled with shredded yellow squash,
topped with Mint Dressing
Water chestnuts, bean sprouts and Jerusalem Artichoke salad
Vinaigrette Dressing
Greenhouse Orange with Grand Marnier

Molded Gazpacho ring filled with lobster salad
Chicken Sauté with Mushrooms flamed with brandy
Lettuce Soufflé
Snow eggs in Low-Calorie Soft Custard

Artichoke Soup
Marinated tiny shrimp and snow peas in Boston lettuce rose
Homemade Melba toast
Russian Cream with raspberries

Fresh pineapple frappé
(Fresh ripe pineapple put in your blender
with ice and mint.)
Fresh artichoke filled with chicken salad
Mocha Sponge

Hot tomato bouillon
Filet of Sole Mold with Shrimp and Dill Sauce
Zucchini and mushrooms Chinese style
Lemon ice with blueberries

Mushroom Consommé
Lemon broiled Cornish hen
Julienne of carrots and white grapes
Strawberry whip with puréed raspberries

Cold sliced tongue
Eggs en gelée
Celery salad with Mustard Horseradish Dressing
Persimmon ice with mandarin oranges

Chicken gumbo filé
Crudités with dried beef roulades
Lemon Sherbet Mousse with slivered pineapple and ginger

Cold boiled salmon steak with Horseradish Mustard Sauce
Small Swiss Cheese Soufflé
Tomato filled with cold Ratatouille
Sherry lemon parfait

Dinners

Cream of Curry Soup
Cucumber and celery sticks
Roasted Rack of Veal with Chanterelles in pan juices
Salsify Persillade
Zucchini Fans Parmesan
Artichoke heart salad vinaigrette
Warm Fresh Steamed Peaches with Puréed Strawberries

Baked Shrimp with Lime Sauce
Broiled butterfly leg of lamb basted with gin
Stir-Fried Spinach with steamed onion rings
Celery Salad with Mimosa Dressing
Raspberry ice ring filled with fresh fruits in season (strawberries,
blueberries, sliced peaches) and Almond Soft Custard

Iceland Trout with Mustard Sauce
Thin Melba toast
Lemon Broiled Squab Chicken with Papaya
(added the last 10 minutes to the broiling pan)
Spiced yellow squash
Cold fresh artichoke with Sauce Verte
Eggnog Mousse

Chicken Consommé Oriental
Marinated Flank Steak
Chinese Style Vegetables
Sweet red pepper and romaine salad with Sherry French Dressing
Low-Calorie Cheese Cake with raspberry sauce

Fresh asparagus Parmesan
Filet of Sole Roulade filled with Caper Sauce
Artichoke soufflé ring with julienne carrots cooked in vodka
and orange peel
Watercress salad with Vinaigrette Dressing
Fresh fruit and Ricotta cheese
Toasted water crackers

Clam and chicken consommé with sliced mushrooms
Tandoori Roast Chicken
Baked white squash, paprika
Green bean purée
Crudités salad
Apricot Sherbet in orange cups

Jellied chicken consommé with slivers of chicken and salami
Lamb and vegetable kabobs
Carrot pudding
Fresh fruit salad with Apple Dressing
Cold Chocolate Soufflé with Rum Custard

Tuna Surprise
Veal Birds with Mushroom Sauce
Eggplant Provençale
Grapefruit and Spinach Salad with Green Herb Dressing
Pears Alaska

Cold Tomato Soup
Tarragon Roasted Chicken
Braised cucumbers
Dilled green beans with slivered celery
Chinese cabbage with Roquefort Dressing
Hot apricot soufflé

JERUSALEM ARTICHOKE

Strictly American, this vegetable does not look or taste like the green artichoke. Where did the name come from? It belongs to the sunflower family and its name came from the word "girasol" meaning "turning to the sun." You find it in some markets under the name "sun 'chokes." The French found this vegetable among the American Indians, took it back home and improved it through selective breeding. It tastes something like a potato. While potatoes average 279 calories per pound, the artichokes have about 22 calories per pound. Think about it. You may simply wash, slice thin and add Jerusalem artichokes to salads, relish trays, or cook and treat as another vegetable.

Remember, use sparingly when dieting. It is only the flavor that should interest you.

VINAIGRETTE DRESSING

1 tablespoon Dijon mustard	6 tablespoons olive oil
2 tablespoons lemon juice	6 tablespoons salad oil
2 tablespoons vinegar	Salt and pepper

Put all ingredients in a bowl and beat for 1 minute with a French whip. Toss with greens or whatever.

Use it as a base for Mimosa Dressing: add 1 chopped hard-cooked egg white and 2 tablespoons chopped parsley. Add finely diced onion and garlic for a Niçoise Dressing.

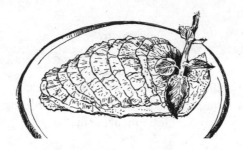

The Greenhouse, a health and beauty spa located between Fort Worth and Dallas, Texas, serves low calorie food to its guests. I have always felt that regardless of what you eat, you enjoy it better if the food is pretty. Guests at The Greenhouse think our way of slicing an orange is beautiful and have named it The Greenhouse Orange. You may use this fruit for any meal. I find men succumb to its beauty with equal enthusiasm.

GREENHOUSE ORANGE

8 navel oranges   Grand Marnier

With a sharp knife, start at the flat end of the orange and peel round and round until you come to the end, leaving about ¼ inch of the peeling on so you can hang onto the orange. If you use a sawing motion instead of a pulling one you will peel it easily. When only the flesh of the orange is showing, start at the peeled end and slice with very thin slices almost all the way through. When you reach the end, take the point of your knife and fan out the slices. I leave the peel end on and place a sprig of fresh mint, a half strawberry or any fresh fruit garnish between the peel and the last slice. Use anything but a maraschino cherry. Sprinkle Grand Marnier or Cointreau over when you use the orange for lunch or dinner.

CHICKEN SAUTE WITH MUSHROOMS

4 2-pound broiling chickens
Flour, salt and paprika
½ cup whipped margarine or
    butter

1½ cups beef consommé
⅓ cup Cognac
8 or 10 large mushrooms
Salt and pepper

Wash, split chickens and remove the back bone and any fat (or have the butcher do it). Sprinkle the chickens very lightly with flour, salt and paprika. Melt the margarine in a skillet and sauté the chicken slowly until brown on both sides. Add the consommé and deglaze the skillet. Heat the Cognac, ignite and pour over the chicken. Cover and cook 20 minutes. Remove cover and cook 5 minutes more, basting with the drippings in the pan. Remove to serving platter, add mushrooms to the pot and cook in drippings for 1 minute or until translucent. Correct seasonings. Pour over the chicken and serve.

This is a popular soufflé at The Greenhouse. You must use iceberg lettuce.

LETTUCE SOUFFLE

1 large head iceberg lettuce, slivered
1 tablespoon grated onion
½ cup whipped butter or margarine
5 tablespoons flour
1½ cups skim milk
6 egg yolks, beaten
Salt and pepper
6 egg whites

Pour boiling water over lettuce and onion; let drain. Melt butter, add flour and cook until bubbly. Pour in milk; cook until smooth and thick. Add egg yolks slowly, beating all the time. Cool, add lettuce and, when you can hold your hand comfortably on bottom of pan, season with salt and pepper. Beat the egg whites until stiff. Stir one third of them into the mixture; fold in the rest. Pour into a buttered 2-quart soufflé dish. Bake at 350° for 35 to 40 minutes.

LOW-CALORIE SOFT CUSTARD

2 cups skim milk   1 teaspoon sugar substitute
4 egg yolks

Heat the milk with the sugar substitute in top of double boiler. Beat the egg yolks until lemon colored; slowly stir milk into the eggs, beating with a French whip. Pour back into top of double boiler and cook over hot water, not boiling, until custard coats the spoon. Add whatever flavoring you wish.

ARTICHOKE SOUP

1 14-ounce can artichoke bottoms
3 10½-ounce cans chicken
   consommé
1 clove garlic (you may omit)

Approximately 1 cup dry white
   wine
Salt and pepper

Mash the artichoke bottoms. Add the consommé and garlic. Bring to a
boil. Pour in the wine, reheat, season with salt and pepper, and a dash
of Tabasco if you wish it spicier. Remove garlic before serving.

RUSSIAN CREAM

1¾ cups skim milk
  4 teaspoons sugar substitute
  1 tablespoon plus 1 teaspoon
    unflavored gelatin
  ½ cup cold water

1 cup plain yogurt
1 teaspoon vanilla
½ cup sour cream
Raspberries

Heat the milk and sugar substitute. Add the gelatin, which has been dissolved in the cold water. Mix thoroughly. Cool. Stir in the yogurt,
vanilla and sour cream. Pour into individual molds and refrigerate. Unmold and serve with fresh or frozen raspberries, whole or puréed in a
blender and strained.

MOCHA SPONGE

2 tablespoons unflavored gelatin
½ cup cold skim milk
4 teaspoons unsweetened cocoa
2 teaspoons instant coffee

1½ cups hot skim milk
Sugar substitute, about 1 teaspoon
  4 egg whites, beaten stiff

Soften gelatin in the cold milk. Mix together cocoa, coffee and hot milk;
blend in with the gelatin. Add sugar substitute to suit your taste. Cool.
When partially congealed, fold in the egg whites. Pour into a 1½-quart
mold and chill until firm. Serve with Low-Calorie Soft Custard or with
orange sections and sprigs of fresh mint.

FILET OF SOLE MOLD

4 filets of sole
Juice of 1 lemon
1 cup finely chopped mushrooms
4 tablespoons whipped butter
1 pound white crabmeat or any white fish, flaked
½ cup soft white bread crumbs

¾ cup skim milk
4 eggs, beaten
3 tablespoons melted whipped butter
2 tablespoons lemon juice
Salt and white pepper

Line a lightly buttered 2-quart Pyrex bowl or soufflé dish with the sole filets sprinkled with the lemon juice. Lightly sauté the mushrooms in the butter. Mix with the crabmeat or white fish. Soak the bread in the milk and squeeze dry. Add to the crab mixture. Pour in the beaten eggs and melted butter. Blend in the 2 tablespoons lemon juice and season with salt and white pepper. Pour into the fish-lined mold. Cover with foil or wax paper. Place in a pan of hot water and bake at 350° for 1 hour. Unmold on a heated serving tray and serve with:

SHRIMP AND DILL SAUCE

2 tablespoons whipped butter
1 cup uncooked small shrimp
2 tablespoons flour
2 cups skim milk

2 teaspoons lemon juice
1 teaspoon dill weed
Dash of cayenne

Melt butter, add shrimp and sauté until pink (about 1 minute). Add flour; cook 1 minute. Pour in milk and cook until thickened. Add lemon juice, dill and cayenne.

LEMON SHERBET MOUSSE

1 6-ounce package lemon-flavored gelatin
1 cup boiling water
1½ tablespoons lemon juice

1½ pints lemon sherbet
1 cup slivered fresh pineapple, any fresh fruit or ¼ cup slivered preserved ginger

Dissolve gelatin in boiling water. Cool. Add lemon juice; blend in lemon sherbet. Pour into a ring mold and chill until firm. Unmold and decorate with fresh fruit, or slivered preserved ginger.

A simple addition *when not dieting*: pass one cup whipped cream seasoned with 4 tablespoons sugar, ¼ cup lemon juice and grated rind of 1 lemon.

You may make various cold soups with yogurt, and if you keep still everyone will like them — but don't advertise!

CREAM OF CURRY SOUP

3 cups yogurt
3 cups chicken or beef consommé
1 clove garlic (you may omit)

1½ teaspoons curry powder (more if you wish)

Mix all ingredients in a blender. Chill. Serve very cold with minced chives (grow your own) or parsley. This soup will keep in the refrigerator for days. Add slivers of chicken or shrimp if you like. Omit the curry and add 1 cup peeled and seeded tomatoes for a cold tomato soup.

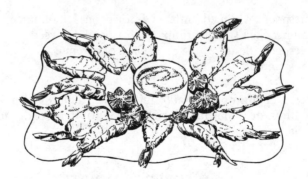

Shrimp cocktails are overworked, but baked or broiled shrimp are not. I like this recipe either as a first course or as an entrée.

BAKED SHRIMP

Use as large a shrimp as you can obtain in the shell. Remove small legs and then split the shrimp over the black intestinal tract and down the back shell as far as the tail. Rinse and remove black tract but do not remove the shrimp from the shell. Flatten shrimp meat with palm of hand. Put shell side down on a baking sheet, sprinkle with salt and a little white pepper and brush with melted whipped butter or margarine. Bake 15 minutes in a 350° oven. The best way I know to tell when shrimp is properly cooked is to observe the shell; when it changes from an opaque to a translucent appearance the shrimp is cooked enough. Overcooking shrimp is far worse than having them slightly underdone. Arrange shrimp on a plate with the tails to the outside and halves of fresh limes for a garnish — and lime juice and melted whipped butter for a sauce. It depends on the size of the shrimp how many you serve: if very large, 5; if smaller, 7. An odd number on the plate looks better than an even one.

CELERY SALAD

4 cups slivered celery, cut on the bias	1½ tablespoons Dijon mustard
2 heads Boston lettuce	4 tablespoons finely chopped parsley
1½ cups yogurt	Salt and pepper
1½ tablespoons lemon juice	

Cover and cook celery in very little boiling water for 3 minutes. Drain and cool. Arrange on lettuce cups. Mix yogurt, lemon juice, mustard and parsley. Season to your taste and pour dressing over. This dressing is good on seafood with 2 tablespoons horseradish or ¼ cup horseradish sauce added.

ICELAND TROUT WITH MUSTARD SAUCE

Today in most markets you will find a canned fish that is delicious, Iceland trout. There are five in a can. As a first course serve one very cold with a lemon cup filled with Mustard Sauce: 1 cup yogurt, 1½ tablespoons Dijon mustard. You will find you will be using these fish whether you are counting calories or not.

LEMON BROILED SQUAB WITH PAPAYA

The flavor of lemon helps one to enjoy any fowl preparation. Prepare for broiling, Rock Cornish hens, squabs or squab chickens by rubbing inside and out with lemon juice to which a little Tabasco has been added (about ⅛ teaspoon to ½ cup of lemon juice). Place fowl on broiling racks bone side up and sprinkle with finely minced shallots, salt and white pepper. Broil about 5 inches from heat for 15 minutes. Turn, rub again with the lemon juice and seasonings; broil another 15 minutes. If you like a more definite color, rub with paprika also.

SAUCE VERTE
(*1 cup*)

1 cup yogurt
1 hard-cooked egg, finely chopped
2 teaspoons lemon juice
2 tablespoons green onion or
chives, finely chopped

2 tablespoons chopped parsley
Few drops of Tabasco
Salt and pepper to taste

Mix and refrigerate. Good on green salads also.

EGGNOG MOUSSE

1 tablespoon unflavored gelatin
¼ cup cold water
4 eggs, separated
3 cups hot skim milk
4 teaspoons granulated artificial
sweetener

½ teaspoon vanilla
3 tablespoons bourbon
¼ teaspoon nutmeg

Dissolve gelatin in cold water. Beat the yolks until lemon yellow. Stir into the hot milk and cook over hot water until thickened. Remove; add the gelatin. Sweeten to your taste. Add vanilla, bourbon and nutmeg. When the custard begins to congeal, fold it into the stiffly beaten egg whites. Pour into a 1½-quart soufflé dish or into individual serving cups and refrigerate overnight.

You may use this as a basic recipe. For a Cold Chocolate Soufflé, add 3 tablespoons of unsweetened cocoa to the custard and correct the artificial sweetener to suit your taste.

CHICKEN CONSOMME ORIENTAL

5 cups canned chicken
consommé or make your own
½ cup diced water chestnuts
½ cup sliced canned or fresh
mushrooms

1 cup fresh spinach leaves, slivered
1 egg white
Salt and white pepper

Bring consommé to a boil. Add the water chestnuts and mushrooms. Cook 1 minute. Add spinach, again cooking 1 minute only. Pour egg white in slowly, stirring with a fork. Correct seasonings and serve at once. For a few more calories, add a handful of bean threads (rain noodles) and cook until transparent before adding the spinach.

FLANK STEAK

Flank steak is a good cut of meat for dieting. What little fat there is can be trimmed off easily along with the tough membrane. Because I think flavor is so important in low-calorie planning, I like to marinate flank steak in half soy sauce, half water or white or red wine for an hour, then broil medium rare, 4 minutes on each side; baste once with some of the marinade. Let rest about 3 minutes, place on a board, then slice across the grain in thin slices; start at the small end of the steak, almost paralleling the board. But be sure the slices are thin or the steak will be tough. If you do not like the flavor of soy sauce, marinate the meat in red wine and garlic instead, or in nothing at all.

I use the Oriental approach to some vegetables. Stir-frying is quick and I find that men eat with gusto the vegetables prepared this way.

CHINESE STYLE VEGETABLES

You may use any vegetable combination, but this is one I like.

2 tablespoons salad oil (not olive oil)
1 pound slivered green beans, cut on the bias
2 cups slivered celery, cut on the bias

½ cup chicken broth or water
1 cup bean sprouts (fresh if available)
2 teaspoons cornstarch, mixed with a little water
Salt and pepper
Chopped parsley

Heat oil, add beans, sauté at high heat for 2 minutes, stirring constantly. Add celery; cook 1 minute. Stir in chicken broth and bean sprouts (be sure to wash sprouts with cold water). Cover and cook 1 minute. Add cornstarch and cook until clear. Correct seasonings. Sprinkle with chopped parsley.

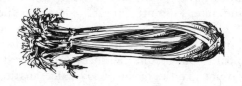

LOW-CALORIE CHEESE CAKE

1 tablespoon unflavored gelatin
2 tablespoons lemon juice
½ cup hot skim milk
2 eggs, separated

2 teaspoons sugar substitute
2½ cups Ricotta cheese
1 cup crushed ice
1 teaspoon grated orange peel

Dissolve gelatin in lemon juice; add hot skim milk. Put in blender. Add egg yolks, sugar substitute and cheese. Whip at high speed for 2 minutes. Add 1 cup crushed ice. Continue running at high speed until thoroughly blended. Beat egg whites until stiff. Add orange peel. Fold into the cheese mixture. Pour into an 8-inch spring-form mold. Chill until firm, about 24 hours. Serve with any kind of puréed fresh fruit.

No one will argue that fish has fewer calories than meat. This recipe may be used whether you think thin or not.

FILET OF SOLE ROULADE

3 pounds filet of sole (of equal size and thickness)
½ pound fresh salmon, boned
2 tablespoons whipped butter or margarine, melted

1 teaspoon salt
Water
Dry white wine
1 lemon, sliced

Wash sole and salmon in cold water and pat dry. Lay the filets of sole on a piece of foil, and brush them with the melted butter. Sprinkle with salt. Start at narrow end of fish and roll just enough to hold a slice of salmon securely, then finish rolling loosely and insert a toothpick crosswise to hold the roll together. This may be done early in the day and refrigerated. Place in a shallow pan lined with foil, the shiny side up. Cover with half water, half dry white wine. Add the sliced lemon. Bring to a full boil. Lower the heat to simmer; cover and steam for 8 to 10 minutes. Remove with a slotted spoon to a heated serving tray and serve with:

CAPER SAUCE

1 tablespoon whipped butter
1 tablespoon flour
1½ cups yogurt
½ cup liquid from poaching

¼ cup capers
2 tablespoons chopped parsley
Salt and white pepper to taste

Melt the butter, add the flour and cook until foamy. Add yogurt and liquid; cook over hot water until thickened. Add capers and parsley. Correct seasonings. Substitute small shrimp or thinly sliced cucumbers for the capers.

If I believed in reincarnation, I would like to return as a rich woman of India. I love everything about India (except their poverty), and I especially like their food. The idea of men carrying their spices with them as they hunt quail and such intrigues me.

TANDOORI ROAST CHICKEN

3 cups plain yogurt	2 tablespoons ground coriander
6 cloves garlic, crushed	1 tablespoon cumin
1½ tablespoons fresh grated ginger	1 teaspoon cayenne pepper
	1 teaspoon powdered anise
¾ cup lime juice	4 1¾-pound roasting chickens

Mix yogurt, garlic, ginger, lime juice and spices. Rub chicken inside and out with mixture. Place in a bowl and pour rest of marinade over. Cover and marinate in the refrigerator for 24 to 48 hours. Turn chickens, if not completely covered in marinade, at least once. Remove from marinade and roast in a 375° oven until done, about 1 hour. Baste with the marinade. Disjoint and serve with a wedge of lime and steamed, thinly sliced onion. Use this recipe when not dieting and baste with butter also. Do turkey the same way.

APRICOT SHERBET
(1½ quarts)

4 cups apricot nectar	1 3-ounce package lemon gelatin
1 cup water-packed apricots, chopped	Juice of 1 lemon
	Artificial sugar (if necessary)

Mix and freeze in ice cream freezer, 6 parts of ice to 1 of ice cream salt. Or freeze in your deep freeze and whip when partially frozen in your electric mixer and return to freezer.

TUNA SURPRISE

4 medium tomatoes
2 4-ounce cans white water-
  packed tuna
½ cup finely diced celery
2 teaspoons Dijon mustard
1 tablespoon seedless raisins

2 tablespoons yogurt
Salt and pepper
2 hard-cooked eggs, put through a
  sieve
Chopped parsley

Cut peeled tomatoes in half. Remove as many seeds as possible. Mix the tuna with the celery, mustard and raisins. Add enough of the yogurt to hold the tuna together. Correct seasonings. Pile the tuna on top of the tomato. Coat with the sieved eggs and sprinkle with chopped parsley. Serve cold with a lemon wedge.

VEAL BIRDS WITH MUSHROOM SAUCE

2 pounds lean veal, cut into 16
  thin even-sized slices
1 teaspoon salt
¼ teaspoon sage
16 small pieces Swiss-type cheese
4 tablespoons whipped butter or
  margarine

2 tablespoons chopped shallots
1½ cups chicken consommé
¼ cup Madeira wine
2½ cups canned sliced
  mushrooms
2 tablespoons chopped parsley
Salt and white pepper

Place each veal slice between 2 pieces of foil and pound with a wooden mallet until very thin. Sprinkle with the salt and sage. Place a small finger of cheese in center of veal; roll up and tie each piece with a string. Melt the butter in a skillet. Add the shallots and cook 1 minute. Add the veal and brown quickly over high heat, turning once. Transfer to a shallow casserole. Add the consommé to the skillet and bring to a boil. Pour over the veal with the wine. Bake at 350° for 30 minutes, basting frequently. Add the mushrooms and heat only. Remove from oven; take off strings and sprinkle veal with the parsley. Correct seasonings. Serve from casserole or transfer to a hot platter. Allow two per person.

EGGPLANT PROVENÇALE

3 medium-sized eggplants, peeled
   and cut in 1-inch cubes
3 large fresh tomatoes, peeled
   and chopped
½ cup coarsely chopped onion
1 clove garlic, minced

2 tablespoons lemon juice
A pinch of tarragon, fresh or dried
Chopped parsley
1 tablespoon grated Parmesan
   cheese
Salt and pepper

Place eggplant and tomatoes in a skillet with the onion, garlic, lemon juice and tarragon. Cover and simmer over low heat until vegetables are tender. Correct seasoning. Transfer to a heated serving dish. Sprinkle with parsley and Parmesan cheese.

GRAPEFRUIT AND SPINACH SALAD

1½ pounds fresh spinach
4 pink grapefruit
2 tablespoons Roquefort cheese

½ cup Sherry French Dressing
Salt and cracked pepper

Remove stems from spinach. Wash thoroughly and put in a closed plastic bag to crisp. (Do the day before if you wish.) Peel and section the grapefruit. Mix the Roquefort cheese with the Sherry French Dressing and toss with the spinach and fruit. Correct seasonings. Sprinkle with cracked pepper. Substitute orange for the grapefruit sometimes.

ROQUEFORT DRESSING
(1½ cups)

3 tablespoons Roquefort or Blue
   cheese
1 cup tomato juice
2 tablespoons finely chopped
   green onion

1 clove garlic
3 tablespoons lemon juice
¼ cup catsup
Salt and pepper to taste

Mash cheese, add rest of ingredients and mix with an egg beater. Good on shrimp, salads or cocktails.

13

Lagniappe

LAGNIAPPE may seem an esoteric word for a native of upstate New York to be using, but remember I came to Texas in 1940 and have been in Louisiana many many times with stops to lecture in Baton Rouge, New Orleans, Shreveport and some of the smaller towns. If I didn't want to use the Creole definition of the word I could use the Peruvian since in the Quechua language *lagniappe* means "a small present to a customer." My meaning here is a "small present to the reader." I hope you will enjoy these additional recipes which I could not bear to omit — some, my favorites and others, mostly requests. When my friends heard I was doing a new cookbook my telephone rang with "be sure to put in" and so, without much organization, your *lagniappe*.

About Bread

Your bread recipe reads: "knead until smooth and satiny." How long is that? You've never made bread before! Most doughs require from 8 to 10 minutes of kneading before you recognize a smooth and satiny surface. After 10 minutes, grasp the dough in one hand, squeezing it slightly with your fingers. If fully developed, the opposite side of the dough ball should feel smoothly taut; you will see bubbly blisters under the surface.

Yeast bread likes a warm, draft-free and moist place for rising. If you don't have a cozy, private nook for "proofing" (rising) dough, make a "mini sauna" of your oven. Turn your oven to 400° for one minute only and then turn it off. It should have reached a temperature between 80° and 100° — just what the dough likes. Situate your dough in the warm oven so it has plenty of room to rise. Place a pan of hot water on the oven floor before closing the door. Or place dough in bowl beside your stove, turn one burner on to low. Be sure to cover the bread with a towel or napkin if proofing outside the oven.

Almost any yeast dough or batter may be refrigerated if the amount of yeast in the recipe is doubled. A sweet dough, that is, high in sugar, refrigerates best. You can refrigerate the dough immediately after mixing, kneading or after it has risen once and been punched down. Proofing before refrigeration, however, helps the dough retain its rising power.

If storing the dough in the refrigerator, grease the bowl well. I use butter or margarine and cover with plastic wrap or a tight bowl cover. The best refrigerator temperature is 45° to 50°. Most refrigerator doughs may be kept three or four days with portions removed as desired. Some rising will take place in the refrigerator, but the dough can be punched down if it gets too high.

After refrigeration you can either shape the dough immediately or allow it to come to room temperature — about 1 to 3 hours — before shaping. Then let the shaped dough rise again before baking at the required time and temperature.

I think it confusing to have a different bread recipe for each idea you have. A few good basic ones are enough. The following recipe you can use for bread, rolls, sweet rolls or any variation you would care to make. It takes little time; it's worth the little effort. A hamburger or frankfurter made on a roll from this dough will make you wonder why you'd ever eaten cardboard market buns.

BASIC RECIPE
(2 loaves)

1 package compressed or 1 package dry yeast	¼ cup sugar
¼ cup lukewarm water	1 teaspoon salt
1 cup milk	4 cups sifted flour (about)
¼ cup shortening	2 eggs

Soften yeast in water. Heat milk and shortening together until melted. (Do not boil.) Measure sugar and salt into large bowl; add hot milk mixture, stir until dissolved and cool to lukewarm. Add 2 cups flour to milk and mix until well blended, 1 minute on electric mixer. Stir in softened yeast and eggs, beat well and add more flour to make a thick batter. Beat thoroughly until smooth and elastic, 2 minutes on electric mixer. Cover and let rise in warm place (80° to 85°) until bubbly, about 1 hour. Stir down. Put on a floured board, knead lightly and shape dough into desired form; let rise in warm place for 30 minutes. Bake in moderate oven (375°) for 20 to 30 minutes or until golden brown.

Variations:

Marmalade Rolls. Follow Basic Recipe through stir down step. Prepare muffin pans by placing ½ teaspoon melted butter or margarine and 2 teaspoons of any kind of marmalade in each cup. Drop dough into greased muffin tins, one-half full. Let rise and bake as for Basic Recipe. Invert pans and remove rolls immediately after baking. Makes two dozen rolls. Make them in the small muffin tins (48 to 60 rolls) for your morning coffee parties.

Honey Cinnamon Buns. Sprinkle bottom of buttered muffin pan with brown sugar, add ½ cup honey, 1 teaspoon cinnamon and ¾ cup pecans. Proceed as in Basic Recipe.

Marble Nut Coffee Cake. Follow the Basic Recipe through stir down step. Combine ⅓ cup butter or margarine, melted, ⅔ cup brown sugar and 2 tablespoons water. Spread half of mixture in each of two 9-inch round pans. Divide batter in half. To one-half part add ½ cup brown sugar, ½ cup chopped nuts and 1 teaspoon cinnamon. Beat until thoroughly blended. Divide both parts of batter in half again, making four equal parts. Combine 1 plain part of batter with 1 brown sugar part by lightly stirring them together for 15 seconds. Spread batter evenly in prepared pan. Repeat. Bake as for Basic Recipe. Invert pan and remove coffee cake immediately after baking. Makes two 9-inch coffee cakes.

Merry Christmas Coffee Cake. Follow Basic Recipe through stir down step. Combine ½ cup sifted flour, ¼ cup fine bread crumbs or nut meats, ¼ cup sugar and 1 teaspoon cinnamon. Cut or rub in an additional ¼ cup butter or margarine until mixture is crumbly. Drop batter by tablespoonfuls into crumbly mixture and gently roll to form coated balls. Shape two coffee cakes by arranging balls a layer deep on greased baking sheet or in a round pan. Let rise and bake as for Basic Recipe. Decorate with Confectioners' Sugar Icing: beat together ½ cup confectioners' sugar and 1 to 2 teaspoons milk until smooth; add candied fruit and halves of pecans. Makes two coffee cakes.

Sausage Bread. Use a mildly smoked sausage (the kind that comes by the foot), beef stick or salami. Roll out the Basic Recipe dough to desired length. I make it about 12 inches long. Put the meat in the center and form the bread dough around it, about ½ inch thick. Let rise to double in bulk and bake at 375° until golden brown. If I use a beef stick (hickory smoked) or salami, I trim it to about 1 inch to 1½ inches in diameter. The trimmings I use for omelettes or in scrambled eggs or sandwiches. Don't throw them away. Serve the bread warm, sliced about ½ inch thick. 'Tis tasty-nice with cocktails too.

When you need bread crumbs, use your blender. Trim away the crusts, break bread into pieces, put into the blender, cover and turn to high speed until finely crumbled. For buttered crumbs, butter the bread before putting it in the blender. Use dry bread crumbs for coating foods and for stuffings. Use soft crumbs for fondues, timbales, thickening sauces and soups.

MONKEY BREAD

Many people claim the original Monkey Bread recipe. I do not. A customer called me out of the blue one day, read it over the telephone and this is my interpretation. I usually make it in a bundt pan because it looks attractive. It freezes well and may be reheated. Great toasted.

1½ yeast cakes or 2 packages dry
    yeast
1 cup milk, heated to lukewarm
4 tablespoons sugar

1 teaspoon salt
½ cup melted butter or
    margarine
3½ cups sifted flour (about)

Dissolve yeast in lukewarm milk. Stir in sugar, salt and butter. Add flour and beat well. Let rise to almost double in bulk. Punch down and roll out on lightly floured board to ¼-inch thickness. Cut in about 2-inch pieces: round, diamond or square. Dip each piece in melted butter. Pile in buttered pans until half full. Let rise to double in bulk. Bake at 400° for 30 minutes or until golden brown. If I use margarine in place of butter, I increase the salt to 1½ teaspoons and add some salt to the melted margarine.

You serve loaf uncut; let people pull off whatever amount they wish. It is already buttered, so no bread and butter plate is needed. It always is a favorite.

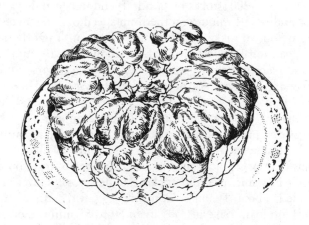

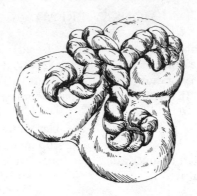

MAPLE TRINITY BREAD
(*1 loaf*)

4½ to 5 cups flour	½ cup salad oil
2 packages dry yeast	2 teaspoons salt
¾ cup maple syrup	1 egg
½ cup milk	1 egg yolk
½ cup plus 1 tablespoon water	1 egg white, slightly beaten

Stir together 2 cups flour and yeast. Heat syrup, milk, ½ cup water, oil and salt over low heat until warm, stirring to blend. Pour into flour-yeast mixture and beat until smooth, about 2 minutes on medium speed of electric mixer or 300 strokes by hand. Blend in egg and egg yolk. Add 1 cup flour and beat 1 minute on medium speed or 150 strokes by hand. Stir in more flour to make a soft dough. Turn onto lightly floured surface and knead until smooth and satiny, about 8 to 10 minutes. Shape into ball and place in lightly greased bowl, turning to grease bread on all sides. Cover and let rise in warm place (80° to 85°) until doubled, about 2½ hours. Punch down. Divide into fourths, cover and let rest 10 minutes. Shape three portions into balls; place on greased baking sheet in cloverleaf design; flatten each to 1 inch high. Cut remaining dough into fourths; shape each with palm of hands into 20-inch ropes. Twist ropes together in pairs; press ends to seal. Arrange to form on cloverleaf, curving ends in semicircles and tucking under cross. Cover and let rise until doubled, about 1 hour. Combine egg white and 1 tablespoon water; brush on loaf. Bake in 350° oven 50 to 55 minutes or until done. Remove from baking sheet immediately after baking.

I had this bread made for the Easter season. It was hard to say no to good customers other times of the year, so you can make it anytime. This is beautiful on a brunch buffet and a good neighbor gift.

Sourdough Bread is the most sought after bread in America. This recipe is good.

SOURDOUGH BREAD STARTER

2 cups flour   1 package dry yeast
2 cups warm water

Combine ingredients in large bowl (not metal); mix together until well blended. Let stand uncovered in warm place (80° to 85°) for 48 hours; stir occasionally. Stir well before use. Pour out required amount and replenish remaining starter by mixing in 1 cup each flour and warm water. Let stand uncovered in a warm place a few hours (until it bubbles again) before covering loosely and refrigerating. Use and replenish every two weeks.

SOURDOUGH BREAD
(2 1½-pound loaves)

3 cups plus 3½ cups flour   1 tablespoon salt
1 cup Starter   1 teaspoon baking soda
2 cups warm water   Cornmeal
2 tablespoons sugar   Melted butter

Measure 3 cups flour, Starter, water, sugar, salt and baking soda into large mixing bowl (not metal); beat until smooth. Cover loosely with waxed paper and let stand in warm place (80° to 85°) at least 18 hours. Stir batter down. Mix in more flour to make a moderately stiff dough. Turn onto lightly floured surface and knead until smooth and satiny, about 8 to 10 minutes. Shape dough, place on greased baking sheets that have been sprinkled with cornmeal; brush with butter. Cover and let rise in warm place until doubled, about 1½ hours. Bake in 400° oven 40 to 50 minutes or until done. Brush with butter after baking.

REFRIGERATOR WHEAT BREAD
(2 1-pound loaves)

3½ to 4 cups white flour	3 tablespoons sugar
2 packages dry yeast	1 tablespoon salt
2 cups milk	4 cups whole-wheat flour
¾ cup water	Oil
¼ cup salad oil	

Mix 2½ cups flour with yeast. Heat milk, water, ¼ cup oil, sugar and salt over low heat until warm (120° to 130°). Add liquid ingredients to flour-yeast mixture and beat 3 minutes on high speed of electric mixer. Add whole-wheat flour; gradually stir in more white flour to make a stiff dough. Turn out onto lightly floured surface and knead 5 to 10 minutes. Cover dough with bowl or pan; let rest 20 minutes. Divide in half. Roll each out to 7 x 14-inch rectangle. Roll from narrow side, pressing dough into roll at each turn. Press ends to seal and fold under loaf. Place in 2 greased 4½ x 8½-inch loaf pans. Brush loaves with oil or melted butter. Or make into rolls, 2 dozen medium size. Cover with plastic wrap and refrigerate 2 to 24 hours. When ready to use, let stand at room temperature 10 minutes. Puncture any gas bubbles with skewer. Bake in 400° oven 40 minutes. Remove immediately from pans and brush with oil or butter. Cool on wire rack.

WHITE BREAD
(2 1-pound loaves or 1 2-pound loaf)

5½ to 6 cups flour	2 tablespoons sugar
2 packages dry yeast	2 tablespoons oil
1 cup milk	2 teaspoons salt
1 cup water	Oil

Stir together 2 cups flour and yeast. Heat milk, water, sugar, 2 tablespoons oil and salt over low heat until warm (120° to 130°). Add liquid ingredients to flour-yeast mixture and beat until smooth, about 3 minutes on high speed of electric mixer. Stir in more flour to make a moderately soft dough. Turn out onto lightly floured surface and knead until smooth and satiny, about 5 to 10 minutes. Cover dough with bowl or pan; let rest 20 minutes. For two loaves, divide dough in half and roll out into two 7 x 14-inch rectangles; for one loaf, roll out to a single

8 x 16-inch rectangle. Roll from narrow side, pressing dough into roll at each turn. Press ends to seal and fold under loaf. Place in 2 greased 4½ x 8½-inch loaf pans *or* 1 greased 5½ x 9¼-inch loaf pan; brush with oil. Let rise in warm place (80° to 85°) until doubled, about 30 to 45 minutes. Bake in 400° oven 35 to 40 minutes. Remove immediately from pans and brush with oil or butter. Cool on wire rack.

POTECA
(3 *Christmas Breads*)

2 packages yeast, compressed or dry	½ cup sugar
	2 teaspoons salt
¼ cup water (lukewarm for compressed yeast, warm for dry)	5 cups sifted flour (about)
	2 eggs
1 cup milk	Walnut Filling
¼ cup shortening	Melted butter or margarine

Soften yeast in water. Heat milk and shortening until melted. (Do not boil.) Measure sugar and salt into large bowl; add hot milk mixture and stir until dissolved. Cool to lukewarm. Add about 1½ cups flour and beat well. Add softened yeast and eggs. Beat well. Add enough more flour to make a soft dough. Turn out on lightly floured board or pastry cloth and knead until smooth and satiny, about 5 to 8 minutes. Shape into ball and place in greased bowl. Grease surface of dough lightly. Cover and let rise in warm place (80° to 85°) until doubled in bulk, about 1 hour and 15 minutes. Punch down. Let rest 10 minutes. Divide dough into thirds. Roll out each portion to rectangle about 10 x 20 inches. (Dough will be very thin.) Spread with Walnut Filling. Roll up like jelly roll, starting with narrow edge, sealing edges to underside. Place on greased baking sheets and brush tops lightly with melted butter or margarine. Let rise until doubled, about 30 minutes. Bake in moderate oven (375°) for 30 to 35 minutes or until golden brown. Brush with melted butter or margarine.

Walnut Filling:

2 cups ground walnuts	¾ cup honey
¾ cup milk	⅓ cup sugar

Mix ingredients together in large heavy saucepan. Bring to boil and cook about 5 minutes, stirring occasionally. Remove from heat and cool.

Spread on dough. Sometimes I make this in small bread pans, wrap loaves and tie to give my guests as they leave my Christmas parties.

PEASANT BREAD

2 packages dry yeast
3 to 4 cups flour, unbleached if possible
1 tablespoon salt

½ tablespoon sugar
1¼ cups lukewarm water (120° to 130°)
Cornmeal

Mix yeast with 1 cup of the flour, salt, and sugar. Add the warm water, and beat 2 minutes at medium speed of your electric mixer or beat by hand. Add enough flour to make a stiff dough. Beat at high speed for 2 minutes more, scraping sides of bowl frequently. Turn out dough on a floured board and knead until smooth and elastic, about 5 or 6 minutes. Place dough in bowl and dust lightly with flour. Cover and put in a warm place; let rise to double in bulk, about 1 hour. Punch it down; divide in 2 pieces. Shape each section by rolling and stretching into a long loaf, about 1½ inches in diameter. Place well apart on ungreased baking pan, which has been sprinkled with cornmeal. Brush with water and slash diagonally across top 3 or 4 times. Place on lowest rack in a cold oven. Bake at 350° for 1 hour or until a golden brown. The bread will rise in the oven. Vary by using half whole-wheat, half white flour.

BRIOCHE
(about 3 dozen small)

1 package dry yeast
½ cup warm water
¼ cup sugar
2 teaspoons salt
1 egg yolk, mixed with 2 teaspoons water

1 cup butter or whipped margarine, softened
6 eggs, at room temperature
4½ cups sifted flour

Sprinkle yeast over water in large bowl of electric mixer; stir until yeast is dissolved. Add sugar, salt, butter, eggs, and 3 cups flour. Beat at medium speed 4 minutes, occasionally scraping side of bowl and beaters with rubber scraper. Add remaining flour. Beat at low speed or until smooth (dough will be soft). Cover bowl with foil. Let rise in warm place free from drafts until double in bulk for about 1½ hours. Using a rubber scraper, beat down dough. Then refrigerate, covered with foil, overnight.

Next day, generously grease small brioche, tart or muffin tins. With a sharp knife cut off pieces of dough about the size of an egg or 2 ounces in weight. On a slightly floured board shape into a ball. Fit into the greased pans. With your fingers make a slight indentation in each center. Insert a small ball of dough for the cap. Cover with a towel; let rise in a warm place until dough reaches top of pan, about 1 hour. Beat 1 egg yolk with 2 teaspoons water. Brush cap only. Bake at 375° for 10 minutes. Cover loosely with foil and bake about 20 minutes longer, or until cake tester inserted in center under the cap comes out clean. Let stand in pan for 10 to 15 minutes. With a spatula carefully loosen from side of pans, then remove.

LEMON FAN-TAN BREAD
(2 loaves)

4½ to 5 cups flour	2 teaspoons salt
2 packages dry yeast	2 eggs, lightly beaten
½ cup milk	2 teaspoons grated lemon rind
½ cup water	2 tablespoons lemon juice
½ cup plus 1 cup sugar	½ cup chopped nuts
¼ cup oil	Streusel Topping

Stir together 2 cups flour and yeast. Heat milk, water, ½ cup sugar, oil and salt over low heat only until warm, stirring to blend. Add liquid ingredients to flour-yeast mixture and beat until smooth, about 2 minutes on medium speed of electric mixer or 300 strokes by hand. Blend in eggs and lemon rind. Add 1 cup flour and beat 1 minute on medium speed or 150 strokes by hand. Stir in more flour to make a moderately stiff dough. Turn onto lightly floured surface and knead until smooth and satiny, about 8 to 10 minutes. Shape into ball and place in lightly greased bowl, turning to grease all sides. Cover and let rise in warm place (80° to 85°) until doubled, about 1½ hours. Punch down. Divide dough in half; shape into balls. Let rest 10 minutes. Roll one portion into 10 x 16-inch rectangle. Stir together 1 cup sugar, lemon juice and nuts; spread half of mixture over rectangle. Cut into four 4 x 10-inch rectangles; stack on top of each other. Cut these rectangles into 5 stacks, 2 inches wide and 4 inches long. Place stacks in row in greased 4½ x 8½-inch loaf pan, long side down. Repeat procedure with remaining portion of dough for second loaf. Sprinkle loaves with Streusel Topping. Let rise in warm place until doubled, about 45 minutes. Bake in 400° oven 30 to 35 minutes or until done. Remove from pans immediately.

STREUSEL TOPPING

2 tablespoons flour   2 tablespoons sugar
1 tablespoon butter

Stir together flour and sugar. Cut in butter until mixture resembles coarse crumbs.

Quick Breads

DANISH

2 8-ounce packages refrigerator
  crescent rolls
2 tablespoons butter
1 tablespoon melted butter
1 cup puréed cooked prunes or
  apricots

1 teaspoon lemon juice
¼ cup finely chopped pecans
½ cup confectioners' sugar
2 or 3 teaspoons milk

Roll out 1 package of the rolls. Shape into a rectangle approximately 12 x 8 inches. Soften but do not melt the butter and spread about 4 inches wide down center of rectangle. Unroll second package of rolls and place over the first, completely covering the butter. Brush top dough with melted butter. Spread puréed fruit and lemon juice down center of top dough. Sprinkle with nuts. Cut parallel pieces, about 2 inches long and 2 inches apart. Fold dough pieces over filling. Place on a buttered cookie sheet and bake at 375° until golden brown. Mix confectioners' sugar and milk and dribble over warm Danish. Cut and serve. Use same method but substitute marmalades, jams, marzipan or butter for a richer and more flaky roll.

CROQUEMBOUCHE

3 cups milk
2 pieces vanilla bean or 2 teaspoons vanilla
1 cup sugar
8 egg yolks

½ cup flour
2 cups whipped cream
Small cream puffs, ½ inch in
   diameter

Scald milk with beans. Mix sugar and egg yolks until lemon yellow. Add flour to blend. Add milk, gradually stirring with a French whip. Cook until mixture *begins* to boil. Strain and cool, stirring to prevent a crust from forming. Fold in 1 cup of whipped cream. Fill small cream puffs when cold. Dip in Caramelized Sugar and attach in a circle to a Sugar Crust. Repeat circles a smaller one each time to build a pyramid. Fill center, as you build, with cream filling and whipped cream. Dribble Caramelized Sugar all over.

The Houston *Post* started me on the road to writing about food. The Food Editor, Ann Valentine, sent me the following cake recipe to include in this book. Good for holiday snacking and gifts.

BOURBON NUT CAKE

½ pound margarine
2 cups sugar
6 eggs
4 cups sifted flour
2 teaspoons baking powder
2 teaspoons nutmeg

1 cup bourbon
1 pound finely chopped pecans
7¼ ounces dates
3 tablespoons coconut
¼ teaspoon almond extract
1 teaspoon vanilla

Cream margarine and sugar, drop in whole eggs one at a time and stir after each addition. Add flour, baking powder, nutmeg, almond extract, vanilla and bourbon. Flour nuts; add nuts, coconut and dates to cake lightly. Pour into buttered and floured angel food tin. Cook in slow (250°) oven for 6 hours. Place a pan of water in the oven to prevent cracking. Also cover cake with aluminum foil for the first few hours of the baking period.

ORANGE COFFEE CAKE
(for 8 to 10)

2 eggs, separated	2 cups flour
1 cup sugar	2 teaspoons grated orange rind
1 cup sour cream	2 teaspoons baking powder
½ teaspoon baking soda	¾ teaspoon salt

Topping:

1 cup sour cream	¼ cup brown sugar
¼ cup dry bread crumbs	1 teaspoon grated orange rind
Chopped almonds and cinnamon	

Beat egg yolks until foamy, add sugar and beat until light. Add sour cream, soda, flour, grated orange rind, baking powder and salt. Mix well. Fold in stiffly beaten egg whites. Spread in a buttered 9-inch square cake tin. For the topping, mix sour cream, dry bread crumbs, brown sugar and grated orange rind. Spread on top and sprinkle with chopped almonds and cinnamon. Bake at 375° for 40 minutes. Cut in squares and serve warm.

SPICY SPECULAAS COOKIES
(6 dozen small cookies)

3 cups flour	¼ teaspoon salt
3 teaspoons cinnamon	1 cup softened butter
1 teaspoon cloves	½ cup shortening
1 teaspoon nutmeg	1½ cups light brown sugar
½ teaspoon baking powder	2 to 3 tablespoons milk

Sift together flour, cinnamon, cloves, nutmeg, baking powder and salt. Add butter, shortening and brown sugar. Mix at low speed on mixer or with wooden spoon until mixture is crumbly and well blended. Add milk, a tablespoon at a time, to form a very stiff dough. Press small amount of dough into each carved section of speculaas board and press down firmly with palm of hand to completely fill mold. With sharp knife, gently cut away excess dough by using a sawing motion with the knife across top of board. Invert board over ungreased baking sheet and tap one end so cookies fall onto sheet. If some cookies break, gently push together. Place cookies close together on sheet. Repeat with remaining dough. Bake in moderate oven (350°) about 15 minutes or until cookies are lightly browned around edges.

Cookies will come out of carved sections more easily if board has been seasoned first. To season, fill sections with solid shortening, using about 2 tablespoons total, and place board on aluminum foil or baking pan. Place in a slow oven (300°) for about 45 minutes. Remove from oven and wipe off excess shortening. Cool board before using.

A favorite party cookie:

PECAN BALLS
(*about 5 dozen*)

½ cup shortening	2½ cups cake flour
½ cup butter	½ teaspoon salt
½ cup sugar	2 egg whites, slightly beaten
2 egg yolks, beaten	1½ cups finely chopped pecans
2 tablespoons grated orange peel	½ pound glazed cherries (you
2 teaspoons grated lemon peel	may omit)
2 teaspoons lemon juice	

You may substitute margarine for the shortening or butter, but the texture and flavor is better if you do not. Cream the shortening, butter and sugar. Add egg yolks, peels and juice; stir and add flour and salt.

Stir, but do not beat. Chill for 30 minutes. Form into small balls. Roll in the egg whites, then in the nuts. Place on a greased cookie sheet. Make an impression in the center of each ball. Cut the cherries in half and press in the cookie. Bake at 325° for 25 minutes. Nice for Christmas.

Any cookie tray looks better with some rolled cookies on it. They are not hard to do, but you have to be quick in their preparation.

ROLLED NUT COOKIES
(about 3 dozen)

⅓ cup shortening	¼ teaspoon salt
1 cup light brown sugar	½ cup finely chopped pecans
2 eggs	½ teaspoon vanilla
½ cup flour	

Cream shortening, add sugar and beat until light. Beat eggs well and blend into the sugar mixture. Add flour and salt. Mix thoroughly. Add pecans and vanilla. Drop from tip end of teaspoon on a lightly greased cookie sheet, which is turned flat side up so you can remove cookies easily when they are done. Put only two or three at a time on the sheet as they spread very thin. Bake at 325° for 5 to 8 minutes. Remove with spatula and roll over the handle of a wooden spoon on a chopping board — be quick! If you do not roll the hot cookie, you will have a crisp lace wafer.

If you are a purist, make your own curry seasoning.

CURRY POWDER
(1½ cups)

½ cup coriander seed	½ teaspoon mustard seed
½ cup red chili pepper	½ teaspoon fenugreek seed
5 tablespoons cumin seed	6 whole cloves
3 tablespoons ground turmeric	6 cardamom seeds
1 tablespoon peppercorns	1 2-inch piece cinnamon stick

Put in blender. Store in an airtight container.

For Round Robin dinners I am often asked to make Crêpes Suzette, which I like to do, and here is my recipe.

CREPES SUZETTE

¾ cup plus 1 tablespoon butter,
 no substitute
½ cup orange juice
2 teaspoons lemon juice
½ cup Curaçao
½ cup Grand Marnier

½ cup sugar
2 teaspoons grated orange peel
24 thin crêpes (allow 3 crêpes per
 person)
Granulated sugar
Cognac

Bring the ¾ cup butter, orange juice, lemon juice, Curaçao and Grand Marnier to a boil. Remove from heat, add the ½ cup sugar and orange peel. This may be done ahead of time. In fact, I keep this mixture in a covered jar in my refrigerator. When ready to make the dessert melt the 1 tablespoon butter in the crêpe pan or skillet. Place the crêpes in the pan a few at a time. Spoon some of the sauce over and heat over sterno or on the stove. Fold or roll, sprinkle lightly with sugar, add warm Cognac or brandy and ignite; serve with some of the sauce. I sometimes heat and add to the sauce Elberta peach halves and serve with the crêpes, but then I am apt to add most anything.

After serving She-Crab Bisque at a gourmet dinner, I received many requests for the recipe. You do have to order the she-crab with eggs ahead of time from your fish man.

SHE-CRAB BISQUE

2 tablespoons butter
1 tablespoon onion, chopped
 fine
¼ teaspoon dry mustard
1 tablespoon flour
1½ cups milk
1½ cups half-and-half

1½ cups she-crabmeat with eggs
1 teaspoon salt
1 teaspoon chopped parsley
 (you may omit)
A pinch of white pepper
Dry sherry

Melt butter, add onion and sauté until soft. Add mustard, flour and cook until well blended. Pour in milk and cream; bring to a boil. Remove from stove to add crabmeat and seasonings. Return pot to stove and keep over hot water until ready to serve. Add parsley before serving. I like to put a teaspoon of hot sherry into the hot cups before ladling the soup. You may add hot sherry to a soup tureen when serving from it. If you cannot obtain she-crab with eggs, use lump crab and add ¼ cup riced egg yolk.

There is no vegetable more exciting to the taste buds than fennel, either in a salad or a vegetable.

FENNEL AU GRATIN

4 bulbs fennel	Salt and white pepper
⅓ cup butter	¼ cup grated Parmesan cheese
⅔ cups whipping cream or thin cream sauce	¼ cup grated Gruyère cheese

Wash fennel well, trim and discard the tops. Slice the bulbs and cook in boiling salted water until tender, not soft. Melt the butter and sauté until a light brown. Transfer to serving casserole, cover with the cream, sprinkle with salt and pepper. Cover with the cheese. Run under broiler to brown. You can prepare this vegetable ahead of time and refrigerate. To warm, bake at 350°.

CHEESE CAKE

¼ pound butter	1 teaspoon cinnamon
1 pound graham crackers, rolled into crumbs	½ cup sugar

Melt butter, add crumbs, cinnamon and sugar. Mix thoroughly and line sides and bottom of 9-inch spring mold or pie pan.

1½ pounds cream cheese	1 cup sugar
4 eggs	1 teaspoon vanilla

Mix cheese until creamy in your electric mixer. Beat the eggs, add sugar and vanilla. Add to cheese and beat together until light. Pour into

prepared crumbed mold and bake at 375° for 25 minutes or until cake is
firm. Remove and cool 10 minutes.

   Mix:

2 tablespoons sugar   1 cup sour cream
½ teaspoon vanilla

Spread on top of cheese cake and return to a 475° oven for 5 minutes.
Cool and refrigerate for 24 hours. Spread with sour cream before serving.

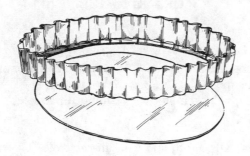

Rice has been mentioned as far back as 3000 B.C. in India. Rice came by
way of Madagascar to this country 275 years ago when a ship enroute
from Madagascar to England was blown off course and put in at Charles-
ton, South Carolina. The captain of the ship gave the governor a small
amount of rice as a token of gratitude, and so began a great industry in
America. Rice around the world has many ways of being prepared and
many recipes are similar. For instance Pais Pidgeon in Jamaica is Hop-
ping John in the Southeast. Rice and Almond Pudding in Sweden has
only one almond; the boy or girl who finds it in his serving will be the
first to marry. In Finland, the finder will have a year of good luck. At
any rate, Americans consume about eight pounds of rice per person each
year, and New Yorkers use more than Southerners.

   As far as I am concerned there is a genie in my kitchen — and it is
rice. It will also fit if you are budget-minded. You may never find the
end to the various things you can do with it. Uncle Ben's Converted
Rice and I have had a love affair for years. I know others are good; I just
like Uncle Ben's. You do not need a fancy gadget to cook rice; simply

follow the directions on the package. The rice processers know what they are doing, but I always cook rice in the oven in a covered casserole for 45 minutes at 350°, regardless of how I may vary the preparation. I do not have to worry about its boiling dry. To me the taste and texture is better. For day-before preparation I put everything in the casserole, refrigerate, then put it in the oven at 350° 1½ hours before serving.

These are some of my favorite rice recipes.

ORANGE RICE
(for 6)

¼ cup butter	Juice of 1 orange
1 cup rice	Grated rind of 1 orange
½ teaspoon salt	Salt and pepper
2 cups chicken broth	Chopped parsley
½ cup dry white wine	

Place butter, rice, salt, broth and wine in casserole. Cover and bake at 350° until light and feathery, about 45 minutes. Add juice and rind; return to oven for 10 minutes. Correct seasonings, toss with a fork and sprinkle with chopped parsley or slivered almonds.

MUSHROOM RICE (RISOTTO WITH MUSHROOMS)

¼ cup butter	1 cup rice
¼ cup thinly sliced onion	2½ cups beef or chicken broth
¾ cup thinly sliced mushrooms (about 4)	½ teaspoon salt
½ cup dry white wine	2 tablespoons grated Parmesan cheese

Melt butter; add the onion, sauté until soft, but do not brown. Add mushrooms, pour in wine and cook until the liquid has evaporated. Add rice, cook 1 minute. Pour in broth, cover and bake at 350° about 45 minutes or until rice is tender. Remove from oven, add salt and cheese; fork stir before serving. (I save my mushroom stems for this recipe and chop instead of slice.)

FRIED RICE
(for 6)

2 tablespoons vegetable oil	1 egg, well beaten
½ cup finely diced cooked ham or pork	Salt and white pepper
	Sesame oil
¼ cup finely diced green onion	Dry sherry
3 cups cooked rice, cold	
1½ tablespoons Kikkoman soy sauce	

Heat vegetable oil, add onion and meat. Cook 1 minute at high heat. Reduce to medium heat; add rice and soy sauce. Fork stir thoroughly. Mix in egg with a fork. Correct seasonings. Add a few drops of sesame oil and dry sherry (the secret ingredient). This will hold successfully and reheats well if leftover. Be sure rice is cold or this dish will be gummy.

A rice soufflé is an impressive accompaniment for any entrée and a good lower-in-cost carrier for any creamed food. I like it with Prime Rib of Beef.

RICE SOUFFLE
(for 6)

¼ cup butter	1 cup cooked rice
3 tablespoons flour	4 eggs, separated
1 cup milk	Few drops Worcestershire sauce
1 teaspoon salt	1 tablespoon Parmesan cheese
⅛ teaspoon white pepper	(you may omit)

Melt butter, stir in flour and cook until bubbly. Add milk and stir with a French whip until smooth and thick. Remove from heat; add seasonings, rice and beaten egg yolks. Beat the egg whites until stiff. Stir 2 tablespoons into the rice mixture; fold in the rest. Sprinkle Parmesan cheese on top. Bake in an ungreased 2-quart casserole at 350° about 45 minutes.

RICE CAKES

2 cups cooked rice
2 egg yolks
1 teaspoon salt
⅛ teaspoon cayenne pepper
3 tablespoons grated sharp
   cheese

½ cup thick cream sauce (2
   tablespoons flour, 2
   tablespoons butter, ½ cup
   milk)
1 egg white, slightly beaten
Dry white bread crumbs

Mix rice and egg yolks, seasonings, cheese and cream sauce. Chill.
Shape into flat cakes. Dip in the egg white and dry crumbs. Fry until
light brown, or bake on a buttered cookie pan at 375° until light brown.
I like to serve them with warmed butter and grated orange or lemon peel.

There are many flavored rices on the markets today, so use them. They
will add spice and rice to your menus.

CARAMEL RICE PUDDING
(for 6 to 8)

½ cup plus ¾ cup sugar
2 tablespoons water
6 eggs
½ teaspoon salt

½ teaspoon vanilla
3 cups scalded milk
1½ cups cooked rice

Place ½ cup sugar in a heavy skillet. Cook over medium heat, stirring
constantly until a light brown. Add water and cook until caramelized.
Pour into a 2-quart see-through casserole. Let cool; then butter the casserole and cooled caramel. Beat eggs slightly, add ¾ cup sugar, salt and
vanilla. Pour in the scalded milk, stirring rapidly with a whip or fork.
Strain, add rice and pour into the casserole. Place in a pan of water and
bake at 350° for 1 hour and 15 minutes. Serve from casserole with the
caramel syrup. You may also let the pudding cool, then put into a pan
of boiling water for 10 minutes and turn out onto a serving tray.

14

Much More This and That

I DISLIKE INTENSELY the term *creamed* so I never use it. I refer to *chicken in cream, mushrooms in cream* or whatever in cream. Don't you think it sounds better?

Dust with candied violets, ground pistachio nuts, almond! Roll any of these ingredients between two sheets of foil or brown paper until dusty. Store in covered containers to dust at will.

Correct seasoning means add salt and pepper to suit your taste.

I use *snipped* frequently. I mean cut in ¼-inch pieces, especially for fresh green beans and asparagus. The frozen kitchen cut are similar, but not small enough.

I say *ignite* brandy or Cognac because it takes away the raw taste of either. Also you destroy the calories and the sin — both go up in the air!

A Word about Wine

Wine complements any meal with the exception of breakfast. The maxim of white wine with white meat and red wine with red meat will keep you out of trouble with the wine snobs. The wine you like may be used with both.

The vintage of wine depends on the weather, the soil and the producer. You should buy your wines, if you are really interested, from merchants who have this information. It is the "in" occupation today to attend wine seminars, so do!

Simple wine rules to follow:

Dry or medium dry white wines with fish and seafood, sweetbreads and fowl. Dry red wines with beef, lamb, game and pasta dishes.

Either white or red dry or medium with roast chicken, turkey, veal; use only white if in a cream sauce.

Rosé may be served with any dish, but cold meats and aspics are better attuned to it. Dry champagne may be served with any food before, during and after a meal. Red wines usually are served at room temperature, white wines usually served chilled and champagne always served chilled. A famous gourmet and wine expert was once asked to give some words of wisdom concerning the serving of wine. He stood up and said: "Never put the Cognac in the refrigerator." I interpret this as serve what you like.

A Word about Herbs

Much has been written about herbs for centuries. Women in Biblical times took them for granted. Through history men have fought wars over them. The modern cook, with an imaginative use of herbs, transforms an ordinary dish into an inspired creation. It has been said herbs are the wit of cooking, but even wit should be tempered. So herbs and spices should be used not with a heavy hand, but with a light and disciplined one, thus producing a subtle delight for the taste buds. Buy as small a package as possible. Keep tightly covered, store away from heat.

A Word about Cheese

Every country has its cheeses which now have almost world-wide distribution. Their versatility is boundless. You may serve cheese before or after a meal, any time of the day. It is a good source of vitamin A, protein and fat; it is also high in calories. These are a few cheeses I like to use.

For cooking: American Cheddar, Swiss Gruyère and Italian Parmesan and Bel Paese.

For sandwiches and salads: French Roquefort, American Blue and Muenster, cream cheese and Monterey Jack.

For hors d'oeuvres: French Brie (to me the King of cheeses), Boursault and Boursin, New York State Cheddar, Port Salut.

For dessert to serve with fruit or crackers: Brie, Reblochon, Gourmandise with Kirsch, French Grape, Roquefort, English Stilton, Danish Crema Danica.

Cheeses are better with unsalted or very lightly salted crackers or Lahvash; they should be served at room temperature. I usually take my cheese out of the refrigerator early in the afternoon.

A Word about Equipment

Everyone has his own ideas of the equipment with which he needs to cook and entertain. I have been asked to list absolute essential items. I am flip when I say only a *French knife,* a *French whip,* a *bowl,* and a *skillet,* but you do not need to clutter up your life with too many kitchen tools. Add a good *chopping board* 24 x 10-inch; the heavy plastic chopping board is great. You can scrub it and hang it up out of the way. My chopping block I attached to a two-drawer, two-cabinet standard kitchen cabinet. An electric mixer comes in handy.

It is not necessary to have a copper bowl; *a stainless steel* or *hard plastic* will do as well. You need *measuring cups* and *spoons,* a *cook's fork* to stir with, a *scale* (as more and more recipes call for weights rather than measurements); I think you need a *thermometer* (a meat and a candy one), a *double boiler,* a *pot with a handle.* A cover is not necessary, you can always cover with foil, and squeeze around the edge of the pot. I suggest a small and large *skillet* with a heavy bottom, a large *spoon* to stir with, either stainless steel or hard plastic. I have never been a wooden spoon fancier — my hospital training no doubt. A *strainer* and one *shallow* and one *deep casserole*. Gourmet shops and housewares departments are busting out all over with various kinds of colorful casseroles and other items you would like to have; they are good investments as they make entertaining easier and cooking more pleasant. However, it is not necessary to own chafing dishes and silver trays galore. You can rent almost any serving piece you need in most cities, or you can borrow; however, extra dollars spent in outfitting your kitchen and pantry will make you happy.

Most Everyone Should Know

a dash or a pinch:	less than ⅛ teaspoon
small t:	teaspoon
large T:	tablespoon
3 t:	1 tablespoon
16 T:	1 cup
2 cups:	1 pint
2 pints:	1 quart
1 liter:	1.06 quarts (it won't appear in this book but it might in another)
4 quarts:	1 gallon
8 quarts:	1 peck
4 pecks:	1 bushel
16 ounces (dry):	1 pound
1 8 oz. can:	about 1 cup
1 No. 1 can:	2 cups
1 No. 2 can:	2½ cups
1 No. 3 can:	4 cups
1 No. 10 can:	12 to 13 cups

You need 1 tablespoon unflavored gelatin for 1 pint of liquid; put in 1 more teaspoon gelatin if you are adding cut-up fruit — and *never* use fresh pineapple; add another teaspoon if you are adding to whipped cream or egg white. If using commercial gelatin desserts such as Jell-o or

Royal follow the directions on the box for quantity and preparation; if adding fruits, whipped cream or egg whites be sure and count them as liquids.

Quantities You Should Know

butter:	1 pound of butter will serve 50 people
cake:	3 layer cakes or 3 Angel Food cakes for 50 (18 to 20 slices per cake)
candy:	1 pound of hard candy for a party of 50
chicken:	(see hen)
chicken salad:	2½ gallons chicken salad for 50
coffee:	1 pound coffee will yield 50 cups (for stronger, add ¼ to ½ pound more coffee)
punch:	2 gallons for 50
sandwich bread:	1 loaf of unsliced sandwich bread will yield 22 slices
meats:	a minimum of 4 ounces of meat, fish or poultry per person (if you want people to like you)
turkey:	two 18- to 20-pound turkeys will feed 50 people
vegetables:	about 6 quarts of cooked vegetables (fresh or canned) for 50 persons; allows for those who want seconds and others who skip them
whipping cream:	1 quart of whipping cream will provide dollops for 50
ham:	a 16- to 18-pound ham will feed 50 people
hen:	one 5-pound hen will yield 1 quart cooked diced meat
ice cream:	2 gallons ice cream for 50 people (using a No. 12 dipper)
iced tea:	3 gallons for 50
iced tea sugar:	¾ pound granulated sugar for 50
lemons:	6 lemons for 50 people (one lemon should cut 8 wedges for tea)
mayonnaise:	2 quarts of mayonnaise or cream type dressing for 50

I was brought up with a healthy respect for rhubarb. I like this recipe with meats of all kind but chicken or pork in particular.

RHUBARB CRISP
(for 6)

1 package frozen rhubarb or
1 pound of fresh hot-house
rhubarb
2 tablespoons orange juice
½ cup sugar
1 teaspoon grated orange rind

¾ cup white bread crumbs, dried
out in a 200° oven
Pinch of salt
4 tablespoons butter or
margarine

Place rhubarb in a buttered shallow casserole. Pour orange juice over. Mix half the sugar and all the rind together and sprinkle over. Mix crumbs with rest of sugar, salt and butter to make crumbs. Spread over rhubarb. Bake at 350° for about 35 minutes if frozen fruit is used, about 60 minutes if fresh. The crust should be a golden brown.

You may substitute margarine for butter if you wish. I did when I tested the recipes and no one complained. You usually need to add more salt when you do.

If you cannot find a convenient spot on your buffet table for your forks, stand them up in a vase or goblet. I use an old spoon holder.

You will always brew good coffee if you start with a thoroughly clean coffee maker; no one calls it a pot any more. Buy coffee in the size package that will be used within a week or ten days after opening. It is a good idea to refrigerate unused coffee. Coffee cannot be stretched, so use a standard coffee measure (2 level tablespoons equals a standard coffee measure) and use as a basis for a good cup of coffee 1 coffee measure of coffee to ¾ of a measuring cup. Be consistent! Serve as soon as possible after brewing, and be sure to use freshly drawn cold water in making coffee, Sanka or tea.

My good friend Margaret Hull makes the best Bread and Butter Pickles I have ever eaten. She brings me some every time she visits, and I do not share them with anyone. Her pickled okra is the best too. Her secret is using small cucumbers and okra.

BREAD AND BUTTER PICKLES

1 gallon cucumbers (small in circumference), about 6 pounds
2 green peppers
8 small white onions
½ cup salt (do not use Iodized salt)

Slice vegetables thin. Cover with salt and stir. Mix ice cubes through and cover with ice. Let stand 3 hours in a cool place. Take ice out and *drain thoroughly.*

Pickling Syrup:

5 cups sugar
1½ teaspoons turmeric
½ teaspoon ground cloves
1 teaspoon celery seed
2 tablespoons mustard seed
5 cups vinegar (cider)

Boil syrup. Add vegetables, heat to boiling but do not boil. Put in jars. Cover with melted sealing wax. Let stand at least 3 months before using.

PICKLED OKRA

Choose small okra; wash and leave stem ends on. Fill each jar tightly, but do not bruise okra. For each *pint:*

2 teaspoons dill seed
2 strips jalapeño peppers
½ teaspoon red chili
2 cloves garlic, cut in half

Cover with the following which have been boiled together:

1 quart *white* vinegar
1 cup water
½ cup salt (do not use Iodized salt)

This syrup is enough for 4 to 6 pints. One pound okra fills 2 pints. Seal jars as soon as filled. Pour paraffin on top to seal properly.

If you are using canned vegetables such as green beans or peas, drain them and reduce by one-half the liquid they are canned in by cooking it on top of the stove. Then put the vegetables back in pot and heat. Add your seasonings and butter. They will taste better.

Whether you buy or bake cookies, store them properly by keeping them at room temperature; crisp ones in a container with a loose cover, soft ones with a tight fitting cover. A wedge of fresh apple will keep them moist. If crisp ones become limp, place on an ungreased baking sheet and put in a 300° oven for 5 minutes.

Cookies are a sign of hospitality and are as old as 1563. The American "cookie" comes to us from the Dutch who settled New Amsterdam (New York). The Dutch called a cookie a "koekje," a diminutive of "koek," meaning cake. As in many cases when adopting new food, the English took the sound and gave it their own spelling. The British today call our cookie and/or cracker a "biscuit" and sometimes a "tea cake."

When cutting cookies dip the cutters in flour before pressing into the dough. When rerolling the trimmings, lay them together. Wadding them together before rolling out toughens them.

If you wish to mail homemade cookies to your children, pack them in popcorn to prevent breakage. They can eat the popcorn too.

When using noodles or any pasta as part of a casserole, reduce the cooking time by one-third. The noodles finish cooking in the oven. Casseroles containing cheese should be baked at low to moderate temperatures.

Asparagus has been claimed the "aristocrat" of the vegetable world. It comes from the royal family of the orchid and lily and has been held in high esteem for at least 2000 years. It is believed to be a native of the eastern Mediterranean and Asia Minor and grows wild over much of that area today. The Greeks and the Romans cultivated it; they cooked it quickly. The saying "quicker than you cook asparagus" is said to have been originated by the Emperor Augustus. At any rate, asparagus adds a touch of elegance to any dinner, so treat it with the respect due it.

Magnesium plays an indispensable role in the body's use of food for energy. Usually if your meals contain enough protein and calcium you also get enough magnesium — and phosphorus, another important mineral. Magnesium is found in nuts, whole-grain products, dry beans, dry peas, and dark green vegetables.

Light destroys riboflavin. It may also cause an off-flavor in milk products. So don't let milk and cream stand in the light. Put these products in the refrigerator as soon as possible.

Buying fresh pineapple? Look for the heavy pineapples; they are usually the better quality ones. Ripe pineapples have a fragrant, fruity aroma. Buying fresh coconut? Good fresh coconut is heavy for its size.

Young whole chickens can be roasted at 400° instead of 325°, the latter being the temperature generally recommended for whole poultry.

A barbecue originally referred to a whole animal roasted or broiled for a feast. Derived from the French "barbe-a-gueve," meaning from snout to tail, the popular version of the word barbecue or cook-out was first known in Virginia before 1700.

Don't forget the secret of barbecuing is a solid bed of glowing coals. Whether charcoal, wood or other fuel is used, light the fire at least 30 minutes ahead of time so that it will burn down to ash-gray coals before cooking starts.

Rub the outsides of pots and pans with soap before using over an open fire. They will be much easier to clean afterward.

Do not partially cook poultry one day and complete cooking the following day, according to the U.S. Department of Agriculture. This is not considered a good procedure, as it would give bacteria an additional opportunity to grow.

The U.S.D.A. also warns against roasting your turkey in the oven all night long at a low temperature. Don't be tempted. Instead, roast the turkey at a proper, higher temperature for fewer hours in the morning. When done, internally it should be 180° to 185°.

How do you prevent mushrooms from darkening during cooking? Use a little lemon juice. Wash fresh mushrooms in water, dry and cut off the tips of the stems. It's not necessary to peel mushrooms.

Making gravy? The real secret of making smooth gravy is to blend flour thoroughly with fat or with cold liquid before combining it with hot liquid.

Mock sour cream may be made from equal amounts of creamed cottage cheese and buttermilk; add a couple of teaspoons of lemon juice. It's easy to make in a blender.

The term "fry poaching" is rather new. Try it. Melt a little fat in a fry-pan over low heat, just enough to grease the bottom of the pan. Add eggs one at a time, pour in two or three tablespoons of water, cover pan tightly, and steam until eggs are done.

Easy pickled prunes. Take pitted prunes and any spiced sweet syrup, such as syrup left from watermelon or peach pickles, heat the syrup to boiling and pour over prunes.

Cured meats should not be frozen because seasonings added during curing accelerate the development of rancidity.

Have you thought to check the temperature in your frozen food cabinet lately? The temperature should be 0°.

Freezing does not kill the bacteria in food; it simply stops their multiplication. Bacteria continue to multiply after the food is thawed.

If you're planning to make homemade ice cream, you can substitute chilled evaporated milk (not diluted) in place of light cream. You might call it a weight watcher's ice cream because it is only about 140 calories per serving.

Shredding cheese? A good rule of thumb concerning cheese: one-half pound of cheese yields about two cups of shredded cheese. If you want to keep a large piece of cheese for an extended time, dip the cut surface in melted paraffin.

What is freezer burn? It is the drying out of the surface tissues of food resulting in a white appearance. Freezer burn is not harmful, but does make the dehydrated area tough and tasteless when cooked.

If you store fruits in a plastic bag, wash the fruit first, make a few small holes in the bag to provide ventilation and let out some of the moisture which accumulates.

These are good with a salad meal.

INDIVIDUAL CHEESE BREADS

Diagonally slash hard rolls at one-inch intervals. Do not cut all the way through. Place small squares or strips of Mozzarella or Swiss cheese in each gash. Warm rolls in preheated 375° oven, 3 to 5 minutes or until cheese melts. Serve hot.

Words to the wise cook! Unless it is specifically called for, don't use whipped butter in a recipe since the shortening power is not the same as for unwhipped butter.

What are "pine nuts?" There are many varieties of pine seeds under the name of "pignolas." The most common are "piñon" (Spanish for pine). Add them to rice, noodles, green salads, for a change of flavor.

Surprises with prunes:
When making muffins, fill pans about one-third with batter, drop in a pitted, uncooked prune for each muffin and add batter to the usual two-thirds level. Sprinkle tops with cinnamon sugar before baking. Fragrant and delicious.
Thread skewers with plump prunes and your choice of the following: cherry tomatoes or tomato wedges, pieces of green pepper, mushrooms, canned whole onions, cooked Brussels sprouts or marinated artichoke hearts. Brush with melted butter or margarine, broil gently and serve with any main dish.

And Zoe Thompson's

SHERRIED PRUNES

1½ pounds pitted dried prunes   1 tablespoon vanilla
  2 cups sherry (I use Almaden's   1½ cups sugar
    Golden Sherry)

Rinse prunes in hot water. In crock type container mix sherry and vanilla; add prunes. Pour sugar over prunes and cover. Keep at room temperature, stirring every day or so, until sugar dissolves. Allow to stand at least a week before serving.

Stuff prunes with walnuts, Cheddar cheese and pineapple. Cover with sweet sherry. Chill. Drain and serve with a fruit salad or cottage cheese.

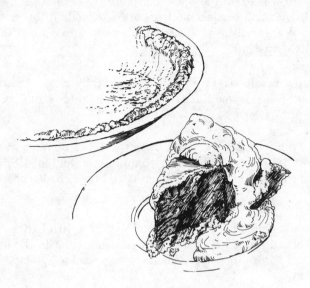

An interesting crust:

COCONUT CRUMB CRUST

1½ cups tender-thin flaked
    coconut
2 tablespoons butter, melted
2 tablespoons sugar

¼ cup finely crushed graham
    crackers, ginger snaps, vanilla
    wafers, or chocolate wafers
A pinch of cinnamon

Combine coconut and butter and mix well. Add sugar and cookie crumbs, mixing thoroughly. Press firmly on bottom and sides of 9-inch pie pan. Bake in moderate oven (375°) for 10 to 12 minutes or until lightly browned. Cool.

To serve, fill crust with ice cream. Serve immediately, or deep freeze to serve later. An all-time favorite, coffee ice cream in Coconut Crust with butterscotch sauce and whipped cream. Or fill with chiffon or cream pie filling and chill until firm.

If you wish to keep brownies and similar cookies a longer time, cut and wrap individually in foil or clear plastic before storing.

Add ⅓ cup of toasted sesame seeds to ingredients for a single pie crust when making a quiche or a meat pie.

For summertime:

CHICKEN AND FRUIT SALAD

1 quart diced white meat of chicken
1 cup grapes, seeded and cut in half
½ cup salted almonds

½ cup mayonnaise plus ¼ cup whipped cream, salt and white pepper to taste
2 tablespoons capers

Toss chicken, grapes and almonds with mayonnaise. Mix. Season to your taste. Pile on Boston lettuce leaves and sprinkle with capers, or place in center of an avocado mousse and surround with pineapple fingers dusted with ground pistachio nuts.

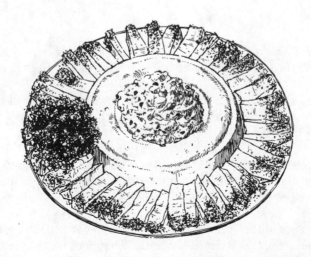

To avoid "pulling" an angel food cake down when you cut it, slice with a pronged divider or two forks back to back.

Start with a chilled bowl and beaters if you're planning on whipping cream. Cream is easiest to whip when it is chilled between 35° and 40°.

When heating sour cream, remember that it reacts as milk does to high temperature, and it may curdle. So use medium heat.

Add a little warm liquid to slightly beaten egg before combining the egg with a hot liquid or mixture.

A good dessert for any time:

MELBA FRUIT

2 cups frozen raspberries	8 frozen, canned or poached fresh
3 tablespoons sugar	peach halves
3 grapefruit, sectioned	

Purée raspberries, strain, add sugar, pour over fruit and refrigerate overnight.

Sometimes it's a good idea to serve frozen fruits with some ice crystals still in them; the texture will be firmer, more like that of fresh fruits.

A light soup the Zodiac customers enjoyed was of thin slices of avocado, mushrooms and water chestnuts added to chicken broth. We never found a name for it.

Danish Kitchen Finesse: Don't weep, says an old Danish proverb, when peeling or slicing onions. Place a small piece of bread between the teeth and breathe through the mouth.

I like to use out-of-the-ordinary canned vegetables at times; one that you find in gourmet shops today is cardons. They look like celery, taste a bit like asparagus, but will keep guests guessing. This recipe is so easy. You merely drain the cardons, place flat in a buttered shallow casserole or crêpe pan, sprinkle with cream, melted butter, salt, pepper and fresh grated Parmesan cheese. Run under the broiler until they are sizzling.

Did you know that small dandelion leaves, nasturtium leaves and beet greens added to a green salad make for a sprightly one? Try fennel salad, if you can find fennel (you cannot in Texas).

A really good chutney made with green pears comes from Meg Healy of radio fame via Cris Millard of General Foods. I like it as well as the famous Major Grey's — and it's less expensive.

CHUTNEY SAUCE
(12 pints)

¼ tablespoon Worcestershire sauce
1½ ground peppers
1 tablespoon cloves
1½ tablespoons ground cinnamon
Dash of red pepper
4½ pounds sliced green pears
4 lemons, peeled and sliced (cut peels in strips)
¾ pound dark raisins
3 pounds dark brown sugar
8 buds garlic
3 large onions, sliced
⅔ cup crystalized ginger, cut fine
7 cups canned pineapple chunks, drained
1 quart plus 1 cup vinegar
3 tablespoons mustard seed
½ cup soy sauce
Tamarind root, boil and use 3 tablespoons of juice (you may omit entirely)

Mix all ingredients and cook slowly until fruit is done, 45 minutes to 1 hour after boiling. This does not spoil and does not need to be sealed. Good with lamb, chicken, roast beef, etc.

If you insist on boiling your vegetables, use less water! One-half to one cup water usually is enough water to boil for 6 servings of fresh, young and tender vegetables. You must cook over low heat in a pan with a tight-fitting lid. Watch them — they boil fast.

How many beans? One cup of uncooked dried beans yields about 2½ cups cooked beans.

In making crêpes, if you find yourself with a hole in the crêpe, simply add more batter while the crêpe cooks. Who will know?

Choux designates a cream puff mixture. Why? It looks like a cabbage or chow.

Having a few canned cold soups in the refrigerator is a good time saver in planning a menu. Anyone who spends the time and money to make jellied consommé today has more time and money than I. Dressing up the canned variety is fun. For instance:

Jellied Madrilene with a teaspoon of sour cream and a bit of red caviar on top; or a tablespoon of ripe avocado mashed with lime, both pretty and tasty; or chopped chives and black olives on sour cream, or even both at times, or a few grains of curry powder; a tablespoonful of chopped fresh vegetables such as beans, peas, carrots and summer squash.

Jellied chicken consommé is made pleasing by adding fresh mint or rosemary with cooked fresh vegetables spooned in before serving; or try slivers of chicken or ham and white grapes.

Jellied beef consommé with a dash of sour cream and caviar becomes a gourmet dish. Substitute any seafood for the caviar.

Jellied green turtle soup with lump crabmeat. Why go on? Use your imagination and dress up cold soup with anything.

Condensed cream of chicken soup becomes a specialty when finely shredded cucumber is added with the cream or milk to dilute it. Heat long enough to blend the flavors, then chill; or prepare in a blender and sprinkle with chopped chives or watercress. This I think could make a quick delightful supper dish when served with whole cold shrimp and halves of hard-cooked eggs, mayonnaise whipped up with lime juice in which to dunk the eggs and with salty rye crisp wafers.

Canned *condensed cream of celery soup* diluted with cream, generously combined with finely chopped cooked broccoli or raw spinach served icy cold with chopped fresh tomato floating in the center and a faint dusting of curry powder, goes well with a make-your-own sandwich tray of assorted breads and cheeses.

Cream of green pea combined with fresh mint, served cold with well-chilled fresh fruit and Lime Dressing would make a summer luncheon party a joy for both hostess and guests. Serve with crisp cheese wafers — packaged and bought, of course.

The Mauna Kea Hotel in Hawaii has a favorite soup, most often requested too. It is good!

COLD BANANA BISQUE

> 1 quart half-and-half
> 4 large peeled ripe bananas

Put in the blender until thoroughly mixed and creamy. Chill. Serve with cinnamon croutons made as follows:

> 3 slices thin-sliced crustless white   3 tablespoons sugar, mixed with
>   bread, diced   ½ teaspoon cinnamon
> ⅓ cup melted butter

Place the diced bread in a buttered shallow pan. Mix with the butter and sugar mix. Put in a 300° oven until lightly caramelized, stirring frequently. These are good with cold avocado soup too.

Young appetites take to this casserole developed by Nell Morris, the manager of consumer service for Frito-Lay. With great success it has been used to promote less expensive beef for the Texas Agriculture Department.

MONTERREY CASSEROLE

1 pound ground lean beef	4 cups Taco-flavored tortilla
2 tablespoons chopped onion	chips (Doritos brand)
¾ teaspoon seasoning salt	2 cups grated Cheddar cheese
2 cans (8-ounce) tomato sauce	½ cup ripe olives

Cook beef in skillet for 5 minutes until crumbly and light in color. Add onion, salt and tomato sauce. Simmer for 5 minutes. Place 3 cups of chips in a 2-quart casserole. Sprinkle 1 cup of grated cheese over the tortilla chips. Pour over the meat sauce and top with the remaining grated cheese. Garnish with the last cup of tortilla chips. Bake at 350° for 15 minutes. Top with ripe olives before serving.

One pastime that Stanley Marcus enjoys is eating, and he likes to try new foods. He is not a beef-and-potato man, thank goodness. He often came back from a trip with a new dish to try to stump me. I usually was a jump ahead of him or else Billie (his Frau) warned me, but "Maigret" left me with mud on my face. This recipe turned out to be the breast of a heavy duck broiled.

BROILED DUCK MAIGRET

Have the butcher remove the breast from a 6-pound or heavier duck. Cut the breast in half. Marinate with 4 tablespoons lemon juice, 2 teaspoons salt, 1 teaspoon ground ginger; let stand 1 hour. Arrange the duck skin side down on a rack and broil as far from the heat as possible, about 20 minutes. Turn and continue broiling but do not overcook. It should be medium rare. Brush with melted butter and lemon juice and serve at once.

South Americans use sweetened fruit, especially bananas, with their main courses. This recipe I like — and it is good for you.

6 medium bananas	2 tablespoons butter
2 tablespoons butter or margarine, melted	½ cup milk
¼ cup firmly packed light brown sugar	1 cup cottage cheese

Peel the bananas and cut in half. Add to the melted butter and fry until light brown. Place in a 1½-quart casserole. Sprinkle with brown sugar, butter and milk. Bake at 350° for 30 minutes. Remove from oven and serve with cottage cheese.

SPANOKOPITA
(for 6 to 8)

Spanokopita is a Greek spinach that goes well with everything and is delicious.

2 pounds spinach, washed and trimmed of heavy ribs	1 package Strudel leaves
¼ cup chopped onion	Gruyère cheese

Drain spinach and chop fine with onion or put in a blender. Brush a shallow 2-quart casserole with melted butter. Cover with a layer of strudel leaves. Brush with melted butter. Repeat 4 times. Place a layer of the spinach, sprinkle with ¾ cup shredded Gruyère cheese. Repeat until spinach is used. Cover with 4 more strudel leaves, each one lightly buttered. Bake at 350° for 40 minutes or until top is golden brown. Cool and serve either hot or cold. The authentic Greek recipe calls for Feta cheese, but I like the Swiss Gruyère better.

A good summertime vegetable:

FRESH CORN AND YELLOW SQUASH

4 tablespoons butter
½ cup thinly sliced onion
4 ears of corn, cut off, or 1
    package frozen corn kernels
3 cups diced fresh tomatoes

1 pound sliced yellow squash
1 teaspoon salt
White pepper
¼ cup chopped parsley

Melt butter, add onion; cook until limp, but not brown. Add rest of ingredients except parsley. Cover and cook 10 minutes. Correct seasonings if needed. Sprinkle with parsley and serve.

APRICOT SOUFFLE
(for 6)

1 8-ounce package dried apricots
¼ cup water
¼ cup sugar

5 egg whites
Confectioners' sugar

Cook apricots and water until water has completely evaporated. Purée apricots in a blender or put through a sieve with the sugar. Cool. Beat the egg whites until stiff. Stir one third of them into the apricots, then fold in the rest. Butter a double boiler and its cover and sprinkle both with granulated sugar. Add the apricot whip and cover. Put over just simmering water and cook 1¼ hours. Do not remove cover while cooking. Turn out onto a serving dish. Sprinkle with confectioners' sugar. Serve with Soft Custard or surround with fresh strawberries.

Mark Twain quote: "An American man without American cookery would gradually waste away and eventually die."

A quick appetizer:

Mash together equal quantities of sweet butter and Roquefort or Danish Blue cheese. Sandwich a little of the mixture between two walnut or pecan halves. Chill before serving.

This is a lovely dessert.

GLORIFIED PEACHES

1½ cups canned peach juice
½ cup water
2 cloves
1 orange, sliced thin with skin on
1 cinnamon stick

3 tablespoons honey
8 canned Elberta peach halves
1 quart vanilla ice cream
Cognac
Macaroons

Boil juice, water, cloves, orange, cinnamon and honey for 10 minutes. Strain, pour over peaches and refrigerate overnight. Put peaches in a serving dish, top with ice cream, pour sauce over. Heat 2 jiggers of Cognac, ignite and pour over. Sprinkle crushed macaroons over all.

Try fresh Brussels sprouts, sliced, cooked 6 minutes in a small amount of water. Drain, add butter and grapes. Season to your taste with salt and pepper and a tiny dash of cinnamon.

Thread on a skewer chunks of pineapple, zucchini squash, tomatoes, canned mushrooms, green pepper and onions. Brush with butter, salt and pepper and sprinkle with brown sugar and broil or bake. A way to tempt children and men who are in a rut as to their vegetable consumption.

Liederkranz cheese, strictly American, and fresh pears or apples make a good dessert. Smelly, but good!

"How can I tell a mushroom from a toadstool? Remember this: There is no difference except in nomenclature between the two. We may say an edible mushroom or an edible toadstool, a poisonous mushroom or a poisonous toadstool. You must learn the difference in appearance [between edible and poisonous] just as we learn the difference between a carrot and a beet. Beauty has nothing to do with it. Some of the most beautiful mushrooms are poisonous and the little brown fellows at your feet may make a succulent dish." So says Margaret McKinney, mushroom authority.

Don't you sometimes want just a plain sugar cookie? A delightful neighbor of mine, Ethylleen Dodson Wright, who believes in grandmothers, gave me her recipe.

PLAIN SUGAR COOKIES

Cream together:

1 cup sugar   1 cup butter

Add:

½ teaspoon salt   1½ teaspoons baking powder
3 cups sifted flour

Beat one egg with 3 tablespoons of cream (I substitute 1 teaspoon of vanilla for part of the cream).

Mix well and turn onto well-floured board. Roll about ⅛ inch thick, cut and bake carefully in moderate oven on a buttered cookie sheet until lightly brown. Sprinkle with granulated sugar before baking if you like.

In Italy basil is called "Kiss-me-Nicholas" and any girl approaching a favorite young man with her basil sprig is hoping to be kissed.

Ripe olives lend extra-special appeal to any relish or canapé tray. To provide a rich gloss, drain olives well and pat dry with paper towels, then roll in a bowl with a few drops of salad oil. Serve some of the olives with coatings of parsley, toasted sesame seeds or instant minced onion.

The Arabs knew about the lemon a long time before the medical researchers discovered Vitamin C. Its culture was preserved in the 12th and 13th centuries in Spain. The Spanish in turn brought lemons to America. In these days of salt-free diets, a squeeze of lemon juice gives the magic that salt normally provides. At any rate use lemons, Vitamin C and all. Flavor water for ice cubes with lemon juice for beverages, add a mint leaf or olive too. Combine with a little olive oil for vegetables and fish. Let celery stand in cold water and lemon juice for an hour. The celery will be more crisp, white and tender. Add lemon juice to water for pie crust. Use it in place of vinegar for dressings, and for a change make:

LEMON MARMALADE

4 lemons, sliced very thin   5 cups water
4 cups sugar

Cover lemon slices with water. Bring to a boil. Simmer, covered, for 2 hours. Measure, add enough water to make 4 cups of the fruit mixture. Add the sugar. Cook at high heat until the syrup sheets from a testing spoon. Pour into hot clean glasses. Seal.

When you want to serve pancakes family-style and prepare them all at once, keep them warm until serving time by placing between cloth towels in a 200° oven.

Use cocoa in place of flour to dust pans for chocolate cake.

Remember that lemons should have a glossy skin, according to U.S. Department of Agriculture marketing specialists. A slightly green tint on the skin has no effect on juiciness, but smooth-skinned lemons usually have more juice than rough-skinned types.

In buying canned pears be sure to look for the count on the label. For the best all around use, buy a 5-to-6 or a 6-to-8 count. Anything smaller will not make an attractive service unless you are cutting them up. For instance, diced pears, walnuts and celery tossed with mayonnaise, is a nice change from the traditional Waldorf salad. Decorate with slices of avocado for a holiday salad.

How do you skin green peppers? Roast the peppers in an oven until the skins are well blistered (no harm will be done if they blacken a little). Then remove them from the oven, put them at once in a pot, and cover. Let the peppers stand (off the heat) for about five minutes. The steam will have loosened the skins and they can be easily removed.

Potato salad will have more flavor if you add your dressing and seasonings while the potatoes are hot. The French do.

Do not use fresh pineapple with gelatin unless you first cook this fruit.

What is tripe? It consists of the plain or smooth lining from the cow's first stomach and the honeycombed lining from the second stomach. Honeycombed tripe is considered a delicacy.

If using a meat thermometer to check your turkey for doneness, insert the thermometer into the center of the inner thigh muscle of the whole turkey. This is the slowest heating part of the bird. (Don't let the thermometer touch the bone.)

About 1 cup of stuffing for each pound of poultry is a safe rule to follow.

A bushel of peaches can give you a very fine time, especially during the peach season. It brings a color and flavor to your table that everyone enjoys, and who knows, it may even inspire your mate to pass you the most superb compliment I know: "You look just like peaches and cream."

Parisian cooking is a phenomenon that few people enjoy at home because (1) they stand in awe of the Frenchman's way of fashioning his vittles, and (2) they are quite sure it is too complicated to accomplish in a kitchen that is not lined with copper pots or with a cook who lacks ingenuity. Both need constant polishing.

I am amazed at the requests I receive for pralines. I like this one.

PRALINES
(3 dozen small)

2 cups sugar	¾ cup butter or margarine
1 teaspoon soda	2 cups pecan halves
1 cup buttermilk	1 teaspoon vanilla

Cook sugar, soda, buttermilk and butter to soft ball stage, 240° on candy thermometer. Stir from bottom frequently. Remove from stove, beat for 5 minutes. Add pecans and vanilla. Beat until the mixture drops easily onto wax paper. When cool, wrap individually in clear plastic. These keep indefinitely.

Did you know that white bread was made only for royalty in Roman times? (Now royalty is looking for some good whole-wheat or rye bread.) And that Egyptians made the first yeast raised bread?

To test bread dough to see if it has doubled in bulk, press the tips of two fingers lightly and quickly about ½ inch into the top of the dough. If the dent stays, the dough is light enough to have doubled in bulk.

When baking bread, if you like a hard crust, set a pan of warm water in the bottom of the oven while baking, and brush the crust when partially baked with ½ cup of water mixed with 1 teaspoon of salt. For a soft crust, brush with melted butter before and after baking.

When baking yeast breads, test for doneness by first turning pan over and tapping the bottom to release the loaf. Thump the bottom of the loaf. If there is a hollow sound, it is done; if not, return bread to pan and bake a few minutes longer.

Be sure you do not use cake flour for bread making. Use all-purpose flour because it has the protein to form an elastic framework strong enough for bread making. How is cake flour different from all-purpose flour? Cake flour, milled from soft wheat, is lower in protein than all-purpose flour and usually is not enriched. Cake flour is very fine, uniform and makes tender, delicate cakes.

If you like a brown pie crust, sprinkle a little granulated sugar on the top or brush lightly with an egg beaten with a little water.

Eggs are considered a liquid ingredient in recipes, so their size will affect the "wetness" of a mixture. Extra large eggs may necessitate adding a little more flour; very small eggs make it necessary to add less flour than the recipe calls for. A large egg is a safer size.

If the meringue topping on your pie shrinks from the crust, it is because you did not seal it properly before putting in the oven. Be sure the meringue touches the edge of the crust.

Place baking pans in the center of the oven to permit free circulation of air and heat on all sides. When putting two or more pans in the oven at the same time, stagger them on different shelves, so that one is not directly above the other. There should be at least one inch between two pans on the same shelf; otherwise the trapped heat will cause a "hot spot."

Do you bake with your oven light on? If so, the light throws extra heat into that corner of the oven, possibly causing uneven baking.

Biscuits will take on a light brown finish if the tops are brushed with milk or butter before baking. If you want biscuits to be crusty, place cut dough one inch apart on baking sheet; if soft, place next to each other.

If you cut off the crust before freezing bread, you will find the loaf will not crumble when you slice.

Lumpy — that's the batter for perfect muffins. Overbeaten batter will cause peaks, tunnels and toughness in the muffins because the gluten in the flour is overdeveloped.

To convert between self-rising and all-purpose flour or cornmeal, remember that every cup of the self-rising product contains exactly 1½ teaspoons baking powder and ½ teaspoon salt, which must be added or deleted from the recipe, depending on which way you are converting.

Here's a biscuit recipe that calls for only two ingredients: 2 cups enriched self-rising flour and 1 cup dairy sour cream! Blend the two together, knead slightly, roll, cut and bake at 450° for 15 minutes. It's a light, tasty biscuit.

If you have only one cookie sheet, cut pieces of foil to fit, shiny side up. You do not have to wait then for pan to cool. Just shift foil onto cookie sheet. Then throw away the foil — no pan to wash.

Unless your recipe states otherwise, preheat the oven at the correct temperature for at least 10 minutes before you begin baking cookies or anything else. When making puff pastry and the like, you especially must have your oven already preheated. The cooled pastry coming in contact with the hot oven causes rapid air expansion, resulting in light pastry.

Dark or dull pans absorb heat with the result that foods actually bake faster and crusts are browner than in shiny pans that reflect the heat.

Leftover yeast rolls? They will obtain a fresh-baked taste by being sprinkled lightly with water, covered and rewarmed in a 400° oven. Store-bought rolls likewise.

Baking custard? Try substituting two leftover egg yolks for one whole egg. It works.

To bake a frozen unbaked pie, bake in a 425° oven adding 15 minutes to regular baking time. If the pie is already baked, thaw at room temperature for ½ hour. Then bake at 375° for 30 minutes.

A quick raclette: place Monterey Jack cheese on an oven-proof plate, bake in a 450° oven until it begins to melt. Serve as a cocktail tidbit with small (hot) boiled potato and green onions.

A quick and easy dressing for fruit salad: Mix ¼ cup mayonnaise, ¼ cup vanilla ice cream, 2 teaspoons chunky peanut butter, 2 tablespoons pineapple juice. Add ¼ teaspoon grated orange peel for a change of flavor.

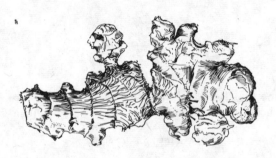

This is a good salad to accompany any fish entrée. I like to make it in a ring mold for a buffet and fill the center with seafood salad.

CUCUMBER MOUSSE

¾ cup boiling water
1 package lime-flavored gelatin
1 cup cottage cheese
1 cup mayonnaise
2 tablespoons grated onion

¾ cup grated cucumber with peeling left on
1 cup slivered almonds (you may omit)

Pour boiling water on gelatin, cool; add cheese, mayonnaise, grated onion, cucumber and nuts. Pour into a wet mold and refrigerate.

Everyone has a boss whether they realize it or not. Mine is Josie Calhoun, my twice-a-week maid and friend. She scolds me when I get too tired or continue to go on the run. Josie has a dessert recipe that everyone asks for.

PINEAPPLE CRUNCH

1 box yellow cake mix
½ cup flour
2½ cups canned crushed
    pineapple

1 cup pecans or more
1 cup butter

Heavily butter a 2-quart shallow casserole. Pour the pineapple over the bottom. Mix the cake mix with the flour and the pecans. Pour over the pineapple. Melt the butter and pour over all. Bake at 350° for 1 hour.

It seems to me that the reputation of Carrot Cake has deteriorated. It is such a good cake it should stay popular. This is the one I use.

CARROT CAKE

3 cups sifted flour
1½ teaspoons soda
1 teaspoon cinnamon
½ teaspoon salt
1½ cups liquid corn oil
2 cups sugar

2 cups grated raw carrots
1 8½-ounce can crushed pineapple with juice
1½ cups chopped pecans
2 teaspoons vanilla
3 eggs

Sift flour, soda, cinnamon and salt. Mix oil and sugar. Add half the dry ingredients. Mix well and beat in carrots and pineapple, nuts and vanilla. Add remaining dry ingredients and beat until well blended. Drop in eggs one at a time, beating after each addition. Pour batter into well buttered and floured 10-inch tube pan. Bake at 350° for 1½ hours. When done leave in pan for 10 minutes then remove. Cool thoroughly before icing.

CREAM CHEESE ICING

1 8-ounce package cream cheese	1 teaspoon vanilla
½ cup butter	1 cup chopped pecans
1 box confectioners' sugar	

Cream the cheese and butter. Add sugar, vanilla and pecans. Add a little milk, if necessary, to aid in spreading.

A sauce for asparagus or broccoli:

PIQUANTE SAUCE

1 cup mayonnaise	1 cup peeled, seeded and diced
1 tablespoon lemon juice	tomatoes
½ teaspoon salt	

Mix mayonnaise, lemon juice and salt. Keep hot over water. Add tomatoes when ready to serve.

Candied bacon, a wonderful breakfast treat. Blanche bacon in hot water for five minutes, dry, place on broiler pan, sprinkle with brown sugar and broil.

You can always fall back on turnips.

MASHED TURNIPS

Mix 4 pounds white or yellow turnips, cooked and mashed, with 1 table-spoon sugar, ¼ teaspoon mace, ¾ stick butter, ½ cup sour cream, salt and pepper. Put in buttered casserole and bake at 350° until hot.

Whipped cream mixed with puréed and strained frozen raspberries is divine for icing an angel food cake.

A good quick soup for 8: two cans cream of celery soup, 1 medium-sized onion which has been grated or put in blender, ½ cup milk, pinch of nutmeg. Heat but do not boil. Add 1 pound fresh crabmeat, ¾ cup sherry. Reheat but do not boil.

ORANGE BOWLE

Put in a crystal bowl 6 seedless oranges, peeled and sectioned. Cover with:

1 tablespoon honey	1 teaspoon scotch
1 tablespoon bitter orange marmalade	1 teaspoon lemon juice
	1 tablespoon cold water
1 teaspoon Grand Marnier	

Refrigerate overnight. Test for sweetness and add sugar if necessary. Serve very cold with almond dust.

If you are in the vicinity of Harbor Springs, Michigan, be sure to stop and buy the miniature vegetables at Bluff Gardens. The tiny new potatoes would make a cocktail tidbit worth remembering. Boil and dip the potato in hot sour cream and dill or caviar.

Chopped thin mints on peppermint ice cream, cinnamon candy stick crumbs on coffee ice cream with crème de cacao, apricot purée mixed with Cointreau on orange ice or vanilla ice cream or both, crushed Almond Roca candy on strawberry ice cream, fresh or frozen blueberries mixed with crème de cassis on lemon ice — all good.

Cocktail wafers on tap: 1 cup flour, 2 cups grated cheddar cheese, ¾ cup chopped pecans, ¼ teaspoon minced garlic, ½ cup margarine. Mix, form into a log, chill. Slice when ready to serve and bake at 350°, 10 to 12 minutes.

Would you like to decorate with chocolate leaves? Melt semi-sweet chocolate, pour over leaves from your garden. Mark veins with a knife. Let chocolate harden, then peel the leaves.

HOT STRAWBERRY PIE

1 unbaked 9-inch pie shell	½ cup sugar
1 quart whole strawberries	½ cup flour
3 egg yolks	3 egg whites, beaten stiff

Fill unbaked pie shell with strawberries. Beat the egg yolks, add sugar. Whip until fluffy. Add flour and beat until smooth. Fold in egg whites. Pour mixture over the berries. Bake at 375° for 8 minutes, then lower to 325°. Bake until set and golden brown. Serve hot with whipped cream.

Sauce for steak: 6 ounces Roquefort cheese, 2 tablespoons cream cheese, 1 teaspoon Worcestershire sauce, 1 teaspoon mushroom catsup, 1 garlic clove — minced, few drops Tabasco. Mix.

Chocolate, vanilla and coffee ice cream over fresh fruit in Galliano's liqueur — a nice ending.

A different twist to a salad: hot broiled pineapple chunks, over chunky pieces of iceberg lettuce with Sesame Dressing or French Dressing.

A bit of horseradish sauce added to any salad dressing will give it the push it sometimes needs.

Frozen fish poached in cider and butter takes on a better flavor. Cover fish with whipping cream and mushrooms and sauté until cream is thickened. An Irish cooking secret.

Garlic is a strong and pungent herb. Use with discretion.

Sour cream never hurt anything. It will pep up a mayonnaise, give life to frozen vegetables, make a cream sauce creamier.

Suggestion from Club fare — a Shrimp Peel. Hot and cold shrimp with sauce, shrimp gumbo, shrimp salad, shrimp Newburg, rice and salad — some or all, if you catch the shrimp; otherwise you need a pot of gold to buy them.

Cooking takes positive thinking and, of course, some time. Where are you going when you say to yourself and all who can hear you: I do not have time to make even a good pot of coffee or soup — as you pour hot water on those little flavor buds of instants and shove a pre-packaged meal into the oven? We go this way only once and you can make it as pleasant as possible, gastronomically speaking. Many troubled waters may be smoothed with a well-planned and -prepared meal.

TUNNEL OF FUDGE CAKE

Beat 1½ cups soft butter at high speed until fluffy. Beat in 6 eggs, one at a time. Gradually whip in 1½ cups sugar: beat until fluffy. By hand, stir in 2 cups flour, 1 package dry frosting mix (Double Dutch) and 2 cups chopped walnuts until blended. Bake in greased bundt or 10-inch tube pan at 350° for 55 to 60 minutes, until top is dry and shiny. Cool in pan for 2 hours.

The frosting mix and nuts are essential for success. Cake has a soft fudgy interior.

If you dilute your frozen orange juice with apricot nectar, you will enjoy it more.

You'll need the following for an inexpensive spaghetti sauce, good for a late supper: 12 slices of bacon, minced and fried in 2 tablespoons olive oil, 3 eggs, ⅓ cup grated Parmesan, salt and cracked pepper. Beat eggs, add to hot spaghetti, toss and toss. Add bacon and oil, toss again; stir in cheese and salt and pepper. Enough for 1 pound pasta.

An apple tart I like. Line a tart pan with removable bottom with pie crust. Slice apples (Greenings are best) and overlap in circles to fill bottom. Bake at 400° for 10 minutes. Mix ½ cup flour, ½ cup sugar, ½ cup cream, pour over and bake at 350° until apples are tender.

When buying a whole fish in the market, be sure the fish looks you in the eye with a healthy stare. You cannot tell about one that has been skinned and boned, so smell it and cook as soon as possible after you buy or catch, or freeze it. Don't overcook. For once in your life follow the rules.

A taste for all ages:

BAKED ALASKA PIE

Melt in a saucepan:

1 stick butter   1 square bitter chocolate

Add 1 cup sugar, mix. Beat 2 eggs until very light. Add ⅓ cup flour, pour in chocolate mixture, beat. Add 1 teaspoon vanilla. Butter 9-inch glass pie pan and add mixture. Bake 35 minutes at 325°. Cool. Prepare a meringue — beat 5 egg whites until frothy, gradually add ½ cup sugar, ⅛ teaspoon salt, beat until stiff and glossy. Pile peppermint candy ice cream on top of pie. Completely cover with the meringue, sealing the ice cream in. Run under broiler to brown. Do ahead and deep freeze if you like.

A pretty dessert from Mrs. Fred Jones of Oklahoma City, is Grape Freeze: 3 cups grape juice, juice of 1½ lemons, 2 cups sugar. Mix, add 3 cups whipping cream, whipped. Freeze. Put scoops of it in the middle of a silver tray, surround with clusters of black grapes on grape or ivy leaves.

A sweet ending to a luncheon or dinner:

THE SWAN

Make a meringue ring. Then with a pastry tube create a right and left
wing, a neck and head (a letter S will do) and a tail — all of meringue.
Bake as you would any meringue. Place a ball of ice cream in the ring,
attach the wings and neck and tail. Sprinkle fresh coconut over the top
of the ice cream ball; float on strawberries or any other fruit.

Next time you make a cream pie, any kind, put a layer of whipped cream
on top, then the meringue and you have three textures to savor. Or you
may substitute ice cream for the whipped cream.

You all should learn to like rabbit, which you can roast, broil, fry or
barbecue. You will see more rabbits in the markets, I bet you.

All Fun — No Fat with Chinese Cookery is a good book for low cholesterol diets. Put out by the Palm Beach Heart Association.

Do not discard your mushroom stems. Chop, sauté in butter, freeze in
small packages to use in sauces, soups and such.

If you like the flavor of almonds, grind them in your blender, season with
salt and roll boned and skinned chicken breasts in them. Sauté in butter
and serve with the nut-flavored butter they have cooked in.

You cannot buy in the supermarket Crème Fraiche, so make it. This recipe is excellent when you want a special sauce for fresh berries, especially wild ones.

CREME FRAICHE

2 cups whipping cream   1 tablespoon buttermilk

Mix the cream and buttermilk together. Heat over low flame until just warm, 85° if you have a thermometer (and you should by now). Remove mixture and put in warm oven; stir every once in a while for 8 hours. It will be thick. Refrigerate before serving.

A dessert party is the answer at times. It's good for late afternoon all-women gatherings, conventions and the like, or after an early lecture or early theater. But be sure to serve enough of each dessert for everyone as your guests will eat all of everything. At least my guests do.

Words of wisdom from Lin Yutang: If there is anything we are serious about it is neither religion nor learning, but food. We acclaim eating as one of the few joys of life.

LA JOLLA POTATOES

You'll need: 6 medium-sized cooked potatoes, 1 cup cream sauce (2 tablespoons butter, 1½ tablespoons flour, 1 cup milk), 1½ cups grated sharp cheddar cheese, 1 large banana, salt and pepper. Dice potatoes and banana, mix. Put in 1-quart buttered baking dish. Add cheese and cream sauce, salt and pepper. Bake at 350° until fluffy.

There are as many recipes for chutney as time and people who make it. This one from Mae Walker of Warner Springs, California, has a different taste I like.

EAST INDIAN CHUTNEY

3 pounds peeled and cored apples (weigh after peeling)
3 pounds sugar
4 ounces green ginger root, scraped and sliced in long thin slivers
½ ounce red chili, pounded or almost pulverized
4 ounces garlic, peeled and sliced the short way of the small clove

1 tablespoon salt
1 pound apricots, dried and cut in strips, large enough to both see and really taste in the chutney
½ pound raisins, seeded and cut, not put through blender
1 pint apple cider vinegar

Cook apples into an applesauce. Add sugar, ginger, chili, garlic and salt. Cook down to a jam. Stir from bottom of pot as this mixture will burn easily. Add apricots and raisins; continue cooking about 20 minutes. Add the vinegar and bring to a rolling boil. Pour into jars and seal.

There is nothing better (nor higher in calories) with sautéed chicken livers than Béarnaise Sauce — a good cocktail tidbit.

Sauté walnut meats with chives in butter and serve with roasted or broiled chicken.

Jessie was one of my cooks at the Driskill Hotel in Austin, and he made the chili. I still use his method and keep the chili frozen. Using this recipe I have substituted lower-in-calorie chicken and turkey for the beef.

JESSIE'S CHILI
(4 quarts)

¼ pound chili pods (1 package)
1 quart water
1 pound coarsely ground beef suet
5 pounds coarsely ground beef
3 to 4 cloves garlic, finely chopped, or 1 tablespoon garlic powder
2 teaspoons ground comino (cumin)

¾ cup chili powder
2 cups chopped onion
2 cups canned tomatoes
4 tablespoons cornmeal
2 tablespoons flour
Water
Salt

Boil the chili pods covered in a pot with 1 quart of water for 15 minutes. Remove the pods, and save the water they have boiled in. Remove pods' stems, seeds and slip off the skins. Chop the pods. Sauté the suet, beef and garlic until meat is thoroughly cooked, about 40 minutes, with the comino and chili powder. Add the onions and cook 10 minutes, add tomatoes mixed with the cornmeal, flour and chopped pods. Cook another 5 minutes. Add the chili water and enough water to make 2 quarts. Simmer for about 45 minutes or until all the flavors are well blended. Correct seasonings.

When I substitute coarsely ground turkey or chicken for the beef I add ½ cup of butter or salad oil in place of the suet.

When I make Enchiladas I dip each tortilla in the fat from making the chili, or in broth or salad oil, fill with chili, grated cheddar cheese or half cheddar, half provolone cheese and grated onion. Roll up and arrange side by side, seam side down, in a shallow casserole. Pour chili over and grated cheese. Bake at 350° for 15 minutes. Run under broiler until piping hot. Serve right away, but you may assemble them ahead of time and freeze before baking.

Ann Creswell of Houston has a good recipe for Turkey Enchiladas using cooked turkey, developed by the Texas Department of Agriculture.

TURKEY ENCHILADAS
(for 15)

Oil
2 4-ounce cans green chiles
1 large clove garlic, minced
1 1 pound 12-ounce can tomatoes, drained and liquid reserved
2 cups chopped onion
2 teaspoons salt

½ teaspoon oregano
½ cup water or tomato liquid
3 cups shredded cooked turkey
2 cups sour cream non-dairy substitute
2 cups grated Cheddar cheese
1 package (15) corn tortillas

Preheat 2 tablespoons oil in electric skillet at 300°. Rinse seeds from chiles and chop (use rubber gloves and don't touch eyes). Sauté with minced garlic in oil. Drain and break up tomatoes. Reserve ½ cup liquid. Add tomatoes, onion, 1 teaspoon salt, oregano and reserved liquid. Simmer at 200° uncovered until thick, about 30 minutes. Remove from fry pan and set aside. Combine turkey with sour cream, grated cheese and remaining salt. Heat ⅓ cup oil and dip tortillas until they become limp. Drain well on paper towels. Fill tortillas with turkey mixture; roll up and arrange side by side, seam side down in electric skillet. Pour chili sauce over top and cook at 250° until heated through, about 20 minutes. Can be prepared as a casserole in a 13 x 9 x 2-inch baking dish in a 350° oven.

PATE

This pâté substitutes very well for the imported pâté de foie gras. Bring 1 pound chicken livers to a boil in chicken broth barely to cover and simmer them for 15 to 20 minutes in a covered saucepan. Drain and put the hot livers through the finest blade of the food chopper. Mix this with 2 teaspoons salt, a pinch cayenne, ½ cup softened butter, ½ teaspoon dry mustard and 2 tablespoons finely minced onion. Blend well, add 1 tablespoon dry sherry; pack the mixture in a crock and chill in the refrigerator. You may freeze.

When combining seafood and other foods with a sauce, mix with a fork; also use a fork to stir-fry when you want food to be stirred rapidly.

Add a can of beer to meats you boil or braise or roast. It will act both as a tenderizer and a flavor bud.

A celebration dessert to use for birthdays, anniversaries, holidays. Any cake, any pie, strawberry shortcake, anything that will hold extra-long skinny tapers. You merely push them into the dessert and light. It is a blaze of glory, and that is what a celebration should be.

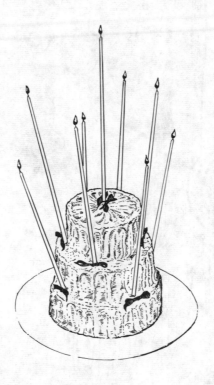

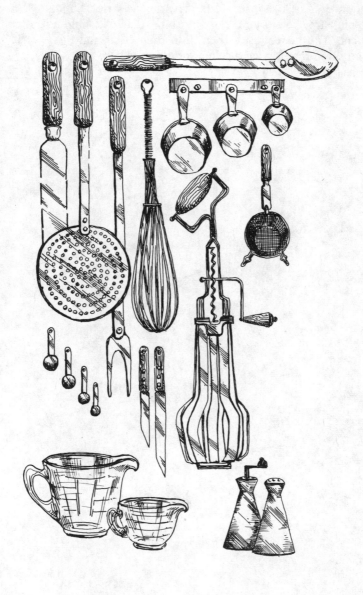

Index